Income Tax:
Shattering The Myths

by Dave Champion

Income Tax: Shattering The Myths

Copyright © 2010 by Dave Champion

All rights reserved. No part of this book may be used or reproduced by any means, graphic, electronic, or mechanical, including photocopying, recording, taping or by any information storage retrieval system without the written permission of the publisher except in the case of brief quotations embodied in critical articles or reviews.

Because of the dynamic nature of the Internet, any web addresses or links contained in this book may have changed since its publication and may no longer be valid.

Second Printing: March, 2012

ISBN: 978-0-615-35685-3

Published by Dave Champion

Dedication

This book is dedicated to every American who understands that "patriotism" means standing up for liberty, and that government only deserves the support of We The People to the exact extent that it fosters and promotes an environment of personal liberty for its citizens.

"Guard against the impostures of pretended patriotism."

George Washington

DISCLAIMER

I am not an attorney. This book does not provide legal advice. I am not an accountant or CPA and this book does not give tax advice.

I am an American who loves liberty.

This book contains what the U.S. Supreme Court calls "political free speech". It is me speaking out about a subject I've been researching and working within for nearly two decades. It contains a message I believe all Americans must hear.

The government would tell you I'm not an "expert" so you should ignore what I say. What the government really means is that I am not approved by them – the government – to speak on the subject. Fortunately, at least for now, Americans don't need to be "approved" by the government to speak out.

Am I an expert at the subject contained in this book? I am. In fact, I am likely the most knowledgeable person in the nation on the material contained in this book. With that said, I am not providing the information contained in this book to establish myself as an expert, but rather to insure that you understand what is being done to you at the hands of dishonest law-breaking United States government officials. While I share with you at the end of the book what steps I think all Americans should take to end this travesty, ultimately the matter is in your hands.

In response to this book, the government (and its minions) will tell you that I am trying to harm America. They will likely even go to the absurd length of saying that if Americans act upon the information in this book, America will not be able to win the "War of Terror". They will predict doom and gloom if you agree with what is in this book and you choose to take action to restore our Republic.

Allow me to take a moment to assure you that what I want is freedom and liberty for you! Would we not live in a strange country indeed if the government contends that your freedom and liberty are dangerous to the nation!

There will be disagreement about the macro political conclusion contained in this book because people have different visions for where America should be going. I want America to return to the principles of Jefferson and Madison – the men who contributed so profoundly to the design and concept of American government. Others want a different America. Their America is not an America of freedom and liberty.

Do I intend harm to the United States? Well, that depends on how you define "United States". If the United States means the collective citizenry of the states of the Union, then I mean to restore a greater degree of freedom and liberty to you, your children, and your grandchildren. If "United States" means the felonious and unconstitutional rape of the American people by power-hungry government officials, then yes, I mean this book to do them harm.

A long habit of not thinking a thing wrong
gives it a superficial appearance of being right.
    Thomas Paine

Table of Contents

Disclaimer

Introduction

How To Read This Book

Chapter 1: Rules of The Game 1
    The Constitution 2
    Statutes 6
    Regulations 7
    Treasury Decisions 9
    Other Resources 10
    Definitions 11

Chapter 2: Origins and Evolution 12
    Indirect Tax 17
    Direct Tax 18
    The Coming Storm 20
    The 16th Amendment 22

Chapter 3: Interpretations and Perceptions 25
    Other Decisions 33

Chapter 4: Income v. Income 41

Chapter 5: Then as Now 55

Chapter 6: If Not You, Then Who? 77
    Corporations 85
    Individuals 92

Chapter 7: In Their Own Words 100
    Internal Revenue Districts 106
    26 CFR, Part 601 111
    Withholding of Tax at Source 115

Illegal Withholding	118
Illegal Backup Withholding	119
Withholding Agent	121
Payor	123
Treasury Decision 8734	127
Those Grand Old Letters	142
IRS Organization and Staffing	142
Form 1040	148
T.D. 1928	149
T.D. 2313	151
T.D. 2401	154
T.D. 2815	155
T.D. 2988	156
T.D. 6500	157
OMB Control Number Chart at 602.101	160

Chapter 8: "Employee" – Who, Me? **164**
Trade or Business	171
Statutory Definitions Control	172
Includes and Including	173
Employee	180
Form W-2	186
F.I.C.A isn't "Social Security"	188
How do "Employment Taxes" break down?	190
Form W-4	204
Form W-2	216

Chapter 9: Working the Marks **225**
Indirectly Working The Mark	227
Ignorant Frank	231
Informed Frank	233
Informed Janice	234
Ignorant Janice	234
Ignorant and Malicious Janice	235

Table of Contents

Ignorant and Criminal Janice 236
Directly Working The Mark 237
Tax Terrorism Season 238
The IRS says… 241
What Happens When… 242
Financial Institutions 258
What of Employment Taxes? 265

Chapter 10: The Lies They Tell To Cover The Lies They've Told **267**
    Current IRS Responses 269
    Employee 269
    Wages, Tips, Etc 270
    Foreign Source Income 271
    A Direct Tax 275
    The Quislings 276
    Freedom of Information Act and other IRS Scams 281
    Court Precedent 284

Chapter 11: The Good, The Bad, And The Mistaken **286**
    UCC Controls 287
    Expatriation/Repatriation 288
    861 Position 290
    Filing A "Zero" Return 294
    The "Cracking The Code" Method 296

Chapter 12: Tricks Of The Trade **299**
    IRS Summons 299
    Levy 305

Chapter 13: This and That **311**
    Willful Failure to File 311
    System of Records 318
    More Systems of Records 319
    State Income Tax 320

Thrashing About **323**
    Fair Tax 324
    Flat Tax 330
    Value Added Tax – VAT 332

And The Answer Is… **334**
    Grand Jury 355
    Trial Jury 356
    In The Marketplace 359
    Financial Institutions 373
    Shunning 390

Admonition **398**

The Dave Champion Show and Other Resources **399**

The Right Handgun **400**

Acknowledgments **403**

Table of Authorities & Notes **407**

Index **416**

Introduction

"During times of universal deceit, telling the truth becomes a revolutionary act."
~ George Orwell

Over the years there has been a lot of talk about America's tax system; its benefits and its hardships; what is right and what is wrong with it. This book is not about those things. This book is not intended to spark tax reform or have you send a copy to your Congressman or Senator as evidence that he should seek to restructure the IRS (yet again) or implement one of the various alternative tax schemes that have been bandied about over the last several years. There are plenty of web sites, books, speakers, and political organizations out there that one can turn to if one desires to "build a better tax system". Good luck with that!

This book is for those who want to know the hard-core no-holds-barred truth about the current "income tax" – the one that has existed since 1913!

While this book will cover a lot of ground, the single most important question this book answers – indisputably and once and for all – is, "Upon whom has Congress actually imposed the income tax?". I will also answer the question, "What are the income tax's true legal and constitutional boundaries?" The answers to these questions (accompanied by irrefutable evidence) will surprise you. You'll also likely end up very angry.

Most Americans have never read a single word of tax law. Amazingly, that includes most people whose job it is to collect (alleged) taxes from you and/or report your "income" to the IRS.

Throughout this book I will share stories with you of my encounters over nearly two decades with people who claim they "have to" do various things that are harmful to you because "it is the law", yet cannot even tell me (or you) what the law is that they claim to be required to follow! You will discover that the entire "tax system" operates – to the detriment of hundreds of millions of Americans – on a myriad of "tax myths" that cannot be found anywhere in the law!

Dave Champion

For decades the government held all the cards in this game. It was the only source of information and the dominant media was all too happy to parrot the government's "party line" on the income tax. Technology has changed all that! Thanks to the internet, and other technical advances, information on virtually any subject is now readily available to the average man. The internet has also had a profound impact on how people get their news – and from whom!

Those who see a "wrong" being committed can now do a lot with the information available on the internet. Not only is it much easier today to ferret out legal or technical details, but the fruits of such efforts can be distributed widely at virtually no cost and with little effort.

While there have always been people who have managed to discover the truth of the income tax, they were numerically few and scattered across our vast nation with little opportunity or means to get the message to others. With the advent of new technologies (such as the internet), concerned, passionate, patriotic Americans were able to come together, in both the virtual and physical worlds, and the "Tax Honesty Movement" was born!

For the first time in history researchers could easily locate one another and work together. The fruits of their labor could be published for everyone to see. This dynamic was crucial because researching U.S. tax law is very much like the old story of the blind men touching different parts of an elephant – it can be difficult to see what the entire animal looks like.

When the Tax Honesty Movement came into being, a war began. For the first time in history the U.S. government was faced with a relatively large, reasonably well organized, body of citizens that knew that the government's "party line" on the income tax was an unabashed lie and were unwilling to buy it. Worse yet, this new Movement now had the ability to share its information with the public-at-large easily and with little expense.

As in any struggle against a powerful and dangerous adversary, many in the ranks of the Tax Honesty Movement have been mercilessly mowed down by the government. The government has branded these people "tax protesters" and, more recently, "tax deniers", and has embarked on a systematic program to demonize and discredit those who would dare to question or oppose the government's "party

Introduction

line" on the income tax. Many leaders of the Movement have been jailed or been enjoined by federal courts from writing or speaking about the income tax.

Because the message of the Tax Honesty Movement and that of the federal government are so thoroughly at odds, only one side can be telling the truth. And only one side can win the battle.

At the beginning of my Tax Honesty journey I was naïve enough to think that the government was simply confused or mistaken; if the law was brought to its attention it would stop attacking innocent people and follow the law. At the conclusion of this book many of you may feel the same way. You may feel that if you can get this information into the hands of the right people, then the problem can be resolved. I'm sorry to tell you that is not going to happen. After almost two decades in the trenches I can tell you without a shred of doubt that the government is fully aware of the facts in this book and it is dedicated to keeping the host [you] ignorant and complacent so that it can continue its parasitic behavior, and the law be damned!

Tax laws (passed by Congress) and tax regulations (created by the Secretary of the Treasury), as well as Treasury Decisions, Treasury Orders, IRS Determination Letters, the Cumulative Bulletin, the Internal Revenue Manual, etc., comprise literally hundreds of thousands of pages. If we look at all these documents as they've been printed since 1913, there are likely millions of pages of various tax materials available for review.

With this in mind it is easy to understand why some Tax Honesty researchers have at times propounded incorrect legal theories. The government has used these occurrences to attack the Movement and attempt to discredit it on a wholesale basis. With the cooperation of the dominant media, the government has been successful to some extent.

What does the government offer in rebuttal to the truth about the income tax? Absolutely nothing! The government has refused every opportunity to talk about the income tax and clarify to whom it applies and under what circumstances. Millions of Americans have asked the government to provide the law that requires the average American to file a Form 1040 and pay income tax. Instead of providing the law Americans have asked to see, the government provides meaningless platitudes and warns the inquiring citizen not to fall prey to "tax protester" arguments.

Dave Champion

For those who think the government has this issue well in hand, you will be shocked at how flimsy and transparent the government's propaganda really is.

The main difference between the government and the Tax Honesty Movement is that those within the Tax Honesty Movement have been attempting to get the truth out to their fellow Americans. By contrast, the government knows the truth and is engaged in a massive disinformation campaign to hide the truth from an entire nation!

To be blunt, the U.S government is guilty of committing the largest financial crime in history. Worse yet, it is fully aware that it is doing so and it has no intention of stopping.

I do not want you to take my word for it! I want you to see the facts for yourself. Facts are stubborn things.

One of the most disturbing elements of this book may be that the government's #1 co-conspirator in this crime is the average American! Very possibly you will see yourself described in the book, either as a victim, violator, or both. You will discover that the IRS rarely commits any direct action against anyone. The IRS simply sends out mail – and the recipients of that mail then voluntarily harm the innocent – usually out of ignorance, fear, or both. Many readers will have to come to terms with how many lives they've damaged or destroyed by enforcing nothing more than "tax myths" upon innocent Americans.

During the Cold War most of us were taught that the KGB was an evil organization that had wound its tentacles around every aspect of Soviet life. We were told that one of the most evil aspects of that system was that the KGB had coerced so many Soviet citizens [one out of every three by some reports] into "snitching" on their neighbors and coworkers. And Americans don't like a snitch! As you continue through this book you will find that by intentional misapplication of the income tax laws, the U.S. government has achieved a level of "snitching" by the American people that would make the most hardened KGB agent weep tears of admiration.

I long ago came to the realization that the only way to end the fraudulent application of the income tax was to come directly before the American people and provide them with the necessary information in such a way that they can see the situation for what it is, and then act accordingly.

Income Tax: Shattering The Myths

What will amaze you the most when you reflect on what you have read in this book is how simple the issue really is. At its core, the income tax is surprisingly straightforward!

No one can tell you what the truth is. You must decide that for yourself. In order to do so the entire matter must be laid before you clearly and without equivocation. This book does that for you.

So join me as we journey into the labyrinth of facts, law, lies, truths, half-truths, distortions, and deception that characterizes the search for the truth about the income tax and the government's efforts to keep that truth suppressed!

Dave Champion

How To Read This Book

After some reflection, I thought it necessary to include a brief statement about how this book will best be read. I think it necessary to make these suggestions because the subject matter is very likely foreign to most of you and the language of the statutes and regulations may appear quite odd; almost as if it's not English at all at some moments.

Accordingly, here are my suggestions to you concerning how to get the most out of this book.

1. Forget what you think you know about income tax and payroll tax. If you've read the law on this subject in agonizing detail, then you're the exception and you can ignore this advice. However, if you're the more common reader who's never read a word of tax law, or you're in the "tax industry" and you've read just the sections you have been told to read in order to "do your job", then your investment in this book (i.e. the money you paid for it) will be maximized by starting out with the mindset that you know nothing at all about tax law, and every socialized belief you hold (even if taught to you at an institution of higher learning) should be suspended. You'll eventually get it all figured out no matter how you approach it, but if you cling to what you now believe to be true, you may have to read the book again and again in order for everything to sink in and displace the "socialized" view you currently hold. In other words, suspending your "socialized" beliefs concerning taxation will likely result in less frustration for you and save you time in the long run.

2. Don't stop and mentally dispute every point you come to simply because it may be in conflict with your "socialized" view of how the income tax or payroll taxes work. [See suggestion #1!] If you battle in your mind over each point as they are made, this will likely be a long and frustrating read for you. I'm not saying you should agree with everything in this book without critical analysis. Doing what you're told without critical analysis is the government's expectation of you, not mine! I have no doubt that upon critical analysis you will agree with every fact in this book. There will be plenty of time to mentally kick around any questions that come to mind as you read. After reading each portion of this book I suspect your mind will percolate on the things you've read. A natural part of that process will

be comparing the evidence in this book against whatever it is you've been told over the years. If you are a rational human being I presume you will choose evidence over what people have told you – even if it's been told to you all your life. My point is that you should read the book straight through without making yourself nuts by mentally fighting anything and everything that cuts across the grain of what you've been told. Just read it. There will be plenty of time to go back over the material and give it your personal "acid test", whatever form that may take for you.

3. Do not spend too much time struggling over arcane language of old court decisions or the stilted language of the statutes or regulations. As you progress through the book this unfamiliar use of the English language will start to feel more familiar and less daunting. Just like exploring all the evidence in this book [suggestion #2], you'll have plenty of time to go back over it. My suggestion is to just read the book through and take in what is being presented. Go back over it as often as you feel you need to in order to insure you properly understand the decisions, statutes, and regulations.

4. Keep a yellow highlighter and two pens handy, one red and one blue. If something strikes you as quite significant, highlight it! If you don't understand something as well as you might like, place a small blue mark in the border next to that segment as a marker to use later when/if you choose to re-read it. If there is something that troubles you, or you want to research it for yourself, place a small red mark next it. Again, this will help you locate those segments later. You may also want to keep a notebook handy so you can write down your questions as they come up, though I believe you will find that most are answered as you continue reading.

5. Don't get part way through the book and run around telling others how the tax system works. If you're only part way through, you only know part of the story! I had a friend years ago who often heard me talk about the reality of the income tax. One night at a large get-together at his father's house, over dinner he attempted to tell the guests about the income tax. A number of the guests were attorneys, as is his father. Since he didn't know the material well, he got beat up pretty badly in the conversation and felt humiliated in front of his family and friends. After that evening he never wanted to hear another word about the income tax. Don't get yourself in that position. Know the material thoroughly before you speak up. But once you're confident that you really know the material, SHOUT IT FROM THE ROOFTOPS!

How To Read This Book

6. Do not immediately jump on the IRS's website the first time you think you've found something which the IRS might disagree with. I encourage you to do that, just not right away. There is an entire chapter of this book in which we explore the things the IRS has to say, in their own words, about numerous issues, including the things the IRS has to say about those wacky "tax protesters"! After you've completed chapter 10, feel free to roam the IRS's website to your heart's content. Until we've covered the material you're all too likely to fall prey to the government's intentional trickery. The IRS has been playing this game for a long time. They are experts at deceit. Let me show you (in chapter 10) exactly how they pull their little con job. After that, YOU be the judge!

7. I've been told that my animosity for the IRS comes through loud and clear in this book. I have no doubt that it does. How would you feel about a man who raped your wife or daughter? I'd bet the word "animosity" wouldn't begin to describe your feelings. Well, for nearly two decades I've been watching the United States government knowingly and intentionally rape hundreds of millions of Americans every year. I've seen people commit suicide because of the IRS. Americans who are as innocent as the day is long are languishing in federal prisons for alleged "tax crimes". Some of these innocent people will likely die in jail without ever again seeing their spouses or children – for a crime they never committed. So yes, I do feel animosity toward the IRS. It's likely you will too when you've finished this book. If you are uncomfortable with my animosity as you're reading, just move right past it and focus on the information you purchased the book to acquire.

8. Remember, in the end you are the judge. I am merely the messenger.

Rules of The Game

Chapter 1

"Knowledge will forever govern ignorance; and a people who mean to be their own governors must arm themselves with the power which knowledge gives."
~James Madison

All games have rules. That is no less true of taxation. But taxation in America is an odd game in that it has two different sets of rules.

The first set of rules is called "the law." Insofar as taxation is concerned, the law consists of the Constitution of the United States, the statutes created in pursuance thereof, and the regulations promulgated behind the statutes.

The second set of rules we shall call, "How things work on the street." In other words, what actually happens on Main Street – on your street – in America.

The problem we face as Americans is that these two sets of rules are in conflict. The law says one thing (quite clearly in most cases), while something entirely different is being done on the streets of America.

If these conflicting rules created nothing more than a benign sense of confusion, we'd have a relatively insignificant problem. However, the problem these conflicting rules create is not benign. The problem is insidious and malevolent, and it is harming every man, woman, and child in America.

As you proceed through this book, I will reveal to you how what is happening in virtually every home and business in America is completely adverse to what the law says, and why. But in order to understand that what is happening "on the street" is in conflict with the law, we must begin by looking at the law.

Lawyers go to school for years to learn various aspects of law. Law is so complex that it requires very specialized training if one wishes to make it a career. Since we aren't concerned with making the law a career, we don't need to go to law school! All we need to do is learn enough about the inner workings of law so that we can make some informed decisions concerning what the law really does, or doesn't say. Fortunately, everything we need to know has been laid out clearly for us and all we need to do is spend a little time exploring it!

No one can understand tax law without getting certain legal fundamentals under his/her belt. The lack of such fundamentals is precisely why the public has been so vulnerable to the government's mischaracterization of tax law. The good news is that any person of at least average intelligence can readily understand everything that is needed to discover the truth about our tax system!

THE CONSTITUTION

The structure and boundaries of the national government are found in the Constitution of the United States. Whenever we are looking at a question of federal authority or federal law, such a question always begins with the Constitution. Since that is true of every inquiry relating to federal law; that includes U.S. tax law.

It should be pointed out that the Constitution does not create or grant rights of any kind to American citizens. The Constitution lays out the structure of the federal government, grants to it authority in enumerated areas, restricts the states from doing several things, and defines a few national crimes, such as treason.

Some readers may be thinking, "But wait! The Bill of Rights grants us rights!" Not so! The Bill of Rights simply highlights certain rights that the federal government is powerless to legislate (or otherwise act) against. It should be pointed out that the list is not complete; it is merely those rights that were felt to be most worthy of mention. Amendment IX tells us that when it states, "The enumeration in the Constitution, of certain rights, shall not be construed to deny or disparage others retained by the people." In other words, the Bill of Rights is only a "Top Ten" list!

It should also be pointed out that the government must go about its business without infringing upon the individual rights of the American people.

For example, clearly it would be more convenient and efficacious for the government to prosecute alleged criminals without the restrictions of the 4th and 5th Amendments. Nevertheless, the Constitutional power to prosecute a person accused of a crime does not permit the government to violate a defendant's rights. We would be in a sorry state indeed if our rights were subject to being brushed aside any time the government wished to exercise one of its powers!

The point is that our rights remain in place and unaffected even as the government performs the functions for which it was created. The government has no authority or power to abridge, alter, or abolish our rights simply because the government has chosen to move in any particular direction.

Over the last hundred years or so, Americans have come to mistakenly believe that their rights must yield in the face of government action. This unfortunate and incorrect perspective has only intensified since 9/11. Too many Americans appear to have come to the erroneous conclusion that if the government chooses to pursue a certain course, it then has the authority to alter, modify, or even abolish our rights if doing so is thought necessary to achieve the government's desired ends. Nothing could be further from the truth!

This sad and inaccurate view is almost universally held by Americans when it comes to tax law. A view that is almost universal in America is that our rights must yield when it comes to taxation. Even those who work to defend our rights in many other areas of life fall completely silent on the question of whether taxation trumps the individual rights of the American people. Actually, there is no question. Our rights remain just as powerful and vibrant in the face of taxation as they do in any other activity where the government touches The People!

In 1819 the U.S. Supreme Court, in <u>McCulloch v. Maryland</u> 17 U.S. 327, enunciated a universal truth - "The power to tax is the power to destroy." What the Court meant is that if the government has the power to tax something, it can continue to raise the rate of the tax on that thing until it is destroyed. Let me give you an example.

Let's say that, at this time, milk costs $4.00 a gallon. At this price you may be willing to buy milk for your family. If the government places a 25% tax on milk, your cost becomes $5.00 a gallon. Would you buy it at that price? Now imagine that the government increases the tax to 50%. A gallon of milk would now be

$6.00. Still willing to buy it? Of course, if the government has the authority to tax milk, then it can set that tax at any rate it pleases. [More on that later.] Imagine that the government increases the tax again, now to 100%, making a gallon of milk $8.00. And, of course, at 200% that same gallon would cost $12.00! How many of you would still be willing to buy milk?

As you can imagine, very few people would be buying milk at these tax-inflated prices. Let's speculate that these tax increases on milk reduce milk purchases by 95%. That, of course, means that the revenue of the dairies which produce milk will decrease by 95%. So what industry is it that can survive a 95% reduction in its revenue? If you said no industry can survive such a reduction of revenue, you'd be right. This illustrates how taxation can destroy anything that is subject to taxation.

Now let's look at a far more disturbing proposition.

The Declaration of Independence states, "...that all men are created equal, that they are endowed by their Creator with certain unalienable Rights, that among these are Life, Liberty and the pursuit of Happiness." The point I want you to focus on is the unalienable rights of "Life, Liberty and the pursuit of Happiness."

A well-settled point of law is that once a legislature has the power to tax a thing, the rate of tax is completely at the discretion of the legislature. In other words, if Congress can tax a thing at 1%, it can tax that thing at 1000%!

If the Unites States government had the authority to tax the fruits of your labor, i.e. your income, then it would be free to tax your income at **whatever** rate it wishes! So, let me ask you a few questions.

1. If Congress were to tax your income at 100%, would you be able to sustain your "life"?
2. If Congress were to tax your income at 100%, would you be able to sustain (or retain) your "liberty"?
3. If Congress were to tax your income at 100%, would you be able to "pursue your Happiness"?

The answer to all these questions is plainly "no"!

If Congress could take (tax) 100% of your pay, then you'd have nothing left on which to survive. You could not pay for food, shelter, clothing, medical care, etc.

If Congress could take (tax) 100% of your pay, you would be destitute. You would not be destitute because of some calamity or natural disaster; you would be destitute due to the actions of your government. That would certainly rule out your "liberty."

And if you were rendered destitute by the actions of your government, I don't think we need to discuss your "pursuit of Happiness"!

It should be noted that the U.S. Supreme Court has stated that our "unalienable rights" can never be altered, modified, or abolished by government, because these rights existed in The People before the formation of either the states or the federal government.

We can summarize as follows: American citizens have unalienable Rights. These unalienable Rights include (among others) the right to Life, Liberty, and the pursuit of Happiness. The U.S. Supreme Court has ruled that it is outside of, and beyond, the power of government to alter, modify, or abolish our unalienable Rights. Once Congress has the power to tax a thing, it is free to increase the rate of tax as it wishes, even to the point of destroying the thing taxed.

Yet, if we believe the U.S. government's position concerning the income tax, we would have to somehow believe that the government possesses the power to destroy every single one of our unalienable Rights (although we've only focused on three of them so far) through the (alleged) power to tax our labor!

Now, some readers might be saying, "Come on, the government would never tax our income at 100%!" And you may well be right about that. However, this section addresses the foundation of federal taxing power, which is Congress's authority under the U.S. Constitution. We are discussing whether Congress has the Constitutional authority to take away (i.e. tax away) your unalienable Rights. Whether or not they would choose to exercise such power is another discussion altogether.

It should be manifestly obvious to all but the most hardened Federalists that Congress does not have, and cannot have, any authority that if used would eviscerate our unalienable Rights. Not only would the Founding Fathers never have vested the national government with such a power, but the U.S. Supreme Court has ruled that no government in this nation has, or can have, such authority.

Earlier in this section, I said that, "the government must go about its business without infringing the individual rights of the American people." Hopefully, you now have a better appreciation of why that principle is true.

STATUTES

After the U.S. Constitution, the next level of government authority is to be found in the statutes passed by Congress. Statutes passed by Congress are commonly called the "laws of the United States."

We must remember at all times that statutes passed by Congress may never exceed Congress's authority as expressed in the Constitution. We have all heard of federal laws being declared "unconstitutional." Those are cases in which the statutes Congress enacted have exceeded the authority given to it in the Constitution.

When statutes enacted by Congress fall within its constitutionally granted authority, they represent (at least in theory) the will of the American people as expressed through their elected representatives. These laws address matters within the realm of federal authority and include the tax laws of the United States.

The United States government imposes many different types of taxes. This book will not address the vast array of taxes imposed by the federal government, most of which are straightforward and completely legitimate. This book will only explore the "income tax" [26 USC, subtitle 'A'] and "employment tax" [26 USC, subtitle 'C'.

Statutes are rarely written by our elected officials. They are usually written by interested parties who hire attorneys specializing in drafting legislation. If you visit with your Representative or Senator and he is interested in creating legislation, he will turn to legislative draftsmen (attorneys who work for Congress) to have the desired statute drafted.

The language of a statute is very important. Not only should the language allow a person of average intelligence to determine what Congress is requiring (or prohibiting) by the statute (which the language rarely achieves), but courts must turn to the language of the statute if a person is accused of violating the law, or the law is challenged on constitutional grounds.

Statutes were originally designated only by "Statute-At-Large" numbers. In recent decades a dual identification system has evolved wherein each statute that is enacted by Congress receives a "Statute-At-Large" number as well as a "Public Law" number. Either of these numbers can be used to locate a particular statute in the appropriate law book.

As the decades passed and Congress enacted thousands of statutes, the task of finding each and every statute pertaining to a particular subject became daunting, if not impossible. An orderly and logical system of "codification" was needed that would allow a person to locate all the statutes on any particular subject. Further, that system would have to allow a person to find statutes addressing specific particulars within that subject matter. The system that was established to meet these needs is what we know today as the "United States Code" or USC.

It is impossible for Congressmen and Senators to be experts concerning every subject upon which they may be called to legislate. The U.S. Supreme Court has acknowledged this and stated that Congress speaks with "the broad language of the statute." In other words, the language of a statute often creates a broad framework that requires additional clarification in order for people to understand how the Executive Branch will implement Congress's intent. That "additional clarification" is provided in the form of federal regulations.

REGULATIONS

Regulations are created by the cabinet officer who has authority over a particular area of federal law. As an example, the U.S. Secretary of the Treasury is the cabinet officer who has authority over the administration of U.S. tax law. As such, the Treasury Secretary writes and issues tax regulations. Of course just as individual Representatives and Senators do not write statutes personally, neither does the Treasury Secretary write regulations. He has legislative draftsmen on his staff who perform that task for him.

The most important thing to know about regulations is that while they are not actual "laws," they have the "full force and effect of law."

Federal agencies are charged with faithful implementation and enforcement of the laws [statutes] through the regulations they promulgate [create].

Like statutes, regulations are also codified. The system of codification for the regulations is called the Code of Federal Regulations, known more commonly as the CFR.

The purpose of the CFR is to provide a system of categorization whereby all the regulations created by a federal department or agency on a given subject can be located with relative ease and sourced to the corresponding statute. The CFR does an admirable job of providing that service.

The form and structure of regulatory law is very complex. So complex, in fact, that few Americans have any idea how regulatory law really works. Most attorneys do not truly understand its intricacies. The relatively few attorneys who have a complete understanding of how the regulatory law system really operates are paid substantial sums of money by America's largest corporations to address regulatory issues.

Sadly, the average American citizen stands little chance of prevailing in the regulatory environment. It is the proverbial "David and Goliath" story, but in the regulatory world Goliath [the government] almost always wins. Adding insult to injury is the fact that almost every area of federal law has been established as "regulatory" in nature. It is for these reasons that I believe all regulatory laws should be held as unconstitutional – but I digress.

In order to make sense of the U.S. tax law, and understand its limitations, it is necessary for us to be familiar with just a few key principles of regulatory law.

1. As I stated a moment ago, regulations have "the full force and effect of law." That means if you violate a regulation it is exactly the same as having violated the law [statute].

2. Regulations may not exceed the scope of the statute. This means that when writing regulations a department or agency may explain how the intent of Congress is going to be carried forward, but it may not

use the regulation to expand the scope of the law beyond what Congress intended.

3. Regulations that are to have "general applicability" to the public, or impose a penalty on someone outside the government, must be published in the Federal Register.

4. While a department or agency is generally required to create regulations to clarify statutes, there is an exception. The federal courts have held that if a statute is so short and clear that it cannot be misunderstood, no regulation is required. Few statutes meet that standard.

TREASURY DECISIONS

So far, we have discussed actual laws (the U.S. Constitution and federal statutes) as well as the regulations, which are not law, but on a practical basis, must be treated as if they are.

We now enter into a discussion of an item that is not law, nor is it to be treated as law, yet it is an essential element in understanding tax law.

Treasury Decisions provide the details behind the regulations.

I've often said that a statute can be three paragraphs, while the regulation providing additional clarification to that statute can be eight pages. Likewise, a regulation can be eight pages and the Treasury Decision providing the details behind the regulation can be 30 pages!

Some of you may be thinking that this system is insane. You may be saying, "What rational form of law has a four-tier system in which one cannot know what a law actually means until he has 'drilled down' through all four levels?!" I am with you 100%, but this is the system the government has put in place to keep you ignorant and confused.

A retired FBI agent once stated that because during his career he had worked with numerous criminal statutes from various titles [areas of law] within the

United Stated Code, he thought he was well versed at making sense of statutes. But, after a lifetime of dealing with federal law, when he looked into the Internal Revenue Code, he found a maze that was impossible even for him to fathom.

OTHER RESOURCES

While we will generally stick to the Constitution, statutes, regulations, and Treasury Decisions during the course of our exploration, there are other resources that can be helpful in completing the picture.

Some of these are Treasury Orders, Memorandums of Decision, the Internal Revenue Manual, the system of codification used in constructing the USC and CFR, various government "systems of record," etc.

It should be noted that the statutes and regulations are 'the law' which the courts must use. And, the federal courts are required by statute to take "judicial notice" of the Federal Register. Additionally, federal *decisional law* [decisions of the federal appellate courts that create "precedent"] says that for federal tax purposes the *regulations control* (not the statutes).

Beyond the statutes, the regulations, and the Federal Register, everything else is merely for our education. The courts are not required to take notice of any of it or even admit such "persuasive" items into a proceeding.

At this point, some of you may be wondering how these underlying information sources that are necessary to actually understand tax law do not need to be considered by a court, and in some cases may not even be admissible as evidence. Welcome to the America you never knew existed!

As you will discover vividly in this book, the United States government is not at all interested in honesty or truth. It is interested only in your *obedience,* which in relationship to tax law means that you surrender your money to them for a "tax" that has never been imposed upon you. And the worst part is that the government knows everything in this book because they designed the system, and they enforce it everyday on its unsuspecting targets – the American People.

DEFINITIONS

There are a number of "legal terms" that we will encounter as we move forward. Oftentimes, these "legal terms" may appear to be familiar English words that you can find in the dictionary and that you believe you know the meaning of. Unless you have some familiarity with "law," what you do not know is that words used in law frequently have a completely different meaning, or no meaning at all, outside the confines of "the law." A wise man will never assume he knows what a "legal term" means unless he has already explored its special legal meaning.

So, what is the difference between a "word" and a "legal term"? "Words" are not defined by the legislature, while "legal terms" are. If a word is not defined by the legislature for use within the law you are reading, then it is indeed a "word" and you must use the dictionary definition or the commonly held societal meaning of the "word". This is what the U.S. Supreme Court has called "the plain meaning rule."

However, if the legislature has provided its own definition for a word, then it ceases to be a "word" (subject to the "plain meaning rule") and becomes a "legal term," subject only to the definition provided by the legislature. It is important to note that in three separate U.S. Supreme Court cases, the Court has held that once the legislature (in this case, Congress) has provided its own definition for a "legal term", we are barred from applying the "plain meaning rule" (i.e. using the dictionary definition) and may use *only* the definition provided by the legislature.

As we move through the book we will encounter these issues again in greater detail, but it is important that you understand the basics from the beginning.

Origins and Evolution

Chapter 2

"The time is near at hand which must determine whether Americans are to be free men or slaves"
~George Washington

In order to properly understand the boundaries and limitations that Congress has when creating federal tax law, it is first necessary to understand what the Constitution permits and doesn't permit. In order to gain an appreciation for this subject, it is necessary to put one's self in the shoes of the men who conceptualized the structure of the federal government, who debated one another as to what the final result might look like, and who eventually cast their votes for the U.S. Constitution.

Most Americans think of "states" as merely constituent components of the national government. Such a narrow view comes from America's current state of existence, as well as schools that don't teach our children actual history, but rather politically correct history.

One point of fact, the word "state," as used internationally, means an individual independent sovereign nation. When England recognized the independence of her former colonies, she did so by acceding to the independence of each colony on an independent and separate basis. Each former colony became an individual independent sovereign nation! At that time, each of the former colonies became "states"—and referred to themselves as such—even though there was no federal government.

These independent States eventually came together in a confederation. The first form was under the "Articles of Confederation and Perpetual Union" (known commonly as the "Articles of Confederation"). It should be noted that from 1776 until 1781 (when the Articles of Confederation were ratified), the thirteen States existed as completely independent nations—otherwise known as "states".

Each of these States had the powers possessed by every nation on earth. Each possessed the power to create money, make war, make treaties, and so on. Given their co-location on the same continent, their mutual experiences prior to and during the Revolution, and the fact that they'd seen the strife between nations in such close proximity in Europe, these independent States thought it best to establish a "union of states." The Articles of Confederation was the first form of that union.

When the independent States created the Articles of Confederation, they gave the government of the Union only certain (few) limited powers and retained all other powers unto themselves. The States had just thrown off an abusive national sovereign and were not willing to create another entity that would be sovereign over them. In other words, they retained their complete independence and sovereignty, except in those few areas where they had delegated specific powers to the Confederation.

Over the next few years, it became apparent to many people in the governments of the States that the Articles of Confederation was inadequate to achieve some of the ideals that were the original reasons for creating a Confederation. The most notable of these shortcomings was in the area of revenue.

Under the Articles of Confederation, the "national government" was charged with performing certain functions. Of course, no government can do anything unless it has the resources [money] to pay personnel and purchase materials. Despite being charged with performing various "national" functions, the Confederation had not been given the power to enforce financial contributions from the States to pay for the tasks that were expected. In other words, the national government would request the States to pay what was needed, but could not force them to do so.

This situation created a dilemma for the States. Each State had agreed to delegate some of its sovereign powers to the new national government. It was in the interest of the independent States that the new national government actually do the things for which it was created. Some of the States paid their necessary contributions, while others did not.

With some States paying and others falling short, the new government did not have the resources to do the things it was charged with accomplishing on behalf of the States. This meant that the governments of the irresponsible States were depriving every State of the benefits of the new national government. Furthermore, if the goals of the States in creating the confederation were not being met, why would the responsible State governments continue to make financial contributions? Clearly the revenue provisions for the confederation were not adequate to the requirements, and placed the future of a workable union in serious doubt.

Therefore, the States sent delegates to a convention with instructions to find suitable methods by which to correct the inadequacies of the Articles of Confederation. Today we know that meeting as the "Constitutional Convention".

Many delegates arrived at the convention planning to follow their orders; they were merely there to "fix" the Articles of Confederation. Other delegates—most notably James Madison—came to the convention having made the decision that a stronger alliance of the States was desirable and that the Articles of Confederation, even if "fixed," would not provide the level of alliance thought necessary or desirable. These delegates came not to fix the Articles of Confederation, but to use the opportunity of the convention to create something new. They came, as the Preamble of the U.S. Constitution says, "to create a more perfect Union."

The convention covered virtually every issue that one might imagine would be important when laying the foundation for a new national government. On various points there were heated debates, as regional and conceptual differences were hammered out.

While the story of the convention is fascinating in its own right, for the purposes of this book we are primarily concerned with the taxing provisions that were agreed upon and thus appear in the Constitution today.

The first reference to the taxing power of Congress is found in Article I, Section 2, Clause 3:

> *"Representatives and direct Taxes shall be apportioned among the several States which may be included within this Union, according to their respective Numbers...."*

This section does not specifically authorize Congress to lay direct taxes, but rather sets out a specific requirement of apportionment upon such taxes.

As we move on, we find the next taxing provision in Article I, Section 8, Clause 1:

> "The Congress shall have the power to lay and collect taxes, duties, imposts and excises...but all duties, imposts and excises shall be uniform through the United States."

As you can see, this provision grants Congress authority to "lay and collect taxes." Additionally, we see that certain species of taxes—duties, imposts and excises—must be imposed in a uniform manner throughout the nation.

The third reference to taxation is found in Article I, Section 9, Clause 4:

> "No capitation, or other direct, tax shall be laid, unless in proportion to the census or enumeration herein before directed to be taken."

Again, we see that this provision does not grant any taxing authority, but rather lays out what the U.S. Supreme Court has called the "Constitutional regulations" that establish requirements for Congress if it wishes to impose a "capitation" or other "direct" tax.

It should be noted that the provision reads, "...capitation, or other direct [tax]..." That is because "direct" is a category of taxation and a capitation tax is a form of a direct tax. Or phrased another way, a capitation tax is a tax that fits within the larger category of "direct taxes."

One should also understand that the first and third tax provisions within the Constitution address the same matter:

> Article I, Section 2, Clause 3— "...direct Taxes shall be apportioned among the several States..."

> Article I, Section 9, Clause 4— "No...direct, tax shall be laid, unless in proportion to the census or enumeration..."

At this point, you might have noticed that the Constitution references two different categories [what the law calls "classes"] of tax.

1. Direct taxes.
2. Duties, imposts and excises.

"Duties, imposts and excises" fall within a category [class] of taxation called "indirect taxes."

Once we understand that "duties, imposts and excises" are indirect taxes, we can then clearly see that the Constitution addresses two categories of tax—direct and indirect. The US Supreme Court has referred to these as "the two great tax classes." There is no third class.

Let's take a moment and do a quick recap.

- There are only three provisions of the Constitution that address taxation.
- Two of the three do not grant Congress any taxing power, but rather specify a mandatory mechanism [apportionment] that must be adhered to for a direct tax to be constitutionally valid.
- Only one provision [Article I, Section 8, Clause 1] grants Congress its taxing authority.
- Article I, Section 8, Clause 1 grants Congress the power to "lay and collect taxes, duties, imposts, and excises."
- "Taxes" (as used in Article I, Section 8, Clause 1) refers to direct taxes, which are twice restricted to the rule of apportionment.
- Duties, imposts and excises are indirect taxes.
- Article I, Section 8, Clause 1 mandates that indirect taxes are to be uniform throughout the United States.
- Direct and Indirect taxes have been referred to by the US Supreme Court as "the two great tax classes."
- There is no third class.

With those fundamentals under our belts, let's proceed to finding out how we can distinguish Direct and Indirect taxes from each other.

INDIRECT TAX

As a general descriptor, an Indirect tax is one that can be avoided by simply not engaging in a specific activity upon which the Indirect tax has been imposed.

A simple example of an Indirect tax would be a toll-road. In virtually every case I've seen, a toll-road is not the only route to a given location, but it is the more desirable route. In other words, if you do not wish to pay [if you wish to avoid] the Indirect tax, you can use the older, less efficient (slower) route to your destination. In Constitutional terms, this form of an Indirect tax would be referred to as an "impost."

Another form of an Indirect [avoidable] tax is "duties." One type of "duty" that most Americans have heard of is the "Customs duties" required to be paid when bringing foreign products into the U.S. Before returning to the U.S., many Americans buy foreign products at a "duty free" store. If one does not wish to pay [if one wishes to avoid] Customs' duties, one can simply choose not to bring foreign products into the U.S.

This brings us to the third type of Indirect tax—the excise tax. Here are two court cases that quite clearly state the nature of an excise tax:

> "The term '**excise** tax' and '**privilege** tax' are synonymous. The two are often used interchangeably."
> American Airways v. Wallace, 57 F.2d 877, 880

> "The obligation to pay an excise is based upon the voluntary action of the person taxed in performing the act, enjoying the privilege or engaging in the privilege which is the subject of the excise, and the element of absolute unavoidable demand is lacking."
> People ex rel, Atty Gen v. Naglee, 1 Cal 232;
> Bank of Commerce & T. Co. v. Senter, 149 Tenn 441SW, 144

The excise tax is by far the most common type of tax in America. Unfortunately, because of the almost complete ignorance of the American public about the nature of taxation, most Americans routinely pay excise taxes without ever knowing that such taxes are limited to the exercise of a government-granted privilege. "Sales tax" is a prime example of an excise tax that Americans participate in without ever understanding that it is limited to the exercise of a privilege! [More on that later!]

DIRECT TAX

Let's begin with another quote from the courts; this time from the U.S. Supreme Court:

> "Direct taxes bear upon **persons**, upon **possessions**, and **enjoyment of rights**". Knowlton v. Moore, 178 US 41 (1900)

Since "bear upon" may not be clear to everyone, we'll individually explore these three stated categories.

An example of a Direct tax upon "persons" would be a "head tax". A head tax is one in which the government lays a tax upon a person for simply existing.

An example of a Direct tax upon "possessions" would be a tax upon something you own, such as land.

In order to give you an example of a Direct tax upon the "enjoyment of rights," let me return to the toll-road scenario. In my example of the toll-road as an Indirect tax, I stated that there is always an older, slower alternative that will take you to your intended destination. Because there is an alternative route (even if slower), you are not "forced" to pay the toll for the toll-road. The lack of an "absolute unavoidable demand" is what renders it an Indirect tax.

Conversely, if there were no other route to your destination, the toll at a toll-road would no longer be an Indirect tax, but would be a Direct tax. Why? Because the U.S. Supreme Court has held that Americans have a constitutional "right to travel." If you cannot travel to your desired destination without being "forced" to pay a toll [tax] – because there is no alternative route – then your "right to travel" is being taxed, which makes such a tax, Direct.

Earlier I said that a "head tax" – i.e., a tax upon "persons" – is more limited than you might imagine. Allow me to explain.

The Founding Fathers and their generation never used the phrase "head tax" or "taxes upon persons" in relation to American citizens. These phrases were used exclusively in relation to taxing slaves.

Americans know next to nothing about "law" these days. Even many attorneys lack the requisite fundamentals. The public and attorneys have been "dumbed down" concerning certain important legal principles. [Most Americans are not aware that only a handful of law schools today still require a student to take a constitutional law class, and many law schools no longer even offer training in constitutional law!]

One of the early principles of law in this nation was that, when analyzing constitutional questions, the term "person" did not include a citizen. This rule was an active and vibrant part of constitutional and criminal law in the Revolutionary era and for more than a hundred years thereafter.

When the men who debated, wrote, and ratified the U.S. Constitution used a phrase such as "taxes upon persons," they never meant anything such as a head tax upon citizens.

In Hylton v US, 3 US 171 (1796), when addressing the matter of Direct taxes as authorized in the Constitution, the U.S. Supreme Court said the following:

> "The constitution declares, that a capitation tax is a direct tax; and both in theory and practice, a tax on land is deemed to be a direct tax...
> The provision was made in favor of the southern states; they possessed a large number of slaves; they had extensive tracts of territory, thinly settled and not very productive. A majority of the states had but few slaves, and several of them a limited territory, well settled, and in a high state of cultivation. The southern states, if no provision had been introduced in the constitution, would have been wholly at the mercy of the other states. Congress in such case, might tax slaves, at discretion or arbitrarily, and land in every part of the Union, after the same rate or measure: so much a head, in the first instance, and so much an acre, in the second. To guard them against imposition, in these particulars, was the reasons of introducing the clause in the constitution."

There you have the U.S. Supreme Court explaining what the meaning of the "capitation" [head] tax is as used in the reference to Direct taxes in the Constitution. Nowhere in the Court's decision is there any reference to a capitation tax being applicable to citizens of this country! In other words, Direct taxes, as such term is used in the Constitution, deal with land and slaves, and Congress may not extend them to just any object it chooses. [As much as we might not like it today, when the Constitution was written, black slaves were not citizens, but were considered in law to be merely "persons."]

There are some "Hamiltonians" [i.e. those who seek enlarged powers for Congress] who believe that the Direct tax authority of Congress is all-embracing and permits Congress to tax anything it sets its eyes upon. While it is not difficult to determine the motives of people who would put forth such an interpretation, for such an interpretation to be true, we'd need to toss aside the first rule of constitutional construction/interpretation; namely, that the Constitution means what the men who wrote it, debated it, and ratified it, meant when they constructed it! In other words, one can only posit the idea that Congress can lay any Direct tax it wants if one is also willing to throw out the rulebook for constitutional interpretation – and where does that leave America?

No income tax was imposed during the first 88 years of this nation.

The first "income tax" was imposed briefly by the Union during the Civil War. Its form was a tax upon certain government workers – much like today's "payroll withholding tax." [More on that later.]

THE COMING STORM

While there were minor skirmishes over Congress's taxing authority, the constitutional tax landscape remained relatively unchanged until the U.S. Supreme Court decision in <u>Pollock v. Farmers' Loan & Trust Company</u>, 157 U.S. 429 (1895).

In Pollock, the Court held that since taxes on real estate and personal property were Direct taxes, a tax upon the profits derived from such properties – such as rent from real estate – must also then be Direct taxes and subject to apportionment. Because Congress (in the Wilson-Gorman Tariff Act [1894]) had imposed such taxes without the constitutionally required apportionment, the Court held those taxes to be unconstitutional. The government's position (with which the Court did not agree) was that such taxes were Indirect and therefore not subject to apportionment!

[Note: In Pollock, the Court never addressed the question of whether Congress had the constitutional authority to impose a Direct tax on the fruits of real and/or personal property. The Court stopped at the point where it determined that such taxes were Direct and therefore unconstitutional due to a lack of apportionment. In his suit, Charles Pollock never challenged the constitutional authority of Congress to impose such a tax, therefore, the Court did not presume to address an issue that was not positioned as a part of the controversy before the Court.]

Here are two quotes from the Pollock decision:

> *"First. We adhere to the opinion already announced—that, taxes on real estate being indisputably direct taxes, taxes on the rents or income of real estate are equally direct taxes."*

> *"Second. We are of the opinion that taxes on personal property, or on the income of personal property, are likewise direct taxes."*

1895 was just a few years into what historians have dubbed the "Progressive Era." Today some people prefer to be called "progressives" rather than "leftist." The meaning of "progressive" in 1895 was no different than it is today. The euphemistically named "Progressive Era" would be more forthrightly entitled, "The Era of the Popularity of Socialism in America."

Socialism was in vogue during this "progressive" era [1890 to 1929] and the Pollock ruling was seen by socialists, and those sympathetic to the socialists' view of "class warfare," as a ruling that benefited only the wealthy. The "progressive" view was that only the wealthy generated income in the form of rentals, dividends, and interest, therefore a decision that rendered a tax upon those items unconstitutional must be a conspiracy to make the rich richer and the poor poorer. Typical socialist blather that we still hear today.

In reality, the Pollock decision was constitutionally correct. The taxes in question were clearly not "duties," nor were they "excises." They could not be "imposts" because there must be some government provided benefit for there to be an impost.

In this case, Congress was attempting to lay an Indirect tax upon the private transactions of private citizens within the states of the Union. But such transactions do not fall into any of the categories of Indirect taxation. Not only do such transactions not fall into any of the categories of Indirect taxation, but under the established definitions for each of the two "great tax classes," the taxes at issue in Pollock were most certainly Direct.

THE 16TH AMENDMENT

The 16th Amendment is commonly known as the "income tax amendment." and is arguably the most controversial of any of the amendments to the U.S. Constitution.

Not only is it controversial in its purpose, but there is also substantial evidence that it was never properly ratified, but instead was certified as such by Philander Knox, a corrupt U.S. Secretary of State who was politically beholden to the men behind the 16th Amendment. You can investigate these facts for yourself, and reach your own conclusions, by reading "The Law That Never Was" by Bill Benson and M. J. "Red" Beckman.

For the purpose of this book, we shall consider that the 16th Amendment was ratified.

The origin of the 16th Amendment is typically seen as the Pollock decision. As stated earlier, the Pollock decision was seen as a decision made in the interest of the wealthy. Socialist politicians and newspaper owners/editors wasted no time in holding the Pollock decision up as proof that there was a conspiracy afoot to keep the rich in power and deprive "the masses" of a voice in America.

The "class warfare" pitch was that Americans who were more financially successful had a duty to pay for a far greater percentage of the revenues needed by the Federal government than the "average man." Despite the fact that the more financially successful American receives no more protections or services from the federal government than does a poor man, and therefore has no duty to shoulder any greater burden than his fellow Americans, it was nevertheless persuasive to many people.

Congress passed the proposed amendment in 1909. Philander Knox certified ratification in 1913. The text of the Amendment reads as follows:

"The Congress shall have power to lay and collect taxes on incomes, from whatever source derived, without apportionment among the several states, and without regard to any census or enumeration."

Just 30 words; these thirty words changed a nation.

Not long after the 16th Amendment was certified as having been ratified, Congress passed the first income tax act. Provisions of that act were challenged and came before the U.S. Supreme Court in 1916.

However, before I begin laying out the various Supreme Court cases that address the 16th Amendment, let me make a brief aside to tell you what the practical ramifications of the Amendment have been.

If you write to the Internal Revenue Service (IRS) and ask them what their authority is to administrate the income tax, they will write back and tell you their authority is the 16th Amendment. [If you choose to send that inquiry, hang on to the response letter. In my experience, that reply will be the only time the IRS will tell you the truth when you ask questions about the income tax.]

The 16th Amendment ushered in such fundamental changes to this nation, and the lives of its people, that it is hard to paint a complete picture, but here is what it is safe to say:

- Financial privacy is virtually non-existent.
- Americans now live in fear of the federal government.
- Americans now work the better part of 5 months each year to pay taxes.
- Working Americans suffer a lower standard of living because of the income tax.
- The income tax poured fuel on the fire of socialism in America and has now entrenched socialism as the American way of life.
- It is not really a tax system as much as it is a wealth redistribution scheme.
- A strong graduated income tax (which is what we have in America) is one of the ten planks of the Communist Manifesto.

- The income tax has made possible the obscene usurpation of power we've seen from Washington D.C.
- There is no way to return America to greatness as long as the income tax remains in existence (or any of the various suggested alternative schemes).

Is this the America in which you want to live?

While I do not see the 16th Amendment as the bane of freedom – because of what I know about how the income tax REALLY operates – I do think it should be repealed, simply to end the federal government's disastrous and criminal misapplication of the income tax. Without the 16th Amendment, the federal government would have no claim of authority to administrate what is today called "income tax" in the manner they do, and as such the largest financial crime in the history of the world would end.

Interpretations and Perceptions

Chapter 3

"America will never be destroyed from the outside. If we falter and lose our freedoms, it will be because we destroyed ourselves."
~ Abraham Lincoln

The first case to reach the U.S. Supreme Court regarding the effect of the 16th Amendment was <u>Brushaber v. Union Pacific Railroad</u>, 240 U.S. 1 (1916). After all these years, and despite a number of subsequent 16th Amendment decisions, *Brushaber* is still the seminal case.

Brushaber provides a look at a number of constitutional aspects of U.S. tax law.

I previously mentioned that the men who wrote the Constitution viewed Direct taxation as being limited to slaves and land – and since the cardinal rule of constitutional interpretation is that the Constitution means what the men who wrote the words said it meant – then the government's authority to impose a Direct tax is properly (constitutionally) limited to slaves and land.

In *Brushaber*, Justice White, writing the decision of the Court (and who wrote the dissent in *Pollock*), reviews in brief the *Pollock* decision. During this review he summarizes Direct taxes in the following manner:

> "On the one hand, that the tax was not in the class of direct taxes requiring apportionment, because it was not levied directly on property because of its ownership, but rather on its use, and was therefore an excise, duty, or impost; and on the other, that <u>in any event the class of</u>

<u>direct taxes included only taxes directly levied on real estate</u> because of its ownership." [Underline added by author for emphasis]

The Court then buttresses this observation with the following statement:

> "In the first place this is shown by the fact that wherever (and there were a number of cases of that kind) a tax was levied directly on real estate or slaves because of ownership, it was treated as coming within the direct class and apportionment was provided for, <u>while no instance of apportionment as to any other kind of tax is afforded</u>."

[Underline added by author for emphasis]

The last line of the above quote should settle this debate once and for all in the minds of any rational, thinking person. Justice White is clearly saying the following:

- The Constitution requires apportionment on any and all Direct taxes.
- Taxes on real estate and slaves are Direct taxes.
- In the history of U.S. taxation there was "no instance" in which a tax on any other form of property was apportioned.

After almost two decades of research, it is my well-considered opinion that the U.S. government's authority to impose a Direct tax is restricted to slaves and land. And I am not alone in this determination. The U.S. Supreme Court said as much in 1796 in *Hylton*. Then in *Pollock* (99 years after *Hylton*) the Court once again concludes that Congress' Direct taxation power is limited to slaves and real estate.

Eighteen years after *Pollock*, the Court reinforces this doctrine yet again by using *Pollock*'s explanation as the foundation from which to announce the Court's position in *Brushaber*.

Of course it should be noted that as of 1865 slavery became constitutionally impermissible, so after that date Congress' authority to impose a Direct tax was limited to real estate.

So what was the overarching purpose in the minds of the men who constructed the Constitution when they included the requirement of apportionment for Direct taxes? Again, Justice White, writing in *Brushaber* gives us the answer:

Interpretations and Perceptions

"Concluding that the classification of direct was adopted for the purpose of rendering it impossible to burden by taxation accumulations of property, real or personal, except subject to the regulation of apportionment, it was held that the duty existed to fix what was a direct tax in the constitutional sense so as to accomplish this purpose contemplated by the Constitution."

The Founding Fathers were cultured, intelligent men who were well schooled in history. The history of the conduct of governments since the beginning of time was no mystery to the Founders.

Knowing the propensity of government to rape the people of their property through the power of taxation, the Founders chose to protect the American people from a "burden by taxation accumulations of property, real or personal, except subject to the regulation of apportionment".

Another way to phrase the intention of the Founders is that they desired every American – folks just like you and me – to be able to accumulate wealth –in the form of real and personal property – without that process of accumulation being burdened by taxation. In other words, the requirement of apportionment was intended to be a powerful disincentive to Congress interfering in our right to accumulate property/wealth.

But let us continue with Justice White's *Brushaber* review of *Pollock* (while keeping in mind that White sat on the *Pollock* Court).

> "Moreover, in addition, the conclusion reached in the *Pollock* Case did not in any degree involve holding that income taxes generically and necessarily came within the class of direct taxes on property, but, on the contrary, recognized the fact that taxation on income was in its nature an excise entitled to be enforced as such unless and until it was concluded that to enforce it would amount to accomplishing the result which the requirement as to apportionment of direct taxation was adopted to prevent....'

What is White saying here? Let's break it down.

First, White is stating that *Pollock* did not hold that "income taxes" were Direct taxes. He continues by saying "...on the contrary...taxation on income was in its nature an excise...." In other words, **taxation on income is, in its proper**

constitutional role, an excise tax. [This is a critical point to keep in mind as we move forward!]

Since income taxes are, in a proper constitutional sense, excise taxes, obviously the *Pollock* Court found there was something different or unusual about the particular tax being challenged in that case, because the Court held that it was a Direct tax. [You are likely wondering what that distinction was. All will be revealed in good time, my friends, but I have not yet laid the necessary foundation to reveal that pivotal fact. It's coming!]

In the above quote, White goes on to say that a constitutionally proper income tax – that is, an excise – is *"entitled to be enforced as such unless and until it was concluded that to enforce it would amount to accomplishing the result which the requirement as to apportionment of direct taxation was adopted to prevent...."*

Note that White has shifted from discussing the proper nature of an income tax, (it is an excise, not a Direct tax), to remarking upon the manner in which the income tax is enforced. Why did he do that? Do we imagine that his line of commentary is merely a flight of fancy?

To imagine it so would be a mistake for several reasons. First, there is nothing in White's various decisions that would indicate he is prone to flights of fancy. Second, White's style is to make the most of every word he uses. (I have yet to read a single word that White has written in any decision that is in any way irrelevant or surplus to the topic being commented upon.) And third, White is drawing the reader to a specific and important conclusion, derived from the intent of the men who wrote the Constitution.

White is saying that an income tax – which is imposed as an excise – is 100% constitutional, BUT if that tax is enforced (aka; administered) in such a way that it runs afoul of the intent of the apportionment clause, then the tax must be declared Direct because it is then burdening "by taxation accumulations of property, real or personal", which would then force that tax into the Direct class.

[**Author's Note**: If your head is starting to swim a bit at this point, it's OK. I'm throwing a lot at you on a subject with which you are unfamiliar. You may wish to stop here and re-read the previous chapter, and this chapter up to this point, until you are certain you understand the concepts. I say this because it is difficult to make sense of all the issues we will be discussing if you are unclear about the foundational blocks upon which the future discussions rest.]

Now that White has made it crystal clear that the proper constitutional nature of an income tax is an excise, let us revisit what an excise tax is.

"The term '**excise** tax' and '**privilege** tax' are synonymous. The two are often used interchangeably." <u>American Airways v Wallace</u>, 57 F.2d 877, 880

An excise tax is a privilege tax. Simple enough. So what is a "privilege"?

Privilege – A special benefit, exemption from a duty, or immunity from penalty, given to a particular person, a group or a class of people. <u>Law.Com Dictionary</u>

Privilege – A right, license, or exemption from duty or liability granted as a special benefit, advantage. <u>Findlaw.com</u>

Privilege – This word, taken in its active sense, is a particular law, or a particular disposition of the law, which grants certain special prerogatives to some persons, contrary to common right. <u>Bouvier's Law Dictionary</u>

As you can see, a "privilege" is when someone is being treated in a special manner under the law, which does not apply to others. Or phrased another way, a person receiving a privilege is one who has been granted the right to do something that others in his same class are not permitted to do and would be penalized for doing absent special government dispensation.

What this means is that income tax, in its proper constitutional nature, is a tax imposed on a person who is receiving a privilege, under the law, from government.

I have my own personal definition of a "privilege". **Anything you do not have a <u>right</u> to do.** I prefer this definition because, when used, it consistently begs the question, "Is this something I have a right to do as an American citizen?" and that focuses our attention on our rights!

Let's also now recall another facet of an excise:

"The obligation to pay an excise is based upon the voluntary action of the person taxed in performing the act, enjoying the privilege or

engaging in the privilege which is the subject of the excise, and the element of absolute unavoidable demand is lacking."
People ex rel, Atty Gen v. Naglee, 1 Cal 232; Bank of Commerce & T. Co. v. Senter, 149 Tenn 441SW 144

If an income tax – operating in its proper constitutional nature – is one that is applied to the exercise of a privilege, one must also be free to reject the privilege, and thus place himself outside the reach of a "privilege tax" because there can be no "absolute unavoidable demand" associated with an excise tax.

Let's take a moment for a short summarization:

- An income tax, in its proper constitutional nature, is an excise.
- An excise is a tax upon the acceptance/exercise of a governmentally granted privilege.
- In order for a tax to be sustained as an excise there can never be an absolute unavoidable demand.
- Although the tax being challenged in *Pollock* was called an "income tax", the U.S. Supreme Court decided that it was not really an income tax (an excise), but rather was a Direct tax (and unconstitutional for want of apportionment).

Having completed our summary, I wish to take a moment to note that everything we've covered so far is pre-16th Amendment. We have been in the midst of exploring *Brushaber* because it is the first U.S. Supreme Court case to rule on the meaning of the 16th Amendment. So let us continue.

There is much debate – even today – about what *Brushaber* did or did not do. In fact, it has caused so much confusion that half of the United States Circuit Courts hold that today's income tax is an unapportioned Direct tax, while the other half hold that it is an excise.

This confusion is not without cause. White's style of writing is unusual and he often approaches his point from the back end. In other words, he often presents a contention that cannot be true under the 16th Amendment and then "reverse engineers" the logic of why the contention cannot be valid. Combine his unusual prose with this unconventional method of articulating his point, and the *Brushaber* decision can be a read that will make you want to pull your hair out in frustration! That said, the decision is not inscrutable, merely challenging.

I will now tell you what the Court's position is in *Brushaber*. I'm going to tell you in plain English. After I tell you what the Court's position is, I'm going to prove their interpretation by using White's words from the decision.

> **Brushaber's holding is that the income tax is an excise and that the 16th Amendment merely blocked future courts from declaring an income tax to be a Direct tax on the basis that Congress had imposed the tax on the fruits [income] of property that could not itself be taxed without that tax being Direct.**

I hope that's clear, but let me give you an example.

A man owns a home. A federal tax upon that home would be, without question (before and after the 16th Amendment) a Direct tax with the attendant requirement of apportionment. Prior to the 16th Amendment, taxing the fruits of his home [rent] would also be a Direct tax because under *Pollock* taxing the fruits of the property was considered a burden on the property itself. After the 16th Amendment an income tax (excise) could not be said by a court to be Direct merely because it taxed the fruit of property that could not itself be taxed as an excise.

I know that many readers are now struggling with the concept that Congress can now, under the 16th Amendment, impose an income tax, which is presumed to be an excise, but the courts cannot rule that Congress actually imposed a Direct tax. It would seem like the 16th Amendment acts to bar the courts from making an all-important determination about the true constitutional nature of a tax. And you'd be right – to an extent.

White is very clear (as have been other decisions) that since income tax remains an excise, there must be the exercise of a privilege as the basis of the tax. What White is saying is that the 16th Amendment means that if a true privilege is being exercised, and is thus subject to a proper constitutional income tax, then the fact that it is imposed on the fruits of property, which cannot itself be taxed other than by a Direct tax, does not permit that income tax to be forced (by court determination) into the class of Direct, and thus subject to apportionment (or being declared unconstitutional for the want of apportionment).

So…while the decision is not as evil as some have accused it of being, it nevertheless provides substantial room for shenanigans by federal taxing authorities – and they have made full use of this unfortunate "loophole" created by the 16th Amendment.

Now we get on the language of the decision itself.

> "…there is no escape from the conclusion that the Amendment was drawn for the purpose of doing away for the future with the principle upon which the *Pollock* Case was decided; that is, of determining whether a tax on income was direct not by a consideration of the burden placed on the taxed income upon which it directly operated, but by taking into view the burden which resulted on the property from which the income was derived, since in express terms the Amendment provides that income taxes, from whatever source the income may be derived, shall not be subject to the regulation of apportionment."

Here White is telling us that the purpose of the Amendment was to insure that the *Pollock* doctrine had been rendered void by the Amendment. In other words, if an income tax (excise) was imposed on the fruits of property that could only be taxed itself by a Direct tax, that would not be sufficient for a court to declare the income tax Direct also.

And here is more from *Brushaber*:

> "…the contention that the Amendment treats a tax on income as a direct tax although it is relieved from apportionment and is necessarily therefore not subject to the rule of uniformity as such rule only applies to taxes which are not direct, thus destroying the two great classifications which have been recognized and enforced from the beginning, is also wholly without foundation since the command of the Amendment that all income taxes shall not be subject to apportionment by a consideration of the sources from which the taxed income may be derived forbids the application to such taxes of the rule applied in the *Pollock* Case by which alone such taxes were removed from the great class of excises, duties, and imposts subject to the rule of uniformity, and were placed under the other or direct class."

Here White is telling us that simply because the Amendment bars an excise from being declared a Direct tax due to its source, that should not be construed to mean that there is now such a thing as a Direct tax without the requirement of apportionment, but rather that all income taxes are excises and it is for that reason, and that reason alone, that they do not require apportionment. The Amendment did not bar the courts from distinguishing between a Direct and Indirect tax, but merely barred the courts from pushing an excise into the Direct category due to the fact that the underlying property could not be taxed in any manner other than a Direct tax.

OTHER DECISIONS

Although *Brushaber* is the seminal case concerning the 16th Amendment and controls the issue entirely, other U.S. Supreme Court decisions have mentioned *Brushaber* or relied upon it as the foundation of the various cases before the Court.

In my opinion, the most notable of these subsequent cases is Stanton v. Baltic Mining Co., 240 U.S. 103 (1916). It is notable due to its short, crisp, clear statement concerning what the 16th Amendment did not do!

In the Court's decision, Justice White [again writing the decision of the U.S. Supreme Court in a tax case] reviews the reasons (alleged by the appellant) that the tax he is challenging is unconstitutional. While there are several allegations of unconstitutionality, there are two based on the 16th Amendment. The second one is irrelevant to our inquiry, but the first is most revealing.

White here summarizes the first allegation of 16th Amendment unconstitutionality:

> "(1) That, as the Sixteenth Amendment authorizes only an exceptional direct income tax without apportionment, to which the tax in question does not conform, it is therefore not within the authority of that Amendment."

White answers that allegation this way:

"As the first proposition is plainly in conflict with the meaning of the Sixteenth Amendment as interpreted in the *Brushaber* case, it may also be put out of view."

As we can clearly see, White completely rejects the proposition that the 16th Amendment authorized a Direct tax without apportionment. So not only do we have the *Brushaber* decision in which White was clear about the purpose and effect of the 16th Amendment, we now have him declaring that the 16th Amendment did **not** permit Congress to impose a Direct tax absent apportionment!

Given the clear message of the U.S. Supreme Court on this subject, do you not find it amazing – and thoroughly bizarre – that half of the federal circuit courts hold that the 16th Amendment authorized a Direct tax absent apportionment?

I point this out because those who support the illegal and unconstitutional misapplication of the income tax will point to these circuit court decisions as evidence that you are mistaken in your understanding.

In order for those who support the illegal and unconstitutional misapplication of the income tax to be right, they would have to jettison two pivotal rules that control our system of jurisprudence in the United States.

First, they would have to jettison the rule that decisions of the United States Supreme Court are binding on the lower courts. They would have to jettison that rule because since *Brushaber*, and certainly since *Stanton*, it is impossible for a circuit court to hold that the 16th Amendment authorizes a Direct tax absent apportionment.

Second, there is a rule of judicial interpretation that says when a modern court is reviewing the meaning of a constitutional provision it is to give greater weight to those decisions made closer to the date of enactment than to later cases. This is because it is understood that the men who lived in the era of the enactment, or closer to that era, were better able to ascertain the intent of the framers and/or the ratifying states, than are later generations. Accordingly, if one wishes to say that the 16th Amendment authorizes a Direct tax absent apportionment, one would have to ignore both *Brushaber* and *Stanton* – and that would constitute jettisoning the principle of giving greater weight to court decisions closer to the time of enactment.

Isn't it interesting that in order to attempt to get you to believe their corrupt position, those who support the illegal and unconstitutional misapplication of the income tax have to ignore these two judicial principles that are universally applied in every other case!

Since these two rules/principles have to be abandoned in order to hold the view that the 16th Amendment authorizes a Direct tax absent apportionment, how is it then that half the federal circuits so hold? That is an excellent question!

Since the U.S. Supreme Court has spoken so plainly on this issue, there can really only be two possible conclusions.

1) The judges on those circuits are unable to make sense of the same statements that you and I just read. This is disturbing because it means that the judges on these circuit courts are too stupid to be on the bench. I hate to use language such as "too stupid" in a situation like this, but since you are likely not a member of Mensa, and yet you were able to understand it without too much difficulty, what then are we to say about men who are trained in the law, yet cannot understand something so plainly stated by Justice White in both *Brushaber* and *Stanton*?

2) Of course this brings us to the more disturbing second possibility. The circuit court judges can read and make sense of *Brushaber* and *Stanton* yet choose to hold the exact opposite of what the U.S. Supreme Court has established in both those cases!

There is no third choice that I have been able to discover.

This presents half the people of this nation with a terrible dilemma: people in the half of the country within the jurisdiction of the circuit courts that hold incorrectly on the 16th Amendment have the miserable choice of determining whether the judges in those circuits are morons or treasonous criminals!

Further, this horrible dilemma brings us to another question. Can we – or should we – trust the government to tell us what the truth is on this subject (or any subject, for that matter)? And make no mistake; the federal courts are a part of the federal government!

Americans are basically forthright and honest people. We've been told that the Judicial Branch is independent and stands between us and the overreaching of government. But is that really true?

On August 22, 2006, Chief Judge Douglas H. Ginsburg, joined by judges Judith Rogers and Janice Rogers-Brown, sitting on the United States Court of Appeals for the District of Columbia Circuit [aka - First Circuit] issued an amazing decision adverse to the Internal Revenue Service (IRS). The case is Murphy v. U.S.

What made the decision amazing was that the Court stated that Murphy's income, which was the result of an emotional distress ruling, could not be constitutionally considered to be income under the 16th Amendment. Even more startling was that the Court's logic was based on the same line of precedent we have been examining here, as well as those we will get into shortly.

This case was a real problem for the government. Here we had an important appellate court of the United States holding that the 16th Amendment did not confer upon Congress the power to tax anything it wanted and call it "income" (subject to the 16th Amendment). Worse yet for the government, the Court had relied on arguments that honest Americans, who've taken the time to read the relevant court cases, have always known were true. These were the same arguments that are often called "frivolous tax protestor arguments" by those – including the IRS – who support the illegal and unconstitutional misapplication of the income tax!

What did those who support the illegal and unconstitutional misapplication of the income tax do? They excoriated the decision. I paid careful attention to the articles they wrote about the Murphy decision. While much ado was made about the "consequences" of the decision, hardly a word was spoken concerning the actual positions held by the Court! If the decision was so terrible, surely there should have been detailed analysis of why the Court's underlying positions were in error. Yet that did not occur!

So what happened in this case?

The government predictably filed a "Motion for Reconsideration". This is where the losing party asks the Court to reconsider its decision and offers what it hopes are persuasive arguments as to why the Court's decision is mistaken. Motions for reconsideration rarely achieve much, because all the arguments (from both sides) are to have already been put before the Court at trial and therefore all the moving party can attempt is to paint a picture that the Court didn't view the arguments in the proper light.

Here comes the troubling part.

The Court did not rule on the government's Motion for Reconsideration. Instead, on December 22, 2006, the Court acting of its own volition, without urging from either party, vacated its decision and decided to write an entirely new one. The subsequent decision (issued July 3, 2007) read like a complete repudiation of the original. It read like a decision written by three different judges who vehemently disagreed with Ginsburg, Rogers and Rogers-Brown!

Anyone who has followed the careers and decisions of Ginsburg, Rogers and Rogers-Brown knows that these three are diligent jurists. In Murphy, after hearing the numerous positions of both parties, they took months to construct a well-reasoned decision that could not be assailed by its opponents on the merits.

Shortly after vacating its original decision, the Court entertained brief oral arguments. Then – miraculously – this court of competent and prestigious judges issued a new decision that was in complete conflict with its original decision!

These events leave the American people with yet again a set of very unpleasant options to explain this unheard of turn of events. The choices are few:

1) The Court's original decision, the products of months of research and reflection upon the meaning of the original taxing provisions of the U.S. Constitution as well as the 16th Amendment, by three of the most professional judges on the federal bench, was just an "oopsy". And not a small "oopsy" but a screw-up of monumental proportions!

2) Someone threatened these judges to the point where they felt they had no choice but to completely reverse themselves.

Which do you imagine is more likely to be the case?

So…now I will repeat my question: Can we – or should we – trust the government to tell us what the truth is on this subject (or any subject, for that matter)? In this author's mind, the answer is clear.

Returning to the *Stanton* decision:

> "But, aside from the obvious error of the proposition, intrinsically considered, it manifestly disregards the fact that, by the previous ruling, it was settled that the provisions of the Sixteenth Amendment conferred no new power of taxation, but simply prohibited the previous complete and plenary power of income taxation possessed by Congress from the beginning from being taken out of the category of indirect taxation to which it inherently belonged, and being placed in the category of direct taxation subject to apportionment by a consideration of the sources from which the income was derived -- that is, by testing the tax not by what it was, a tax on income, but by a mistaken theory deduced from the origin or source of the income taxed. <u>Mark, of course, in saying this we are not here considering a tax not within the provisions of the Sixteenth Amendment -- that is, one in which the regulation of apportionment or the rule of uniformity is wholly negligible because the tax is one entirely beyond the scope of the taxing power of Congress, and where consequently no authority to impose a burden, either direct or indirect, exists.</u>"
> [Underline added by author for emphasis]

Pay careful attention to the portion I underlined. This is Justice White writing for the U.S. Supreme Court. Do you understand what he is writing for all of posterity [YOU!] to read? Remember I said earlier that White does not waste words or indulge in irrelevant flights of fancy? White is saying this for a reason. He is making sure that Americans in all future generations will be able to read those words.

He starts with "Mark". In the vernacular of the day, "mark" (as used in this context) meant "to give heed or attention to" or "pay attention to this". White is calling our attention to something of which he wants us to take particular note. His next words are "of course". In the context White places it, that phrase should be understood as, "it goes without saying".

White then briefly mentions apportionment and uniformity. What he then says is the truly significant part. He lets us know that in the *Stanton* decision the Court is not addressing a tax that is "entirely beyond the scope of the taxing power of Congress, and where consequently no authority to impose a burden, either direct or indirect, exists."

This dovetails perfectly with other statements by the Court concerning Congress' power of taxation.

> "As pointed out in recent decisions, it [16th Amendment] does not extend the taxing power to new or excepted subjects…"
> William E. Peck and Co. v. Lowe, 247 U.S. 165 (1918)

If, as the Hamiltonians [those who support the illegal and unconstitutional misapplication of the income tax] would have us believe, the federal government can tax anything and everyone it might care to, how could there be any "new subject" to which to apply the tax? Additionally, who (or what) are those "excepted subjects"? The Court is saying that before the 16th Amendment there were subjects [in the legal vernacular of the day, "subject" could be either a person or an activity] that were exempt from Congress' taxing power under the Constitution. How come you were never taught **that** in school? And who (or what) are these "excepted subjects"?

And *Peck* relied on *Stanton*, in which the Court said:

> "The provisions of the Sixteenth Amendment conferred no new powers of taxation…." Stanton v. Baltic Mining Co., 240 U.S. 103 (1916)

If there were constitutionally "excepted subjects" prior to the adoption of the 16th Amendment, and the Amendment "conferred no new powers of taxation", then plainly those subjects remain constitutionally excepted today.

Because there are always those Hamiltonians who will use any argument, no matter how meritless, in an attempt to pull the wool over people's eyes, some might say that my use of the word "today" in the previous sentence is inappropriate because things have changed since the early 1900s. And indeed they have! But in all the time since *Brushaber*, *Stanton* and *Peck*, there has been no constitutional alteration in the authority of the federal government to tax. As far as the fundamentals of constitutional taxation in America, what was true then is still true now!

And finally, South Carolina v. Baker, 485 U.S. 505 (1988) in which the Court said:

> "The legislative history merely shows…that the sole purpose of the Sixteenth Amendment was to remove the apportionment requirement for whichever incomes were *otherwise* taxable." [Bold/italicized by author for emphasis] South Carolina v. Baker, 485 U.S. 505 (1988)

Two things are significant about Baker. First, the decision was issued in 1988, thus dispensing with the Hamiltonians' feigned anxiety that things have changed since the early 1900s.

Second, the Court uses very specific language here. It does *not* say the purpose of the Sixteenth Amendment was to remove the apportionment requirement for *all* incomes, which is the known inaccurate position put forth by the United States government every day in furtherance of the largest financial crime in the history of the world.

The Baker decision is carefully crafted to give the reader the necessary information. That carefully crafted language says the purpose of the "…Sixteenth Amendment was to remove the apportionment requirement for whichever incomes were *otherwise* taxable." In other words, it has to first be an excise tax, which means the activity has to be a privilege, and because of that proper constitutional nature of the income tax (an excise), apportionment cannot be required by looking at the source (i.e. the underlying property itself could only be taxed as a Direct tax), nor can the tax be declared unconstitutional for want of apportionment, because an excise tax is not constitutionally required to be apportioned, only uniform.

I suspect that at this point many of you are wondering what exactly is the unspoken element that is repeatedly hinted at by the U.S. Supreme Court which would render one's income "entirely beyond the scope of the taxing power of Congress, and where consequently no authority to impose a burden, either direct or indirect, exists." [Stanton]

We're not quite there yet, but we're getting there – I promise!

Income v. Income

Chapter 4

"Our lives begin to end the day we become silent about things that matter."
~ Dr. Martin Luther King, Jr.

Although everyone has heard the phrase "income tax", few Americans have stopped to wonder what actually constitutes "income". This is, of course, because Americans mistakenly believe they know what "income tax" is, and they feel there is little purpose in exploring such matters because, "You can't fight City Hall" and the income tax is the ultimate manifestation of "City Hall".

Should we really be looking into such things? Well, that depends. If you like being the host from which the malicious parasite sucks away your lifeblood and infects you with an illness, then by all means, look the other way. On the other hand, if you believe that Americans are – or should be – a free people, and that the government **must** follow the law, especially in areas as important as your property rights, then you might want to pay attention.

I say "property rights" because that's exactly what the fundamental issue is which underlies the income tax.

When you received payment in exchange for a physical object, or for your labor, that payment is your _property_. This is a significant fundamental in understanding the income tax and the limits of Congress' tax authority. This is not some banal or esoteric discussion. It is the core issue!

Let us for a moment explore how a typical American small business operates. For the sake of this illustration, let's say the owner, Joe, earns his living selling "widgets."

If Joe is a savvy businessman he knows that the game is all about buying low and selling high, thus maximizing profits. Accordingly, Joe shops a number of providers for the lowest possible price on his widgets. Let's say Joe ends up buying his widgets for $50.00 each. Widgets happen to be in vogue at the time so Joe is able to sell them for $100.00 to the public. Joe makes $50.00 profit per widget.

Americans use all sorts of euphemisms to refer to property. In the illustration just provided, people might use words such as "profit", "margin", "income", "cash flow", "revenue stream", etc., to describe the $50.00 per widget profit that Joe has made. The one word you will never hear is "property"!

Using euphemisms to describe your property programs you not to think of your property as – **your property**!

Joe acquired certain property at $50.00 a unit. Let's say Joe purchases 100 units. He now has $5,000.00 worth of his property sitting on the shelf. It's fine to describe that property as "merchandise" or "goods," as long as we never lose sight of the fact that it is – in reality – above all else – **his property!**

Joe then sells 40 units of his property. At $100 a unit (to the public), Joe receives $4,000.00 in exchange for the 40 units. So now Joe has $4,000.00 of **his property** in the form of cash, and 60 units of **his property** sitting on the shelf in the form of product. At this moment in time, Joe has turned $5,000.00 of **his property** [original capital investment] into $7,000.00 of **his property** [cash and product on the shelf].

As time goes by, Joe sells the remaining 60 units and has no more product on the shelf. But what Joe now has is $10,000 of **his property** in the form of cash. Joe has taken $5,000.00 of his property [cash] and exchanged it for 100 widgets [product], which he then exchanged with other people at a higher price, thus doubling **his property** from $5,000.00 to $10,000.00. God bless free enterprise!

Some of you may be saying that the example I just provided is self-evident. Is it? The truth be told, most American business owners don't think of their goods/products or receipts as their **property.** They tend to think of their big screen TV as their property, or their bowling ball as their property, or their furniture as their property. They may think of the shelving at their store as their property, or the cash register as their property, but they do not generally think of the goods/products or the return of capital with profit, as **property**. That subtle distinction is significant.

You will recall that the U.S. Supreme Court, in *Pollock* and in *Brushaber*, stated that the income tax is an excise. You will also recall that it is a well-settled point of law that an excise is a tax upon a privilege.

Now, let's dovetail these legal facts with Joe's situation. Joe buys **property**. He then sells that **property**. At the point of sale, Joe's **property** becomes the **property** of another. As payment, Joe receives other **property** (in this illustration, cash). So you see, all that happened is that different forms of property were exchanged. So we might ask, "Where's the privilege that would make this transaction subject to an excise tax?"

At this point, those who support the illegal and unconstitutional misapplication of the income tax will offer all sorts of worthless platitudes and screwball responses. They will say things like:

- An excise tax is not upon property, but upon the "happening of an event."
- There is no privilege, unless all of that occurred in the course of "business."
- The privilege is upon the transfer of property.
- The profit is the privilege.

If these answers seem screwy to you, you're on the right path! Let's take a brief moment and examine their nonsense.

There are court cases which have said that an excise tax is imposed on the "happening of an event," but that "event" still has to be a government-permitted privilege before an excise can be applied. An example of this would be the sale of tobacco products. Selling tobacco is a government permitted privilege. The "event" that is taxable is the "sale" of tobacco between the retailer and the consumer.

There is no distinction in constitutional law between property I own for pleasure and property I own for the purpose of re-selling it for profit [which is its own form of pleasure!].

Transferring ownership of property is not a privilege, nor is there any law that would make it so. [Later we will take a brief journey into the issue of "sales tax".]

Making a profit is not a privilege – despite the best efforts of socialists to create that impression!

Now that we have dispensed with the ridiculous responses of those who support the illegal and unconstitutional misapplication of the income tax, what have the courts said about property ownership?

> "…the individuals' Right to live and own property are natural rights for the enjoyment of which an excise cannot be imposed."
> Corn v. Fort, 95 S.W.2d 620 (1936)

> "The property that every man has is his personal labor, as it is the original foundation of all other property so it is the most sacred and inviolable…to hinder his employing [it]…in what manner he thinks proper, without injury to his neighbor, is a plain violation of the most sacred property."
> Butcher's Union Co. v. Crescent City Co., 111 US 746 (1884)

> "Included in the right of personal liberty…is the right to make contracts for the acquisition of property. Chief among such contracts is that of personal employment, by which labor and other services are exchanged for money and other forms of property."
> Coppage v. Kansas, 236 US 1 (1915)

As you can see, the U.S. Supreme Court has confirmed that personal property (which includes one's labor) is "inviolable."

What does "inviolable" mean?

    1. Secure from violation...
    2. Impregnable to assault or trespass; invincible American Heritage Dictionary, Fourth Edition

    1. Incapable of being transgressed or dishonored
    2. Immune to attack; incapable of being tampered with
    3. Must be kept sacred

4. Not capable of being violated or infringed
   WordNet 3.0, Princeton University

In *Coppage*, the Court says that "personal liberty" includes (among many other rights) the right to make contracts for the acquisition of property.

In *Butcher's Union*, the Court tells us that to hinder a man's use of his property in any manner he thinks proper – without injuring the rights of others – "is a plain violation of the most sacred property."

The Court in *Butcher's Union* is drawing upon these words from Justice Story in his commentaries on the U.S. Constitution:

> "The sacred rights of property are to be guarded at every point. I call them sacred, because, if they are unprotected, all other rights become worthless or visionary. What is personal liberty, if it does not draw after it the right to enjoy the fruits of our own industry? What is political liberty, if it imparts only perpetual poverty to us and all our posterity? What is the privilege of a vote, if the majority of the hour may sweep away the earnings of our whole lives, to gratify the rapacity of the indolent, the cunning, or the profligate, who are borne into power upon the tide of a temporary popularity?"
> -- Judge Joseph Story, 1852

And Judge Story may well have been drawing on the words of John Locke:

> "Whenever legislators endeavor to take away and destroy the property of the people…they put themselves into a state of war with the people…." -- John Locke (1690)

It should be noted that Thomas Jefferson incorporated Locke's writings on personal liberty into the Declaration of Independence.

Jefferson wrote in the Declaration of Independence that we have the right to "life, liberty, and the pursuit of happiness." As Murray Rothbard points out in "Conceived in Liberty," Jefferson's phrase was merely a contraction of George Mason's sentence from the Virginia Declaration of Rights, [keeping in mind that Jefferson was a Virginian], which said that among man's natural rights "are the enjoyment of life and liberty, with the means of acquiring and possessing property, and pursuing and obtaining happiness and safety."

So what are we to make of all this?

Quite clearly, we see that in a republican form of government, property rights have been paramount from the beginning.

> "The United States shall guarantee to every State in this Union a Republican Form of Government..." United States Constitution, Article IV, Section 4

It should be clear that acquiring, utilizing, and disposing of property are among our numerous unalienable Rights. As such, these Rights cannot be infringed upon.

The Founding Fathers gave the new federal government limited power in this area, allowing Direct taxes on real estate and slaves, while also permitting the government to impose excise taxes upon those involving themselves in government-created privileges. Taken along with imposts and duties, this conglomeration of constitutionally permitted taxing methods was viewed as sufficient by the Founders to sustain a federal government operating within its enumerated powers.

So now we know that "income tax," in its proper constitutional nature, is an excise. And, we know that property (as well as the fruits of property) are unalienable Rights that cannot be constitutionally infringed upon by the federal government, except in the case of real estate or slaves (in the form of a Direct tax). So, what then is the "income" to which the 16th Amendment refers?

I started this chapter by saying that most Americans have never shown the slightest interest in what "income" means as it is used in the 16th Amendment.

And we have arrived back at that point.

While the courts have done an admirable job of detailing the exact and specific meaning of "income" as used in the 16th Amendment, their words do not express or convey what "income" – as used in the Amendment – cannot mean! Before exploring the words of the federal courts, it was necessary to insure that you had a firm grasp of what the word could not mean, and why.

The U.S. Supreme Court, speaking again in the era of *Pollock*, the 16th Amendment, and *Brushaber*, states the following:

> "As has been repeatedly remarked, the corporation tax act of 1909 was not intended to be and is not, in any proper sense, an income tax law. This court had decided in the Pollock Case that the income tax law of 1894 amounted in effect to a direct tax upon property, and was invalid because not apportioned according to populations, as prescribed by the Constitution. The act of 1909 avoided this difficulty by imposing not an income tax, but an excise tax upon the conduct of business in a corporate capacity, measuring, however, the amount of tax by the income of the corporation...." Stratton's Independence, LTD. v. Howbert, 231 US 399, 414 (1913)

One should take note that the Corporation Tax Act of 1909 (which the Stratton Court is ruling upon) was passed by Congress four years before the [alleged] ratification of the 16th Amendment and there was no presumption that it was unconstitutional, nor was the Act ever declared so by the any court.

In 1918, the Supreme Court again considered a case dealing with the Corporation Tax Act of 1909:

> "Whatever difficulty there may be about a precise and scientific definition of 'income', it imports, as used here [in the 1909 Act], something entirely distinct from principle or capital either as a subject of taxation or as a measure of the tax; conveying rather the idea of gain or increase arising from corporate activities." Doyle v. Mitchell Brother, Co., 247 US 179 (1918)

Now we move to post-16th Amendment cases.

In Towne v. Eisner, 245 U.S. 418 (1918), the U.S. government stated (as part of a motion to dismiss) that the term "income" as used within the Income Tax Law of 1913 (which was enacted based on the 16th Amendment) had to have the same meaning as in the Amendment if it were to be held as constitutional.

Accordingly, we can see that the Corporation Tax Act of 1909 and the Income Tax Act of 1913 are not necessarily the same tax. This is important, because there are those on both sides of the fence who mistakenly believe that the tax imposed under the 1909 Act [pre-16th Amendment] is the same tax later imposed by the 1913 Act [post-16th Amendment].

Clearly the Corporation Tax Act of 1909 could not have been an act under the authority of the 16th Amendment because the Amendment had not yet been created!

In <u>Eisner v. Macomber</u>, 252 US 189 (1920), the U.S. Supreme Court addressed the 16th Amendment, and an act pursuant thereto, as related to the definition of "income":

"This case presents the question whether, by virtue of the Sixteenth Amendment, Congress has the power to tax, as income of the stockholder and without apportionment, a stock dividend…"

The Court continues:

"It [the controversy] arises under the Revenue Act of September 8, 1916."

Therefore we know that the Court is addressing an Income Tax Act enacted after the 16th Amendment, and that the question before the Court is whether or not the authority of the Amendment permits Congress to tax a stock dividend.

The Court did not believe the case turned on the definition of "income" but did feel that establishing a solid definition of income would be essential to the proper understanding of the 16th Amendment and would assist in proper administration of tax acts which did rely upon the Amendment for their authority.

Here is the Eisner Court's definition of 16th Amendment "income":

"[Income is] derived--from--capitol--the--gain--derived--from--capitol, etc. Here we have the essential matter--not gain accruing to capitol, not growth or increment of value in the investment; but a gain, a profit, something of exchangeable value…severed from capitol however invested or employed and coming in, being "derived", that is received or drawn by the recipient for his separate use, benefit and disposal--that is the income derived from property. Nothing else answers the description…". [emphasis in original] <u>Eisner v. Macomber</u>, 252 US 189 (1920)

Then in 1921:

> "[Income] must be given the same meaning, in all the Income Tax Acts [1913, 1916, 1917] of Congress that it was given in the Corporate Excise Tax Act, and what that meaning is has become definitely settled by the decisions of this court". Merchants Loan & Trust v. Smietanka, 255 US 509 (1921)

The Court continues in *Merchant* with:

> "In determining the definition of the word 'income' thus arrived at, this Court has consistently refused to enter into the refinements of lexicographers or economists, and has approved, in the definitions quoted, what it believed to be the commonly understood meaning of the term which must have been in the minds of the people when they adopted the Sixteenth Amendment to the Constitution."

By the *Merchant* decision, the Court declared that the Corporation Tax Act of 1909 [pre-16th Amendment] and the Income Tax Act of 1913, 1916, and 1917 [relying on the 16th Amendment for their authority] must have possessed one single cohesive definition of "income." This was the first time the Court made a solid connection between the pre-16th Amendment definition of "income" in the 1909 Act and the definition of the word as used in the 16th Amendment itself.

This is likely a good time to pause and point out that we are only talking about the meaning of the word "income" for the purposes of the 16th Amendment. The Court did not say that a "tax" under the authority of the 16th Amendment had to be the same tax as the 1909 Corporation Tax Act.

We know from *Brushaber* that the 16th Amendment merely prevented an excise tax from being declared a Direct tax by considering the means by which the underlying property would have to be taxed [which is by a Direct tax]. By contrast, the 1909 Corporation Tax Act was limited solely to corporate activity.

However, by its decision in *Merchant* regarding the meaning of "income," the Court narrowed the application of the 16th Amendment to the boundaries of the 1909 Act. It became impossible to apply the Amendment broadly once the Court had stated that "income," as used in the 16th Amendment, meant "gain or increase arising from corporate activities".

It is extremely important to take stock of the fact that the federal government has always had, and still has, the constitutional authority to impose any excise tax it deems appropriate without regard to the 16th Amendment. The 16th Amendment only operates upon an excise tax in a particular (narrow) set of circumstances and does not affect any excise tax outside that narrow set of circumstances.

I raise this issue because all too often people misunderstand the nature of the government's overall taxing authority and the purpose of the 16th Amendment. They somehow get it in their heads that if a tax isn't "authorized by the 16th Amendment," then it's not valid. That position is not legally accurate, and the results of such an erroneous view, if acted upon, can be damaging.

That said, it is critical to understand that the courts have consistently held that an excise may only be imposed on that which is actually – in reality – the exercise of a privilege. Congress may not declare something to be a privilege, that is not in reality a privilege, just so it can then tax the activity. This is why I prefer my definition of "privilege" to that of the courts. The courts are free to use any language they want to attempt to explain or define a 'privileged activity', but the only test that really matters is whether we, as Americans, have a *right* to do a particular thing. If we do indeed have a *right* to do that thing, then it cannot be taxed as an excise.

You can now see that "income," as that word is used in the 16th Amendment, is something that the Courts have defined quite narrowly. Further, the 16th Amendment confirmed that the "income tax" to which it applies is an excise.

Outside of the narrow species of income applicable to the 16th Amendment, generic income has never been defined. And there is no need to define it.

Congress can tax privileged activities in the form of excise taxes, or it can tax real property as a Direct tax subject to apportionment.

Do lawyers know the things discussed in this book? Most don't, because tax law is thought to be very complex. Additionally, lawyers attend schools that are "accredited." The standards for accreditation are established by the government. This guarantees that the truth will not be taught in law school.

I've often said that if any college or university hired me to teach tax law, that school's accreditation would be threatened by the government within weeks.

That is the government's way of controlling what is taught in America's halls of upper education.

Despite the government's best efforts, however, the truth is out there. This book evidences that fact.

"Westlaw" is one of the nation's premier resources to legal professionals. You'd be hard pressed to find a lawyer or law firm that does not subscribe to Westlaw's services. I have a number of law books published by Westlaw's publishing arm.

Westlaw's books offer "keys." These "keys" are succinct statements that Westlaw has concluded are legally true, based on such things as the U.S. Constitution, statutes, and court decisions. These "keys" are numbered so that one may verify the source information, and easily cite them in legal arguments.

In their volumes addressing taxation, we find two pertinent and interesting "keys":

> **Taxation Key, West 53** - The legislature cannot name something to be a taxable privilege unless it is first a privilege.
>
> **Taxation Key, West 933** - The right to receive income or earnings is a right belonging to every person and realization and receipts of income is therefore not a "privilege that can be taxed."

Given these legal facts, is it any wonder that the government has to practice massive sophistry about the "income tax"?

The U.S. Supreme Court has held that the "income tax" authorized by the 16th Amendment is an excise [privilege] tax. Yet hundreds of millions of Americans go to work, exchange their labor for compensation, and are told that now they owe "income tax." Have they exercised any government-created privilege? To answer that question, I draw your attention to two resources. First, the West Taxation Key 933 we just read. Second, three Court cases: two of which we read earlier in this chapter.

> "The property that every man has is his personal labor, as it is the original foundation of all other property so it is the most sacred and inviolable...to hinder his employing [it]...in what manner he thinks

> proper, without injury to his neighbor, is a plain violation of the most sacred property."
> Butcher's Union Co. v. Crescent City Co., 111 US 746 (1884)

> "In our opinion that section, in the particular mentioned, is an invasion of the personal liberty, as well as of the right of property, guaranteed by that [5th] Amendment. Such liberty and right embraces the right to make contracts for the purchase of the labor of others and equally the right to make contracts for the sale of one's own labor." Adair v. United States, 208 U.S. 161, 172 (1908)

> "Included in the right of personal liberty…is the right to make contracts for the acquisition of property. Chief among such contracts is that of personal employment, by which labor and other services are exchanged for money and other forms of property." Coppage v. Kansas, 236 US 1 (1915)

As you can clearly see, there is no question that simply working for a living is a **right**, not a privilege. As such, it cannot possibly be subject to an excise tax upon the exercise of a privilege!

Since working for a living is a **right**, not a privilege, and therefore cannot be the object of an excise tax, how does the government get away with convincing hundreds of millions of Americans that they owe an excise tax on a **right**? At this point, I am merely demonstrating that the government's "party line" cannot possibly be true – or legal! In the chapters ahead, I will explain how America has been bamboozled for decades by a duplicitous and self-serving government that doesn't give a damn about you or your family. You may consider those hard words, but when you've completed this book, you may find your words harsher than mine.

In closing this chapter, I'd like to remark upon a strange statement made by Justice White. In *Brushaber*, White suggested that the *Pollock* court "impliedly" accepted the proposition that a Direct tax can be imposed on things other than real property because the Court did not use the "real estate and slaves only" argument to strike down the tax as unconstitutional. This is a strange argument indeed.

Imagine that your 16-year-old daughter came home and announced that she was going away for five days with a group of Hell's Angels. She did not ask permission to do so; she merely announced it to you.

You respond immediately that she is not going anywhere with the Hell's Angels and you don't want to hear another word about it! Your daughter leaves the room crestfallen. Does this now mean that she can go away with someone other than the Hell's Angels for five days without your consent? Of course not. The fact that you saw the Hell's Angels as the predominant violation, made clear your rules, and thus saw no reason to explore the equation further, does not suddenly make the lesser violations (such as going away with someone else without your consent) any more acceptable or permissible.

Likewise, the fact that the *Pollock* court decided the controversy on the "fruits of property" issue does not imply that other aspects of the tax, that are clearly unconstitutional but were not a part of the Court's holding, are somehow then sanctioned as constitutional.

Prior to *Brushaber*, there was no case in the history of U.S. jurisprudence that suggested that a Direct tax could be imposed by the federal government on any objects other than real estate and slaves. There is no writing of any Founding Father that suggests any other application of the Direct tax provision in the Constitution than toward land and slaves. By contrast, there are court decisions and writings of the Founders that substantiate that a Direct tax – as such phrase is used in the U.S. Constitution – is limited to land and slaves.

The fact that the *Pollock* court chose to decide the matter on other grounds cannot change the original intent of the Constitutional provision concerning Direct taxation, nor can White's speculative remark that the *Pollock* court somehow "impliedly" sanctioned a broader power than the Constitution grants. And it should be self-evident that if the Constitution permitted a Direct tax on anything other than land and slaves, White's comment would have been wholly unnecessary.

Thankfully for us, the U.S. Supreme Court has stated that taxes cannot be imposed by implication.

> "In the interpretation of statutes levying taxes it is the established rule not to extend their provisions, by implication, beyond the clear import of the language used, or to enlarge their operations so as to embrace matters not specifically pointed out. In case of doubt they are construed most strongly against the government, and in favor of the citizen."
> Gould v. Gould 245 U.S. 151 (1917); United States v. Wigglesworth,

2 Story, 369, Fed. Case No. 16,690; American Net & Twine Co. v. Worthington, 141 U.S. 468, 474 , 12 S. Sup. Ct. 55; Benziger v. United States, 192 U.S. 38, 55 , 24 S. Sup. Ct. 189.

If the U.S. Supreme Court does not feel that taxes can be imposed by loose construction (mere "implication") of a *statute,* how then can one imagine that a breed of taxes hitherto constitutionally unknown (i.e. a Direct tax on anything other than land and slaves) can be sanctioned by loose construction (mere "implication") of the Constitution!

Then as Now

Chapter 5

" Only the State obtains its revenue by coercion."
~ Murray Rothbard

There have been no changes in the federal government's constitutional taxing powers since the creation of this nation. As the Court pointed out in *Brushaber*, the purpose of the 16th Amendment was to "harmonize" the government's taxing powers, not change them.

At this point, you have a superficial understanding of the tax scheme. I say "superficial" because there is more that has yet to be revealed. Nevertheless, if you stopped reading this book right now, you'd still know more about the federal government's powers of taxation than 99% of the American public. You'd just be missing the most critical part!

Before I reveal the hidden reality the government desperately does not want you to know about, let's explore what the tax code looks like today. After all, if there have been no changes in the government's taxing powers in more than 200 years, and only a "harmonizing" in 1913, we should be able to get a pretty clear picture of what tax has been imposed upon whom and for what activity.

Let's start at the beginning of the Tax Code with section 1(a).

There is hereby imposed on the taxable income of —

(1) every married individual (as defined in section 7703) who makes a single return jointly with his spouse under section 6013, and

(2) every surviving spouse (as defined in section 2 (a)),

If we resist the temptation to assume we know what that statement means and focus solely on the words Congress has chosen to use in this, the opening section of the Tax Code, how could we possibly know if that section is referring to us?

I say that we should "resist the temptation to assume we know" because most Americans have been socialized to believe they "know" what the income tax is. The fact that by this point in the book you have almost certainly learned all manner of things about the income tax you never knew before should serve as a warning that presuming you "know" about the income tax is unwise. If you're reading this book, I presume you're looking for the truth about the income tax. If that is your goal, you'll need to put aside all the things you *think* you know, and concentrate on what's actually there – without any preconceived ideas based on years, or possibly decades, of erroneous socialization.

Let's look at the phrase "every married individual". Does that refer to an American citizen who is married, or does is refer to a foreign person who is married and living in the U.S.? Based solely on the words Congress has chosen to use in the very first section of the Code, can you say which is true? No.

Further, is it married people living in the U.S. or Americans who are married but living outside the U.S.? (You may not find that question so odd as we continue.) Based solely on the words Congress has chosen to use in the very first section of the Code, can you say which is true? No.

And note that the statute says you are taxed on "taxable income". Based solely on the words used in this statute, can you tell me what specific type of income that is or who might be earning that specific type of income? No. Clearly, Congress didn't mean *all* income or the statute would say that. Accordingly, we know that the tax being imposed is only upon a particular species of income known as "taxable income". (We'll get into that in a little bit.)

It should be obvious that the statute doesn't tell us all that we might want to know – or all that we *must* know – in order to make an informed decision about whether or not the tax in question has been imposed on us.

I've often referred to the Regulations as that which "puts the meat on the bone". Since the statute in this instance is clearly a bone with no meat on it, let's have a look at the corresponding regulation.

1.1-1(a) – Section 1 of the Code imposes an income tax on the income of every individual who is a citizen or resident of the United States and, to the extent provided by section 871(b) or 877(b), on the income of a nonresident alien individual. The tax imposed is upon taxable income.

1.1-1(b) – In general, all citizens of the United States, wherever resident, and all resident alien individuals are liable to the income taxes imposed by the Code whether the income is received from sources within or without the United States.

Does this regulation provide any additional clarity or certainty? Not much. It is nearly as vague as the statute.

Section 1.1-1(a) tells us that an income tax is imposed "on the income of every individual who is a citizen or resident of the United States." This statement begs far more questions than it offers clarity.

Let's see how this breaks down.

First, the tax is imposed "on the income of every...." Laying a tax "on income" is straight out of the 16th Amendment. So at least initially, we can presume that the tax being imposed is an excise. The U.S. Supreme Court has repeatedly held that the value of a privilege may be determined, and taxed, based on the amount of income generated by the privileged activity. So what we see in 1.1-1 is that the Secretary (who writes the regulations) is confirming that this is a tax upon a privilege.

What privileged activity is being taxed? That's impossible to say from reading this regulation because it does not tell us that. How then shall we know if 1.1-1 is speaking to us? Might this hidden element have to do with the fact that the statute specifies "taxable income"? Possibly. We'll look at that shortly.

Next, we see that the regulation tells us that this tax is upon the income of "a citizen or resident of the United States". Please note that it says a citizen **or** resident of the United States. It does **not** say citizen <u>and</u> resident...." There is a very good reason for this.

The legal term "resident" has numerous meanings in law. Each of these numerous meanings is specific to the area (or type) of law in which the term is being employed. As an example, the term may have one meaning in tax law, but a completely different meaning in your state's real estate statutes.

In tax law, "resident" means a foreign person who is residing in the United States. For the purposes of U.S. tax law, "resident" means "resident alien".

What is a "resident alien"?

7701(b)(1)(A) Resident alien

> An alien individual shall be treated as a resident of the United States with respect to any calendar year if (and only if) such individual meets the requirements of clause (i), (ii), or (iii):
> (i) Lawfully admitted for permanent residence. Such individual is a lawful permanent resident of the United States at any time during such calendar year.
> (ii) Substantial presence test. Such individual meets the substantial presence test of paragraph (3).
> (iii) First year election. Such individual makes the election provided in paragraph (4).

The regulation also mentions a "citizen". There shouldn't be much debate as to who is an American citizen.

What is missing from the regulation is any description of what this citizen must be doing to be embraced by this law, as well as where he may have to be geographically to be affected by this law. Since a foreigner must be "resident" in the U.S. for this statute/regulation to embrace him, where must the citizen be? The natural socialized (and possibly "common wisdom") reply might be, "Here in the U.S., of course". Yet we have already discovered that our socialized opinion is not worth much when we explore the actual law, and "common wisdom" has precious little to do with tax law. In fact, the best way to misunderstand tax law is to believe it can, or should be, read within the context of one's own socialized perceptions.

Returning to 1.1-1; this is how it would read if it had been written with the intent to provide clarity to you:

> "Section 1 of the Code imposes an excise tax on every specific individual, who is either a citizen of the United States or a resident alien in the U.S."

Yet even this would not provide the necessary clarity or certainty because it does not reveal the activity in which the citizen would need to be engaged to have this excise tax imposed upon him, nor where he might need to be geographically as he engages in it.

Again, I remind you that these are not things you can simply presume. The law must spell out each of these specifics in order for said law to have authority over you and thus compel you to obey it.

I should also draw your attention to the use of the phrase "specific individuals" in the restructured example of 1.1-1 (above). That phrase is significant because "individual" has been modified with "specific". Synonyms for specific are: distinct, special, peculiar, specified, different, appropriate, exclusive, particular, etc. In other words, if the Secretary wanted to let you know the actual meaning of 1.1-1 he would have said the tax is imposed on **certain** "specific individuals" who are distinct from the general population by virtue of some identifiable *particular*. But of course the Secretary is doing everything he can here to be intentionally vague. We'll find out soon enough where he gets specific!

The next issue I'd like to draw your attention to is that 1.1-1(a) speaks (in vague terms) about those upon whom the tax has been **imposed,** and 1.1-1(b) speaks (also in vague terms) about those who have been made *liable* for the tax.

These two sections – nearly identical, yet wholly different – are necessary, because the federal income tax is one of the few taxes in this country in which the tax can be imposed on one person, but another person is made liable for paying the tax and filing the return for the person upon whom the tax was imposed!

You may have noticed that I keep repeating that your socialized view, or your common sense perspective, of tax law will get you into trouble. Re-read the paragraph above and tell me how well the fact stated there comports itself with your socialized view or common sense perspective of income tax!

Clearly, if imposing the tax on a person also made that very same person exclusively liable for the tax, the Secretary would not have created two virtually identical regulations [1.1-1(a) and 1.1-1(b)] that only differ in that one "imposes" the tax and the other tells the reader who is made "liable" for the tax.

So, what does it mean to be made "liable"?

Liable - responsible or obligated. Thus, a person or entity may be liable for damages due to negligence, liable to pay a debt, liable to perform an act which he/it contracted to do, or liable to punishment for commission of a crime. Failure to meet the responsibility or obligation opens one up to a lawsuit, and committing a crime can lead to a criminal prosecution. Dictionary.law.com

The very first word of the definition above – "responsible" – is all we really need in order to understand. For the purposes of the income tax, the person made "liable" is the one who is made "responsible" for the payment of the tax (and the filing of a return). And of course because one is made responsible/liable for the tax by law, one is also "obligated" to fulfill the "responsibility".

Obligation - a legal duty to pay or do something. Dictionary.law.com

We can see that, in tax law, an obligation is a "legal duty to pay".

Since we've now broken down these various terms to their core meanings, let's have a look at 1.1-1(b) again. Here is the original version as written by the Secretary:

> "In general, all citizens of the United States, wherever resident, and all resident alien individuals are liable to the income taxes imposed by the Code whether the income is received from sources within or without the United States."

Here is the way it would read if it were being written with an eye to having the American people better understand what is actually being said:

In general, all citizens of the United States, wherever they may be living, and all alien individuals legally residing in the U.S., who elsewhere in the Code have been designated as the person responsible for filing a return and paying the tax of any person upon whom a tax has been imposed, shall be the person liable for said tax.

While it doesn't resolve all of the "missing pieces", this version does start to bring some clarity to what the Secretary's words are really conveying.

I'll give you a little peek into what is ahead, and tell you that for the purposes of subtitle 'A' (known as "income tax"), the person upon whom the tax has been imposed is ***not*** always the same person who has been made liable! As I said, when it comes to the income tax, "common wisdom" has no role – except to lead you astray!

At this point you may be asking yourself why the income tax laws have been written in such a confusing manner when obviously they don't have to be. There are two reasons for this.

The first reason is fairly generic. Lawyers like to construct laws in "legalese" (i.e. a bizarre use of language that is designed to intentionally prevent most "common folk" from being able to understand the true meaning) so you will feel lost, confused, and incapable of dealing with the law unless you hire a lawyer!

The second reason is specif to income tax. Do you remember the movie, "The Wizard of Oz"? In the movie, the great and terrifying "Oz" turned out to be something entirely different than what people perceived him to be. In the movie, "the man behind the curtain" was simply creating a facade for the people. In the tax code, special lawyers (remember the "legislative draftsmen" of Chapter 1?) have created not merely a facade, but a legal landscape so vast and confusing that virtually no one can understand it. The fact that it is so vast is mainly due to the nature of the beast, but the fact that it is so utterly confusing is intentional. It is confusing by design.

In "The Wizard of Oz" a false image was constructed to fool the people. In subtitle 'A' of the U.S. Tax Code (entitled "income tax") a series of seemingly endless and meaningless concentric circles have purposely been created to wear down and confuse all but the most dedicated adversary. These legislative draftsmen have created a "legal obstacle course" to render the true application of the law nearly impenetrable.

Why would they do this?

As we've already seen, an "income tax" is, in its proper constitutional nature, an excise. [Congress is free to create a Direct tax and call it "income tax;" but as a Direct tax, it would still require apportionment.] From *Brushaber* we learned that the income tax (as created by Congress) is an excise.

Let me pause to ask you a question. Prior to reading this book, when have you ever been told that the income tax (subtitle 'A') is a tax upon the exercise of a privilege established in law by government? I'm betting that for 99.9% of you the answer is "Never."

Why do you imagine that is?

It's because the federal government could not possibly hope to steal…I mean "collect"…the revenue it *wants* to collect under the restraints imposed on it by the Constitution! It's that simple, my friends. It's all about the money. And since the Constitution allows only an 'excise' or a 'Direct tax requiring apportionment' upon "The People", the federal government had to find a way to get you to swallow something else.

Admittedly, their plan has been amazingly effective! They constructed a huge, complex, almost impenetrable maze of sophistry. Today we call that the "Tax Code". The income tax laws are so complex and highly detailed that discussions revolve almost exclusively around such questions as, "What does it mean?" and, "What does it permit?", and "How are things to be done?". The complexity and highly detailed nature of the income tax have created so much "clutter" that almost no one ever thinks to go to a deeper level and ask questions such as, "What is the Constitutional nature of this tax?" or "Upon whom has this tax actually been imposed?"

When people do ask such questions, or act pursuant to the answers, the government implements the second element of its plan – it attacks the person asking the questions or acting on the answers he discovered through years of research.

I told you in the Introduction that the government will attempt to discredit or jail anyone who asks the right questions or finds out the truth and has the audacity to stand upon it. That is "part 2" of their plan to steal…I mean "collect"… money by any means possible. The first part is to construct a series of statutes and regulations that almost no one can fathom. The second part is to attack anyone who threatens to break through the government-created "fog". The government's attack will be all the more severe against those who would show others how to see through the fog.

And yes, I expect to be criminally prosecuted by the federal government shortly after this book is released. They cannot afford to leave me "unstained". They have a "playbook" for protecting the theft…I mean "collection"…of money to which they are not legally entitled. One element of the "playbook" is to attack people like me. The IRS actually has "legal hit teams" whose mission is to "take down" people like me by whatever means possible. They already attempted to silence me through a civil action. That effort failed. Once this book is released, the "legal hit team" will come under intense pressure from Washington, DC to discredit and/or silence me. While the federal government is extremely powerful, it only has a fixed number of tools at its disposal. In a matter such as this, it has three choices:

1) A civil action to enjoin me from speaking publicly about the Income Tax. (Despite the fact that we [supposedly] have "freedom of speech" in America, the government routinely uses this method to silence people in the Tax Honesty Movement.)

2) A criminal prosecution to tarnish my reputation, and possibly – if all goes well for the government – lock me up for awhile and hope I thereafter choose to remain silent.

3) Silence me permanently. This is easier than you might think. Here's how it could look like it was done "legally": Two federal agents approach me in such a way that it is obvious they are "moving to positions of tactical advantage". This would instantly get my attention. They do not identify themselves as federal agents but begin to draw their sidearms. I then quite naturally act to defend myself by drawing my own weapon (which the government is already aware I carry daily). As I attempt to draw my weapon a "designated sniper" secreted nearby engages me with a rifle. As I'm hit by the rifle rounds, the agents on foot fire rounds into me as well. The sniper says that he was forced to shoot to protect the agents on foot. When the "incident" is investigated, the agents simply swear under oath that they identified themselves as federal agents and that's when I drew my gun. I am no longer alive to dispute their false testimony. I am then portrayed by the dominant media as a violent anti-government "domestic terrorist" [and let's not forget "tax protester"!] who attempted to kill the upstanding righteous servants of the people. Case closed.

You can see that option 3 is simple enough to accomplish. All it takes is the will. Does the government have such men in its employ? Of course. When the government filed its civil action against me, its "front man" for the "legal hit team" filled his sworn affidavit to the court with one outright fabrication after another.

I would tell you the name of the "front man" except he acknowledged in the court documents that he was using an IRS-approved pseudonym!

The third leg of the government's "playbook" for keeping the fraud going is "disinformation". It is ironic that many Americans know the federal government uses disinformation as a standard tool all over the world to accomplish its goals, but somehow believe that "their government" would never use this same tool to manipulate Americans.

The government (on its own and in conjunction with the dominant media) puts out more disinformation in this country concerning the income tax than all the disinformation it puts out in other parts of the world combined! If you doubt this, at the end of this book ask yourself why your perception of the income tax was shockingly different than the reality of it. Every single bit of disinformation you've ever received concerning the income tax has originated with our federal government.

One of the maxims of any criminal investigation is to look at/for the person who benefited from the crime. So, let's do that here. Who is the recipient of the money that is stolen…I mean "collected"…due to the public's completely inaccurate view of what the income tax is and to whom it applies? No more need be said.

Earlier in this chapter I told you that the government attacks those who tell the truth, or act upon it, because the government could not possibly hope to steal…I mean "collect"…the revenue it *wants* to collect under the restraints imposed by the Constitution! Do you think the Founding Fathers put those restraints there by accident? The Founders put those restrictions in the Constitution to forbid the federal government from doing exactly what is doing today – stealing the wealth of The People.

The Founders knew that the future federal government would want every penny it could steal from the people under the guise of taxation. That is one immutable truth about every government, and the Founders knew that.

In *Brushaber*, White told us that an excise is entitled to be enforced as such, until the manner of its enforcement burdens the accumulation of property, which (he told us) the apportionment clause was put in place to prevent. In other words, when the *enforcement* (also known as *"administration"*) of tax law becomes such that an excise is being enforced as if it were a Direct tax, then the government has violated a constitutional prohibition. When a case is brought alleging such a constitutional breach, the Court is to look at "substance over the form" and rule it unconstitutional as a Direct tax absent apportionment – not because of how the law reads on paper, but because of how the government has enforced it in practice. That is precisely where we are today.

I also mentioned earlier that the lawyers who created the Tax Code constructed "seemingly endless and meaningless concentric circles" within the Code. Let's look at some of those.

In court cases over time, the U.S. Department of Justice Tax Division has put forth a number of different answers to what requires a person to pay income tax. Some may seem (on the surface) to make sense; others don't.

Section 6001 - Every person liable for any tax imposed by this title, or for the collection thereof, shall keep such records, render such statements, make such returns, and comply with such rules and regulations as the Secretary may from time to time prescribe.

You will note that the sole description of the person whom this statute applies to is "Every person liable". Read the statute carefully. Can you find anything there that would tell you who the "person liable" is? I've been looking at such statutes for more than 15 years and I can't find anything. Additionally, I've asked licensed attorneys and accountants to tell me who is the "person liable" in sections such as this, and they can't find it either!

Another interesting part of 6001 is this:

> "Whenever in the judgment of the Secretary it is necessary, he may require any person, by notice served upon such person or by regulations, to make such returns, render such statements, or keep such records, as the Secretary deems sufficient to show ***whether or not such person is liable*** for tax under this title." [Italics in bold by author.]

This is yet another clear indicator that the tax applies to an excise. For you to be engaged in a privileged activity, the government would have to know about it. Why? Because in order so that people do not engage in a privileged activity without paying the tax, privileges activities are almost universally "criminalized" unless the person exercising the privilege has permission [such as a license] from the government to do so.

If the Secretary had the power – without prior knowledge that you were involved in an excise taxable activity – to demand you surrender your financial records simply to determine that you're *not* a 'person liable', there would have to be some "income tax exception" to the restrictions placed on the government by the 5th Amendment. But no such "income tax exception" exists in the law.

Having shown that 6001 must apply to some privileged activity of which the government is already aware – in other words, an excise taxable activity – let's look at the regulation for 6001.

> 1.6001 – (a) In general. Except as provided in paragraph (b) of this section, any person subject to tax under subtitle A of the Code…or any person required to file a return of information with respect to income, shall keep such permanent books of account or records, including inventories, as are sufficient to establish the amount of gross income, deductions, credits, or other matters required to be shown by such person in any return of such tax or information.

And there we have it! After I showed you that the statute can only pertain to an excise taxable activity, we find that the Secretary agrees. While the statute mentions nothing about subtitle 'A', the Secretary tells us that the relevant part of the statute pertains to subtitle 'A', which is, according to *Brushaber*, an excise.

But how attuned and attentive would a person have to be to notice the phrase "whether or not such person is liable", no less grasp the fine distinction that the language used can only apply to an excise without violating the prohibition upon the government under the 5th Amendment? I see it only because I have been steeped in this subject for nearly two decades.

Do you feel that it is appropriate for the government to expect Americans, such as you, to devote nearly two decades of their lives to the Tax Code in order not to be stolen from?

> Section 6151 - (a) General rule - Except as otherwise provided in this subchapter, when a return of tax is required under this title or regulations, the person required to make such return shall, without assessment or notice and

demand from the Secretary, pay such tax to the internal revenue officer with whom the return is filed, and shall pay such tax at the time and place fixed for filing the return.

Section 6151 deals with two issues: filing a return and paying a tax.

It states that a "person required to make such return" shall do so. It then states that the person "required to make such return" must also pay the tax to the IRS officer with whom the return was filed.

So, who is the "person required to make such return"? It doesn't say. It simply says that the person who is required to file a return is "required under this title or regulations". Are you starting to see the concentric circles?

Here's one of the sections I just love when the government puts it forth as the statute that makes a person liable!

Section 61 - (a) General definition

Except as otherwise provided in this subtitle, gross income means all income from whatever source derived, including (but not limited to) the following items:
(1) Compensation for services, including fees, commissions, fringe benefits, and similar items;
(2) Gross income derived from business;
(3) Gains derived from dealings in property;
(4) Interest;
(5) Rents;
(6) Royalties;
(7) Dividends;
(8) Alimony and separate maintenance payments;
(9) Annuities;
(10) Income from life insurance and endowment contracts;
(11) Pensions;
(12) Income from discharge of indebtedness;
(13) Distributive share of partnership gross income;
(14) Income in respect of a decedent; and
(15) Income from an interest in an estate or trust.

Yes my friends, the government has claimed in some court cases that the definition of "gross income" is where we are to find upon whom the tax is imposed and/or who has been made liable. Amazing! But do you know what is even more amazing? Federal judges universally accept whatever the government proffers as evidence that the defendant has had the tax imposed upon him or that he has been made liable! No rational thinking person has ever been able to identify upon whom the tax has been imposed or who has been made liable in the text of these statutes/regulations, but somehow a federal judge can mysteriously see something that no one else on the planet has been able to see. Now *that's* amazing!

Why would federal judges act this way? There are two reasons. They have been instructed not to force the Department of Justice to prove liability. And, they are cowards.

Each year federal judges attend several "Judicial Conferences". These are group meetings where judges supposedly learn to do their jobs better and are exposed to theories or concepts on how best to handle various issues that may come before the courts. Attending these "conferences" is a part of their responsibility as a federal judge. Seems benign enough, right? The problem is that these "conferences" are put on by the U.S. Department of Justice; the same organization that will appear before these very judges in various types of cases – including tax cases!

So, federal judges attend "Judicial Conferences" which are put on by the U.S. Department of Justice. The U.S. Department of Justice (DOJ) controls the material presented to the judges. Federal judges are told (by the DOJ) not to force the DOJ to prove the liability of a person brought before the court in a tax case. The judges are told that case law dictates that the actions of the Secretary are presumed correct unless the opposing party can provide **substantial** evidence that the Secretary's procedures that led to the court case are somehow improper or incorrect. However, in the same breath the judges are told not to allow any "tax protestor" arguments into their courtrooms. They are instructed specifically on how to dispose of these supposed "tax protestor" arguments.

Of course this is all put forth as being necessary to move cases forward expeditiously in an over-burdened judicial system. The problem is that the training material in these "conferences" casts as a "tax protestor argument" any argument that challenges the constitutionality of the income tax. Sound arguments – based on the law – based on what you will read in this book – are thrown out just as rapidly as oddball arguments that have no legal merit at all. In the judicial version of "throw the baby out with the bath water", the courts immediately reject *any* argument that begins with the premise that the income tax does not apply to the average American.

The disturbing part is that what the law says – what Congress enacted into law – does not matter to federal judges when it comes to income tax. It's all about the money!

This brings me to cowardice.

Some federal judges are truly stupid; most are not. Since most are not, how can we explain the instant rejection of any argument that begins with the premise that the income tax does not apply to the average American?

What you have seen in this book so far, and what you will see as we move forward, are not concepts that are hard to understand. I think you will agree that the facts are clear and the conclusions are plain enough. The problem is not that these things are difficult to grasp, it is that Americans have never been told the truth. And of course, that is not an accident.

Given that the facts and conclusion are clear, what reason would a court have to immediately reject any argument that begins with the premise that the income tax does not apply to the average American? The answer is simple: They've been told that they are not to rule on the question of whether or not the income tax applies to the average American.

As we move into the chapters ahead, you will learn how "the tax system" is designed to *ensnare* you into the *presumption* that you are a person upon whom the tax has been imposed and/or a person made liable for the tax.

This system of ensnaring you into this presumption is well known by federal judges. They know the established judicial principle that says the Secretary of the Treasury is to be given the *presumption* [there's that word again!] *of correctness* unless you can overcome that presumption by weight of evidence. While I strongly disagree with this doctrine in a free country where individual rights – and the right of property – are supposed to be respected by government, nonetheless the battle could still be won except for two factors.

The first factor is that once the "presumption of correctness" has been given to the Secretary, the doctrine states that the evidence required to overcome the presumption must be "substantial". The Secretary has reams of computer-generated documentation that he can submit to the court. He has "examination reports", "information returns", "RACS reports", copies of letters the IRS has sent you, "Notices of Proposed Assessment", assessment documents, "Notice of Final Demand", "Notice of Federal Lien", etc., etc. You, on the other hand, have nothing but the fact that the law never imposed the income tax on you (or made you liable for it) in the first place! Which brings us the second factor.

The second factor is that although the IRS had no legal authority to do any of the things it did, or have you in its computer system, or create any of the documents mentioned above, the court will not allow you to present the law in your defense.

The court will not allow you to present the law in your defense because the court knows what you do not know – that you have personally attested, again and again and again, that you are a person upon whom the income tax has been imposed and/or you are the person made liable for the tax. The fact that you have provided – out of complete ignorance, of course – these repeated *attestations* results in the court granting the Secretary the "presumption of correctness" and refusing you to be allowed to present the law in your defense. The underlying premise is that if you wanted to stand upon the law (that says you are a nontaxpayer), you would never have made the *attestations* of being a taxpayer! Or phrased another way, the job of the entry level court [the United States District Court] is not to rule on the law, but only to determine if the Secretary's actions are in compliance with administrative procedure. And if you made the *attestations* of being a taxpayer, then the court's view is that the Secretary is 100% within his rights to do all the things to which you are objecting. You lose!

The problem with this entire line of "reasoning" is that every judge knows that the American citizen standing before the court has no idea what tax law really says and that the citizen made his *attestations* because he was told he **had to** in order to be employed or get paid for a job he completed.

Imagine sitting on a federal bench – a position of immense trust by The People – and continuously sacrificing innocent Americans upon the altar of the mantra, "Get the money!" These judges have been told not to interfere in the tax system. They are not **allowed** to rule on the fundamental question of the income tax, i.e., "Does the income tax apply to the average American?"

We should also not forget that federal judgeships are highly political in nature because <u>every single federal judge is appointed by politicians</u>. These district court judges rely on politicians to nominate them for promotion to seats on the Circuit Courts, which is where the real power is. Accordingly, every single federal judge owes his job, and his possible upward mobility, to politicians. And what have national politicians been doing for the last 50 years? Buying votes by spending *your* money! This "vote buying" process is called "pork projects", "corporate welfare", "social spending", "entitlement programs", etc. Since national politicians (upon whose favor judges rely) *want* your property to be stolen from you by force, why would they permit their judges to interfere with that?

Let us return to the various sections of the Code and the "concentric circles" they create!

Clearly, section 61 (definition of "gross income") is merely a list of things that are within the statutory definition of "gross income". This may seem elementary, but we know it is merely a list of items because is says, "*...including (but not limited to) the following items:*". After that there appears the following:

(1) Compensation for services, including fees, commissions, fringe benefits, and similar items;
(2) Gross income derived from business;
(3) Gains derived from dealings in property;
(4) Interest;
(5) Rents;
(6) Royalties;

And so on.

I think you will agree it is a list. And we know it is a list of "items" because it tells us so. But more importantly, the definition of "gross income" does not identify the person who has had the tax imposed upon him or who has been made liable.

And here's a pivotal aspect to keep in mind: Section 61 is not within the "General Definition" section of the Tax Code (found at section 7701). Section 61 is within subtitle 'A' and is therefore a definition *exclusive* to subtitle 'A' alone.

Why is this important?

It's important because it means that the definition of "gross income" is *only* applicable to those persons upon whom subtitle 'A' has been imposed. In other words, if a person has had the subtitle 'A' tax imposed on him, then the list of "items of gross income" that appears within section 61 would indeed constitute his "gross income". However, if a person upon whom Congress has *not* imposed subtitle 'A' was to receive "gains derived from dealings in property, interest, rents, royalties, dividends," etc., he would merely be receiving personal *property*.

This demonstrates two important principles. First, that we must always look at objects/items (as well as your labor) as *property*. Second, that it is imperative that we know *whom* subtitle 'A' has been imposed upon and/or who has been made liable. Without this critical piece of the puzzle, we are left spinning in the breeze with no way to resolve the matter.

It is important that we understand that "gross income" is merely a statutory definition created by Congress. There is no magic in it. It is simply a list of items (actually, a partial list) that constitutes "gross income" *only* for a person upon whom Congress has imposed subtitle 'A'. And, as of this point, we've not covered a single statute or regulation that would tell us who that actually is!

It is critical that you understand that receiving a form of property that is on that list does not make you liable for income tax or make you a person upon whom the income tax has been imposed! If that were the case, then the income tax would be a Direct tax, and we have already established the U.S. Supreme Court ruled that it is not a Direct tax and that Direct taxes would still require apportionment to be constitutional. Since it is an excise, you must be a person involved in a privileged activity upon which Congress has imposed the income tax. Only then would one's interest, rents, royalties, etc., be a part of the statutory definition of "gross income".

[As a brief aside, it is theoretically possible for you to engage in a government privilege that has not been taxed. That's another reason we *must* know what privileged activity is the object of the tax.]

Here is an example of a statute that relies on "gross income" as the standard, which is why it is so important that we understand it only applies to those upon whom the tax has already been imposed.

> Section 6012 - (a) General rule (1)(A) Every individual having for the taxable year gross income which equals or exceeds the exemption amount...

If one simply accepted the list of items as applying to everyone, then under 6012 everyone would have to file a tax return. Clearly at that point we would be talking about a Direct tax requiring apportionment, and not an excise tax. However, if subtitle 'A' has been imposed only upon those persons exercising a privilege, then as White noted in *Brushaber*, the taxing provisions of the Constitution are operating "harmoniously".

Another section often cited to explain why one needs to file an income tax return is Section 6011. Would there be two such sections – 6011 and 6012 – to accomplish the exact same objective? Of course not. Nor do they accomplish the same objective. Let's look at 6011.

> Section 6011(a) - When required by regulations prescribed by the Secretary any person made liable for any tax imposed by this title, or with respect to the collection thereof, shall make a return or statement according to the forms and regulations prescribed by the Secretary.

What meaningful difference do you see between 6011 and 6012?

Section 6012 specifically states the requirement of "gross income", which as we've discussed is only defined for the purposes of subtitle 'A'. Section 6011, on the other hand, makes no mention of "gross income", so it contains the filing requirement for all taxes contained in the Code, except those in subtitle 'A'. This makes 6012 the filing requirement exclusively for subtitle 'A'.

Can we buttress this understanding further? Absolutely. Section 6072 addresses the time and place for the filing of a return. Here is the opening sentence of the statute:

> 6072(a) - In the case of returns under section 6012, 6013, 6017, or 6031 (relating to income tax under subtitle A)... [Parenthesis in original]

We can clearly see, in statutes enacted by Congress, that when Congress is speaking of a requirement to file a subtitle 'A' return, Section 6011 is not mentioned at all!

When people (including the government) cite Section 6011 as the section requiring the filing of a tax return for subtitle 'A', you should immediately understand that they have no idea what they're talking about.

It is clear that the sections of the Code (or the regulations) that the government and others put forth as "evidence" that *you* are required to file an income tax return falls far short of establishing that contention.

Many of the disturbing facts I have raised in this chapter will be treated more extensively in the coming chapters. But what is clear even now is that "the system" is closed to any discussion of upon whom the income tax has been imposed.

The District Courts are "closed" in this regard, except when it's DOJ making the argument, and then whatever DOJ says – no matter how ridiculous – is automatically accepted by the court without the slightest critical evaluation whatsoever.

But why is all this so?

I named this chapter "Then as Now". I did so because since the 16th Amendment was adopted – since the time of *Brushaber* – nothing has changed in regard to the government's constitutional authority to tax you! The "income tax" (subtitle 'A') remains an excise tax. Direct taxes still require apportionment (though there are none in effect in this nation). In short, what was true in 1916 is equally true right now as you are reading these words. Nothing has changed. What was true then is true now.

The government knows perfectly well that nothing has changed. The government desperately wishes that it were free to "burden the wealth" of Americans through a Direct tax without the requirement of apportionment. But the government knows that the Constitution does not permit that. A solution had to be found because the U.S. government made the decision long ago to attempt to solve all the world's problems – with *your* money. You didn't imagine that the movers and shakers in government over the last several decades were going to let a little thing like Constitutional restrictions stop them, did you?

Self-promotial politicians, self-perpetuating big government, marching down the corrosive road of Socialism, taking on the role of the world's policeman, etc. – you didn't think all those (supposed) lofty goals were going to be stopped by a little thing like the Constitution, did you?

The Founders wrote the Constitution to do exactly that – to stop that kind of conduct before it ever got started by restricting the federal government's power of taxation to Indirect taxes (which includes excises) and Direct taxes subject to apportionment.

As we've seen, the 16th Amendment didn't change any of that.

Those with the unconstitutional "lofty goals" were not going to be thwarted in their endeavors by the restrictive revenue boundaries of the Constitution. In their minds, their goals are so lofty that *nothing* – including your Rights – can be allowed to stand in their way. The Constitution is used by them if it can somehow support their goals, but ignored when its words stand in their way.

Their answer was to create a taxing scheme that would be so complex, yet so vague, that almost no one could make sense of it. Then they implemented an immense and on-going disinformation campaign to "teach" people that the tax applies to everyone. Then they created a dense thicket of statutory/regulatory "snares" to entrap nearly every American into falsely attesting (out of utter ignorance) to his/her own liability for the tax and then they closed the courts to any argument other than the government's "party line", even when the government's positions are absurd.

By this multi-layered plan, the government has committed a crime. It has knowingly, willfully, and intentionally conducted an end-run around the United States Constitution. It has intentionally breached the faith between the federal government and the states of the Union. The Constitution guarantees the states a republic, but the federal government has set out to destroy that as our national system of government. The federal government has silently declared war on the rights and property of 300 million Americans. The federal government has silently declared war on the states of the Union.

In technical and practical terms the federal government has instituted a Direct tax without apportionment in direct violation of the Constitution and maintains it by sophistry and brute force (i.e. violence against *you*).

The federal government has done so intentionally and without remorse and without any signs that it has any intention of ever altering its conduct.

Two words come to mind:

Tyranny.

Treason.

And this thought also comes to mind:

Is it not time to *force* the government to change its conduct?

If Not You, Then Who?

Chapter 6

"An error does not become truth by reason of multiplied propagation, nor does truth become error because nobody sees it."
~ Mohandas Gandhi

The information we covered thus far should convince anyone but the most intransigent or evil among us that subtitle 'A' does not apply to the vast majority of Americans. The question many will be asking now is, "Then to whom ***does*** the income tax apply?"

A number of people have attempted comment upon this over time. Most have not even come close to being factual or accurate.

Irwin Schiff likely deserves the title "Grandfather of the Tax Honesty Movement." I heard Irwin's name connected with questions about the income tax when I was a young man, though at that point in my life the subject held no interest for me. [The government had not yet ***made*** me interested! It is telling that most Americans who come to the Tax Honesty Movement are propelled into it after being victimized by the dishonesty and abuse of the income tax system.]

Irwin is a perfect example of a gentleman who is 100% dedicated to getting the truth out about the income tax, but who is mistaken in his legal views concerning the income tax.

Another example is Larken Rose. For many years Larken was an eminent voice in the Tax Honesty Movement. I have immense respect for Larken. He has endured a stint in federal prison because he stood upon his beliefs and refused to knuckle under to tyranny. There is much to be admired and respected in such a man, yet his legal position is also errant.

[I will address inaccurate legal arguments concerning the income tax in another chapter.]

There is a wonderful documentary – "America: Freedom to Fascism" – which highlights the sophistry of the government's position on the income tax. In this documentary, former IRS Chief Counsel and IRS Commissioner, Sheldon Cohen, is unable to answer even the most rudimentary questions concerning the income tax and its proper application. The interview with Cohen shows that even the "expert's expert" cannot intelligently respond to questions about the income tax. I might also add that no one from the IRS or the Treasury Department was even willing to be interviewed for the movie.

"America: Freedom to Fascism" was produced and directed by Hollywood mogul, Aaron Russo. Aaron had fought and beaten cancer several times in his life. The cancer had come for him once again as he began to create "America: Freedom to Fascism". This documentary was a passion for Aaron. Aside from his wife and two sons, "America: Freedom to Fascism" was, to him, his legacy – his gift to the country that had given him so much.

I am honored to have had a hand in the movie.

I first heard about the project from my peers in the Tax Honesty community. I called Aaron and asked to contribute in whatever capacity he might consider using me. Being in Hollywood, and being asked for a great many things by a lot of people, Aaron was at first wary. He imagined I was seeking something for myself.

As time went on, we moved past that and worked well together. Aaron used me as his resource for judging the correctness of the myriad of legal arguments that others put before him concerning the income tax. Aaron would call me and give me the "quick and dirty" on some legal position concerning the income tax that had been represented to him. He never told me who brought these arguments to him, and I never asked. I would simply explain why the various arguments were not legally accurate. He'd usually ask me a few follow-up questions; I would answer, and that would be the end of it.

Aaron had me to his office a number of times to kick around various issues. Additionally, he invited me on three particular occasions to view different versions of the movie and give him my feedback. The first two versions were significantly different than the one that was released to the public. The third was very close to the release version.

After viewing the third version, I said, "Aaron, your movie does a fantastic job of showing that the income tax doesn't apply to most Americans and that the government has been lying to the American people. But I want to bring up that the film never discusses to whom the tax actually does apply."

I was a bit nervous raising the subject because I knew the film was near completion and that Aaron considered filmmaking his "art". I was honored to have participated at the level I had, and I did not want to be perceived as attempting to involve myself in matters beyond the role he'd given me. Nevertheless, I felt compelled to raise the matter.

Aaron could be a tough man to collaborate with (because his vision for the project was so clear in his head), but on this subject he showed immediate interest. He expressed concern about any major revisions to the film at such a late date, but was interested in the material. He said, "Tell me who it applies to." And so I told him. His response amazed me. He said, "OK. Write it up and I'll put it in."

I told him that we couldn't do it that way! I said the movie was **his** work and every question or criticism about the content of the film would be directed at **him**. I expressed that while I wanted the information to be included in the film, he would need to understand the legal realities behind it because he would be the lightning rod for the film's critics, not me! Aaron stated tersely that he didn't have time to learn the information and therefore it would not be included in the film. And that's where the conversation ended.

I was floored. I did not understand why he would not take the time for what I felt was a critical aspect of the message. I did not know that, even as Aaron and I sat there talking, he knew he was dying and had little time left to complete his gift to America. I wish I had known. Roughly 18 months later, on August 24, 2007, Aaron succumbed to bladder cancer.

In retrospect I am flattered that he had come to trust me to the extent that he would include the information in his film – his deeply personal gift to America – without researching it personally. Aaron was not a man who trusted easily.

I tell you all of that to make the point that the vast majority of information currently available to the public talks about what the income tax is not. There is little information about what the tax really is, and most of that is inaccurate.

There are a number of reasons for the scarcity of information and its inaccuracy.

As I mentioned in the Introduction, the government has gone after virtually anyone who threatens the "party line" concerning income tax. This has resulted in few people being willing to speak out. And this is exactly the government's intention when it attacks people who do speak out. While the government paints its efforts as legitimate actions to protect the revenue of the United States, it's true purpose is to create a chilling effect on the willingness of Americans to speak out on the subject.

Another reason for the scarcity of information about the income tax is that the government will not publicly discuss the proper application of the income tax – ever! Isn't that fascinating in a supposedly free country!

Over the years, on my radio show – The Dave Champion Show (formerly "American Radio") – I have invited many high profile "tax experts" to come on the show and engage in a real-time, no-holds-barred (except for rudeness), debate about the true application of the income tax. Here are some of the people I have invited:

1. U.S. Secretary of the Treasury (Snow)
2. The Commission of the Internal Revenue Service (Everson)
3. Assistant Commissioner of the Internal Revenue Service (Hart)
4. The Chief Counsel of the Internal Revenue Service
5. The national director of the IRS's Criminal Investigation Division
6. A regional director of the IRS's Criminal Investigation Division
7. U.S. Attorney in charge of the Department of Justice's Tax Division
8. Jay D. Adkisson – Creator and editor of Quatloos (a website that derides Tax Honesty advocates)
9. David Cay Johnston – Former senior tax reporter for the New York Times.
10. Numerous CPAs who have written commentaries disparaging the Tax Honesty Movement.

If Not You, Then Who?

My invitation was not only to the specific individual I contacted, but was extended to include any person they would care to designate to participate in the debate. Not one of these alleged "experts" were willing to come on the show or even designate anyone to participate in such a debate.

As it is the government's unofficial policy of "deceit through silence", I never heard back from any of the federal officials I invited to participate in such a debate. I did, however, hear from a few of the private invitees.

Jay Adkisson is an attorney who runs a registered investment advisory firm in Aliso Viejo, California. From all reports he is quite wealthy. His website, Quatloos, is used to mock and deride members of the Tax Honesty Movement. On the website, Adkisson, characterizes those in the Tax Honesty Movement as committing tax scams and tax fraud.

Accusing people of tax fraud is a pretty heavy accusation, wouldn't you agree? And Adkisson is considered a bit of an expert at such matters, having testified before a committee of the U.S. Senate with regard to tax fraud.

Despite all of these credentials, Adkisson adamantly refused to engage in a live, real-time, no-holds-barred debate concerning the proper application of the income tax. His pathetic excuse was to say that he would not debate me because no one cares what I have to say.

Yet my name appears on Adkisson's website – a website that deals with tax scams and tax fraud! Any reasonable person would assume that if I am being derided on his site then he should be salivating for the chance to prove me wrong – publicly – on my own show! If he were to come on my show and decimate my views on the income tax, would it not destroy my show? No audience will tune in when it has been shown that the host has no credibility!

Adkisson created and edits a website that paints the Tax Honesty Movement as somewhere between retarded and criminal. He has testified in front of a Senate committee on the subject. Yet somehow he does not find it appealing to ruin me as a host and silence my Tax Honesty message? Hmmm. How very odd. I wonder why he would shy away from such an opportunity?

Another person I heard back from was David Cay Johnston. Johnston refused to participate, giving as his reason that I have proven that facts do not matter to me. Huh? What?

It hardly matters whether I care about the facts or not. The issue is what those hearing the debate would think. One does not enter into a formal debate to influence one's opponent, but to influence the audience! If during the debate I were to show myself to be a person to whom facts do not matter, then I would lose the debate, right?

Like Adkisson, if Johnston had the facts to prevail in a live, real-time, no-holds-barred debate concerning the proper application of the income tax, he certainly would have done so. Any opponent who can prevail in such a debate would effectively ruin me as a talk-show host and silence me as a Tax Honesty Advocate.

Johnston has also stated that I have no honor. If Johnston believes that I have no honor and that I have no respect for the facts, then wouldn't he want to silence me – if for no other reason than to keep me from putting out (allegedly) false information to the innocent? Isn't that what a responsible member of the community would do?

What reason then can we fairly attribute to these two for having passed on such a splendid opportunity to ruin me as a talk-show host and silence the Tax Honesty message – a message they say is false and a scam. I think it clear that the only rational reason for their refusal to participate in such a debate is that they know they will suffer a devastating defeat. No other motive comports itself with reason.

Faced with a wall of silence from the government and its adherents, is it any wonder that there's a scarcity of information about whom the income tax actually applies to?

With this "wall of silence" from the government and its adherents in place, telling the truth about the income tax would then fall to whom? On the rare occasions a supposed expert – such as Sheldon Cohen – does speak out, they have no rational or cogent answers. They offer what is easily seen as pure sophistry.

Then who is there to speak the truth?

If Not You, Then Who?

Accountants? CPAs? While there are some who know the truth, they will not speak publicly for fear of being disbarred and having their state authority to practice revoked. Just ask former IRS criminal agent Joe Banister about this!

When Joe Banister discovered the truth, he resigned his great paying career as an IRS criminal investigator and started speaking out publicly about the criminal misapplication of the income tax by the government. He also began representing clients in front of the IRS, clients who felt they had no liability for the income tax.

How did the government respond to this? The government attempted to put him in jail by trying him on criminal charges. He was acquitted. Or phrased another way, the jury found him NOT GUILTY of any of the charges alleged by the government. In other words, the government had lied. Gee…there's a shocker!

Thereafter, the IRS moved to disbar him, which would mean he could no longer represent clients before the IRS. In a series of IRS sham proceedings, in which Joe was denied any vestige of due process, he was disbarred.

Shortly after the IRS disbarred him, the State of California moved to revoke his license as a CPA. (Gee whiz…I wonder who was behind that!) State law says that if the IRS has disbarred a CPA, the State can revoke his/her license – and that is exactly what the State of California did!

How may accountants or CPAs do you imagine will now speak out publicly or represent a client before the IRS or state tax agency who believes the income tax has not been imposed on him/her? Of course the government never intended any of this to have a chilling effect on free speech, right?

So, where does this leave us? You're not going to hear it from the government. You're not going to hear it from self-serving minions. You're not going to hear it from cowardly reporters/journalists. You're not going to hear it from accountants or CPAs. Then from whom?

I know several attorneys who know the truth. Most of them refuse to go public for the same reasons as the accountants and CPAs. A few of these attorneys feel passionately about the issue – just not passionately enough to risk the sneering ridicule of their peers or possible disbarment.

So where does that leave us? It leaves us right here – in this book!

I am not an officer or employee of the government so I do not need to enter into the "conspiracy of silence" as a means of continuing fraud against the American people.

I am not a person who has built wealth around the corrupt application of the tax system, so I am free to speak without being muzzled by selfish motivations.

I am not an accountant or CPA who feeds my family by working within the tax system, so I can speak the truth without fearing divorce or the hatred/resentment of a spouse.

I do not possess any sort of government license to earn my living, so I am free to speak without the fear of being impoverished by an evil act of retribution by cowardly bureaucrats.

In short, I am free to speak!

While I am free to speak, am I free of potential consequences of speaking publicly? Hardly! Just as surely as I type these words out on my keyboard I know there will be a price to pay. The U.S. Treasury Department has a standing policy to make people like me pay! How? We will have to wait and see.

Will it be by destroying me financially through on-going costly civil litigation? Possibly. Will it be by trying to imprison me on some trumped up charges brought before a "friendly judge" who will none-too-discreetly give the government every break while barring me from putting on an effective defense? We shall see. Will they take it to a level worse than those possibilities? Time will tell. But punishment will be exacted. Of that, there is no doubt. It is the only thing they know how to do when confronted by the truth on this subject – ATTACK, PUNISH, BRING THE PAIN!

Now that we have all that out of the way, let's talk about the true application of subtitle 'A'.

We've clearly seen that there is nothing in the 16th Amendment that would tax the average American, and the 16th Amendment is the source of authority for subtitle 'A' – at least the portion that taxes individuals.

We've clearly seen that the income tax (subtitle 'A') is an excise/privilege tax, according to the U.S. Supreme Court.

So where is that illusive privilege? Let's see if we can find it!

Subtitle 'A' taxes two types of "persons". One is a real live flesh and blood human; the other is corporations and other "entities".

CORPORATIONS

Given the words of the U.S. Supreme Court concerning the Corporate Excise Tax of 1909, and the definition of "income" for the purposes of the 16th Amendment, one might presume that the tax is upon the "privilege" of operating in the corporate form. Certainly the message of President William Taft before Congress might cause one to think so.

> "I therefore recommend an amendment to the tariff bill imposing upon all corporation and joint stock companies for the profit…an excise tax, measured by 2 percent on the net income of such corporations. This is an excise tax upon the privilege of doing business as an artificial entity…."

And…

> "The decision of the Supreme Court in the case of Speckels Sugar Refining Co. v. McCain (192 U.S. 397) seems clearly to establish the principle that such tax as this is an excise tax upon privilege and not a direct tax on property, and is within the federal power to tax without apportionment according to population."

Despite Taft using the words "all corporations" in his speech, could such a tax really be applied to *all* corporations, or only certain corporations of a particular character?

> [**Author's Note**: The reader should be aware that President Taft was a Yale-trained lawyer, a noted jurist, and was later appointed Chief Justice of the United States Supreme Court. This is significant because lawyers and judges use language differently than do ordinary people.

When a lawyer or judge says "all corporations" it is implicit in their thought process and way of speaking to mean "...all corporations that are within our authority to act upon in this manner...."]

It should be remembered that America was – and still is – a nation of *delegated* powers. All political power is held by The People and is *delegated* to their elected officials. That means two important things.

First, whatever power the elected official exercises must first have resided in the people who elected him/her. If no such power belonged to the people who elected the office holder, then the office holder cannot exercise such power. In America, there is no such thing as an office holder exercising a power not held by The People and then delegated by the election process.

Second, an elected official cannot use your delegation of authority to pass a law that creates some sort of business vehicle and then tell you that it is a privilege for you to utilize it. It is your original authority – being exercised by the office holder – that created the business vehicle in the first place. It is manifestly impossible for you – personally or operating through your delegate – to create something that is then to be construed as a privilege for you (the author of the authority to create it) to use. It is therefore manifestly impossible for a legislator (exercising your delegated authority) to pass laws that create corporations and then tell you that it is a privilege for you to use one!

And, it should never be presumed that because we delegated authority to an office holder we are somehow then disenfranchised as the original source of the power the office holder exercises. We are never disenfranchised as the source of the legislator's power. We are always and at all times the author of the legislator's authority.

If we are not the power behind the legislators then plainly the government would be a totalitarian regime and we would want to stop talking and start taking back our nation by violence, which is the only way to restore a Republic once it has been surreptitiously converted to a totalitarian regime. Or phrased another way, if our legislators (or the courts) believe they can create something under our authority, but then tell us that it is a privilege for us to use that which our authority created, we should initiate violence immediately to regain our freedom and our republican form of government.

Now we have established that it is our own authority that creates corporations for our own use, benefit, and pleasure. And since that which our own authority creates can never be a privilege for us to use, how then can a corporation be a privilege subject to a "corporate income tax"?

Let me ask you a question. If a citizen of Germany were to create a corporation in one of the states of the Union, would he be the "author of the authority" that created the corporation? Clearly not! The authors of the authority for creating corporations are the citizens of the state in which the corporation was created, who delegated their authority to the state legislature to create corporations.

If a French company – say, Peugeot – decided to create a corporation called "Peugeot USA, Inc.", in the state of Delaware, would the French company "Peugeot" be the author of the authority for the legislature of Delaware to create a corporation? Not at all. The good citizens of Delaware would be the authors of that authority.

Since neither the German citizen, nor Peugeot, are the authors of the authority that permits the creation of corporations, then for them to utilize a corporation in America would indeed be a privilege! As such, these *foreign owned* corporations would be subject to "an excise tax upon the privilege of doing business as an artificial entity."

Please note that in President Taft's comments, he used the words "doing business" in connection with the imposition of a corporate excise tax. Again, lawyers and judges use words differently than do ordinary people (outside the legal profession).

Black's Law Dictionary is the gold standard for legal definitions pertaining to statutory law. "Acts of Congress" – what the public calls 'laws' – are more properly called 'statutes'. Congress enacts all tax laws in the form of statutes, so it is proper to refer to Black's when seeking the meaning of a legal term used therein.

> **Doing Business** – Within the meaning of statutes pertaining to service of process on foreign corporations, equivalent to conducting or managing business. A foreign corporation is "doing business" within a state, making it amenable to process therein if it does business therein in such a manner to warrant the inference that it is present there or that it has subjected itself to the jurisdiction and laws in which the service is made. **Black's Law Dictionary, 3rd Edition (1933)**

And there are more than 25 court citations provided in Black's to support this meaning.

Some people may say, "But Dave, that definition only deals with foreign corporations. What about domestic corporations?" Great question. In the dictionaries of that era there is **no other** definition for "doing business"! The phrase "doing business" had no other legal meaning in the era of Taft's speech other than as pertaining to foreign corporations.

In other words, as a trained jurist and future Chief Justice of the United States Supreme Court, Taft said exactly what he meant – he simply did it in "legalese"!

Understanding what the phrase "doing business" actually meant in that era, let's re-read Taft's statement to Congress.

"I therefore recommend an amendment to the tariff bill imposing upon all corporation.... This is an excise tax upon the privilege of ***doing business*** as an artificial entity...." [emphasis added]

As a trained lawyer and respected jurist, Taft knew the limitations of an excise tax (even if the American people did not). He knew that a privilege tax could never be applied to the very people whose authority created the entity for their own use and benefit. Taft also knew that it was indeed a privilege for *foreign persons* to conduct business in America by using a corporation. Using the legal jargon that was so natural and familiar to him (and to most of the lawyers sitting in Congress) he told Congress quite clearly what type of excise tax he was recommending. However, if you don't speak legalese how would YOU know? Shakespeare's line about killing all the lawyers makes a lot more sense now, doesn't it?

Let me pause here to explain something about the law. Most people have heard the old real estate rule, "location, location, location." The legal parallel is "context, context, context." This "context" rule works almost exclusively upon "jurisdiction." Jurisdiction comes in two flavors – *geographic* and *subject matter*.

When it comes to a question such as whether or not the government can impose an excise on the very people who put the government in place and have delegated their powers to the government, we must look at "jurisdiction" in a broader context.

If Not You, Then Who?

Government does not exist naturally. In a free nation, government exists because of a conscious choice of The People. In America that conscious choice initially manifested itself in the form of making war on the British to throw off the governance of the Crown. It was then further manifested when The People created the states (which pre-existed the national government). After the states existed, The People of the states created a national government under the *Article of Confederation*. When the *Article of Confederation* proved to have certain defects, the conscious choice was manifested again – this time by the Constitutional Convention that produced the U.S. Constitution we have today.

With all that said, the most important part of the equation is that this *conscious choice* was first made by **The People!** In other words, The People are the authors of every authority – and most specifically the existence of the government. The People are the creators of the government. As such, the government has no power except that which The People possess. If The People did not possess the power, they could not delegate it to their servant – the government.

This is the "context" in which many questions of government authority – or more accurately, government's **alleged** authority – must be viewed. In its very nature, government always desires more and more power. It is the nature of the beast. That fundamental reality is why it is important for government officials and citizens alike to keep the underlying source of government authority in mind at all times.

There are only two possible sources for the government's authority in this country. One is *We The People;* the other is, as Chairman Mao said, the muzzle of a gun. If it is the former then we are a free nation. If it is the latter, then there is only one answer, and that is to turn our guns on our oppressors; those who would falsely claim to be "our government."

Understanding that we are the sole source of power and authority of any legitimate government, we should now explore whether our "representatives" in government – those we elect – have the power to do anything or everything their constituents say. The answer to this is 'no'.

Remember that your elected official can only exercise the power *you* have, and nothing more. What that means is that if you cannot do it, neither can he/she acting in your name.

Do you have the intrinsic authority to stop your neighbor from painting his house purple? Does another neighbor have that power? Do *any* of your neighbors have that power? If the answer is 'no', then the person all of you elected to the town council does *not* have that power either because he/she has no more power than each of you!

There are a few established exceptions to this rule. These are very narrow circumstances in which lives are at risk and the ordinary citizen may have to resort to violence to protect himself and/or his family. An example of this would be communicable diseases.

You and I do not, in our individual capacities, have the "authority" to command a person to remain indoors and away from us for our protection if that person is diagnosed with a potentially deadly communicable disease. If you saw the infectious person attempting to come in contact with your family members and you wished to protect them, you may have to kill the infectious person as the only practical means of protecting your family.

This desire to protect ourselves would be universal within the affected community. Every member of the community would want to stay uninfected and thus confident of not dying from the disease. To become infected presents the prospect of dying. That means we have a survival issue at hand – and survival is nature's #1 rule!

If there is a chance I will die from the irresponsible actions of a person infected with a deadly disease, then I have the right of self-defense against that person. There is little difference between being attacked by a brick-wielding assailant and being accosted by a person with a deadly contagious infection! Both may justify the use of deadly force as self-defense.

For this reason, legal tradition has always permitted government to take rational and reasonable steps to protect a community from a communicable disease and to set such regulations as are designed to reasonably prevent the spread of dangerous diseases.

Some examples of this type of authority being put into affect by government are regulations that require food handlers to wash their hands after using the restrooms, health inspections of commercial kitchens, fire inspections of commercial buildings, special storage requirements for explosive or highly flammable material, and routine disease testing for licensed prostitutes.

All of these activities have one thing in common: If not subject to advance regulatory intervention there is a very real possibility of widespread <u>unintentional</u> and <u>indiscriminate</u> illness, injury, or death. Both elements - *unintentional* and *indiscriminate* must be present for the government to exercise this type of authority.

These types of dangers are known as "Public Safety" issues. But do not be fooled; the phrase "public safety" has been bandied about by politicians, law enforcement, and the media for decades now to describe *any* situation that may pose any type of danger to the community. That is not the type of "public safety" concern that grants government the authority I am describing. Most of the situations in which politicians, law enforcement, and the media use the term "public safety" lack the requisite *unintentional* aspect. If a dangerous act is intentional, then it's simply a crime and the perpetrator(s) should be dealt with as such!

The vast majority of corporations pose no community danger. However, if a corporation is acting in such a way that there is a risk of *unintentional* and *indiscriminate* harm to the community, it is then subject to the same regulatory powers as anyone else posing such a threat. However – and this is the important part – that situation would still not render a corporation a privilege for you or me!

Were corporations ever a privilege?

In England of old, the King (or Queen) would grant corporations monopolistic powers in a certain subject or geographical area of the world. This was a special (protected) status bestowed upon the shareholders by law and unavailable to any other persons. Additionally, corporations were not, in those days, available to the common man. They were created for these specific monopolistic purposes.

In our country, back in the days of the early railroads, corporations were established to provide for joint ventures between private interests and the U.S. government. The U.S. government was the majority shareholder in these corporations and they exercised prerogatives held solely by the federal government under the U.S. Constitution. This would certainly be a privileged type of corporation.

Today there are many corporations that were/are created by the government to serve as "instrumentalities" of government power. A common example of this type of corporation would be the FDIC (the Federal Deposit Insurance Corporation). Congress created this instrumentality and it is completely owned by the U.S. government. It has little in common with corporations in the private sector, aside from calling it a corporation. Most of these government corporations are treated as "agencies of the federal government" for Congressional budget/appropriation purposes. States also have their own corporate "instrumentalities."

None of these types of corporations have anything to do with traditional corporations which are exclusively private sector. For corporations in the private sector, the subtitle 'A' privilege is *"doing business"*!

INDIVIDUALS

In addition to corporate taxation, subtitle 'A' also imposes an excise tax on the "individual." Thankfully, this subject is far less prone to complexity or confusion than is the subject of corporations. The relationship of the citizen to the government is much more streamlined.

"The individual may stand upon his constitutional rights as a citizen. He is entitled to carry on his private business in his own way. His power to contract is unlimited. He owes no duty to the State or to his neighbors to divulge his business, or to open his doors to an investigation, so far as it may tend to criminate him. He owes no such duty to the State, since he receives nothing therefrom beyond the protection of his life and property. His rights are such as existed by the law of the land long antecedent to the organization of the State, and can only be taken from him by due process of law, and in accordance with the Constitution. Among his rights are a refusal to incriminate himself and the immunity of himself and his property from arrest or seizure except under a warrant of the law. He owes nothing to the public so long as he does not trespass upon their rights."
Hale V. Henkel, 201 U.S. 43 at 74, (1906)

Given the statement by the decision of the U.S. Supreme Court in *Hale*, it would be difficult, if not impossible, to find something in the ordinary affairs of a citizen's life that would be a privilege subject to an excise tax!

Despite what the government might like us to believe, an American citizen exercises almost no privileges (except for "driving") as he goes about his life!

- Is earning a living a right? Yes; so says the U.S. Supreme Court.
- Is contracting your labor to another a right? Yes; so says the U.S. Supreme Court.
- Is contracting with another for his/her labor a right? Yes; so says the U.S. Supreme Court.
- Do you have an "unlimited power to contract"? Yes; so says the U.S. Supreme Court.

Since every money-earning activity in the private sector involves at least one of the four rights mentioned above, what then is the subtitle 'A' privilege for which an excise could be imposed upon a citizen as he earns his living? Obviously, in the vast majority of cases, there isn't any. And the good news is that subtitle 'A' doesn't impose any tax on the ordinary American!

As we discussed previously, the statutes and regulations are not terribly specific concerning whom the tax is imposed upon and under what circumstances.

> Remember this regulation?
> 1.1-1(a) – Section 1 of the Code imposes an income tax on the income of every individual who is a citizen or resident of the United States and, to the extent provided by section 871(b) or 877(b), on the income of a nonresident alien individual.

The tax imposed is upon taxable income. As we established earlier, this section provides nowhere near the specificity required to know whom the tax has been imposed upon and under what circumstances.

> Let's also look again at:
> 1.1-1(b) – In general, all citizens of the United States, wherever resident, and all resident alien individuals are liable to the income taxes imposed by the Code whether the income is received from sources within or without the United States.

Here we start to get a bit of specificity. I was unable to show you this tidbit of specificity in the earlier chapter because you didn't yet have the foundation to understand it. Now we can cover it!

In 1.1-1(b) we see the following two classes:
- ✓ "…citizens of the United States, wherever resident…" and;
- ✓ "…all resident alien individuals are liable to the income taxes imposed by the Code…"

So what are we to derive from the specificity of the language the Secretary has chosen?

First, as discussed earlier, an individual is a "resident" – for the purposes of U.S. tax law – if he is residing in a country other than the one with which he has citizenship. That means that in this regulation the Secretary has given us a critical piece of information.

The regulation tells us that a U.S. citizen has had the subtitle 'A' income tax imposed upon him if he is residing somewhere other than the United States. Yet we do not know what he must be doing there (as far as "income" is concerned) to fall within the boundaries of the tax imposed. In other words, the Secretary has given us one piece of the puzzle, but not all of it. However, since the regulation starts with the words "In general" we should not expect a detailed statement of specifics. Anything that purports to give us a "general" understanding will never contain specifics. That's just one of the rules of how law is written.

The second element of the regulation tells us that "all resident alien individuals are liable to the income taxes imposed…." We know that a "resident alien" is an alien who has been legally admitted to the United States for permanent residency and has a green card.

So…now we know that subtitle 'A' applies to U.S. citizens residing abroad (but without knowing the particulars) and to "resident aliens" (also with zero particulars).

I reviewed these regulations – which are the first regulations you see when you open the Code of Federal Regulations to Title 26 – to make the point (again) that there is a noticeable lack of specificity that would be needed to know exactly whom the tax is imposed upon. Do we then need to read them in light of the broader "context" rule we discussed earlier?

The broad context is that Congress has to identify a privilege in order to impose an excise (income) tax. There is no getting around this simple fundamental fact.

And we must remember this important rule:

Taxation Key, West 53 - The legislature cannot name something to be a taxable privilege unless it is first a privilege.

In other words, it has to be a real honest-to-goodness privilege in the first place. Only then can Congress impose an excise upon the privileged activity.

If income is derived from a subtitle 'A' taxable activity, that income is referred to in the Code as "gross income" (section 61). The amount of tax due is then based on the "taxable income" (section 63), to wit, *"'taxable income' means gross income minus the deductions allowed by this chapter...."*

It bears repeating that income that is *not* subject to the provisions of subtitle 'A' is *not* "gross income", but merely your property!

Since we have discovered that it is virtually impossible for an American to exercise a privilege taxable by the federal government as an excise, upon whom has Congress imposed this privilege tax (subtitle 'A') that we call "income tax"?

As stated previously, Thomas Jefferson was the closest friend and confidante of James Madison. These men were almost single-handedly responsible for the political concept and practical framework of our national government.

Here are a few quotes from Jefferson that may give you a hint as to what "privilege" would be within the proper constitutional boundaries for the federal government to impose an excise upon.

> "I believe the States can best govern our home concerns, and the General Government our foreign ones."

"My general plan would be, to make the States one as to everything connected with foreign nations, and several as to everything purely domestic."

"Our citizens have wisely formed themselves into one nation as to others [foreign nations] and several States as among themselves."

"The radical idea of the character of the constitution of our government, which I have adopted as a key in cases of doubtful construction, is, that the whole field of government is divided into two departments, domestic and foreign; that the former department is reserved exclusively to the respective States within their own limits, and the latter assigned to a separate set of functionaries, constituting what may be called the foreign branch [the general government]."

"To the State governments are reserved all legislation and administration in affairs which concern their own citizens only, and to the federal government is given whatever concerns foreigners or the citizens of other States; these functions alone being made federal."

"The true theory of our Constitution is surely the wisest and best, that the States are independent as to everything within themselves, and united as to everything respecting foreign nations."

"The best general key for the solution of questions of power between our governments is the fact that 'every foreign and federal power is given to the Federal Government, and to the States every power purely domestic.' I recollect but one instance of control vested in the Federal over the State authorities in a matter purely domestic, which is that of metallic tenders. The Federal is, in truth, our foreign government, which department alone is taken from the sovereignty of the separate States."

It should now be crystal clear to you that the authority of the general government is almost exclusively over foreign matters.

Under the *Articles of Confederation* the general government was to go to the state governments for any money it sought domestically in the form of a Direct tax. It was not welcome to go directly to The People. During the debates at the

Constitutional Convention, there was not one utterance from any delegate about permitting the general government (under the proposed constitution) to seek its revenues by operating directly upon The People. In other words, the change from the *Articles of Confederation* to the U.S. Constitution did not in any way change the restriction that general government is not permitted to seek its revenues by direct action upon The People.

If Congress' authority is nearly exclusively "foreign" in nature, and the general government cannot to go directly to The People for revenue, upon whom then would an individual income tax be imposed? Before I answer that question let me remind you that the basic elements of the general government's authority to tax have not changed since the Constitution was written. The 16th Amendment changed nothing, but only clarified an issue.

If Congress is not free to operate directly upon The People for its revenue, and its authority is essentially foreign in nature, would it not make sense that it would seek its revenues from foreigners exercising a privilege in America? And so it has!

Foreigners, except those here legally with a green card, have few rights in this country. [Do not confuse that reality with Congress' **choice** to give illegal aliens numerous welfare benefits.] Specifically, for the purpose of a discussion on taxation, foreigners who are not resident here have no right to invest capital here and reap the profits. ***That*** is a privilege! And it is the privilege that Congress has imposed the income tax upon in subtitle 'A'.

Congress has also imposed subtitle 'A' income tax upon certain U.S. citizens living abroad with foreign income. I will not be delving into that issue in this book as it touches such a narrow slice of the pie; involving only an infinitesimal number of Americans, and it is not a significant part of the "largest financial crime in the history of the world" as is the misapplication of the income tax here at home. I will only say that the proper application of that aspect of the income tax is even narrower that its description would lead one to believe.

In chapter 5 we looked at regulation 1.1-1(a) as it would be worded if the Secretary wanted to provide clarity (instead of vagueness). Let's look at it again:

> *Section 1 of the Code imposes an excise tax on **specific** individuals, who are citizens of the United States or a resident alien in the U.S.*

I'm betting these words makes a lot more sense to you now!

Before I close this chapter I want to ensure that you understand one of the primary elements that restricts the federal government's taxing authority. As mentioned in Chapter 5, the U.S. Constitution guarantees each state a republican form of government. One the critical and defining elements of a republic is that there is a division between state powers and federal powers; each in control of its own sphere, with little, if any, overlap. Jefferson left us with no doubt of where the dividing line is under our Constitution.

Since our Constitutional system has given the federal government "every foreign…power" and the states retained "every power purely domestic" there is no constitutional authority for the federal government to tax citizens of the states of the Union when living and working in their own country!

The way our constitutional system is structured, we have two different governments.

- The individual states of the Union
- The federal government

Each functions within its own sphere, with only scant overlap.

The U.S. Supreme Court has said that Congress' power to tax is "plenary". Plenary means "full and complete in every respect". Some definitions also include the word "absolute". And indeed Congress' power to tax is plenary. However – and this is critical – it is "full and complete" and "absolute" *only within its sphere.* It has no taxing power whatsoever in that sphere of government reserved to the states. Clearly a tax on the earnings of every American living and working within the states would be within the "domestic" sphere.

In upcoming chapters I will discuss two issues that I'm confident are on your mind right now.

First, I will give you the evidence – right from the government's own words – that the income tax pertaining to U.S. source income has only been imposed on *foreign persons* – although some U.S. citizens have been "made liable" for the *foreign person's* tax!

If Not You, Then Who?

Second, I will explain how, despite the fact that the general government is restricted from seeking its revenue by operating directly on The People, most Americans would say it is doing exactly that! Well...they're really not. Remember, they are committing fraud on a grand scale in order to commit the largest financial crime in the history of the world. As with most fraud, "the mark" [that's YOU!] is led to believe one thing when something else entirely is really happening that "the mark" cannot see or understand. And so it is here!

I can still remember how I felt in 1993 when I first discovered that the United States government had knowingly, intentionally, and willfully, decided to commit massive fraud on the American people and make hundreds of millions of citizens the victims of that fraud. I can relate to exactly how you're feeling right now!

The good news is that at the end of this book you will have the tools to do something about it!

In Their Own Words

Chapter 7

"The object of all despotism is revenue."
~ Thomas Paine

There are people who, having read this far in the book, are very upset – with *me*!

I'm used to it. I've been called every name in the book over the last two decades. I'm even aware of cases in which corporate internet servers have blocked access to my websites, with the screen reading "Anti-Government Site" as the explanation. I guess advocating good constitutional government today is the same thing as being anti-government. I think they make my point for me.

I could not be more proud or gratified to be the enemy of such people. Their view of America is an ugly, deranged fantasy. Interestingly, vitriol against the truth comes from both the left and the right.

The "left" despises the message (and by association, me) because it leaves no room for socialism or the welfare/nanny state.

Some on the "right" despise the message (and by association, me) because they fear that if the Constitution is actually adhered to, America will no longer be "strong" and that our position of "world dominance" will come to an end. I guess it depends on what "dominance" means to you.

I would prefer that America be "dominant" in the minds of Americans and others in reference to personal liberty. I could care less about being dominant in the sense that the U.S. military can wipe out 100,000 people on the other side of the world with the touch of a few buttons.

Since socialism and the "welfare state" are completely antithetical to personal liberty, I am pleased that the supporters of such vile schemes view me as their enemy. They are correct in that characterization.

Hatred from both sides of the fence comes from one simple fact: They cannot attain (or continue) their warped fantasy of America without your money – and in ever-increasing amounts I might add! Anyone who threatens the flow of money is their enemy. Adherence to the Constitution is not even a part of their equation.

In their heads they have a vision of what America should be (the Constitution be damned) and that is all that is important to them. They actually define themselves by this vision. To surrender the "vision" is to surrender their very identity (emotionally speaking).

Am I saying that I think having a "vision" of what you want for America is a bad thing? Not at all. But these people want to see their vision realized despite what the Constitution says (though it is the "Supreme Law of the Land"), and despite what The People want.

If the vision these people have is so wonderful, why all the subterfuge? Why lie? Why commit the largest financial crime in the history of the world if they could just explain themselves to The People and The People would amend the Constitution to facilitate their various (though often conflicting) "visions"?

Of course the answer is obvious. Their visions are not the same as those of the hard-working men and women of America. Some Americans may (out of ignorance) be sympathetic to these visions, but they are certainly not willing to surrender their wealth (at whatever level it may exist) so some stranger can take a shot at creating his own personal vision of Utopia.

Those who support the criminal misapplication of the income tax see the refusal of the American people to willingly surrender their wealth to "the anointed ones" as a character flaw. According to these people, YOU – the American citizens – are too selfish and shortsighted to understand what is really important, which is, of course, their vision of Utopia.

As is the way of politics, these vile criminals (i.e. those who would steal your property under the guise of law) will usually ban together in groups. If a group gets big enough, sometimes it becomes a "party". Forming together as a group changes nothing. Instead of one vile criminal, you simply have a group, a collective, of vile criminals.

By contrast, those who believe in personal liberty want nothing from others – except that others do not infringe upon their rights, just as they will not infringe upon the rights of others. They want to live life within the dictates of their own conscience, restrained only by their obligation not to interfere with the equal rights of others.

Because you – the lover of liberty – are so selfish and shortsighted, you cannot be told the truth. If you were told the truth, you'd rebel against it. If you were told the truth, you would not permit your property/wealth to be seized for no better reason than to let some other guy do with it what he thinks is right. Accordingly, you cannot be told the truth. The truth must be hidden from you because you are too stupid to reason things through for yourself. When your property is stolen from you under the guise of law, a crime is being committed against you, but these same people have made the subject so vast and complex that you cannot discover their crime. In your bones you know something is wrong, but you can't quite get your mind around it. That is exactly the way they want it - and that is exactly what you and I are going to end, right now!

In the last chapter I laid out for you who the income tax is actually imposed upon. Many of you are uncertain. Some of you are flabbergasted. That's OK; I understand. It's a lot to process as you simply read through the book. I'm sure many of you will read this book 2 or 3 times to make sure you understand it thoroughly. That's a good idea. Others will ponder the contents of this book for weeks or even months, mentally sorting through the details until your mind comes to the place it needs to be.

In the final analysis, what I have to say doesn't matter. What matters is where you end up. If all this book contained were Dave Champion's *claims,* you'd have wasted your money buying it. What makes it worthwhile is if you learn what the *government* has to say about the income tax!

What the government has to say about subtitle 'A' comes from numerous sources. Some are found in statutes, some in the regulations, some in Treasury Decisions, some in Executive Orders, some in the Internal Revenue Manual, etc., but no matter what the source, all the items form a cohesive and consistent whole in which subtitle 'A' is imposed upon *foreign persons* with U.S. source income, but with certain specific Americans being "made liable" for the filing of returns and for paying the tax imposed upon the *foreign person*.

In a later chapter I will address Tax Honesty arguments that are incorrect. I bring it up here because at this juncture, some people may mistakenly believe that I am putting forth the "861 position"; also know as the "gross income" position. I am not. While there may be some superficial resemblance between the "861 position" and what the law actually says, they are not remotely the same. This will be explained in more detail later.

When I said that this book has been worthwhile if you learn "what the government has to say about the income tax", that should not be taken to mean "the government's public position on the income tax". The government's public position is to use a combination of vague wording and legalistic jargon to give the American public the impression that everyone owes income tax!

What I'm going to show you here is what the government has said that it doesn't want you to see, or figure out. Some of the items I will show you were written in the 1980s – long before the IRS imagined that it would be required by law to post such documents to its website. Faced with doing so, Treasury convinced Congress to pass laws that "obsoleted" many of the documents. Once a document has been declared "obsolete" it is no longer necessary for the IRS to post the document to its website and it is no longer available through the Freedom of Information Act. The government's goal was that those damning documents would never see the light of day. As you are about to discover, their desire to keep the information hidden from you – the American public – didn't work out so well!

As you review these documents, you will also discover that over the last 5-10 years the IRS has pretty much abandoned the law and now hopes that plain old-fashioned *fear* will keep "the marks" [that's YOU!] in line. Tax law is, in its nature, a very specific thing. The very nature of taxation requires that the statutes, regulations, and other supporting documents detail with substantial specificity whom the tax is imposed upon and under what circumstances. That is not true of income tax alone, but of all taxation.

As the public became more dubious of the government's party-line concerning the income tax, and Tax Honesty researchers began organizing on a more efficient level, the government became aware that the end of the fraud was inevitable because, given enough time and effort, the law contains enough evidence of the truth to convince all but the most hardened and irrational opponents.

The government's response to this "threat" (i.e. you finding out the truth) was to "obsolete" all of the documents that provided specifics and to replace them with mountains of documents that are so vague as to be utterly worthless. If it were possible for the government to gather up all the old documents and destroy them, there would be no chance of proving the statements I made to you in the last chapter. Fortunately, that's not possible – even with all the resources of the federal government.

It would be my preference to create a separate chapter for each "fact" or item of evidence as we move through them. That's not going to be possible because many overlap and are relevant to one another. Accordingly, this is just going to be a long chapter.

Let's start with a simple yet pervasive element of U.S. tax law. The *"Internal Revenue Districts"*. I'll start into this area of tax law by showing you a statute that brings the Districts into play.

7601. Canvass of districts for taxable persons and objects

> (a) General rule
> The Secretary shall, to the extent he deems it practicable, cause officers or employees of the Treasury Department to proceed, from time to time, through each internal revenue district and inquire after and concerning all persons therein who may be liable to pay any internal revenue tax, and all persons owning or having the care and management of any objects with respect to which any tax is imposed.

You can see that section 7601 permits the Secretary to have his employees canvass within each "internal revenue district" for the purpose of finding those who ***may be*** liable for any tax.

I emphasized the words "may be" because in order for the Treasury employee to move from "may be" liable, to "is" liable, the employee might have to summons the "books and records" of the party engaged in the excise taxable activity. That authority is found at section 7602.

7602. Examination of books and witnesses

> (a) Authority to summon, etc.
> For the purpose of ascertaining the correctness of any return, making a return where none has been made, determining the liability of any person for any internal revenue tax or…any person in respect of any internal revenue tax, or collecting any such liability, the Secretary is authorized –
>
> (1) To examine any books, papers, records, or other data which may be relevant or material to such inquiry;
>
> (2) To summon the person liable for tax or required to perform the act, or any officer or employee of such person, or any person having possession, custody, or care of books of account containing entries relating to the business of the person liable for tax or required to perform the act, or any other person the Secretary may deem proper, to appear before the Secretary at a time and place named in the summons and to produce such books, papers, records, or other data, and to give such testimony, under oath, as may be relevant or material to such inquiry; and
>
> (3) To take such testimony of the person concerned, under oath, as may be relevant or material to such inquiry.

It is the government's position that these two sections operate together to give the IRS its power to "summons authority".

But let's look at what is being said. 7601, the first section of the two, and the one that would have to come before the issuance of a summons, involves canvassing for persons who may owe a tax. But Congress did not say that revenue officers are free to canvass anywhere they want. Congress specified that revenue officers can only canvass within "each internal revenue district".

Now some might suggest that while 7601 gives revenue officers the authority to canvass within an internal revenue district, possibly they are also free to canvass elsewhere. But that concept cannot withstand constitutional or interpretive scrutiny.

First, a statute that would allow a revenue officer to go anywhere without restriction would immediately run into legal trouble. What would become of the privacy of Americans?

Second, such unrestricted and intrusive authority would run dangerously close to constituting the power of a "general warrant", which is constitutionally impermissible in this country and was one of the offenses of the Crown that led to the American Revolution.

Third, it would offend one of the preeminent rules of statutory construction, *Expressio unius est exclusio alterius*, which means, "what is expressed excludes that which is not expressed". Or in plain English, "If it ain't in there, you ain't got the authority."

And fourth, even the government itself has never contended that revenue officers are permitted to canvass anywhere but within an internal revenue district.

INTERNAL REVENUE DISTRICTS

So what are these strange things known as "internal revenue districts"?

Our little adventure to determine that begins with section 7621 of the Internal Revenue Code where Congress commands the President of the United States to create things called "internal revenue districts":

> "The President shall establish convenient *internal revenue districts* for the purpose of administering the internal revenue laws. The President may from time to time alter such districts."

Interestingly, the Code itself never defines an "internal revenue district". Isn't it odd that the Code commands the President to create something without telling him what it is that he is creating?

So, did the President create these mysterious *"internal revenue districts"* although he was never told (in law) what they are? He did not. Instead, by Executive Order 10289, section 1(g), the President delegated the authority to the Secretary of the Treasury.

This makes sense (in an odd way) because it is usually the Treasury Department that actually writes the taxation legislation that Congress votes upon. So, in this case, Treasury wrote legislation requiring the President to create *"internal revenue districts"* (even though the law doesn't tell him what they are) and he delegated that authority to the Secretary of the Treasury, who actually knows what an "internal revenue district" is!

Now that the authority to create the *districts* is possessed by the Secretary, what has he done?

The Secretary created Treasury Order 150-01 in which he created 33 *internal revenue districts* that span the nation and cover every state in the Union. In doing so, the command Congress made to the President was completed by his subordinate, the Secretary of the Treasury.

All seems to be as it should be. Well, not exactly.

Although most Americans aren't aware of it, federal law requires that, except for Acts of Congress, all written authorities (which purport to have "general applicability" upon any person or group of persons) must have corresponding "regulations", and these regulations must be published in the Federal Register.

There are, however, a few exceptions.

Section 7621 does not require regulations for two reasons. First, the statute is so short and clear that no regulations are required; and second, it has no impact on the public generally because it simply "authorizes" the President to do something and does not lay any duty upon the public.

However, once the President delegated that authority to the Secretary, the Secretary needed to create regulations to let the public know exactly what he was doing and how it would (or might) affect the public. Accordingly, the Secretary created regulations pertaining to the authority the President delegated to him in Executive Order 10289.

The regulations the Secretary created for E.O. 10289 are found in Title 19 of the Code of Federal Regulations (CFR), Part 101. We know this because the nice folks at the National Archive and Records Administration (NARA) have very kindly provided us with a cross-reference index that shows us which regulations correspond to which statutes or Executive Orders (EO). This index is known as the "Parallel Table of Authority and Rules". Here is the entry for EO 10289:

E.O. 10289 ....19 Part 101

So, what does 19 CFR, Part 101, say? Here is the opening statement that defines the scope of the Part 101:

> **Scope.** *This part sets forth general regulations governing the authority of Customs officers, and the <u>location of Customs ports of entry</u>, <u>service ports</u> and of <u>Customs stations</u>. It further sets forth regulations concerning the entry and clearance of vessels at Customs stations and a listing of Customs pre-clearance offices in foreign countries. In addition, this part contains provisions concerning the hours of business of Customs offices, the Customs seal, and the identification cards issued to Customs officers and employees. [underlines added]*

As you can see, the Secretary has not chosen to create *internal revenue districts* for general tax purposes, but has created said districts *only* for certain matters pertaining to the customs laws of the United States - including the collection of customs duties (taxes).

This dovetails perfectly with the CFR's *Parallel Table of Authority and Rules* entries for "canvassing" and "examinations". According to the National Archive and Records Administration (the nice folks who compile and publish the CFR and the Federal Register), the only *implementing regulations* for 26 USC 7601 and 7602 are for issues pertaining to alcohol importation:

7601-7606 ....27 Part 70
7602 ....27 Parts 170, 296

It should be noted that sections 7601 and 7602 are found in the tax regulations of Part 310. But as we discussed earlier, Part 301 is merely the "general guideline" regulations and do not address any particular type of tax. This should not surprise us because sections 7601 and 7602 of the Code are contained within subtitle

'F', which is entitled "Procedures and Administration". In other words, Subtitle F (*Procedures and Administration* of the Code) is the "general guideline" part of the <u>Code</u> that corresponds to *Procedures and Administration* – the "general guideline" part of the <u>regulations</u> – Part 301!

When we look at the Part 1 (income tax) regulations, 7601 and 7602 do *not* appear! In other words, there is no 26 CFR 1.7601 or 1.7602. Additionally, sections 7601 and 7602 of the Code do not have regulations in Part 20 (estate tax) or Part 25 (gift tax).

Clearly then, "canvassing" and "summons" authority has not been extended to the taxes that average Americans may contend with, such as income tax, estate tax, or gift tax. We know this because there are no regulations for "canvassing" or "summons" in Parts 1, 20, or 25.

And there is a very good reason for that, which I will disclose shortly.

The "*internal revenue districts*" named in T.O. 150-01 do not cover the entire area of a county, or part of a state, named as a district. These revenue districts are limited to the boundaries of "Customs ports of entry", "service ports" and "Customs stations".

Let me give an example. I used to live in Los Angeles. The IRS has, on its map of L.A., made a big circle in red (euphemistically speaking) and the IRS calls that the "Los Angeles District". The IRS is free to make a big red circle on a map with a crayon and call that circle anything it wants. But, their authority to "canvass" and "summons" is not associated with, or controlled by, their big red Crayon circle; it is controlled by Treasury Order 150-01.

The average person might imagine that the IRS's authority to "canvass" and "summons" is within the totality of – in other words, within every square inch of – that red crayon circle they call the "Los Angeles District". It is not! In reality the IRS only has the authority to "canvass" and "summons" within the *internal revenue districts* specified within Treasury Order 150-01.

So what are examples of the *internal revenue districts* within the IRS's "Los Angeles" Crayon circle? Examples are places such as the Long Beach and Los Angeles harbors, and the Los Angeles International Airport. (A complete list of ports designated by the Secretary of the Treasury for customs purposes can be found in the 19 CFR, Part 101, pages 314 through 323 [1998 Ed.] Airports so designated can be found in regulations promulgated by the Secretary of Commerce.)

I mentioned earlier that there are very good reasons why the Secretary restricted the authority to "canvass" (section 7601) and "summons" (section 7602) to places associated with customs enforcement (i.e. foreign trade).

Since there is no Direct tax in effect in America, the ability of a tax agency to look within the general population was/is not necessary. Additionally, any Direct tax would be imposed by the federal government upon the states, not upon their citizens directly, so there is no need to inquire of the population generally.

The income tax (subtitle 'A') is an excise tax. The tax is based upon a privilege. Virtually all privileged activities (though not necessarily taxable activities) are permitted by the government by virtue of licenses, permits, etc., or are otherwise monitored by the government. This means that the government knows who is engaging in a privileged activity either by its licensing process, or by otherwise monitoring the privileged activity. So, if the government already knows who is involved in privileged activities why would it need to inquire of the population in general?

Also, the idea that a federal agency could intrude into the lives and finances of virtually any American simply by claiming that person lives (or works) within an arbitrary government *District* simply could not pass constitutional scrutiny. If that were possible it would mean the general government would have the power to draw a crayon line anywhere it wanted and then demand the personal financial records from anyone within that crayon circle.

Right now you may be saying to yourself, "But isn't that how it works today?" No! That is how you've been led to believe it works, but that's not what the law says.

Remember that I said subtitle 'A' has been imposed on foreign persons deriving U.S. source income? Those foreign persons (or their U.S. "withholding agents") must file tax returns. Section 7602 is also a general authority to conduct an "examination" (what the public usually calls an "audit") for the following purpose:

> (a) For the purpose of ascertaining the correctness of any return, making a return where none has been made...."

So, while 7601 restricts the geographic "canvassing" to designated *internal revenue districts*, it permits the Secretary to summons the "books and records" of a person, if that person has filed a return or is required to file a return (on his/her ***privileged*** activity) but has not done so.

In summary, 7602 permits the Secretary to summons the financial records of any person who filed a return (in connection with an excise activity) or was required to file a return (in connection with an excise activity) but who did not do so. Section 7601 permits the Secretary (who has authority over all forms of taxation, including customs duties) to canvass certain specifically designated areas – called *internal revenue districts* – and if he finds a person in that specifically designated location is liable for a tax (i.e. customs duty), he can use 7602 to summons that person's records for the purpose of determining the actual amount owed.

You will notice that there isn't any statute or regulation that permits intrusion into the financial privacy of anyone who is *not* required to file a return and has *not* done so! And here's a newsflash for you – that's the vast majority of you who are reading this book!

> [**Author's Note:** *Within the last few years, it appears that Executive Order 10289 has been cancelled. Treasury Order 150-01 was terminated in March 9, 2001 and thus Internal Revenue Districts no longer exist. The information you just read is provided to give you an understanding of what the government has done, and is doing, to commit fraud against you. Significantly, the statutes and regulations that rely on the Internal Revenue Districts as the basis of tax administration have not been amended since the underlying E.O. and T.O. vanished. In a later chapter I will address why these authorities have disappeared and what, if anything, has replaced them!*]

26 CFR, PART 601

Part 601 of the tax regulations is entitled "General Procedural Rules". It is primarily for IRS internal use, but it contains revealing and useful information for us.

Let's take a look at it. Let's start with 601.101, the "Introduction" (in its relevant part).

(a) General. The Internal Revenue Service is a bureau of the Department of the Treasury under the immediate direction of the Commissioner of Internal Revenue. The Commissioner has general superintendence of the assessment and collection of all taxes imposed by any law providing internal revenue. The Internal Revenue Service is the agency by which these functions are performed. Within an internal revenue district the internal revenue laws are administered by a district director of internal revenue. The Director, Foreign Operations District, administers the internal revenue laws applicable to taxpayers residing or doing business abroad, foreign taxpayers deriving income from sources within the United States, and taxpayers who are required to withhold tax on certain payments to nonresident aliens and foreign corporations, provided the books and records of those taxpayers are located outside the United States.

That's a bit of a mouthful, so let's break it down into bites.

- *"The Internal Revenue Service is a bureau of the Department of the Treasury under the immediate direction of the Commissioner of Internal Revenue."* That's pretty clear and needs no comment.

- *"The Commissioner has general superintendence of the assessment and collection of all taxes imposed by any law providing internal revenue."* This tells us that the Commissioner and all those to whom he delegates authority are in charge of "assessing" and "collecting" *any* tax that is imposed by U.S. law for the purpose of bringing in internal revenue.

- *"The Internal Revenue Service is the agency by which these functions are performed."* Clear enough.

- *"Within an internal revenue district the internal revenue laws are administered by a district director of internal revenue."* Ah, now things get interesting! We see that there is a "district director" and he is in charge of administering the internal revenue laws within the *internal revenue districts*. But you now know what *internal revenue districts* actually are so you understand his very limited reach.

- *"The Director, Foreign Operations District, administers the internal revenue laws applicable to taxpayers residing or doing business abroad, foreign taxpayers deriving income from sources within the United States, and taxpayers who are required to withhold tax on certain payments to nonresident aliens and foreign corporations, provided the books and records of those taxpayers are located outside the United States."* Not much in that description for the vast majority of Americans.

  [**Author's note**: By Treasury Order 150-01, the Secretary of the Treasury changed the title "Director, Foreign Operations District" to "Assistant Commissioner, International". Remember that because you will see the newer title as we proceed!]

Of the 5 bulleted points you just reviewed, only the last two speak of who is to do what under the Commissioner's authority.

The "district directors" have authority over the administration of internal revenue laws within the *internal revenue districts*. That's it; nothing more for them.

The "Director, Foreign Operations District" administers the internal revenue laws relating to various international tax issues.

That's it! In the Secretary's own description of the administration of U.S. tax law by the IRS, its district directors only have authority in the *internal revenue districts* and *international* matters! (Of course the IRS always has authority over the government's own internal tax liabilities, such as when it withholds from its own *employees*.) Where's the rest?! Where's the stuff about the IRS guys who go after American citizens for a tax on their domestic earnings? How could the Secretary have "forgotten" something so *huge*?

The text of 601.101, above, is from Congress' own website and is current for 2009. I have the same regulation on CD ROM, from 1989, and the wording is identical. It would appear that this amazing oversight – i.e. who it is in the IRS that comes after Americans for some alleged tax on their domestic income – has been left un-addressed for *at least* 2 decades.

In reality it is not an "oversight". It is the Secretary telling the truth in his regulations. And as we proceed, you will see that 601.101 merely restates and substantiates what other IRS documents also say. The IRS is consistent when expressing this reality. It's just that no one ever showed it to YOU before!

Section 601.102 lists/identifies the classes of taxes collected by the IRS. This too is revealing and useful. The section is a bit long and contains details not necessary or significant to you, so I'll provide a quick summary here. (Anyone who wants to read the entire section can find it easily enough on the internet.)

According to 601.102, the IRS collects two classes of taxes.

Class 1: Taxes collected by assessment.
Class 2: Taxes collected by revenue stamp.

Taxes collected by assessment are income tax, estate tax, gift tax, employment tax, and miscellaneous excise taxes collected by return.

In this book, there is no reason to discuss taxes collected by stamp, so we will not examine them. The same is true of "miscellaneous excise taxes collected by return". We *will*, however, be addressing *employment taxes* in a future chapter.

Section 601.103 also has something for us!

(a) *Collection procedure*. The Federal tax system is basically one of self assessment. In general each taxpayer (or person required to collect and pay over the tax) is required to file a prescribed form of return which shows the facts upon which tax liability may be determined and assessed. Generally, the taxpayer must compute the tax due on the return and make payment thereof on or before the due date for filing the return. <u>If the taxpayer fails to pay the tax when due, the district director of internal revenue, or the director of the regional service center after assessment issues a notice and demands payment within 10 days from the date of the notice.</u>

Interestingly, when the district director or regional service center sends out a *notice and demand* in reference to income tax, they are acting under the authority of the *Assistant Commissioner, International* (formerly known as the "Director, Foreign Operations District")!

Within 601.101 (the opening "procedures" section) it states, *"For purposes of these procedural rules any reference to a district director or a district office includes the Director, Foreign Operations District, or the District Office, Foreign Operations District, if appropriate."*

In other words, [*pay attention here*] when the procedural regulations say that a particular thing is to be done by the "district director" or the "district office", we have no idea (initially) whether it is done by the *district director* in his role of administrating tax law within the *internal revenue districts* **or** whether he is acting under the authority of the *Assistant Commissioner, International*. The good news is that whichever authority the district director is exercising (*internal revenue districts* or *International*) it has nothing to do with you and me – the average American citizen!

WITHHOLDING OF TAX AT SOURCE

These same procedural regulations we've been reviewing also speak to the issue of the collection of taxes. One of the most revealing elements within the procedural regulations for "collections" is the section on "withholding of tax at source", which is found at 601.104(a)(2):

> "Withholding at the source of income payments is an important method used in collecting taxes. For example, in the case of wage earners, the income tax is collected in large part through the withholding by employers of taxes on wages paid to their employees. The tax withheld at the source on wages is applied as a credit in payment of the individual's income tax liability for the taxable year. In no case does withholding of the tax relieve an individual from the duty of filing a return otherwise required by law. **The chief means of collecting the income tax due from nonresident alien individuals and foreign corporations having United States source gross income which is not effectively connected with the conduct of a trade or business in the United States is the withholding of the tax by the persons paying or remitting the income to the recipients. The tax withheld is allowed as a credit in payment of the tax imposed on such nonresident alien individuals and foreign corporations.**"

You will note that I've <u>underlined</u> one portion and **bolded** another. This is to distinguish the two "classes" that the Secretary is talking about. The underlined part speaks of *wage earners,* while the bolded part speaks of *foreign persons.*

It is important to note that no one else is mentioned. Where is the part about withholding income tax on the average American who is not a *wage earner*? There isn't one – in this section or anywhere else! Hmmm. How odd! A worker's wages can be withheld from, and payment of money to *foreign persons* can be withheld from, but not from anyone else?

If the income tax applies to everyone, why isn't there a command to withhold from everyone?

Let's look at an example. Let's say "Bob" runs a carpet cleaning company and he cleans the carpets of twenty different businesses in town. If ***everyone*** owes income tax – which would mean that Bob would owe it on his carpet cleaning activities – why hasn't Congress commanded every business for whom Bob cleans carpets to withhold a portion of the payment due him?

If Congress has commanded a company to withhold taxes from a worker's paycheck, and Congress has commanded Americans to withhold taxes from money paid to foreigners, why hasn't Congress simplified matters by making it a universal practice?

Is it because Congress perceives it would be too much of a burden on American business? No. First, it is clear from the myriad of laws that Congress has passed, imposing huge administrative burdens on various groups, that Congress doesn't give a fig about placing burdens on businesses. Second, most businesses are already engaged in payroll withholding; it would be relatively trivial to piggyback a "general withholding" on top of payroll withholding.

So…given that Congress has no objection to imposing administrative burdens on business, and that in this scenario there really wouldn't be much of a burden anyway, why hasn't Congress enacted what I call a "general withholding" requirement?

Would there be an up side to Congress doing so? You bet! If it did so, the government would be much more assured of getting its money – and on a more timely basis. Much like payroll withholding, the government would be getting money throughout the year and the taxpayer would be compelled to file a return to get any refund owed. If the government set the withholding percentage high enough, it would virtually guarantee that every business would **have** to file to get a refund. Clearly this would be a powerful tool by which to force many businesses, who haven't been filing, back into the system!

It would appear that there are some very beneficial aspects to "general withholding" (from the government's perspective) and no real down side. So why hasn't it been done?

The answer is simple. It hasn't been done because Congress doesn't have the power to pass such a law. It doesn't have the power to pass such a law because the income tax doesn't apply to the average American or average American business. Remember, the income tax is an excise. There has to be a taxable privilege involved. What taxable privilege is Bob the carpet cleaner exercising? The answer is NONE!

Because the *excise tax* we call "income tax" doesn't apply to the average American or average American business, Congress is without constitutional authority to enact a "general withholding". And let me tell you – if Congress had the authority to enact a "general withholding" requirement, it would have been done long ago!

Let me take a moment to draw your attention to why Congress has, quite properly, enacted withholding on *wage earners* and *foreign persons.*

In the last chapter I told you that subtitle 'A' (income tax) has been imposed on *foreign persons* deriving income from U.S. sources. Accordingly, since U.S. source income being paid to *foreign persons* is a legitimate object of the income tax, Congress is free to enact a withholding requirement upon those payments – and that is exactly what they did. As I said, when it is within Congress' authority to take steps to "get the money", they surely will!

I would ask your indulgence for my not addressing the payroll withholding issue at this point. Payroll tax withholding is done under subtitle 'C' of the Tax Code.

As we close on this issue, it is important for you to understand that for the purposes of subtitle 'A', the only *withholding* permitted is upon *foreign persons.* This brings us directly to the next issue.

ILLEGAL WITHHOLDING

All too often the Tax Code is enforced by extortionate tactics that do not comport themselves with the law. You might think I'm referring to the IRS, but sadly I'm referring to your fellow Americans. Regrettably, some Americans have come to see themselves as the "enforcement thugs" for the IRS. These sorry excuses for Americans can often be found in the accounting departments of businesses across America.

Why would I refer to them as "sorry excuses for Americans"? Aren't these folks just as misled as the rest of us? Is it really their fault? These are good questions.

As I write these words I've been in this field of endeavor for roughly 16 years. During that time quite a number of companies and individuals have threatened to invoke "withholding" against an American who refuses to provide them with a "taxpayer identification number" (TIN).

This process always begins with a request for a TIN by the party making the payments.

> [**Author's note**: As we move forward you will see that there is no requirement in the law for the average American to furnish *any* number to *anyone* in order to be paid for doing a job.]

The American who understands the law will respond by informing the requester that there is no requirement in U.S. tax law for him to furnish a TIN (or any number, for that matter) in order to be paid for work that he has performed. My office suggests that the requester be provided a cogent letter that summarizes what the law says on this subject. Even when the letter is submitted you'd be surprised at the blatantly illegal responses one receives.

Many times the requester will simply refuse to make the payment that is owed to the person who performed the work. When it is pointed out that no law whatsoever – tax law or otherwise – permits refusing to pay a lawful debt based on not getting a TIN, many arrogant and disgusting Americans simply say, "Too bad! You'll knuckle under and give me the number or you won't get paid!" The law simply doesn't matter to these Nazis. Never once in all these years has even one of them proffered a law that would permit them to fail to pay their legitimate debt, since one cannot proffer what does not exist.

Before they were informed that there is no law that exists to permit their illegal behavior, they may well have simply been misinformed. However, after being informed that their actions are not supported in law, when they choose extortion as their illegal and immoral tool, they become "sorry excuses for Americans".

Over the years, a number of my clients have taken such people to court and have won every case. But why should law-abiding Americans have to invest their time and money to go to court to get money due them when the people refusing to pay have been informed that they are, in fact, breaking the law and they cannot put forth any law that would permit their action! For those who choose to commit the heinous act of refusing to pay a man for his honest work, the old punishment of "tar and feathering" sounds perfect!

ILLEGAL BACKUP WITHHOLDING

Another illegal act committed by some requesters who are denied a TIN is to threaten to backup withhold, or actually do so.

Typically these scoundrels will assert that they must do so under section 3406 of the Code:

> (a) Requirement to deduct and withhold
> (1) In general - In the case of any reportable payment, if -
> (A) the payee fails to furnish his TIN to the payor in the manner required...

There are a couple of elements that we should begin with when considering whether or not this section authorizes backup withholding from the average hard-working American.

First, remember that when writing his regulations at 601.104, the Secretary stated that withholding was performed ***only*** upon *foreign persons*. (He included "employees" but that is not subtitle 'A', which we are discussing here.) If the average American is not subject to an "initial" withholding, how could he/she possibly be subject to "backup" withholding?

When the Secretary stated that withholding was only performed upon *foreign persons,* he was merely staying within the statutory boundaries established by Congress in the Tax Code.

As you will see shortly, with one exception, Congress has never authorized *anyone* to backup withhold from an American citizen. (The exception is an American citizen [or a domestic U.S. corporation] handling U.S. source income as it makes its way to its *foreign person* owner.) Are you handling U.S. source income as it makes its way to its *foreign person* owner? If the answer is 'no', then Congress has never authorized anyone to perform backup *withholding* on you, TIN or no TIN!

Next you will notice that the payments subject to *backup withholding* are "reportable payments". I do not want to deluge you with the voluminous and complex regulatory language concerning "reportable payments". It would be brutally complex and your eyes would soon glaze over and you'd stop reading. Instead I will summarize by telling you that "reportable payments" are *only* payments of U.S. source income owned by a *foreign person.*

Lastly, you should note the use of the term "payor". There is no such word in the English language. (Although some dictionaries now include "payor", they reference it as a term used in law, and refer the reader to "payer" for the actual English language definition.)

Since "payer" is a real word, why didn't Congress use that word? Dictionary. com defines "payer" as "A person who pays." Wasn't that Congress' intent? No! Congress chose its own word because using "payer" opened the possibility that the entire reporting scheme would be declared unconstitutional.

Congress has the authority to require reporting by way of "information returns" (e.g. Form 1099, Form W-2, Form 1098, etc.) when one is involved in a privileged activity that is taxable by the general government. Congress does *not* have the authority to require reporting of any or every payment made in America. If Congress used "payer", a court may well have ruled that Congress overstepped its authority by creating the impression that *every* "person who pays" would be required to report the payments to the IRS. By using the term payor Congress was intentionally distinguishing between "every person who pays" and "*certain* persons who pay".

Earlier I said that Congress has only authorized backup withholding on foreign persons or those Americans in possession of the property of foreign persons. Let's have a look at that!

Do you remember what we learned about statutes or regulations that begin with the words, "In general"? When a section begins with "In general" we know that we are seeing the authority expressed in the broadest language without its limiting specifics. Well, the section we've been examining (that purports to authorize backup withholding) begins with the words "In general"!

WITHHOLDING AGENT

Congress has chosen to permit backup withholding *only* by a withholding agent. There is no law or regulation in existence that permits anyone else to perform backup withholding. Accordingly, if someone wishes to initiate backup withholding he must establish that he is a withholding agent under the tax laws of the U.S.

So what does the law say about who is, or can be, a withholding agent?

The term *withholding agent* is very clearly established and delineated in the Internal Revenue Code. There are several citations that are relevant to a withholding agent. They are:

> 26 USC §1441
> 26 USC, subtitle 'A', chapter 3, subchapter 'B'
> 26 USC §7701(a)(16)
> 26 USC §1464
> 26 USC §6414

Let's quickly examine each citation to determine if you can be a withholding agent under the law.

26 USC §1441 – Defines withholding agent as:

> "Except as otherwise provided in subsection (c), all persons, in whatever capacity acting (including lessees or mortgagors of real

or personal property, fiduciaries, employers, and all officers and employees of the United States) having the control, receipt, custody, disposal, or payment of any of the items of income specified in subsection (b) (to the extent that any of such items constitutes gross income from sources within the United States), <u>of any nonresident alien individual or of any foreign partnership</u> shall... ." [emphasis added]

Because you will be seeing the term "withholding agent" again later (and quite a bit), please take note of the fact that the only way a person can be considered a withholding agent is if he has "control, receipt, custody, disposal, or payment of any of the items of income...of any nonresident alien individual or of any foreign partnership." This definition will be important to keep in mind as we proceed.

26 USC, subtitle 'A', chapter 3, subchapter 'B' – Deals exclusively with various income issues concerning nonresident aliens and foreign corporations with domestic source income.

> 26 USC §7701(a)(16) – Defines withholding agent.
> "The term 'withholding agent' means any person required to deduct and withhold any tax under the provisions of section 1441, 1442, 1443, or 1461."

As you probably guessed, sections 1441, 1442, 1443, and 1461 all speak to income tax issues relating exclusively to nonresident aliens and foreign corporations.

> 26 USC §1464 – Deals with refunds and credits with respect to withheld tax by a withholding agent from nonresident aliens and foreign corporations.

> 26 USC §6414 – Deals exclusively with overpayment of tax imposed by chapter 24 [Employment Tax], or by chapter 3 [Withholding of Tax on Nonresident Aliens and Foreign Corporations].

These are the sum total of the sections of the Internal Revenue Code that address the issue of a *withholding agent*. The short list that appears above is complete and exhaustive. There is nothing else.

We must remember that the Secretary stated in 601.104 that withholding was *only* performed on *foreign persons*. Then we find that only a *withholding agent* can engage in withholding, including *backup withholding*. Accordingly, a person attempting to inflict *backup withholding* would first have to be able to show that, under the law, he/she is a *withholding agent*.

Those who wish to punish an American for not giving a TIN, by threatening to initiate (or actually initiating) *backup withholding*, without first being able to show that he/she is a *withholding agent*, are engaged in a completely illegal act. Their actions are no more defensible than the person who refuses to make any payment at all. Over the years my clients have made this legal reality clear to many people who have threatened backup withholding. After seeing the law, most of them simply continued to act as the American Gestapo and illegally harm an innocent American. Is it any wonder I refer to them as "sorry excuses for Americans"? Tar and feathering once again leaps to mind!

PAYOR

I mentioned earlier that *payor* was chosen by Congress because it has a far more limited meaning that "payer". Let me now go further. *Payor* means a very specific *class of person* making a payment of a very specific nature. Let's explore!

Many people presume the term "payor" found in §3406 simply means anyone who pays someone else. Once again the simplistic "common wisdom" is not what the law says.

1.1441-1(c)(19) – Definition of "Payor" – The term payor is defined in Sec. 31.3406(a)-2 of this chapter and Sec. 1.6049-4(a)(2) and generally includes a withholding agent, as defined in Sec. 1.1441-7(a).

Although the definition has more to it - and I'll get to that in a moment - I want to pause for just a moment to make sure you understand that a *payor* is generally a withholding agent.

In law, "generally" (not to be confused with "in general") means that whatever is being expressed is to be considered so at all times unless there is sound legal reason for an exception. Or phrased more particularly, a *payor* is to be considered a *withholding agent* unless there is a contrary indication provided in the law.

The rest of the "payor" definition is:

> "The term also includes any person that makes a payment to an intermediary, flow-through entity, or U.S. branch that is not treated as a *U.S. person* to the extent the intermediary, flow-through, or U.S. branch provides a Form W-9 or other appropriate information relating to a payee so that the payment can be reported under chapter 61 of the Internal Revenue Code and, if required, subject to backup withholding under section 3406. This latter rule does not preclude the intermediary, flow-through entity, or U.S. branch from also being a payor."

Obviously this definition has nothing to do with the average American or domestic firm making a payment to another American or domestic firm in the course of ordinary business. The definition clearly deals with payments made by a *withholding agent* to a *foreign person* through the *foreign person's* agent, in the form of an intermediary, flow-through entity, U.S. branch (of a foreign financial institution), etc.

It is also important to note the last sentence of the definition: *"This latter rule does not preclude the intermediary, flow-through entity, or U.S. branch from also being a payor"*. This provides the circumstance in which a *payor* is someone other than a *withholding agent*. It details the specific exception to the earlier part of the rule that said a payor is "generally" a *withholding agent*.

Before we conclude on the meaning of *payor*, allow me to direct your attention to a particular part of the definition. 1.1441-1(c)(19) – Definition of "Payor" – states, *"The term payor is defined in Sec. 31.3406(a)-2 of this chapter and Sec. 1.6049-4(a)(2) and generally includes a withholding agent...."*

This definition is telling us that the payor at 31.3406(a)-2 is a *withholding agent*.

> [Author's Note: The term "includes" means that *is* the definition, but other persons that are within the same "class" can be added even though they are not enumerated. The "class" addressed here is the person having control, custody, etc. of U.S. source income belonging to a *foreign person*. In other words, anyone else who has control,

custody, etc. of U.S. source income belonging to a *foreign person*, even if technically not a *withholding agent,* may still be considered a *payor.* This principle can be seen in operation in section 1441, when it states, *"...all persons, in whatever capacity acting...having the control, receipt, custody, disposal, or payment of any of the items of income... of any nonresident alien individual or of any foreign partnership shall...deduct and withhold...."* Notice that it says "all persons". That is because while it is describing a *withholding agent,* there may be others who are not technically *withholding agents,* but who are required to withhold. More on "includes" later!]

Now that we know the *payor* at 31.3406(a)-2 is a *withholding agent,* let's find out exactly what 31.3406(a)-2 says!

31.3406(a)-2: (a) In general. *Payor* means the person that is required to make an information return under section 6041, 6041A(a), 6042, 6044, 6045, 6049, 6050A, or 6050N, with respect to any reportable payment (as described in section 3406(b)), or that is described in paragraph (b) of this section.

You may not understand the significance of what you just read. But **"Wow!"** – **what a bombshell!** What 31.3406(a)-2 says may be the most significant revelation in this book concerning one of the "tax myths" I mentioned in the Introduction! Allow me to explain.

We've seen that the *payor* is generally a *withholding agent.* And now we find that the Secretary has specified that the person required to file *information returns* under sections 6041, 6041A(a), 6042, 6044, 6045, 6049, 6050A, or 6050N is the *payor/withholding agent!*

For the sake of simplicity, we'll just focus on section 6041 for the moment. Section 6041 is the section of the Tax Code that millions of businesses (falsely) believe requires them to file an *information return* (such as Form 1099) when paying another person. Here's what 6041(a) says:

"Payments of $600 or more – All persons engaged in a trade or business and making payment in the course of such trade or business to another person… shall render a true and accurate return to the Secretary…"

Sounds pretty compelling, right? Yes, but only until you understand that the Secretary has said that 6041 **only** requires a *payor* to file an *information return,* and that the *payor* is a *withholding agent!*

In other words, if a private sector business makes a payment to a private American citizen, but the party making the payment is not a *withholding agent* (or other person within that same "class") then there is **no requirement (or permission)** to file an *information return!* That means that millions (possibly billions) of *information returns* each year are issued contrary to the law!

We've covered a lot of ground so let's take a moment to recap.

- Congress has said that a *withholding agent* is a person who has control, receipt, custody, disposal, or payment of items of U.S. source income of any *nonresident alien* individual or of any foreign partnership.
- The Secretary has said that the terms *payor* and *withholding agent* are essentially synonymous.
- The Secretary has said that others, who are not technically *withholding agents,* can be a *payor* if and only if they are within the same "class" (i.e. has control, receipt, etc., of any of the items of U.S. source income of any *nonresident alien* individual or of any foreign partnership).
- The Secretary has said that *only* a *payor* is to file *information returns* (i.e. 6041, 6041(a), 6042, etc.).

> [Author's Note: In a later chapter we'll discuss how these illegal *information returns* – issued without a scintilla of legal authority – are shamefully destroying the lives of millions of innocent Americans!]

We can see that the common thread in the definition of *payor* is that the activity being addressed pertains exclusively to payments made to *foreign persons* or their *U.S. person* agents (which can be an intermediary, flow-through entity, or U.S. branch of a foreign financial institution, etc.

You should be able to see now that both *withholding* and *backup withholding* are mechanisms that are only authorized to be affected upon *foreign persons* or their *U.S. Person* agents and have **nothing whatsoever** to do with the ordinary business affairs of the average American citizen or most American companies.

TREASURY DECISION 8734

One helpful thing the Secretary of the Treasury does is to write and publish Treasury Decisions to provide clarity to tax law. Often, Treasury Decisions are written to explain recent regulatory changes. Although written for officers and employees of the Treasury Department and the IRS, any interested person can learn from them. All Treasury Decisions are binding upon all officers and employees both of Treasury and the IRS.

There have been quite a number of significant Treasury Decisions over the years. However, at this moment we're going to examine just one - T.D. 8734.

T.D. 8734 is quite revealing. It explains how certain financial relationships are to operate under U.S. tax law and how various federal tax forms are to be used when administrating tax law in those circumstances. You will also find that it validates much of what we've already discussed.

As we dig into T.D. 8734 you will discover that many of the tax forms commonly thought to be for the use of average Americans, or the average American business, are not intended for those purposes at all, but rather are for very specific and uncommon applications. In short, you will find that many tax forms with which you are familiar have no legal applicability to you, or to the vast majority of your fellow Americans!

T.D. 8734 is 123 pages long in 8-point type. I will not attempt to provide you with the entire document here. You can see it for yourself by visiting any decent law library.

I have read all 123 pages – several times. It is a grueling read because much of it is highly technical and addresses complex financial arrangements in which the vast majority of Americans will never engage. It was nevertheless a worthy read! There is much in T.D. 8734 that explains what most Americans do not understand about U.S. tax law, including the correct applicability of various well-known tax forms.

Before I launch into T.D. 8734, I want to tell you that in a later chapter I will explain *why* these forms are so commonly misused. The misuse of these forms is essential to the continuing commission of the largest financial crime in the history of the world. Section 7701(a) of the Code defines "Taxpayer" as *"any person subject to any internal revenue tax."* The illegal use of these forms, along with a few other nifty little tricks, creates the legal presumption that you are a *"person subject to"* an *"internal revenue tax".*

T.D. 8734 addresses quite a number of issues, but every single one of them concerns **"Section 1441 – Withholding of Tax on Nonresident Aliens".** How do we know this? Because that is the heading of T.D. 8734!

As I said, T.D. 8734 is 123 pages long, so I will only give you the information relevant to the purpose of this book. If you feel that I may have left something out that would be important to you, please go to your local law library and read T.D. 8734 for yourself.

In the "Background" section, which is on the first page, it states that the T.D. *"contains the final amendments to the Income Regulations (CFR Parts 1, 31, 35a and 301) under sections...6041, 6041A, 6042..."* etc. These are the very same sections we just determined require information returns **only** from the *payor/withholding agent.*

Later it continues, *"Reporting to the IRS may be required under sections 6011 and 1461 or under the reporting provisions of chapter 61 of the Code, such as 6041, 6041A, 6042, 6044, 6045, 6049, 6050A, or 6050N, (the 1099 reporting provisions)."* Whoa! Wait a minute! Did you get that?

We have already determined that the *information return* requirement under sections 6041, 6041A, 6042, 6044, 6045, 6049, 6050A, or 6050N pertains **only** to a *payor/withholding agent*. And now the Secretary is referring to these sections as *"the 1099 reporting provisions".* So at least as far as sections 6041, 6041A, 6042, 6044, 6045, 6049, 6050A, or 6050N are concerned, the Form 1099 can only be legally used by a *payor/withholding agent.*

Many of you have received or issued oodles of 1099s over the years based on the erroneous presumption that section 6041 requires everyone who makes a payment to anyone to complete and send off a Form 1099. Now, today, you discover that every single one of those 1099s was issued without the permission of the Secretary!

Remember, if one wishes to be in compliance with tax law, one must obey the regulations written by the Secretary. In other words, "compliance" means doing what the Secretary says in his regulations. If one is doing things outside of, or beyond, what the Secretary has stated in his regulations, then that person is acting without the authority of the law.

On page 2, T.D. 8734 states, *"A payor making payments to foreign persons must also be aware of the information reporting provisions under chapter 61 of the Code and of other withholding regimes, such as section 3406 (backup withholding), and section 3402 (wage withholding), and section 3405 (withholding on pensions, annuities, etc.)."*

Well, well, well. See? The Secretary can be quite forthcoming when he wants to be! In this statement he is telling us that when a payor makes payments to *foreign persons,* he must be aware of his legal duties concerning *backup withholding* (we've covered that), wage withholding (we're going to cover that in a bit) and withholding on certain other types of payments. And all of this is specific! Remember our earlier conversation about specificity versus general language? This isn't broad language such as "Every person making payments...." or "When making payments to a taxpayer...." This is very specific: "A *payor* making payments to *foreign persons* must...."

Since we have this shining example of specificity, let me give you an example of specificity you will ***never*** see in the statutes or the regulations.

You will never see this:

> *"A U.S. citizen, when making a payment to another U.S. citizen, in the course of any private sector transaction of common right, occurring within one of the 50 states of the Union, is required to file an information return with the Secretary".*

You will never see such a command because it would be unconstitutional and the U.S government knows it! Yet if you stop and think about it, is that not the circumstance in which the overwhelming majority of *information returns* are filed? In other words, the overwhelming majority of information returns are created without any legal authority. Or phrased another way, they are illegal!

Further along in the same paragraph T.D. 8734 states, *"Under chapter 61 of the Code, many types of payments, such as interest, dividends, royalties, broker proceeds, etc. (reportable payments) must be reported on a Form 1099 if paid to*

U.S. persons. In addition, section 3406 requires the same U.S. payees to furnish a taxpayer identification number (TIN) to the payor, generally on a Form W-9...."

Again, "Wow!" And again, the Secretary has been wonderfully forthcoming!

I want to remind you that T.D. 8734 deals **exclusively** with "Withholding Tax on Nonresident Aliens". In other words, 100% of T.D. 8734 is talking about the withholding upon nonresident aliens. Understanding that, what does it mean when T.D. 8734 says that certain payments *"must be reported on a Form 1099 if paid to U.S. persons"*? Let's explore!

The answer can be found in the sentence immediately following to wit:

> *"In addition, section 3406 requires the same U.S. payees to furnish a taxpayer identification number (TIN) to the payor, generally on a Form W-9...."*

You will note that the "U.S. payee" (also known as a *U.S. person*) is required to furnish his taxpayer identification number to the *payor*! In other words, the person making the payment is still making a payment to a *foreign person*. (That is the definition of *payor*!)

I can hear some readers saying, "But Dave, doesn't that contradict what you said earlier?" No, not at all. I can only bring so much information into the equation at one time or a lot of readers would be overwhelmed. Accordingly, I hold off presenting some information until the appropriate time. The time is now appropriate for this subject!

Not all payments made by a *payor* to a *foreign person* are made **directly** to the *foreign person*. Earlier we read the second part of the definition of *payor*. Now it will likely be seen with more clarity.

> "The term also includes any person that makes a payment to an intermediary, flow-through entity, or U.S. branch that is not treated as a *U.S. person* to the extent the intermediary, flow-through, or U.S. branch provides a Form W-9 or other appropriate information relating to a payee so that the payment can be reported under chapter 61 of the Internal Revenue Code and, if required, subject to backup withholding under section 3406. This latter rule does not

preclude the intermediary, flow-through entity, or U.S. branch from also being a payor."

In other words, sometimes a payment of income belonging to a *foreign person* is made to an American citizen, or a domestic entity or institution, as it travels on its way to its *foreign person* owner. In this situation, the American citizen, or domestic entity or institution, is the *U.S. person* (also at times referred to as a *U.S. payee*).

You will remember that at the outset of this section I said, "...much of it (T.D. 8734) is highly technical and addresses complex financial arrangements in which the vast majority of Americans will never engage." Those "complex financial arrangements" involve the movement of U.S. source income to a *U.S. person* who is serving as the *intermediary, flow-through entity, U.S. branch*, etc., as the income flows to its *foreign person* owner.

In other words, a <u>U.S. person is an American citizen or domestic entity that is part of a financial "pipeline" through which U.S. source income flows to its foreign destination.</u>

Congress requires that all payments of U.S. source income to *foreign persons* are reported on *information returns*. That reporting starts with the origin of the income – the "U.S. source". If the U.S. source "origin" makes a payment of *foreign person* owed income to a *U.S person*, then that has to be reflected on an *information return*. We see that reflected in T.D. 8734 when it says, "*Reporting to the IRS may be required under sections 6011 and 1461 or under the reporting provisions of chapter 61 of the Code, such as 6041, 6041A, 6042, 6044, 6045, 6049, 6050A, or 6050N, (the 1099 reporting provisions)."*

When payment is made to a *U.S. person* (as part of the income "pipeline" to a foreign destination) and reporting is required under sections such as 6041, 6041A, 6042, 6044, 6045, 6049, 6050A, or 6050N, the regulations of the Secretary require that *U.S. person* – to whom the money was paid as part of the "pipeline" – to furnish a TIN. There is nothing odd, unusual, or mysterious about this. The only thing that is "odd" is that most Americans mistakenly believe that any other American with whom they do business is a *U.S. person*!

Now that you understand how this particular system works, let me give the full text.

"Under chapter 61 of the Code, many types of payments, such as interest, dividends, royalties, brokerage proceeds, etc. (reportable payments) must be reported on a Form 1099 if paid to certain *U.S. persons*. The form is filed with the IRS and a copy is furnished to the recipient of the payment. In addition, section 3406 requires the same U.S. payees to furnish a taxpayer identification number (TIN) to the payor, generally on a Form W-9, and, for reportable interest and dividends, a certification that the payee is not subject to notified payee underreporting."

What can we derive from this section? Quite a lot!

First, we must remember that T.D. 8734 deals *exclusively* with payments made to *foreign persons*. Not one word of T.D. 8734 addresses you or me! I reemphasize this point because we have all been socialized to believe the income tax applies to everyone, including the domestic earnings of the average American. It is only natural for our minds to keep going back there unless we are reminded that the context of T.D. 8734 is *only* payments to *foreign persons*.

With that firmly in mind, let us evaluate the Secretary's statement (above).

The first sentence makes it clear that payments such as interest, dividends, royalties, brokerage proceeds, etc. made to *foreign persons* are "reportable payments". I brought that to your attention earlier, but here we have the Secretary confirming it for you.

It then tells us that when a payment of U.S. source income is made to a *U.S. person* (as it flows through the pipeline to its foreign owner) such payments are to be reported on Form 1099. If you're in business for yourself, how many 1099s have you received over the years? Probably hundreds; maybe thousands. What you didn't know or understand was that each one of those 1099s was a formal legal testament [i.e. evidence!] that you are a *U.S. person* who received income (that didn't belong to you!) as it traveled through the "pipeline" to its foreign owner. Oops! There's a problem!

So how did this "mistake" occur? You created it. And you may say, "But Dave, how did I create it?" Let's continue with what the Secretary has to say, and see if your answer is there.

Go back to the part from which I quoted earlier:

"In addition, section 3406 requires the same U.S. payees to furnish a taxpayer identification number (TIN) to the payor, generally on a Form W-9...."

If you are in business for yourself, you've likely filled out numerous W-9s. Form W-9 is entitled "Request for Taxpayer Identification Number and Certification". You've likely thought that the purpose of Form W-9 was to attain the TIN of any American to whom payments are made in the course of normal everyday business. As you can see, that is hardly the case.

The instructions for the Form W-9 state, "Use Form W-9 only if you are a U.S. person."[1] Note that is says *"only* if you are a U.S. person." Since you now know what a *U.S. person* is, you also now know that Form W-9 is not, and never has been, a form you are **permitted** to sign. Or phrased another way, every time you filled out this form you swore to something that was *not* true!

The language of the Secretary further verifies the limited role of the Form W-9. He says that the Form W-9 is used to provide a TIN to a *payor*. And of course we now know that a *payor* is a person making payment of U.S. source income to *foreign persons* (even if it is initially sent to a *U.S. person*).

Finally, the Form W-9 itself shows its limited application.

One of the elements of the Form W-9 is that Treasury wants you to "certify" the information you put on the form. This "certification" process involves making three representations and then signing, under penalties of perjury, that those representations are true.

The first representation is that the TIN provided is true and correct. Since we've already discovered that a TIN is only required (for subtitle 'A') from a *U.S. person* we immediately know who is supposed to use the form.

The second representation is that you are not subject to *backup withholding*. Once again, we have already learned that *backup withholding* can only be performed by a *payor* against a *U.S. person (or foreign person)*, so that further confirms the form's limited role.

---

[1] IRS Form W-9, October 2007 revision

The third representation is that you are a "U.S. citizen or other U.S. person". This attestation verifies to the U.S. government that you are a person in the pipeline and *not* the actual foreign owner of the income.

I should take a brief moment to draw your attention to the wording of this phrase – *U.S. citizen or other U.S. person.* There are hundreds of millions of U.S. citizens, however there are very few *U.S. persons,* as such term is used in subtitle 'A'. By using the phrase *U.S. citizen or other U.S. person* the form is communicating that it is not for U.S. citizens generally, but *only* for the small number of U.S. citizens who are also *U.S. persons!* (And of course there are "others" who can be *U.S. persons,* but here we are limiting the discussion to you – the American citizen.)

Once you have certified all three representations you are to complete the process by affixing your signature. And what does the form say on the signature line? "Signature of U.S. person."

So, we have discovered that the Secretary has said that a person making payment of U.S. source income to a *foreign person* is to request the TIN of the *U.S. person* to whom the payment is being made, as the income moves through the pipeline to its *foreign person* owner. We've learned that this request for TIN is to be made using Form W-9. And we've seen that the Form W-9 is *only* to be used and signed by a *U.S. person.*

You've probably already answered your own question by now, but you "created" all those improper 1099s that were issued against you by completing W-9s and submitting them to the requesters. In doing so, you stated – under penalties of perjury – that you are a *U.S. citizen or other U.S. person* who has received a payment of U.S. source income that is on its way to its *foreign person* owner. If you're feeling defensive – as if I'm blaming you – I'm not; we've all done it at one time or another. I'm just teaching you how the system works. (I'll be getting into that in much more depth in an upcoming chapter!)

Let's continue with T.D. 8734. *"Payments to foreign persons are exempt from Form 1099 information reporting and backup withholding."* Well of course they are!

The Form 1099 is used to track the payment of U.S. source income from the "origin" through the domestic "pipeline", which may be made up of one or more *U.S. persons.* There is no need for an information return concerning the final transaction that puts the income into the possession of the foreign owner. Allow me to explain.

Section 1441(a) requires the withholding of U.S. income tax to occur **before** the income is paid over to its foreign owner. Remember this section?

> "... all persons, in whatever capacity acting...having the control, receipt, custody, disposal, or payment of any of the items of income...of any nonresident alien individual or of any foreign partnership shall deduct and withhold from such items a tax equal to 30 percent thereof...."

In other words, the *withholding agent* is required to deduct and withhold the tax before the income is paid over to the *foreign person* owner.

In his regulations on this subject, the Secretary addresses many complex financial arrangements that sometimes require different persons to perform the actual withholding at varying times. For instance, in some cases certain foreign financial institutions may be treated as a *U.S. person* and perform the withholding function before the income is paid over to a *foreign person*. Or, a foreign branch of a U.S. financial institution may perform the withholding function. However, I think you would agree that all these various permutations are irrelevant to the average American because we're not involved in making payments of U.S. source income to *foreign persons*. Because these technicalities are not important to you and me, I like to use common speech to illustrate who is required to withhold. Here's how I phrase it: *"The last domestic guy with it has to perform the withholding."* My plain English version may not be as technical as the Secretary's regulations, but it makes the point!

Now that you understand that the tax must be withheld **before** the income is paid to the *foreign person,* we can return to the question of why no information is required of the final transaction when the income is put into the hands of its *foreign person* owner.

Because the tax must be collected by "the last domestic guy with it," the government is only concerned about tracking the income to that point. Once the tax has been collected – or the government knows who the "last domestic guy with it" is – that is where the government's interest ends. The government has no need to know what *foreign person* received the income. But what if "the last domestic guy with it" fails to perform the withholding? Read section 1461:

"Every person required to deduct and withhold any tax under this chapter is hereby made liable for such tax and is hereby indemnified against the claims and demands of any person for the amount of any payments made in accordance with the provisions of this chapter."

As you see, the *withholding agent* is made liable for the tax, not the *foreign person*! That is why the government only cares to track the income to "the last domestic guy with it"; because he's the guy who's liable. If he doesn't withhold the government will simply go after him for the money!

Do you now understand why the Secretary says *"Payments to foreign persons are exempt from Form 1099 information reporting...."*?

The Secretary also said *"foreign persons are exempt from...backup withholding."* I'm sure you can now put this together yourself, but *foreign persons* are exempt from *backup withholding* because the law requires the tax to be withheld *before* the money gets to its *foreign person* owner.

As you can see, T.D. 8734 is replete with revealing information. Here's more!

T.D. 8734 says on page 2, *"...only amounts subject to reporting under the Form 1099 reporting provisions are subject to backup withholding under section 3406..."* and we have already covered that the Secretary has said the "1099 provisions" are exclusively for *payors* making payments of U.S. source income to *foreign persons*.

Isn't it amazing how once you understand what the income tax (subtitle 'A') is really all about, every single element dovetails perfectly with every other? Doesn't it amaze you now that people think the Tax Code is so horribly complex?

Let's look at a few more revealing aspects of the Code.

Earlier in this chapter we looked at section 1441. Let's look at its relevant part again:

> "...all persons, in whatever capacity acting...having the control, receipt, custody, disposal, or payment of any of the ***items*** of income specified in subsection (b).... of any nonresident alien individual or of any foreign partnership" [emphasis added]

You will notice that I emphasized "items" of income. These "items" are those "specified in subsection (b)". But what are those "items"? Let's look at the Secretary's regulations for clarification.

> 1.1441-2(b) – Income Subject to Withholding – (a) *Fixed or determinable annual or periodic income* – (1) In general -- ...fixed or determinable annual or periodical income includes all income included in gross income under section 61.

And what does section 61(a) say?

> "Except as otherwise provided in this subtitle, gross income means all income from whatever source derived, including (but not limited to) the following ***items:***" [emphasis added]

In other words, the ***items*** of income specified in section 1441 of the Code as being subject to withholding are the very same ***items*** of *gross income* in section 61. You should remember that earlier I said that section 61 only applied to persons upon whom Congress had imposed subtitle 'A'. I hope you are starting to see how all the pieces fall right into place when we know where to look!

At this juncture some naysayers may be thinking, "This is all nonsense because most of the persuasive arguments are based on statutes and regulations within chapter 3 of the Code, entitled "Withholding of Tax on Nonresident Aliens and Foreign Corporations. That has nothing to do with us!"

That kind of thinking is one of the several elements that keeps the fraud operating. Any average American who has the gumption to dig into subtitle 'A' will find that it has only three chapters.

1. Normal Taxes and Surtaxes
2. Taxes on Self Employment Income
3. Withholding of Tax on Nonresident Aliens and Foreign Corporations

Most people would get to the title of chapter 3 and think, "I need to read chapters 1 and 2, because 3 is about someone else." That is a natural human response based on being socialized to believe that the tax is upon the average American. It is also 100% wrong.

Do you remember when we discussed how statutes open with general statements of authority and then "drill down" to the actual limits of that authority? What I am about to explain to you is a variation on that theme.

Chapters 1 and 2 discuss what the tax is, not upon whom it is imposed! This is a very important concept.

Sure, chapter 1 begins with "There is hereby imposed on the taxable income of... " and then speaks of married people and surviving spouses, but how would we know who owes the tax by a discussion of marital status? I also draw your attention to the term "taxable income" used in that opening sentence. What is "taxable income"?

Section 63(a) In general - Except as provided in subsection (b), for purposes of this subtitle [subtitle 'A'], the term "taxable income" means gross income minus the deductions allowed by this chapter....

You can plainly see that *taxable income* begins with *gross income,* and we've already discovered that *gross income* is the same thing as the "items of income" listed at 1441 (Items Subject to Withholding by a *withholding agent*)! So you see, while the opening sentence does not, in plain English, impose the tax on any specific class of person, if we examine and understand the legal terms used by Congress we can discern that the tax is limited to *foreign persons*!

Chapters 1 and 2 lay out what I refer to as "the equations for making the tax work." Section 701 is a great example of this concept.

"A partnership as such shall not be subject to the income tax imposed by this chapter. Persons carrying on business as partners shall be liable for income tax only in their separate or individual capacities."

Do you see any specific *class of person* whom the tax is imposed upon in section 701? One might say "partners", but of course nowhere does subtitle 'A' impose the income tax on "partners" or make "partners" liable, so that response is not legally sound. The point is that chapters 1 and 2 tell us the rules pertaining to the proper computation of the tax, but not upon whom the tax is imposed.

Let's look at more examples. Here's 706(a):

> (a) **Year in which partnership income is includible** - In computing the taxable income of a partner for a taxable year, the inclusions required by section 702 and section 707(c) with respect to a partnership shall be based on the income, gain, loss, deduction, or credit of the partnership for any taxable year of the partnership ending within or with the taxable year of the partner.

Again, it clearly lays out the "rules for computation" and nothing more.

How about section 264(a)?

"General rule – No deduction shall be allowed for— " (followed by a list of expenses associated with life insurance policies.)

And how about 272?

> "Where the disposal of coal or iron ore is covered by section 631, no deduction shall be allowed for expenditures attributable to the making and administering of the contract under which such disposition occurs...."

And I could go on endlessly. A casual reading of chapters 1 and 2 should convince even the most obstinate supporter of the government's "party line" that it is impossible to consider these chapters anything more significant than "rules of computation".

Then we come to chapter 3.

Suddenly, when we reach chapter 3, there are no more "computations". That is finished; it is behind us. When we reach chapter 3 there are no more vague references to "the taxpayer" or "any person" or "every person". Suddenly there is complete clarity! There is no vagueness or subterfuge found in chapter 3 or its regulations. How can one explain this?

We have already discussed several times that Americans have been socialized to (incorrectly) believe that the income tax (subtitle 'A') applies to everyone. As such, when they read the "rules of computation" (chapters 1 & 2) it never even enters their minds that these "rules" are separate and distinct from the discussion of whom the "rules" apply to.

The legislative draftsmen who framed chapter 1 included a few vaguely worded sentences about "imposing" the tax and then embarked on their "rules of computation". Only after understanding far more about the Code than most people – even "tax professionals" – ever bother with, we find that those vaguely worded sentences do indeed contain key legal terms that show the tax is imposed on *foreign persons*.

So, one might ask, does it matter where a statute is placed in the Tax Code? The Code itself answers that one.

Section 7806. Construction of title

> (b) Arrangement and classification
> *No inference, implication, or presumption of legislative construction shall be drawn or made by reason of the location or grouping of any particular section or provision or portion of this title, nor shall any table of contents, table of cross references, or similar outline, analysis, or descriptive matter relating to the contents of this title be given any legal effect.*

Here Congress is saying that we cannot make any presumptions, draw any inferences, or take any implication from where a statute has been placed within the Code.

<u>This is a critical point!</u> ***Congress is telling you that it doesn't matter where in the Code the statute has been placed, but that the language of the statute is the only thing we are to rely upon in determining the meaning Congress intends.***

Can you see now why the title of chapter 3, *"Withholding of Tax on Nonresident Aliens and Foreign Corporations"*, gives the casual reader the wrong message? It doesn't matter what the chapter's title is, or where a statute has been placed in the Code. All that matters is what the statute says!

So when a person says "I don't need to read chapter 3 because that's only about foreigners", he is presuming what Congress said he cannot presume – that there is some significance to the name of a chapter or where statutes have been placed in a chapter with such a name.

This lack of understanding the rules Congress has laid out for reading the Code has kept millions of Americans, over many decades, from ever reading chapter 3, when in fact chapter 3 is where we all need to be looking in order to truly make sense out of the tax scheme Congress has created!

And as I said earlier, if the government could constitutionally impose the income tax on all of us they would have AND they would have implemented a "general withholding" to collect the tax.

Let's be straight about something. Any tax that is imposed – *any* tax – comes with a collection mechanism built into the law. There is no such thing as a tax that is imposed without a method of collecting it. Yet somehow we are to believe that the income tax – unlike every other tax – has absolutely no statutory collection mechanism for Americans conducting business domestically. We are to believe that the government simply trusts that Americans will pay their tax. Yeh, sure. The very thought that Congress created a tax without providing a real-time collection mechanism is absurd.

The truth is that Congress **did** provide a real-time collection mechanism for the tax. The tax is collected, under authority of section 1441, "Withholding of tax on nonresident aliens". The *withholding agent* performs the collection before the income is placed in the possession of the owner. That collection mechanism exists because that is whom the tax is imposed upon. There is no mechanism to collect from you and me because the tax has not been imposed on us!

The law then relies on the *withholding agent* to file a return and pay over the tax to the government, but there is no problem (in theory or in practice) with this approach because the *withholding agent* is not being asked to pay over his own money, but is merely paying money that he withheld from a *foreign person*. Predictably, there have been virtually no problems concerning withholding agents filing and paying.

So what does the IRS say about all this?

As I stated in the Introduction, the IRS says nothing at all. When you ask the IRS about subjects such as those raised in this book, you are immediately branded a "tax denier" and warned not to get involved in any "tax scams". Let's see now – hmmm - branded as "tax denier", and told not get involved in tax scams. Do either of those sound like answers to you?

Fortunately, we do have some recourse to information the IRS has published in years past.

THOSE GRAND OLD LETTERS

I was introduced to the Tax Honesty Movement in 1993, though it had no title back then. At that time the IRS was sending out letters to people who wrote to the IRS and told the IRS that they were not liable for the income tax. If the letter was relatively on-point, the IRS response was, *"Based on the information you have provided we have determined that you are not required to file."* How refreshing! And, unfortunately, all too short-lived.

About 1993 the internet started becoming quite popular with the public and so the IRS determined that it could not risk issuing these letters any more. They were concerned that these letters would begin to appear on websites – and then more people would start asking questions. The sad part is that these letters had been sent out for many years. They were routinely sent out because back then the IRS would let us off the hook if we were one of the few who had figured out that the income tax didn't apply to us. With the rising popularity of the internet the IRS began to fear that its own letters would cause more Americans to question their liability, and so the IRS stopped admitting the truth.

IRS ORGANIZATION AND STAFFING

In the intelligence community [CIA, NSA, etc.] analysts sometimes look at an organization's structure to determine how that organization is operating. Finding out how a clandestine organization is structured can be a bit of chore. Fortunately for us, the IRS is not a clandestine organization, or at least not completely.

During the 1980's the IRS did not fear the internet or the Freedom of Information Act, commonly referred to as "FOIA". This was an era when the IRS was still somewhat honest. It had not yet decided to throw a cloak over every meaningful part of its organizational structure, as it does today. (More on that later!)

Because the IRS was still a fairly open organization back then, when they produced internal documents they were written in a very straightforward manner, without being vetted for what might be revealed to the public.

Earlier in the book I mentioned Joseph Banister, the former IRS criminal investigator who discovered the truth and resigned his position. When Joe was troubled by what he was learning, and was struggling with continuing at the IRS, he came across a part of the Internal Revenue Manual (IRM) that troubled him. When he made the decision to resign, he did not take anything with him, including the pages of the IRM that had disturbed him. Since the document was an internal document he thought that it would never see the light of day. Joe was shocked and amazed – and thrilled – when he discovered that I had a copy of it!

The document to which I refer is "Part 1100" of the Internal Revenue Manual. This "Part" no longer exists, so don't jump on the internet to try and find it. You won't find it.

Part 1100 of the IRM is entitled "Organization and Staffing" and it lays out exactly that – the organization and staffing of the entire IRS! It starts with general information about the origins and history of the IRS and then moves directly into the structure of the organization, beginning with the Commissioner's office. It works its way down almost to the guy who polishes the floors at night! It is very thorough and detailed. My copy is about an inch and quarter thick! And it turns out to be very interesting reading indeed!

The most interesting part begins with the "Office of the Assistant Commission (International)". Considering that the income tax has been imposed on *foreign persons* with U.S. source income, and certain U.S. citizens residing abroad with foreign earned income, you can imagine that this section of Part 1100 might be fascinating – and you'd be right!

The IRM uses an "outline numbering scheme". What that means is that it is a numerical system that uses decimals to distinguish areas of authority. You will see how it works as we go along.

Every major player in the IRS is designated with a number. The Office of the Assistant Commission (International) is found at 1132. Offices or specific employees under the authority of the Assistant Commission (International) are designated as 1132.X. I use 'X' merely for illustration purposes.

I won't cover every "function" or "office" under the authority of the Assistant Commission (International) because many of them are mundane and/or irrelevant to this discussion. I will only address those that are significant.

At 1132.12 we find the "Functional Responsibilities" of the Office of the Assistant Commission (International). It states, *"Administers the internal revenue laws and related statutes as they relate to U.S. citizens residing abroad, corporations and businesses whose books and records are maintained outside the U.S. and nonresident aliens deriving income from sources within the United States."* So far, so good. Isn't that what we'd expect from "international"?

The next item of interest is found at 1132.7. In this numbering scheme, "1132" designates that we are looking at something within the *Office of the Assistant Commission (International)* and ".7" means we are looking at the 7th component within the *Office of the Assistant Commission (International)*.

1132.7 is entitled "Office of Taxpayer Service and Compliance". Let me assure you that the IRS is not interested in "service". The only "service" the IRS is interested in providing is that which promotes more "compliance"!

There are several component entities within the *Office of Taxpayer Service and Compliance*.

1132.71 is the first component and that is the "Director, Office of Taxpayer Service and Compliance". Please note the numbering. "1132" tells us we are still within the *Office of the Assistant Commission (International)*. ".7" tells us we are within *Office of Taxpayer Service and Compliance*. And the addition of the digit "1" tell us we are looking at the first component within the *Office of Taxpayer Service and Compliance*.

So what is the duty of the *Director, Office of Taxpayer Service and Compliance?* Here is what it says at 1132.71:

The *Director, Office of Taxpayer Service and Compliance* is "responsible for the operation of a comprehensive enforcement and assistance program for all taxpayers under the immediate jurisdiction of the Assistant Commission (International)."

This is his sole function. There is no indication that the *Director, Office of Taxpayer Service and Compliance* has any authority outside of or beyond the authority of the *Assistant Commissioner (International)*. Or phrased another way, the Director works for the *Assistant Commissioner (International)* and only exercises such authority as the *Assistant Commissioner (International)* has delegated down to the *Director*.

From there we go to 1132.72. Again, let's examine the numbering sequence. "1132" means we're still within the *Office of the Assistant Commission (International)*. ".7" tells us we are within *Office of Taxpayer Service and Compliance*. But this time instead of a "1", we have a "2", indicating we are now looking at the 2nd component within the *Office of Taxpayer Service and Compliance*.

1132.72 is entitled, "Collection Division". Here's its functional description:

> "Executes the full range of collection activities on delinquent accounts, which includes securing delinquent returns involving taxpayers outside the United States and those in United States territories, possessions, and in Puerto Rico. Administers the program for mutual collection assistance under tax treaties."

The next interesting component is found at 1132.74, the 4th component within the *Office of Taxpayer Service and Compliance* (which of course remains within the *Office of the Assistant Commission (International)*).

1132.74 is entitled "Examination Division". Its functional description is:

> "The Examination Division administers an international examination program involving the selection and examination of all types of Federal tax returns filed with Assistant Commission (International)."

And last, but certainly not least, is the Criminal Investigation Division (CID), found at 1132.75. Its functional description is as follows:

> *"The Criminal Investigation Division enforces the criminal statutes applicable to income, estate, gift, employment, and excise tax laws... as well as applicable Title 31[2] and Title 18[3] violations per the IRM, involving United States citizens residing in foreign countries and nonresident aliens subject to Federal income tax filing requirements...."*

One must read CID's functional description with a careful eye. On first blush some folks might think it covers all sorts of things, including domestic concerns, but that is not true. Remember, CID is 1132.75. The fact that it starts with 1132 means it is within the *Office of the Assistant Commissioner (International)*. So let's re-read the authority of the *Assistant Commissioner (International)*.

> *"Administers the internal revenue laws and related statutes as they relate to U.S. citizens residing abroad, corporations and businesses whose books and records are maintained outside the U.S. and nonresident aliens deriving income from sources within the United States."*

As you can readily see, the *Assistant Commissioner (International)* has no domestic authority whatsoever. Accordingly, if he has no domestic authority, he cannot delegate what he does not possess. In other words, because CID is a component within the Office of the *Assistant Commissioner (International)* and he has no domestic authority, CID is also without any domestic authority.

When I first read through Part 1100 and saw what I have just shared with you, I thought, "OK, this is the international Collection, Examination, and Criminal Investigation divisions. I'll keep reading until I find the domestic Collection, Examination, and Criminal Investigation divisions." The funny thing is that I read Part 1100 all the way to the end and there wasn't any other Collection, Examination, and Criminal Investigation divisions. I figured I must have missed them, so I read Part 1100, in its entirety, all over again – and then again. Still no trace of any domestic Collection, Examination, and Criminal Investigation divisions.

---

[2] Entitled "Money and Finance"
[3] Entitled "Crimes and Criminal Procedures"

Isn't that odd. The IRS creates a section of its manual dedicated to outlining its entire organizational structure in great detail, and somehow there is no mention of any Collection, Examination, and Criminal Investigation divisions for domestic purposes. I would say that's more than a little odd, wouldn't you?

In fact, Joe Banister had questioned his IRS superiors about this very issue. He told me they claimed that domestic functions were exercised by the *Assistant Commissioner (Examination), Assistant Commissioner (Collection),* and the *Assistant Commissioner (Criminal Investigation).* However an examination of the functional descriptions for these three officers, as well as organization charts designated in Part 1100 as Exhibit 1130-1 and 1130-3, make it clear that such a statement is not truthful.

None of those offices have a "compliance" office or any enforcement mechanisms. All of those components speak of functions such as "programs", "planning", "coordination", "support systems", and "research". In short, those officers are in charge of "the back office".

They draw up "plans" concerning how the Examination Division can more efficiently conduct examinations. They provide "system support" for the Collection Division. They provide "development" for the Criminal Investigation Division. <u>Nowhere are they tasked with **conducting** examinations, collections or criminal investigations.</u> Only the Collection, Examination, and Criminal Investigation divisions under the *Office of the Assistant Commissioner (International)* are tasked with actually conducting examinations, collections or criminal investigations.

Why is it important that none of these "back office" entities has a "compliance" officer or component? Because the number one objective of the IRS is "compliance." It is a point made again and again in their internal documents. Virtually every change made in IRS policy or procedure is made solely to increase "compliance". "Compliance" is the IRS's Holy Grail. I should also add that "compliance" is really a euphemism for "enforcement". You've heard the old adage, "The carrot or the stick."? The IRS has never heard that one. They only know how to use the "stick".

While I jokingly say that these apparent "omissions" are odd, they really aren't. In my last two chapters, you have read that Congress' own statutes and the Secretary's regulations show that the tax is only upon *foreign persons* with U.S. source income and upon U.S. citizens residing abroad with foreign income.

Although I will not get into it in this book, taxes such as "gift", "estate", "wagering", etc. are all based on this same premise.

Given that all these taxes are based on the same premise as the income tax (subtitle 'A'), is it any wonder that the power to conduct examinations, collections, and criminal investigations is vested in the *Assistant Commissioner (International)*? Where else would it be!

As I close on this subject, I should tell you that the 1998 IRS Reform and Restructuring Act rendered obsolete the entire organizational structure we've been discussing. That was intentional; to forever hide what I just shared with you. By making the structure obsolete, they made Part 1100 obsolete. By making Part 1100 obsolete, it is no longer attainable through FOIA, and therefore there would be no way for anyone to ever again gain access to it.

Wrong. I have made numerous copies of Part 1100 (and other internal IRS documents) and have them secreted in places around the country. In that way, if the IRS serves some trumped-up warrant, issued by a "friendly" federal judge, at my home and/or office, they will not be able to snatch the last remaining copies of Part 1100!

The IRS is required by law to publish its organizational structure. Since 1999, when the Reform and Restructuring Act was put into effect, the IRS has never again published an organizational chart of the agency. I guess they learned their lesson the first time around. And the law be damned!

I will also tell you that the written descriptions of the new IRS structure are very vague. There will be no repeat of the bold and definitive statements made in Part 1100! Despite the best efforts of the IRS to shroud its new structure in secrecy, my staff and I have found key elements that confirm that the authority remains the same – international. It would have to, because the constitutional boundaries imposed on the government's taxing authority have never changed!

FORM 1040

Most Americans have been socialized to believe that each year they have to file a Form 1040. Most Americans believe that Form 1040 is the form that

Americans are to use to report their earnings. But in light of everything we've seen, what are the odds that's true? Not very good.

As I stated earlier, the income tax structure that Congress created in 1913 has remained essentially the same to this day. Yes the Tax Code has gotten much larger and more complex, but those changes have been in the "rules of computation", not in the underlying foundation of the tax scheme. In other words, the changes have been in how much is owed and under what technical circumstances, but nothing has changed concerning who actually owes the tax!

When the tax system was first put into place, the Secretary was far more forthcoming than is the case today. Treasury did not feel the need to hide the truth from the American people as it does today.

Shortly after the creation of the "modern income tax", the Secretary issued a number of Treasury Decisions that speak to who is to use which tax form. He is very clear and does not equivocate in the least. Let's see what he said!

T.D. 1928

This T.D. addresses a couple of different filing requirements. We are only concerned here with the use of the 1040; therefore, I will only reference that part of the T.D. (The parts not associated with the 1040 do not in any manner detract from (or even relate to) the obvious conclusion to be drawn from the part concerning the 1040.

Here is T.D. 1928 in its relevant parts:

The forms numbered and prescribed below, in addition to those previously approved, are prescribed by this department for the purposes indicated in connection with the administration of the Federal income-tax law:

- *Form 1040 is to be used by individuals, or their duly authorized agents, in making the personal return of annual income.*
- *Form 1041 is to be used by fiduciaries in making returns of annual net income on behalf of their beneficiaries and as withholding agents.*
- *Form 1042 is the annual list return of withholding agents of taxes*

withheld by them on income other than that derived from corporate obligations.
- *Form 1043 is a monthly list return of taxes withheld on foreign income by licensed banks or collecting agents.*
- *Form 1043a is the annual list return to be made by licensed banks and collecting agents of taxes withheld by them during the year on foreign items.*
- *Form 1044 is a monthly list return of taxes withheld by the first bank or collecting agency receiving coupons or interest orders not accompanied by certificates of owners.*
- *Form 1044a is the annual list return of taxes withheld during the year by the first bank or collecting agency receiving coupons or interest orders not accompanied by certificates of owner.*

You will note that Form 1040 is to be used by an "individual" and Forms 1041 through 1044a are to be used by *withholding agents* to report the tax they've withheld from the foreign person. In other words, when the *nonresident alien* (*foreign person*) is filing for himself (or his "agent" is filing for him), he is to use Form 1040. When the tax has been withheld before the *foreign person* received the income, the *withholding agents* are to use the various other forms in the 104X series.

But let's button this up a little tighter. T.D. 1928 says that a Form 1040 is to be used by an "individual". The regulation at 1.144-1(c)3 contains the definition of "individual":

Individual —

(i) *Alien individual.* The term alien individual means an individual who is not a citizen or a national of the United States. See Sec. 1.1-1(c).

(ii) *Nonresident alien individual.* The term nonresident alien individual means a person described in section 7701(b)(1)(B), an alien individual who is a resident of a foreign country under the residence article of an income tax treaty and Sec. 301.7701(b)-7(a)(1) of this chapter, or an alien individual who is a resident of Puerto Rico, Guam, the Commonwealth of Northern Mariana Islands, the

U.S. Virgin Islands, or American Samoa as determined under Sec. 301.7701(b)-1(d) of this chapter.

Let me take a moment to provide clarity on one point. The definition above is *only* for the purposes of chapter 3, "Withholding on Nonresident Aliens and Foreign Corporations". The word "individual" is used in chapters 1 and 2 without Congress or the Secretary having provided their own definition. When the government does not provide its own definition, we are to use what the U.S. Supreme Court has called "The Plain Meaning Rule". The Plain Meaning Rule says that if no definition has been provided by the government in its statutes or regulations, we are to use the common meaning of the word, such as one would find in a standard English dictionary. However, if Congress or the Secretary *has* provided a definition, then that is the *only* definition we are permitted to use.

What that means is that when used in chapter 3 an "individual" is an alien. When used in chapter 1 and 2 an "individual" is simply a singular person. However (and this is a huge "however"), we must remember that chapters 1 and 2 are merely the "rules of computation". By contrast, chapter 3 tells us in excruciating detail whom the tax is upon, precisely how it is to be administered, and exactly who is to file and pay! Therefore, how "individual" is defined in chapter 3 [i.e. an "alien"] is how it is used when the Secretary speaks of who is to use which return.

So, in summation, when the Secretary says that an "individual" is to file a Form 1040, the individual he is speaking of is an alien individual, not you and me!

But wait! There's more!

T.D. 2313

This T.D. is well known to those who've spent much time engaged in research into the proper application of the Tax Code. What makes it so well known is that it was issued immediately after the *Brushaber* decision and is Treasury's own in-house interpretation of the meaning of *Brushaber*. It validates all that we've discussed so far.

Here are the opening paragraphs of T.D. 2313:

> "Under the decision of the Supreme Court of the United States in the case of Brushaber v. Union Pacific Railway Co., decided January 24, 1916, it is hereby held that income accruing to nonresident aliens in the form of interest from the bonds and dividends on the stock of domestic corporations is subject to the income tax imposed by the act of October 3, 1913."

> "Nonresident aliens are not entitled to the specific exemption designated in paragraph C of the income-tax law, but are liable for the normal and additional tax upon the entire net income "from all property owned, and of every business, trade, or profession carried on in the United States," computed upon the basis prescribed in the law."

> "The responsible heads, agents, or representatives of nonresident aliens, who are in charge of the *property owned* or *business* carried on within the United States, shall make a full and complete return of the income therefrom on Form 1040, revised, and shall pay any and all tax, normal and additional, assessed upon the income received by them in behalf of their nonresident alien principals."

Wow! This should tie together for you all that we've discussed. You will remember that in chapter 3 we covered *Brushaber* in detail. We showed that in *Brushaber* the U.S. Supreme Court held the income tax (subtitle 'A') to be an excise; a tax upon a privilege. In chapter 6 I revealed to you that the government has a limited sphere from which to tax [i.e. international/foreign matters], and I told you that the subtitle 'A' (income tax) has been imposed on foreigners with U.S. source income as well as certain U.S. citizens with foreign income.

Now, here we have the U.S. Department of Treasury, stating in an official document to its tax collectors across the world[4], that under the *Brushaber* decision the "normal and additional tax" [chapter 1] is upon the nonresident alien! How much more proof do you need?

---

[4] The IRS has tax collectors assigned to duty in numerous foreign countries.

The T.D. goes on to say that the *"responsible heads, agents, or representatives of nonresident aliens, who are in charge of the property owned or business carried on within the United States, shall make a full and complete return of the income therefrom on Form 1040, revised, and shall pay any and all tax, normal and additional, assessed upon the income received by them in behalf of their nonresident alien principals."*

You'll notice that the form for the *"responsible heads, agents, or representatives of nonresident aliens"* is the 1040 "revised". The 1040 (non-revised) is for the use of the actual nonresident alien when filing his own return. If for any reason withholding is not affected upon the income of a nonresident alien, the nonresident alien could file his own return. Also, if withholding was affected, and the nonresident alien feels that too much was withheld [e.g. a *withholding agent* was unaware of a tax treaty providing a lower withholding rate], the nonresident alien can file a return to obtain a refund.

Further along in T.D. 2313, we find this:

> "The person, firm, company, copartnership, corporation, joint-stock company, or association, and insurance company in the United States, citizen or resident alien, in whatever capacity acting, having the control, receipt, disposal, or payment of fixed or determinable annual or periodic gains, profits, and income of whatever kind, to a nonresident alien, under any contract or otherwise, which payment shall represent income of a nonresident alien from the exercise of any *trade* or *profession* within the United States, shall deduct and withhold from such annual periodic gains, profits, and income, regardless of amount, and pay to the officer of the United States Government authorized to receive the same such sum as will be sufficient to pay the normal tax of 1 per cent imposed by law, and shall make an annual return on form 1042."

Again we see the tax under chapter 1 being discussed. Here domestic entities and Americans citizens are being told that if they have control, receipt, disposal, etc., of *"fixed or determinable annual or periodic gains, profits, and income of whatever kind"* [i.e. gross income] belonging to a nonresident alien, they must deduct and withhold the tax and pay it over to the government accompanied by a Form 1042 tax return. Is this all making sense now?

Next it reads: *"The normal tax shall be withheld at the source from income accrued to nonresident aliens from corporate obligations and shall be returned and paid to the Government by debtor corporations and withholding agents as in the case of citizens and resident aliens...."* This is telling corporations that they are to withhold on the *nonresident alien's* income from "corporate obligations" and that the corporation is to pay the withheld money to the government in the same manner as regular Americans (or resident aliens) are required to when they withhold from a nonresident alien.

And, closer to the end of T.D. 2313 you will see this:

> "The liability, under the provisions of the law, to render personal returns, on or before March 1 next succeeding the tax year, of annual net income accrued to them from sources within the United States during the preceding calendar year, attaches to nonresident aliens as in the case of returns required from citizens and resident aliens. Therefore, a return on Form 1040, revised, is required except in cases where the total tax liability has been or is to be satisfied at the source by withholding or has been or is to be satisfied by personal return on Form 1040, revised, rendered in their behalf."

This paragraph tells us that the nonresident alien's liability to pay the tax is the same as that of the American citizens (or resident aliens) who might owe the tax based on foreign-earned income. In other words, if no one else has filed a return and paid the tax of the nonresident alien, the nonresident alien is required to do so no later than March 1st. If, however, the total tax due by the nonresident alien has been collected by the *withholding agent,* or if the nonresident alien's *"responsible heads, agents, or representatives"* have filed a return and paid the tax, then the nonresident alien is not required to file a return.

Isn't it amazing how simple the income tax really is when you understand it!

T.D. 2401

This T.D. begins with a statement of purpose:

> *"Revision of T.D. 2382 of October 19, 1916, and providing certificates to disclose identity of owner of stock where the actual owner is a nonresident alien individual, firm, or corporation, and the stock is registered in the name of a citizen of, or resident alien individual in, the United States or a domestic firm or corporation."*

What this tells us is that stock can be owned by a nonresident alien but actually be registered to a citizen or resident alien or a domestic firm or corporation.

Here is more from T.D. 2382:

> *"...when the actual owner is a nonresident alien individual a return shall be made whenever the amount of dividend is $3,000 or over; and when the net amount thereof exceeds $20,000 said custodian shall also pay the additional tax on such income. The return for nonresident alien corporations shall be made on income-tax Form 1031 (1030 for insurance companies), and return for nonresident alien individuals shall be made on income-tax Form 1040."*

Not only do we have the obvious fact that the Form 1040 – once again – is the designated form to be used by a *nonresident alien*, this T.D. also illustrates that the normal tax and the "additional tax" are both upon foreign persons.

T.D. 2815

This T.D. is very straightforward.

> "Nonresident alien individuals or their authorized agents should use Form 1040, revised, or Form 1040A, revised, in making returns of income derived from sources within the United States, regardless of amount, unless the tax on such income has been fully paid at the source. If a nonresident alien individual is not liable for any tax which has been withheld at the source, no refund of such tax will be permitted unless such a return is filed and a statement is attached thereto indicating the amounts of tax withheld and the names and post-office addresses of all withholding agents. Unless a nonresident alien

individual shall render a return of income, the tax will be collected on the basis of his gross income…from sources within the United States."

As I said, straightforward. The only thing I'd draw your attention to is that it says the *nonresident alien's* income "will be collected on the basis of <u>gross income</u>.…" If you remember from our earlier discussion, *gross income* is the same thing as *fixed or determinable annual or periodic income*, which is subject to withholding by the *withholding agent* at the direction of the Secretary's regulation, 1.1441-2(b). In other words, by using the term "gross income" the Secretary is saying that the tax will be collected from that species of income that is subject to withholding and it will be collected by a *withholding agent* under U.S. tax law.

T.D. 2988

This is another very straightforward Treasury Decision.

> "*Nonresident alien beneficiary — Where a fiduciary in the United States is the recipient of trust income for which there is but one beneficiary and that beneficiary is a nonresident alien, the fiduciary will be required to make full and complete return on income tax Form 1040, or 1040A, as the case may be, for this trust income on behalf of the nonresident alien, and pay any and all normal tax found by such return to be due, and any and all surtax provided the income is not returned for the purpose of the tax by the beneficiary. Where there are two or more beneficiaries, one or all of whom are nonresident aliens, the fiduciary shall render a return on form 1041, and a personal return on form 1040 or 1040A, for each nonresident alien beneficiary.*"

The picture should be getting crystal clear by now!

As we close on the issue of who is required to file a Form 1040, let me address the changes that have occurred over the decades since many of these T.D.s were written.

Tax administration has changed to keep up with various factors, not the least of which involves many more transactions that are far more complex. This has required tax forms to be tailored to reflect the nature of each particular *class of person* or type of transaction. The IRS has made those necessary changes.

Nonresident aliens no longer use Form 1040. They are now directed to use Form 1040NR. The Form 1040 is now to be used *only* by U.S. citizens residing abroad with foreign earned income. People in Puerto Rico are to use the 1040PR, in the Virgin Islands 1040VI, and so on. The complexities of withholding on a *foreign person's* income have increased significantly and there are now a myriad of returns that are used in varying circumstances, including various forms in the 104X series! ('X' designates a variable. It can be a '1' or a '2', or a '3', etc., such as a Form 1042.)

With all that said, there is one salient point that shines like a lighthouse beacon on a moonless night. In reference to subtitle 'A' (income tax), there is no statute, regulation, Treasury Decision, Treasury Order, any part of the Internal Revenue Manual, etc., or any citation whatsoever that says the following:

"A U.S. citizen, living and working in one of the 50 states, earning his own domestic income, is required to file a return of income on Form XXXX."

You will never see any such a command because subtitle 'A' has nothing to do with you and me! It is a tax on U.S. citizens earning foreign income and *foreign persons* deriving U.S. source income – period!

The income tax has existed since 1913. As I sit here writing these words, that's nearly 100 years! Wouldn't it be the world's most incredible oversight if for nearly 100 years the entire U.S. government just *forgot* to write anything about Americans who are earning their own money here in America needing to file a return? Is there anyone in his right mind who would believe that for even a second? The very idea is laughable!

T.D. 6500

This is one of the most extensive Treasury Decisions ever written. I haven't actually counted, but it looks to be about 100 pages long.

Much of it is mundane and not terribly significant to our inquiry here. However, after reading the specificity in the previous T.D.s concerning exactly who is to file a Form 1040, I thought it would be instructive to compare that with the general language we find when reading the "procedures and administration" section.

There is a part within T.D. 6500 that speaks to what form is required to be filed under 1.6012, which is the regulation that contains the "filing requirement" for subtitle 'A'. And of course 6012 is not actually within subtitle 'A', but rather within subtitle 'F' – "Procedures and Administration".

Here is the "general language" that you can always expect to see when dealing with generic "procedures and administration" sections:

> *Form 1040 is prescribed for general use in making the return required under this paragraph [1.6012(a)]. Form 1040A and Form 1040W are optional short forms which, in accordance with subparagraphs (7) and (8), respectively, of this paragraph, may be used by certain taxpayers. A taxpayer entitled to use Form 1040W in making his return for a taxable year may nevertheless use a Form 1040 as his return for such year. A taxpayer otherwise entitled to use Form 1040A as his return for any taxable year may not make return on such form if...*

You can see that when we enter the "general language" realm of the "procedures and administration" sections, gone are the specifics we found in chapter 3, its regulations, and the previous T.D.s. What we find here is loose language such as *"may be used by certain taxpayers"* and *"A taxpayer entitled to use"* and *"A taxpayer otherwise entitled"*. Fortunately, we now know who that "taxpayer" actually is!

T.D. 6500 tells us which "foreign corporations" doing business in the United States are to file.

> "...*every corporation, as defined in 7701(a)(3), <u>subject to taxation under subtitle A</u> of the Code shall make a return of income...*"
> [Underline added]

Please note that the Secretary has carefully qualified which corporations are required to file a return. They are only corporations *"subject to taxation under subtitle A"*. And you and I now know those are foreign corporations deriving U.S. source income!

And which return is to be used by this foreign corporation doing business in the U.S.?

> *"The return required of a corporation under this section shall be made on Form 1120 unless the corporation is of a type for which a special form is prescribed."*

And all this time you thought Form 1120 was for plain old American corporations going about their daily activities here in America!

Are all foreign corporations with U.S. source income required to file a return?

> *"A nonresident foreign corporation is not required to make a return of income if the tax liability of the corporation is fully satisfied at the source."*

In other words, in this respect corporations are just like individuals; if the U.S. tax obligation has been met in full by withholding performed by the *withholding agent*, then a return is not required to be filed by the nonresident foreign corporation.

And just like an *individual* (i.e. nonresident alien) a foreign corporation can file for a return – even if not otherwise required – in order to claim a refund.

> *"If an overpayment has resulted from withholding of tax at source... statements shall be attached to the claim for refund showing the same information as is required...by a nonresident alien."*

> [**Author's Note**: Remember the phrase *"withholding of tax at source."* You'll be seeing it again!]

I hope you can now see the form and structure of subtitle 'A' and how it operates. *Foreign persons* (individuals and corporations) deriving U.S. source income are required to file returns and pay the tax, unless their tax obligation has been satisfied in full through withholding performed by the *withholding agent*. (Notwithstanding withholding, foreign corporations are still required to file a return if they have a place of business within the U.S.) If an individual or corporation feels entitled to a refund, a return can be filed making a claim for refund even if a return is not otherwise required. If an individual or corporation is not present in the U.S., and return is required (or desired for refund purposes), an authorized "agent" within the U.S. can file on behalf of the individual or corporation.

Pretty simple stuff, huh? It's just that no one ever told you about it!

OMB CONTROL NUMBER CHART AT 602.101

The Secretary of the Treasury has constructed a cross-reference chart in the regulations at 602.101. This chart cross-references tax forms to the regulations that each form serves. Or phrased another way, you can look up a regulation and find out what form is appropriate to use if filing a return pursuant to that regulation.

The unfortunate part is that the forms are listed not by their publicly recognized numbers (such as 1040, 1120, W-4, 1099 etc.), but rather by their little known OMB Control Numbers. If you look at any federal tax form (except the W-9) you will find an 8-digit number somewhere near the publicly recognized number. The OMB Control Number is formatted as four numerals, then a dash, followed by four more numerals. An example would be the Form 1040, which is OMB Control Number 1545-0074 (as are a few other forms, but I'll get into that later).

Since late 1980, every tax form has had its own unique OMB Control Number. The Office of Management and Budget issues these numbers under the authority of the Paperwork Reduction Act. The purpose of assigning the numbers is to vet each form to insure that the federal government is only asking you for the information justified by law, and to make sure that the government is not asking for information it could reasonably presume it already possesses. (A few years back, with no change to the Paperwork Reduction Act, the IRS began using the same OMB Control Number on numerous forms. That is a significant departure from 35 years of precedent in which each form had its own unique OMB Control Number.)

We have discussed the opening regulation of Title 26 (1.1-1) quite a few times already. Remember, that's the one that begins with the words, *"Section 1 of the Code imposes an income tax on the income of every individual who is a citizen or resident of the United States...."*

So what does it say when you look up 1.1-1 in the chart at 601.101? For decades there was only *one* form shown in the chart as being applicable to 1.1-1. That was the form bearing OMB Control Number 1545-0067. Want to know what the publicly recognized number is for that form? It's Form 2555, and it's entitled, "Foreign Earned Income".

Remember, we learned that subtitle 'A' has only been imposed on U.S. citizens with foreign earned income and *foreign persons* with U.S. source income. As we've covered in some detail, the statutory/regulatory requirement for *withholding agents* and/*or foreign persons* to file returns is contained in chapter 3. The requirement dictated by Section 1 of the Code is only upon U.S. citizens with foreign-earned income.

A few years back, the IRS suddenly – after decades – moved 1545-0067 from 1.1-1 on their cross-reference chart to 1.6012. Why would they do that? Because too many people were bringing this reality to their attention.

An American would say to an IRS employee, "What part of the Code requires me to file a return or pay a tax?" The IRS employee would respond, "The regulation at 1.1-1 imposes the tax." The citizen would then pull out the Secretary's chart and show the IRS employee (who works for the Secretary) that the only return referenced for use under 1.1-1 was Form 2555.

The IRS couldn't have people actually knowing what was going on, or using such information to thwart the incorrect statements of its employees, so they moved it to correspond with the regulation 1.6012-1. When asked why they moved it, the IRS stated that it has always been in the wrong place! Why, of course!

[**Author's Note**: A few years ago the IRS changed the OMB Control Number of Form 2555 from 1545-0067 to 1545-0074, which is the same as the 1040! (Despite having changed it on the form, Form 2555 remains "0067" when mentioned in the regulations.) Interestingly, at the same time, the IRS also changed the OMB Control Number of the Form W-4 to 1545-0074. It appears that the IRS has recently decided to view the OMB Control Number requirement as pertaining not to each individual form (as had been the original and long-standing view), but rather to all forms that fall within the liability and/or requirement to file for a particular type of tax; in this case taxes on U.S. source income to *foreign persons* and foreign earned income to U.S. citizens.]

This chapter could go on and on. There is no shortage of information/evidence concerning upon whom Congress has actually imposed subtitle 'A' of the Internal Revenue Code. In this chapter I have attempted to give you the statutes, the regulations, court decisions, Treasury Decisions, and Executive Orders that reveal in the most straightforward fashion what the United States government has said about the legally proper application of subtitle 'A'.

The sources I have cited for you in this chapter run the gamut of time as well. Some of the earliest references are from 1914 while others are straight out of the most current edition of the Code of Federal Regulations (2009). I make that point so you understand that the United States government has *always* known to whom the tax properly applies. It is not a "lost secret" from a bygone era nor is it something new that was just uncovered. It has always been so. And the government has always known it.

It is important that you understand the full implication of what I am saying. The United States government has always known that you *never* owed a penny in income tax. And they stole it from you anyway!

In an upcoming chapter I will address an issue I know is in the minds of some readers. Some of you are struggling to believe the staggering implications of what I've shared with you. Not only do you find this difficult to believe after decades of being socialized to believe the "big lie", but you don't *want* to believe it. To believe it means that the federal government – the government you always thought of as "your" government – doesn't give a crap about you. Even worse, it means that the federal government is a criminal organization on an immense scale and you are its intended victim. Not a pretty picture.

In an effort to explain what you cannot believe – what you do not want to believe – some will say that I am focusing only on the "foreign" parts of the Code, regulations, etc., and that I am intentionally leaving out the "other" parts – the parts that say *you* are the person upon whom the tax has imposed. Boy oh boy, wouldn't that make you feel better! I hate to disappoint you, but in an upcoming chapter I will dispel that notion. When it comes to the Code or the regulations imposing the tax upon the average American, the cupboard is bare; there ain't nothin' there. But I promise you we'll take a diligent look together!

I also want to let you know that soon we'll be exploring the "tricks" or "snares" that are used to get you to falsely declare yourself a person upon whom the tax has been imposed (a foreign person), or the person made liable (a withholding agent). We'll also discuss how to stop doing that!

Right now you may be feeling a bit like you've fallen down the *Alice in Wonderland* rabbit hole. Or maybe you feel like you've just been shown there exists a "world that has been pulled over your eyes to blind you from the truth", as stated in the blockbuster movie, The Matrix.

I understand. I was once where you are right now, and I remember the feeling vividly! I know how uncomfortable it feels. If you are angry, you and I share the same emotional response to the largest financial crime in the history of the world – perpetrated against you, and every American, by the United States government. It isn't a good feeling to realize your government is no better than "The Mob". You can almost hear the IRS Commissioner saying to his thugs, "Hey Vinny! That scumbag (that's you!) doesn't want to pay the vig. He thinks he can live in America without paying extortion. Break his legs Vinny! We don't want these assholes to start believing in all that freedom crap!"

" The lie can be maintained only for such time as the State can shield the people from the political, economic and/or military consequences of the lie. It thus becomes vitally important for the State to use all of its powers to repress dissent, for the truth is the mortal enemy of the lie, and thus by extension, the truth becomes the greatest enemy of the State."
~ Dr. Joseph M. Goebbels, Reich Minister of Propaganda (1933 to 1945)

When it comes to certain forms of taxation, the U.S. government learned well the "art of deception" from the likes of Joseph Goebbels. In fact, the U.S. government now makes Goebbels look like a rank amateur.

At this point, some readers may be thinking that I see a lie around every federal government corner. And you'd be right. But I did not start there! I started life as a young, idealistic, middle-class American boy. I grew into a not-so-young patriotic American man. I served my nation and my community. I never thought I would be called upon to write this book, or anything like it. And, I wish there were no need for this book.

The difference between you and me is that I've been at this for nearly two decades. The blush is off the rose; the innocence long gone. I wish it were otherwise.

If I could make the world the way I want it to be, the federal government would truly be a servant to The People of the states and it would act only in pursuance of its enumerated powers, and it would never think of violating the rights of The People it exists to serve. And it certainly would not be targeting the American people as the victims of the largest financial crime in the history of the world!

While I want nothing more than a government which serves and respects The People, that's not remotely what we have. A good friend of mine coined the adage; *"The government lies and lies all the time. It even lies when the truth would serve it well."* After nearly two decades of dealing with the government's claims of power and authority in all manner of subjects, my experience has been that his adage is remarkably accurate.

For many of you, this book will be a life-altering epiphany. For others, it will merely open the door to understanding how the government really operates, and your epiphany will occur sometime down the road. A small minority will (for emotional reasons) reject everything they read in this book and bury their heads in the sand. But try as they might, they cannot un-learn what they've learned. All they can do is run from it.

This "genie" cannot be stuffed back into its bottle!

Some readers will be able to learn the truth and ignore it. They will be able to go along as if nothing has changed in their universe. I believe the word that best describes these people is "sheep". Regrettably, in this country we have far too many "sheep" masquerading as Americans.

Other readers, imbued with character, integrity, honor, and love of liberty, are, in my opinion, the true Americans! Unlike the "sheep", these people will not be able to stand by as our servants steal our wealth and commit violent acts against their masters [us!] in this house we call "America". It is these men and women – citizens of courage, with a love of liberty, or whom I write this book! It is they who will put this nation back on track!

What has come in the preceding chapters should have demonstrated to you that the government is not telling you the truth about subtitle 'A'. Unfortunately, that's not the end of their lies in this area.

Subtitle 'C' is entitled "Employment Taxes". The regulations for subtitle 'C' are contained in Part 31 of the CFR and they are entitled, "Employment Taxes and Collection of Income Tax at Source". (Didn't I tell you we'd be seeing the phrase "Collection of Income Tax at Source" again?)

Under the (presumed) provisions of subtitle 'C', the average American endures something commonly referred to as "payroll withholding". Yet the law requires nothing of the sort! When it comes to average American working men and women, Congress has never passed any law that permits anyone to take anything out of their paychecks.

Let me begin by telling you a true story that illustrates how little people know about this subject. And sadly, those who are supposed to know, don't.

A few years back, during a telephone conference call with the woman who had been in charge of payroll for a medium-size business for 13 years, she kept saying that she had to perform payroll withholding because, "It's the law". She said that 4 or 5 times during the first few minutes, and her tone was quite adamant.

Since she was so adamant that it was "required by law", I asked her to give me the citation of the law so we could look at it together. "Give you the citation?", she responded. "I don't know the citation."

I told her it was OK that she didn't know the citation and instead asked her to quote a bit of the law to me. I explained that I had been doing this for many years and if she could quote just a small portion of the law I was confident that I would be able to recognize it and I'd know the citation.

"Quote it to you?" she replied. "I can't quote it."

Hmmm. She was insistent that what she was doing was "required by law", yet she did not know where the law was, nor anything that it said. How odd.

Always trying to be helpful, I assured her that after all the years I'd been involved in these matters, I knew where "it" was and we could look at it together on the Internet.

When we finished reading the relevant statute, I asked her if there was any way, even if she twisted, bent, or mangled Congress' words, that she could figure out how to apply it to "Tom", the gentleman who'd instructed her to stop withholding from his paycheck. There was a pregnant pause, and then she said:

"I don't want to talk to you about the law anymore."

That story illustrates the ignorance that exists in virtually every payroll department in America. I cannot begin to tell you how many people I've spoken to over the years in "payroll", "human resources", the "accounting department", the "business office", etc. of companies across the nation. Would you like to hazard a guess at how many of those people I've spoken to about payroll withholding knew where to find the law, or what the law said? If you said "none" you'd be right. In all the years I've been doing this, not one single person who has been taking money out of your paycheck, saying they're "required by law" to do so, has ever read the law they say they are relying upon to take your property!

What sort of national dementia must we be experiencing when hundreds of millions of Americans allow their property to be taken from them by people who have never read the law and don't know what it says! Is this not insanity on a national level?

You might be thinking that the actual people who do the payroll withholding don't need to know the law because the attorneys for these companies surely do. And you'd be wrong about that, too!

I have spoken to many attorneys on this exact matter. Just like the folks in payroll, the attorneys could not tell me what the law says (though a few knew where "it" is – they'd just never bothered to read it).

To be a lawyer, one must complete law school. Then, after law school, one must study diligently for the BAR exam and pass it. A lot of work goes into all of that. One would think a lawyer might put all that training and hard work to use. Apparently, not when it comes to this subject!

The most common response I receive from these 'legal eagles' is, "The IRS says we have to." Ah! So we have reached the point in America where the disembodied voice of a low-paid entry-level IRS employee working the "call center" phones, who is doing nothing more than repeating what he's been told to say, is now "the law". (Keep in mind that the "call center" employee has never read the law either!)

In order to make the point that attorneys have no idea what they're talking about in this area, and that they too "make it up as they go", let me tell you two more stories.

Many years ago I was approached by a gentleman who wanted the company he worked for to stop all payroll withholding. He had studied the subject and was relatively well-informed on it. He was an executive and had made his request directly to the company's CEO.

The CEO, in turn, hired the most prestigious human resources law firm in America, asking them to explain to her (and the executive making the request) why discontinuing withholding from his paycheck would be against the law. She paid $2,500.00 to receive a three-page letter from the human resources law firm.

The executive brought the letter to me. I read it and laughed. It was all nonsense and it never did address the law in question. Every single court case cited in the letter was off-point. In short, it was a joke – albeit an expensive joke.

I assisted the executive in drafting a response. The CEO read it and told the executive that it effectively and completely debunked every statement made by the law firm. She admitted to believing that the law firm had taken her money and delivered nothing of value in return.

And remember, that brilliant $2,500.00, three-page piece of "legal analysis" came from the most prestigious human resources law firm in the United States! If that law firm couldn't put together something credible, why should we expect anything more from anyone else?

My second story involves a very large American corporation capitalized by several of the wealthiest men in America. It owns or controls a number of other large and powerful companies. Its Board of Directors has well-known national political figures on it; names you would instantly recognize.

The CEO of one of the subsidiaries of this parent corporation had researched the payroll withholding laws and knew that their very limited application does not apply to the average American, and hence it did not apply to him.

He had not provided the subsidiary with a Social Security Number or signed a Form W-4, and he informed the parent company that he did not want to be withheld from, and that the law did not permit them to do so.

He had some initial conversations with a gentleman who represented the majority shareholders of the parent corporation. He explained the law to the representative. The representative left those conversations without making any commitments one way or another.

The CEO asked me to participate by phone in the next conversation with the representative.

The representative was a warm and intelligent gentleman. He listened to the CEO's position and we all batted the law around for a bit. As the conversation was nearing the end, he stated that the CEO's "interpretation" was the minority view. Huh? Interpretation? The law is perfectly clear. There was no "interpretation" needed.

What he was really saying was that most people don't follow the law and therefore doing so would be adverse to "how things are done". Oh, great! Now we can steal people's property simply because "everyone's doing it" or "it's how things are done".

The CEO was an important player in the parent company's larger strategy, so the issue did not end with that conversation. The representative then arranged for the CEO and me to talk by phone with the company's attorneys. Unbeknownst to me this conversation was not to be with the company's "in-house counsel". Instead, the company had retained one of the most prestigious law firms in all of New York City to address the matter. The New York law firm had several attorneys on the call, including their lead tax attorney.

The call started out civil enough, but began to deteriorate as we explored the actual law at issue. A few of the lesser attorneys attempted to chime in at the beginning but quickly decided they were in over their heads and left the rest of the call to the "expert"; their lead tax attorney.

As we explored the law, the statutory rules of construction, what the courts have ruled, etc., she became more and more aggressive and angry. It was clear that she was ill-equipped to argue the issue effectively. (How could she? She was attempting to convince us that payroll withholding is required even though it does not appear anywhere in the law!)

At one point I asked her how, as an attorney-at-law, she could advise her clients (the majority shareholders of the parent corporation) to steal the property of the CEO without being able to point to any law that would permit such action. She became inflamed that I had used the word "steal". I countered that unless or until she could produce a law that would permit the taking of the CEO's property, it was just plain, old-fashioned theft. She was livid.

But far more important than the precise dialogue we had, or their "expert" tax attorney's emotions, was the fact that she could not bring forth any law that would permit the CEO's property to be taken from him under the guise of "payroll withholding". She is one of the top tax attorneys in all of New York City (which has a few tax attorneys in it!) and she had nothing to offer! But that's really not surprising because, as you will soon see. The IRS has nothing to offer on this subject either!

So how did our conversation end? It ended with her making a not-so-thinly-veiled threat to advise her clients to fire the CEO.

Wow! How's that for the American way of justice and fair dealing? If you can't bring forth a law to authorize your act of theft, simply fire the person who is standing upon the law and his property rights!

Fortunately, the tax attorney did not have the clout to have the CEO fired, but a few months later that is exactly what the majority shareholders threatened to do. One of them, speaking on behalf of the others, told the CEO that <u>they didn't care about the law</u> and there would be no further discussion or debates about what the law did or did not permit. He was told that if he didn't furnish his Social Security Number and sign a Form W-4, he would be terminated. However, given his importance to the company, they bumped his pay 30% to offset the withholding. What a great country we live in!

Let me be frank about something right here. Those majority shareholders are criminals. They are felons. They are taking an American's property without any law that permits them to do so. Their own in-house attorneys, as well as those they retained from the outside, could not identify any law that would permit the company to take the CEO's property. These men have committed conspiracy (a felony), grand theft (a felony) and extortion (another felony). But worse than that, what these men are doing is just plain un-American. Their actions conjure up recollections of Nazi Germany or the old Soviet Union. The fact that these are some of the wealthiest men in America doesn't change a thing. They are scumbags. Every good-hearted American should hold these men in disgust.

So what is the purpose in telling you these stories? It is to illustrate several points.

- The people who handle payroll matters have no idea what they're talking about, and have zero knowledge of what the law says.

- Their bosses, people such as VPs of finance, company presidents, etc., have no knowledge of the law even though they are personally responsible for the actions of their underlings.

- Corporate attorneys and other lawyers have no idea what the law says and are unable to offer any rational arguments to support their position.

- Company management and attorneys alike will often take the absurd position that the law is whatever a disembodied voice at an IRS "call center" says.

Is this the America you want to live in? Well, like it or not, it *is* the America you live in – unless you do something to change it!

Although the last chapter was entitled, "In Their Own Words", that principle carries forth into this chapter and to others as we move forward. As I said previously, it doesn't matter what I say – it only matters what the law says!

Now, it's time to jump back into a discussion of exactly what the law says.

While it might seem like a strange place to begin, let's start by looking at the definition of a legal term that is used repeatedly in the Code and regulations. That legal term is *"trade or business"*.

We see again and again in the Code and the regulations that certain aspects of tax law hinge on whether one is "engaged in *trade or business*".

Most folks assume they know what that means. I think we've come far enough along that you've discovered that making assumptions about tax law, without having the facts, is foolhardy.

The general definition that applies throughout the Tax Code is found at 7701(a)(26):

> *"The term 'trade or business' includes the performance of the functions of a public office."*

I can't tell you how many people have responded to that definition over the years by saying, "Oh, that definition means all ordinary private business activities *plus* the performance of the functions of a public office." That's nice to say, but there is no truth to it.

Legal terms mean what Congress says in the definition section of the statute, not what people make up in their heads that appears nowhere in law. As I stated earlier, The U.S. Supreme Court has said that once the legislature provides its own definition for a word, that is the only definition that can be used. Once Congress has provided its own definition the "Plain Meaning Rule" can no longer be applied.

Here's what the U.S. Supreme Court has said:

"When a statute includes an explicit definition, we must follow that definition, even if it varies from that term's ordinary meaning." Meese v. Keene, 481 U.S. 465, 484-485 (1987)

"It is axiomatic that the statutory definition of the term excludes unstated meanings of that term. Colautti v. Franklin, 439 U.S. 379, 392 (1979)

But what of the person who insists that his personal opinion of the meaning of a legal term should control, and that whatever meaning he believes to be correct is how a statute should be interpreted?

"As judges, it is our duty to construe legislation as it is written, not as it might be read by a layman, or as it might be understood by someone who has not even read it." Meese v. Keene, 481 U.S. 465, 484 (1987)

Boy oh boy; that last part – "…or as it might be understood by someone who has not even read it" – certainly applies to Employment Taxes (and most tax law), since virtually no one who conducts payroll withholding has ever read the law!

Clearly the U.S. Supreme Court does not approve the absurd view that the meaning of a legal term is to be determined by what "some guy" thinks it should mean. There are reasons for Canons of Construction, Rules of Interpretation, legal maxims, etc. These are the tools one must use to make an accurate determination of a statutory definition.

You'll notice that the definition of *"trade or business"* uses yet another legal term: *Includes*. In order to properly understand *trade or business*, as well as many other definitions within the Code, it is important to take a moment at this point to tackle *includes*.

The Code provides its own definition for this term, at 7701(c).

"The terms 'includes' and 'including' when used in a definition contained in this title shall not be deemed to exclude other things otherwise within the meaning of the term defined."

How's that for brainteaser! Actually, it's not as bad as it sounds. It just takes some detailed attention in order to understand it.

It says the following: *Includes and including – when used in a definition within this title....* So...if we see either the term "includes" or the term "including", and either of these terms is found "in this title" – meaning Title 26; the Tax Code – we are then to adhere to what follows.

What follows is that a definition which uses *includes* or *including* "*shall not be deemed to exclude other things otherwise within the meaning....*"

I know this seems like a lot of double speak – and it is. I'll prove that in a moment. But I did warn you that the Tax Code was intentionally written to be a labyrinth that is difficult to penetrate.

So, we cannot exclude *"other things"* that are within the meaning.... In this usage, *"other things"* means things that are not enumerated within the definition. However, if we assume that we can add whatever comes into our heads, then the meaning of every term in the Code (whose definition uses *includes or including*) would be interpreted subjectively by each reader. Clearly the men who wrote these definitions did not intend that each person should come to his own individual conclusions about every term in the Code. If you think the Code is a nightmare the way it is, imagine if every reader were permitted to attribute his own meanings to its terms!

This potential guess-work is removed when the definition then says, *"otherwise within the meaning of the term defined."* So, if something is not enumerated, but is otherwise within the meaning, then it cannot be excluded. Or phased more positively, if something is not enumerated, but is otherwise within the meaning, then it can be covered by the definition.

But where do we find the "meaning of the term defined"? Since it's a statutory definition, and the U.S. Supreme Court has said that once a statutory definition is provided we must use *only* that definition, there is no other permissible place to look for the "meaning" but to the words employed by Congress.

In other words, the words Congress writes in a definition (that uses *includes or including*) circumscribe a category of items, persons, or activities. If a particular thing is not enumerated in the definition, but it is still within the *category* established by the words used in the definition, it may then be considered a part of the definition (i.e. included).

[: In the real world, we use the word "category". In the legal world, they use the term "class". They are synonymous.]

I said a moment ago that the definition of *includes or including* in the Code is a lot of double speak. Allow me to show you how succinctly the exact same meaning of *includes or including* has been defined elsewhere.

Title 27 of the United States Code is entitled "Intoxicating Liquors" and it also involves the imposition, assessment, and collection of taxes. When something other than the income tax is involved, how clearly is *includes or including* defined?

27 CFR 72.11 states, *"The terms 'includes' and 'including' do not exclude things not enumerated which are in the same general class."*

Gee…how simple it can be when they want it to be. The definition above is the simple and rational version of what appears at 7701(c), and has the exact same meaning.

Now that we have an understanding of the meaning (and hence the impact) of *includes* or *including*, let's return to our discussion of the legal term *trade or business*.

Trade or business is a term that is used again and again throughout subtitle 'A' and its regulations. Sometimes something is made mandatory if one is "engaged in" *trade or business*. Other times there are exceptions made from a requirement if one is "involved in" *trade or business*.

If we use Congress' definition for *trade or business* – which of course we must – we see that *trade or business* revolves around what we might describe as "official business", not private enterprise.

In many states, government vehicles and other government property have stickers on them that read, "For official use only". Welcome to *trade or business*!

I'm sure those readers who've made their living from the Tax Code, such as accountants and tax attorneys, are livid right now. After years – or maybe decades – of reading the Code in the "ordinary sense", without ever once thinking to actually read the Congressionally provided definitions, this discussion of *trade or business* is too much!

Sometimes when the con job is so huge it's hard to come back to reality and accept the truth. When the lie has been everything to us, we humans have the propensity to hold onto the lie because it is all we know; the lie is our "comfort zone". Governments have known this forever and have always used it against the People.

"The great mass of people...will more easily fall victim to a big lie than to a small one." Adolph Hitler, Mein Kampf, vol. 1, ch. 10 (1925)

It is amazing – and disgusting – how many similarities there are between the Nazis and the United States government's approach to the income tax. As a matter of fact, I anticipate that the government will attempt to ban this book by claiming that it threatens the revenues, and hence the stability, of the United States government.

In other words, the Right of Free Speech, enshrined in the 1st Amendment to the U.S. Constitution, and which Amendment prohibits the U.S. government from interfering with, will instantly be tossed aside by the federal government when "the State" feels threatened. In other words, the government only accepts the exercise of your rights when your exercising them is something the government is comfortable with. When the government is uncomfortable with your exercising your rights, its perspective is that your rights must yield to the government's concerns. I think it's fair to say that if that be the practical reality of it, we wouldn't be able to say we actually have any rights!

You think we don't ban books in America, right? Well, you are wrong about that too. On June 16, 2003, Federal District Court Judge Lloyd D. George issued an injunction banning the sale and distribution of Irwin Schiff's book entitled, *"The Federal Mafia: How The Government Illegally Imposes And Unlawfully Collects Income Taxes And How Americans Can Fight Back."* On August 9, 2004, the Ninth Circuit Court of Appeals upheld the book banning.

The "angle" that the government used to ban Schiff's book was to assert that it was "false commercial speech". Yet somehow the judge never once required the attorneys for the government to show that the book's content was in any way false!

The government engaged in a lot of "name calling". It referred to Schiff as a "tax protestor" and called his positions in the book "frivolous". Yet the government never once quoted from Schiff's book or made any effort to prove that any portions were false. Despite the government never attempting to show that Schiff's content was "false" (which is an essential element of an allegation of "false commercial speech"), Judge George issued an order banning any future sales of the book.

It should also be noted that while the vast majority of allegations of "false commercial speech" are initiated by the Commerce Department or the Federal Trade Commission, it was the Treasury Department which initiated the effort to ban Schiff's book.

Irwin Schiff is mistaken in his legal positions, but that is hardly the point. The point is that when it comes to taxation, the U.S. government has taken the position that if they don't like what you say they possess the authority to stop you from saying it. Seig heil! Totalitarianism, plain and simple.

Back to *trade or business*. Section 162 of the Code details the "itemized deductions" that can be taken in the course of *trade or business*. The statute opens appropriately with the words, "In general", which we've discussed previously. These words signify that what we are about to be told will be presented in the form of a broad outline, absent specifics or limitations.

Before we explore section 162, allow me to point out that Congress' definition of *trade or business* does not specify that the "performance of the functions of a public office" is limited to a public office within the United States government. Ah ha! Once again you presumed something that is not written in the law!

The opening words of section 162 are:

> "There shall be allowed as a deduction all the ordinary and necessary expenses paid or incurred during the taxable year in carrying on any trade or business...."

I can almost hear the "tax professionals" screaming that this section is about private enterprise! Of course we know that isn't true because in order to make it true we'd need to throw out Congress' statutory definition of *trade or business* and/or completely ignore the Rules of Interpretation and the words of the U.S. Supreme Court.

I should add that those who support the criminal misapplication of the Code absolutely love the *Rules of Interpretation*, the definitions within the Code, and the U.S. Supreme Court holdings concerning construction/interpretation – but only on the rare occasion that these items support their criminal intentions. However, as soon as these same rules/requirements threaten to expose "the big lie", these folks suddenly develop amnesia and can't seem to remember that the *Rules of Interpretation*, the definitions within the Code, and the U.S. Supreme Court holdings concerning construction/interpretation even exist. In other words, those who support the criminal misapplication of the Code make ready reference to these "tools" when it suits their purpose, but pretend that these very same "tools" don't exist when to apply them would reveal the truth. What character! What integrity!

So what might the opening words of section 162 look like if we substituted the actual definition for the term *trade or business*? It would read like this:

> "There shall be allowed as a deduction all the ordinary and necessary expenses paid or incurred during the taxable year in carrying on the performance of the functions of a public office...."

That provision suddenly became quite clear!

Shortly after the opening stanza of section 162, we see this:

> "For purposes of the preceding sentence, the place of residence of a Member of Congress (including any Delegate and Resident Commissioner) within the State, congressional district, or possession which he represents in Congress shall be considered his home.... For

purposes of paragraph (2), the taxpayer shall not be treated as being temporarily away from home during any period of employment if such period exceeds 1 year. The preceding sentence shall not apply to any Federal *employee* during any period for which such *employee* is certified by the Attorney General (or the designee thereof) as traveling on behalf of the United States in temporary duty status to investigate, or provide support services for the investigation of, a Federal crime."

That certainly sounds like "official business" to me. If there's anything there that applies to private enterprise, I don't see it.

And just a bit later we find this:

"No deduction shall be allowed under subsection (a) for any payment made, directly or indirectly, to an official or *employee* of any government, or of any agency or instrumentality of any government, if the payment constitutes an illegal bribe or kickback or, if the payment is to an official or *employee* of a foreign government, the payment is unlawful under the Foreign Corrupt Practices Act of 1977."

In this segment Congress is saying that it will not allow a deduction for an expense that is – under U.S. law – an illegal attempt to influence "the performance of the function of a public office." Remember when I mentioned that the definition of *trade or business* does not distinguish between U.S. or foreign government functions? Please note that in the above portion of section 162, Congress is disallowing a deduction of a bribe or kickback that attempts to influence the function of ***any*** public office, foreign or domestic.

The next subsection deals with "Capital contributions to Federal National Mortgage Association". Of course you know the Federal National Mortgage Association by its more common name – Fannie Mae. And after the 2009 financial meltdown of Fannie Mae everyone should have become aware that it is a wholly-owned Federal corporation. In other words, what Fannie Mae does is *the performance of the functions of a public office.*

From there we go to "Denial of deduction for certain lobbying and political Expenditures". What is the purpose of "lobbying and political expenditures"? *To influence the performance of the functions of a public office*, of course.

Subsection (f) and (g) deal with fines and penalties. Then we go right into "State legislators' travel expenses away from home".

Section 162 is very lengthy and contains a lot of complex issues, but what I've brought to your attention thus far from section 162 should confirm for you that the statutory definition of *trade or business* is indeed limited *to the performance of the functions of a public office*. I will tell you that there is nothing in the entire lengthy content of section 162 that addresses anything other than *the performance of the functions of a public office*!

In discussing *trade or business* I am laying a piece of the foundation for what is to come a bit further in this chapter.

Now, the issue of payroll withholding, and who is an *employee* for the purposes of payroll withholding, is "layered". Let me give you an example of what I mean.

You overhear a judge instruct a bailiff to deliver the convicted defendant to the state prison. Your thought would ordinarily be that the convicted defendant is being taken to the prison to serve out his sentence. Later in the day you're listening to the news and hear that the very same defendant is to be executed at midnight. That added piece of information now changes your earlier perception. Earlier you thought he was going to serve a prison sentence. Now, with additional information, you realize he is going to be executed. That's a significant difference!

The next morning you are surprised to read in the newspaper that after receiving new and compelling evidence, the governor pardoned the defendant of all charges and he is a free man. In the span of less than 24 hours, as new information came to you, you had 3 different understandings of the same situation. At first you thought he was going to serve out a prison sentence. Then you believed he was going to be put to death at midnight. And lastly you learned that he was completely innocent!

That example illustrates how you will experience "Employment Taxes". As I bring the information to you, it will seem like one thing, then another, and then yet another. These changes will occur as we drill through the "layers" of law and regulations.

Subtitle 'C' – Employment Taxes – addresses a number of issues. As an example, it addresses certain railroad taxes. I won't be getting into those. I'm going to stay on track by addressing only those matters that affect the American public at large, not every subset that a statutory scheme may touch upon.

Chapter 24 of subtitle 'C' is entitled, "Collection of Income Tax at Source on Wages".

Before we proceed, I want to take a moment to make the observation that every time the phrase "Collection of Income Tax at Source" is used in subtitle A, it has always referred to the withholding of U.S. tax from monies paid to a *foreign person*. Is this instance any different? Let's find out!

Chapter 24 contains section 3402, which is the command to deduct and withhold from the *wages* of an *employee*. I have italicized *"wages"* and *"employee"* because they are legal terms. If you've been paying attention, you already know that since they are legal terms we ***cannot*** use our common understanding of such terms, but must seek out the Congressionally provided definitions.

The command to deduct and withhold reads as follows:

> "Except as otherwise provided in this section, every <u>employer</u> making payment of <u>wages</u> shall deduct and withhold upon such *wages* a tax determined in accordance with tables or computational procedures prescribed by the Secretary." [Underlines added to identify legal terms]

You will notice that the *employer* "shall" deduct and withhold. Typically in law, "shall" means the act is mandatory. Accordingly, we know that the requirement to deduct and withhold is mandatory upon an *employer* who is paying *wages* to an *employee*.

If you've come to understand that a big part of the "game" being played in tax law is the use of statutory definitions, you should already have a suspicion that this command doesn't apply to those who might think themselves embraced by it under the commonly understood meaning of these words. Your suspicion is well founded!

While the command to deduct and withhold is found at 3402, the definitions that control 3402 are contained in 3401.

I will tell you now that the entire statutory definition framework of chapter 24 pivots on the definition of the term *"employee"*. All other terms key off of *"employee"*. Let's see how that works.

> 3401(a) – Wages: For purposes of this chapter, the term "wages" means all remuneration (other than fees paid to a public official) for services performed by an <u>employee</u> for his employer. [emphasis added]

Let me draw your attention to a couple of things. First, don't be thrown by the words within the parentheses. "Fees" do not belong to the *employee*, but merely pass through his hands. An example would be the fee a federal firearms dealer pays for his license. A government *employee* collects the license fee, but the fee does not belong to the *employee*; the *employee* is required to pass it along to its owner – the U.S. Treasury.

I would also draw your attention to the specific wording of the definition. The remuneration (i.e. pay) is made specifically to the *employee* and no one else. And of course *employee* has its own congressionally provided definition.

> 3401(c) – *Employee*: For purposes of this chapter, the term *"employee"* includes an officer, employee, or elected official of the United States, a State, or any political subdivision thereof, or the District of Columbia, or any agency or instrumentality of any one or more of the foregoing. The term "employee" also includes an officer of a corporation.

[Let's leave the final sentence out of the discussion for just a moment. I'll get back to it a moment.]

Knowing that the U.S. Supreme Court has said we **must** use the definitions Congress has provided, is there any way to make this definition fit anyone other than various government workers? In 16 years I've never met anyone who answered 'yes' to that question.

So now we know that payroll withholding on *wages* applies solely to the pay of "an officer, employee, or elected official of the United States, a State, or any political subdivision thereof, or the District of Columbia, or any agency or instrumentality of any one or more of the foregoing."

Let's restate the definition of "wages" using the full definition of *employee*.

For purposes of this chapter, the term "wages" means all remuneration... for services performed by an officer, employee, or elected official of the United States, a State, or any political subdivision thereof, or the District of Columbia, or any agency or instrumentality of any one or more of the foregoing.

Doesn't it flabbergast you that virtually every private sector company in America says they "have to" deduct money from your paycheck under this section? As I said: the largest financial crime in the history of the world!

Just for the sake of thoroughness, let's look at the definition of *employer*.

3401(d) – *Employer*: For purposes of this chapter, the term "*employer*" means the person for whom an individual performs or performed any service, of whatever nature, **as the <u>employee</u>** of such person…. [emphasis added]

As you can see, *employer* is controlled by the definition of *employee*. To provide additional clarity, let's insert the definition of *employee* into 3401(d).

For purposes of this chapter, the term "employer" means the person for whom an individual performs or performed any service, of whatever nature, as an officer, employee, or elected official of the United States, a State, or any political subdivision thereof, or the District of Columbia, or any agency or instrumentality of any one or more of the foregoing.

Isn't it great how clear things get when we insert the actual definition for the term rather than merely using the term itself, which is prone to be mistakenly read with its commonly understood meaning!

Aside from using the definitions and rules to properly understand the meaning of *employer*, is there anywhere else we might verify the meaning? Yes, there is.

Section 6331 is the section that addresses the Secretary's authority to "levy". Here's a sentence right out of 6331:

> "Levy may be made upon the accrued salary or wages of any officer, *employee*, or elected official, of the United States, the District of Columbia, or any agency or instrumentality of the United States or the District of Columbia, by serving a notice of levy on the **employer**

(as defined in section 3401(d)) of such officer, *employee*, or elected official."
[emphasis added]

As you can see, the statute essentially quotes the definition of *employee* at 3401(c). Then, when it mentions serving a notice of levy on the *employer*, it specifically references 3401(d). My experience has been that the Code is always harmonious, and this example highlights how different (but related) sections within the Code rely on the same operative definitions, with one section validating the proper meaning of the other.

If we take a moment and translate this all into language that's more suitable for the average man, here's what we have.

Employee – Certain government workers.

Employer – Any entity or office for which certain government workers work.

Wages – The pay received by certain government workers.

Plain English is so much better than legalese, isn't it?

I said I would return to the question of the final sentence in the definition of *employee*. That sentence reads, "The term 'employee' also includes an officer of a corporation."

Within the Rules of Construction/Interpretation there are various "legal maxims" at work. A legal maxim is a phrase or sentence that makes a succinct statement about a principle of law that is always operative in a given situation. The maxim that is operative in this instance is *Ejusdem Generis*.

A good definition of *Ejusdem Generis* appears on the internet at www.legal-explanations.com.

> (eh-youse-dem generous) v adj. Latin for "of the same kind," used to interpret loosely written statutes. Where a law lists specific classes of persons or things and then refers to them in general, the general statements only apply to the same kind of persons or things specifically listed. Example: if a law refers to automobiles, trucks, tractors,

motorcycles and other motor-powered vehicles, "vehicles" would not include airplanes, since the list was of land-based transportation.

As we apply *Ejusdem Generis* to the final sentence of *employee*, it means that the "officer of a corporation" must be read in light of the specifically listed entities preceding the final sentence. Thus, the "officer" being referred to in the definition is an officer of a corporation owned by one of the specifically listed entities. That means it is a corporation owned by *the United States, a State, or any political subdivision thereof, or the District of Columbia, or any agency or instrumentality of any one or more of the foregoing.* Examples would be the CEO of the Federal Deposit Insurance Corporation (FDIC) or the President of Federal National Mortgage Association (Fannie Mae), etc.

In short, there is nothing in the Congressionally provided definition of *employee* at 3401(c) that embraces anyone in the private sector.

I am tempted at this point to tackle the subject of how the government responds to the reality I've just shared with you. The government's response is pathetic; maybe even worse than pathetic. For those who imagine the government would respond with the mighty roar of a lion, you'll be disappointed. The government's response is more like the tiny squeak of a mouse. As much as I'd like to jump into it here and now, that discussion will have to wait. Coming up is an entire chapter in which I address the government's "responses" (such as they are) to virtually every point revealed in this book. So we'll both have to be patient and wait until we reach that chapter to discuss the government's frivolous responses. The wait will be worth it. It'll be a lot of fun!

Remember when I said that we'd have to drill down into the layers of "Employment Taxes" (subtitle 'C')? As of this moment we've completed an examination of the outer layer.

At this "outer layer" it appears that the tax is to be withheld from the paychecks of various government workers. As we "drill down" into the layers, what other issues might we find to consider? Possibly the tax is not to be withheld from all of the various government workers, but just a subset within that group. We keep talking about "the tax" being withheld, but what tax are we talking about, exactly? Is it a tax imposed upon working for the government? Maybe, maybe not. You once thought that subtitle 'A' (income tax) had been imposed on every

American who made money. That presumption was wrong, wasn't it? (That's not criticism. I once believed that, too.) As always, let's explore!

Remember chapter 3 of the Code? We've discussed it at some length. It provided the clarity and specificity to understand upon whom Congress has imposed subtitle 'A' and who Congress has made liable for the tax (the withholding agent).

Interestingly, chapter 3 has a lot to say about chapter 24 as well!

If you're like me, that probably shocks you. I know it shocked me. I couldn't immediately get my arms around the idea that a chapter entitled, "Withholding of Tax on Nonresident Aliens and Foreign Corporations" would have anything to do with "Employment Taxes". They're not even in the same subtitle!

Aren't "Employment Taxes" simply taxes imposed upon the *employee* and/or the *employer*? That's what I thought for a number of years. That was before I started really tearing into chapter 3 and its regulations.

At this point allow me to make a statement that may assist you as we proceed. It is a statement that may help you put the pieces together as we go along. It's a statement I wish someone would have made to me years ago. It would have made things so much easier to understand.

Here is the statement:

With that startling (but accurate) statement made, let's begin to "drill down" through the layers!

Most Americans who work for a company or another person are familiar with a Form W-2. It is the "information return" that is filed by the company reflecting the "wages" you earned during the previous year.

Let me say plainly that there is nothing in U.S. tax law that requires – *or permit*s – a private sector firm to create a Form W-2 for the average working American, nor to send one to the IRS.

You may recall that all the "income tax" regulations are in Part 1 of the Code of Federal Regulations (CFR). The regulations for "Employment Taxes" are contained in Part 31 of the CFR.

Here's what the "Employment Taxes" regulations say about Form W-2:

> – "Every employer, as defined in section 3401(d), required to deduct and withhold from an employee a tax under section 3402…shall furnish to each such employee, in respect of the remuneration paid by such employer to such employee during the calendar year, the tax return copy and the employee's copy of a statement on Form W-2."

Note that the *employer* is specifically defined as the *employer* at 3401(d). We've already covered that 3401(d) means "any entity or office for which certain government workers work."

And remember that section 6331 verified this when Congress said:

> "Levy may be made upon the accrued salary or wages of any officer, *employee*, or elected official, of the United States, the District of Columbia, or any agency or instrumentality of the United States or the District of Columbia, by serving a notice of levy on the **employer** (as defined in section 3401(d)) of such officer, *employee*, or elected official." [emphasis added]

There is no doubt that *employer* means the entity that employs and pays the person who is "any officer, *employee*, or elected official, of the United States, the District of Columbia, or any agency or instrumentality of the United States or the District of Columbia."

According to the Secretary of the Treasury, as expressed in his regulations, Form W-2 is to be used ***only*** by the *employer*. So why is the private sector company for which you work conducting payroll withholding and giving you a Form W-2 at the end of the year? I understand you don't have a good explanation for that. Ironically, neither do they!

As I stated earlier, the common (and pathetic) response is, "The IRS says I have to." I guess these people would also murder their children if directed to do so by a disembodied voice at an IRS call center. After all, how can murdering their children be wrong if the IRS directs them to do so? If they're willing to violate your rights and steal your property (which is a part of your *life*) simply because some flunky at the IRS told him to do so, why not murder children too? I'd love to hear the response to that. I can hear it now; "I'm willing to steal and violate the property rights of my fellow Americans because a disembodied voice at the IRS told me to, but I wouldn't murder children if the IRS told me to do so." Well, isn't that person courageous and moral for drawing the line !

Traditionally, the three most common items of withholding on a person's paycheck are FICA, federal income tax withholding, and State income tax withholding. We're going to explore each of these!

Let's begin with FICA.

Many Americans see a deduction on their paycheck that reads, "F.I.C.A." When workers ask what "F.I.C.A." is, they are told that it is their Social Security deduction. That is a complete lie; FICA has **nothing** to do with Social Security. Yes, I'm saying that entire generations of Americans have been lied to about what FICA is!

In 1937 the U.S. Supreme Court decided the case of <u>Charles C. Steward Machine Co. v. Davis</u>, 301 U.S. 548. It delivered its opinion after President Roosevelt had threatened to "pack the court" if it continued to find his *New Deal* legislation unconstitutional. And so, the Court's resistance to the unconstitutional acts of Congress (taken under FDR's leadership) had collapsed in the face of FDR's threat. *Steward Machine Co. v. Davis* is a travesty of justice, an abortion of logic, and a monument to the Court's perfidy against the American people and against the Constitution that the justices swore to uphold.

Despite the decision's corrupt nature, there are a few statements of simple fact that managed to get through unscathed. In *Steward*, the Court is dissecting what we know today as FICA. In doing so the Court states:

> "The proceeds [taxes], when collected, go into the Treasury of the United States like internal revenue collections generally. They are not earmarked in any way."

And when speaking of how the money is paid out, the Court said:

"The appropriations when made were not specifically out of the proceeds of the employment tax, but out of any moneys in the Treasury."

In other words, all FICA taxes are paid directly into the Treasury's general fund and spent in whatever way Congress decides. <u>There is no requirement in law that these funds be set-aside for you, nor are they</u>!

The Court has referred to FICA as merely "an additional income tax". Wow! How come no one ever told you *that* before?

When the Social Security Administration needs to pay out "benefits", it simply asks Congress to make funds available through its annual appropriations process.

Americans falsely believe that Social Security is "their money". They believe that their "contributions" (i.e. FICA payroll withholding) has been put aside with their name on it – like a savings account – growing over time. And when the proper time arrives "their money" will be doled back out to them to assist with retirement. That is not even remotely the legal reality of it. Most Americans believe this hogwash because self-serving politicians have been lying about it since the 1930's.

Remember the "Social Security Trust Fund" you hear about every few years in the news? It doesn't exist. There is no "Social Security Trust Fund". That is a key part of the lie that the politicians love to play on you!

Title 31 of the United States Code (USC) is entitled "Money and Finance" and contains a list of accounts maintained by the U.S. Treasury that Congress has classified as "trust funds". That list is found at section 1321. There is no "Social Security Trust Fund" listed, nor anything that could possibly be construed as having anything to do with what Americans think of as "Social Security".

There is an "account" maintained by the U.S. Treasury called, "Old-Age and Survivors Insurance Trust Fund". But, despite the words "trust fund" in the name of the account, it is *not* a trust fund! This is simply a part of the con-job.

Imagine if you were to break your monthly income/expenses into categories. You might have a rent/mortgage "account", a food "account", a motor vehicle "account", etc. You've created these "accounts" to help you get a better mental picture of what you've got, but in reality these "accounts" are just contrivances for the purpose of organization.

This is exactly the type of "account" that the Treasury keeps and the politicians call the "Social Security Trust Fund". It's just a bookkeeping contrivance. It is not, by any stretch of the imagination, a trust fund. The account maintained by the

Treasury is no more a "trust fund" than your personal checking account would become one if you started calling it your "Family Trust Fund".

Americans see Social Security benefits as "their money". It's not. Your money has long since been spent on whatever suited Congress at the time (which may have been decades ago). Your FICA payments were/are merely an additional income tax. They are *not* Social Security taxes – no matter how many times the lie is repeated. And the money taken from you has never been put away for your future needs.

There are two completely separate mechanisms of law. One is called the Social Security Act and the other is called the Federal Insurance Contribution Act (FICA). The hard part for Americans to understand and believe is that neither has anything to do with the other. Social Security benefits are funded by appropriations from Congress each year and FICA is merely another tax operating under the false "cover story" of having a relationship to Social Security, which it does not.

Now let's look at the regulations under Subtitle 'C'. They are broken down into 7 "subparts":

Subpart A – Introduction
Subpart B – Federal Insurance Contribution Act
Subpart C – Railroad Retirement Tax Act
Subpart D – Federal Unemployment Tax Act
Subpart E – Collection of Income Tax at Source
Subpart F – General Provisions Relating to Employment Taxes
Subpart G – Administrative Provisions of Special Application to Employment Taxes

Did you notice that of the 7 subparts, only 3 address a type of tax?

Clearly the "Introduction" is not a tax! Subpart E mandates the mechanism for collecting the tax, but is not itself a tax. Subpart F is a general discussion of various "procedures" that are to be used when administrating an "Employment Tax". And subpart G discusses how some procedures have special applicability to Employment Taxes. In summary, subparts A, E, F, and G do not impose or even address any specific tax, but only speak to the broad category of taxes known as "Employment Taxes".

More important is that subparts B, C, and D do address specific taxes. Those taxes are: FICA, Railroad Retirement, and Federal Unemployment. That's it! There's nothing more; there's no "other" tax contained in Subtitle 'C'!

Now, the Tax Code (as opposed to the regulations) shows six chapters. Those chapters are:

21 – Federal Insurance Contribution Act
22 – Railroad Retirement Tax Act
23 – Federal Unemployment Tax Act
23A – Railroad Unemployment Repayment Tax
24 – Collection of Income Tax at Source on Wages
25 – General Provision Relating to Employment Taxes

Let's start by looking at chapter 21 – FICA. The Code uses this language to impose FICA on *employees*:

> In addition to other taxes, there is hereby imposed on the income of every individual a tax equal to the following percentages of the wages (as defined in section 3121(a)) received by him with respect to employment (as defined in section 3121(b))

You will note the specific language of "there is hereby ***imposed***...."

Section 3111 uses similar language when addressing the tax on *employer*s:

> "In addition to other taxes, there is hereby ***imposed*** on every employer an excise tax...."

Again we see the specific language, "there is hereby imposed...."

So what's actually in the chapter 21, which is entitled "Federal Insurance Contribution Act"?

Chapter 21 is comprised of 3 subchapters; A, B, and C. Subchapter 'A' is entitled "Tax on *Employees*"; subchapter 'B' is "Tax on *Employer*"; subchapter 'C', "General Provisions". (We have already discussed how subchapters A and B specifically "impose" taxes.) Subchapter 'C' is "General Provisions" and looks like this:

3121 – Definitions.
3122 – Federal service.
3123 – Deductions as constructive payments.
3124 – Estimate of revenue reduction.
3125 – Returns in the case of governmental *employee*s in States, Guam, American Samoa, and the District of Columbia.
3126 – Return and payment by governmental *employer*.
3127 – Exemption for *employer*s and their *employee*s where both are members of religious faiths opposed to participation in Social Security Act programs.
3128 – Short title.

You'll notice there isn't much there. It starts off with the definition section (which we'll get into shortly). It moves immediately to "Federal service", followed by two procedural sections (3123 & 3124). Then it discusses returns in reference to States, Guam, American Samoa, etc. and returns by government *employer*s. We don't need to concern ourselves with religious exemptions and the "Short Title" here.

In summary, subchapter 'C' – which is the general provisions – contains only four meaningful sections:

- Definitions
- Federal Service
- Returns regarding employees of the governments of the States, Guam, American Samoa, etc.
- Return and payment by governmental *employer*

Aside from the definition section, the only meaningful sections pertain to the government. Hmmm. <u>Since virtually every private sector company in America thinks it has to be involved in FICA, where are the "provisions" that address returns and payments for private sector firms in the states of the Union?</u>

Just another case of ignorant people insisting they are required to do what *isn't* anywhere in the law.

[: It is regrettable that subchapter 'C' is named "General Provisions". Do not confuse the title "General Provisions" with our earlier discussion about "general language". Subchapter 'C' is the Secretary's specific language for subchapters 'A' & 'B'.]

Don't most Americans believe that everyone is subject to the Social Security tax? Maybe so, but that's not what the Social Security Administration (SSA) says! The SSA has a Q&A page at http://www.ssa.gov/history/InternetMyths.html (although it may be moved or removed before this book hits the stores). On that page it says:

> "Persons working in employment covered by Social Security are subject to the FICA payroll tax. Like all taxes, this has never been voluntary. From the first days of the program to the present, anyone working on a job covered by Social Security has been obligated to pay their payroll taxes."

Did you see that? The SSA says that you have to be working "in employment covered by Social Security". Note that it is not *you* who is covered by Social Security, but rather, "covered employment". The second sentence uses the language, "a job covered by Social Security". Clearly the key here is that the *nature of the employment* determines whether there is an obligation to pay FICA. Again, why didn't anyone ever tell you *that*! So now I'm sure you're wondering whether what you do is "covered". Great question!

Remember that definition section (at section 3121) that we just mentioned in passing? Well, it's got some rather interesting definitions!

The most fundamental definition is 3121(b):

> - For purposes of this chapter, the term "employment" means any service, of whatever nature, performed (A) by an *employee* for the person employing him, irrespective of the citizenship or residence of either, (i) within the United States, or (ii) on or in connection with an American vessel or American aircraft under a contract of service which is entered into within the United States or during the performance of which and while the *employee* is employed on the vessel or aircraft it touches at a port in the United States, if the *employee* is employed on and in connection with such vessel or aircraft when outside the United States, or (B) outside the United States by a citizen or resident of the United States as an *employee* for an American *employer* (as defined in subsection (h)), or (C) if it is service, regardless of where or

by whom performed, which is designated as employment or recognized as equivalent to employment under an agreement entered into under section 233 of the Social Security Act.

Let's cut out some of the parts that are superfluous to most Americans, such as the parts about vessels and aircraft, and look at it again:

For purposes of this chapter, the term "employment" means any service, of whatever nature, performed

- (A) by an employee for the person employing him, irrespective of the citizenship or residence of either, (i) within the United States, or...
- (B) outside the United States by a citizen or resident of the United States as an employee for an American employer (as defined in subsection (h)), or
- (C) if it is service, regardless of where or by whom performed, which is designated as employment or recognized as equivalent to employment under an agreement entered into under section 233 of the Social Security Act.

The definition above is the description of "covered employment". The tax is imposed upon "employment" (as defined at 3121(b)), and the definition of "employment" is telling you what's covered. Now all we have to do is break down the definition!

Under (A) we see three elements:

- Employment within the *United States*
- Employment outside the U.S. for an *American employer*
- Service performed that is recognized as employment under section 233 of the Social Security Act

I have italicized the legal terms above. These terms have specific legal definitions that control the meaning of the sentences in which they are used, and hence control (limit) the application of the statute.

Subsection 3121(e)(2) contains the definition of "United States". I wish to remind you that there are several definitions of the terms "United States" and "State" (among others) within the Code. The reason that these definitions change at different places in the Code is that Congress is attempting to tailor the legislation to achieve the exact and specific purpose Congress had in mind for that particular legislation.

Subsection 3121(e)(2) is the definition of "United States" for the purposes of FICA.

> *The term "United States" when used in a geographical sense includes the Commonwealth of Puerto Rico, the Virgin Islands, Guam, and American Samoa.*

You remember our earlier discussion of "includes"? In order to determine the meaning of a definition that uses "includes" we must look at the enumerated items Congress listed and find the "class" (or category) that most accurately fits that list.

In the case of "United States", as defined at 3121(e)(2), what category do these enumerated items fall into? If one is not familiar with the options that are available, this may be a difficult task. Accordingly, let's look at the options as expressed by the U.S. Supreme Court.

In Hooven & Allison Co. v. Evatt, 324 U.S. 652 (1945), the U.S. Supreme Court stated that the phrase "United States" can be used in any of three ways.

1. A sovereign nation amongst the community of sovereign nations of the world.

2. The territory over which the sovereignty of the United States extends, *or*...

3. The collective name of the states that are united by and under the Constitution.

In other words, there are 3 separate and distinct meanings that can be intended when using the phrase "United States". I bet no one ever told you *that* before either!

I wish to point out that I italicized the word 'or' at the end of item #2 because that word appears in the *Hooven* decision at precisely that point. I also wish to point out that meanings #2 & #3 are not the same. I raise this issue because some readers will mistakenly assume that "the territory over which the sovereignty of the United

States extends" *is* the "states of the Union". It is not. If it were, the Court in *Hooven* would not have explicitly mentioned them as separate independent meanings.

So that you better understand what is meant by item #2, let me give you a few examples.

- At the outset of the Civil War, southern states declared themselves to be a completely separate and distinct nation from the United States of America. The Confederate States of America then engaged in warfare against the United States and lost. The lands of the Confederate States of America (that the Union then held as victor of the war) would be lands "over which the sovereignty of the United States extends".

- On December 10, 1898, the signing of the Treaty of Paris between Spain and the United States gave the U.S. control of Cuba, the Philippines, Puerto Rico, and Guam. These places thus became lands "over which the sovereignty of the United States extends".

- In early 1917, that portion of the Virgin Islands, today known as the "U.S. Virgin Islands", was sold to the United States by Denmark and treaties were ratified to that end. On March 31, 1917 the Danish government transferred control of the islands to the U.S. government. The U.S. Virgin Islands became lands "over which the sovereignty of the United States extends".

The states of the Union are *not* lands over which the sovereignty of the United States extends. Remember, the original 13 states existed as individual independent sovereign nations before there was a "United States"! The 13 sovereign states chose to create the federal government, and delegate to it certain limited authorities in order to achieve those aims the individual states felt were better managed by a collective body (that today we call Congress). In other words, the federal government was created by the 13 sovereign states to serve certain specific needs of the states. The federal government is not sovereign over the states; it is their creation.

Since we now have a solid understanding of the three possible meanings of "United States", let's go back to the definition of "United States" at 3121(e)(2), addressing FICA.

Which of the 3 definitions do you think Congress is communicating to you when it writes that *United States* includes the "Commonwealth of Puerto Rico, the Virgin Islands, Guam, and American Samoa"? I should also add that the definition states that it is used in a "geographical sense". This is significant, because at times the government can have "personam" or "subject matter" jurisdiction that extends beyond geographical boundaries. In this definition, Congress is telling us that a "covered *employee*" is one who works within the geographic *United States*, as here defined.

I should also point out that Washington D.C. is **not** a state of the Union. Under the U.S. Constitution, Washington D.C. is a place that is under the "exclusive legislative jurisdiction" of Congress. (See Article I, Section 8, Clause 17.) It is also one of those places which, while not specifically enumerated in the 3121(e)(2) definition of United States, is includable because it is in the same "class" as the enumerated items (i.e. "lands over which the sovereignty of the United States extends").

Some of you may be thinking, "Come on Dave; you're being silly. Congress just made a mistake. The definition really means the whole country." Oh, really? How soon we forget! Remember these 3 little ditties?

"When a statute includes an explicit definition, we must follow that definition, even if it varies from that term's ordinary meaning." Meese v. Keene, 481 U.S. 465, 484-485 (1987)

"It is axiomatic that the statutory definition of the term excludes unstated meanings of that term. Colautti v. Franklin, 439 U.S. 379, 392 (1979)

"As judges, it is our duty to construe legislation as it is written, *not as it might be read by a layman, or as it might be understood by someone who has not even read it.*" Meese v. Keene, 481 U.S. 465, 484 (1987) [emphasis added]

Further, if Congress did "just make a mistake", it's a mistake that Congress has left uncorrected for more than 70 years! Who in their right mind would believe that Congress would just leave an "oopsy" in place for 70 years?

Additionally, Congress knows precisely how to write a definition that embraces the 50 states when it wants to.

The definition of "State" for the purposes of FICA (found at 3121(e)(1)) is:

The term "State" includes the District of Columbia, the Commonwealth of Puerto Rico, the Virgin Islands, Guam, and American Samoa.

See anything in there about the 50 states? Now look at another section of the Code in which Congress wants to include the states of the Union in its definition of "State".

26 USC 6103(b)(5)(A)(i) - *<u>any of the 50 States</u>, the District of Columbia, the Commonwealth of Puerto Rico, the Virgin Islands, Guam, American Samoa, and the Commonwealth of the Northern Mariana Islands,...* [underline added]

Well, I'll be damned. It looks like Congress knows exactly how to include the states of the Union in a definition when it chooses to!

So...now that we know that *United States* – as defined for the purposes of FICA – is not an "oopsy" and does not include the states of the Union, we can see that as Congress uses its own definitions to explain to us who is a "*covered employee*", it is not private sector folks within the states of the Union!

The 2nd element of being "covered" is if you are engaged in "employment outside the U.S. for an *American employer.*" Yup, you guessed it; *American employer* has a very specific definition. That definition is found at 3121(h):

For purposes of this chapter, the term "American *employer*" means an *employer* which is—

(1) the United States or any instrumentality thereof,
(2) an individual who is a resident of the United States,
(3) a partnership, if two-thirds or more of the partners are residents of the United States,
(4) a trust, if all of the trustees are residents of the United States, or
(5) a corporation organized under the laws of the United States or of any State.

As always, let's break it down!

First, you'll notice that this definition does not use the term "includes", but instead uses the word "means". This is a significant distinction because, when the word "means" is used, that is the *sole* definition and **nothing** can be added. Where "includes" allows expansion of the definition (as long as it's within the same "class"), "means" does not.

Item #1 is plain enough. It is the United States government or any of its many instrumentalities.

A good working layman's definition of "instrumentality" (as used in federal statutes) is *"any man, woman, or entity, that serves as an intermediary or agent through which one or more functions of the government are carried out."* Since just a bit ago we were discussing places such as the Virgin Islands, a good example of an instrumentality would be the Virgin Islands Corporation. The Virgin Islands Corporation is defined in law as being "under direction of the President of the United States or his representative for promotion of economic development of Virgin Islands."

Item #2 is an alien individual who is residing in the United States. (Remember, for the purposes of U.S. tax law, a person is either a citizen or a resident.)

Item #3 is a partnership in which 2/3 or more of the partners are aliens residing in the U.S.

Item #4 is the same as #3 but deals with trustees instead of partners.

Item #5 is self-explanatory.

Or is it?

What do all these definitions have in common? They all use the term "United States" – and we've already covered that Congress provided a very specific and limited definition for *United States* when used in FICA! Instead of using "United States" in items 2-5, let's use the *definition of United States*, except we'll add the words, "and all other jurisdictions within the same class." The only place we cannot use this "substitution method" is in #1 because it is referring to the government of the United States and is not using the phrase *United States* in its "geographical sense".

Let's now use this "substitution method" on 2-5!

- An individual who is a resident of the Commonwealth of Puerto Rico, the Virgin Islands, Guam, and American Samoa, and all other jurisdictions within the same class.

- A partnership, if two-thirds or more of the partners are residents of the Commonwealth of Puerto Rico, the Virgin Islands, Guam, and American Samoa, and all other jurisdictions within the same class.

- A trust, if all of the trustees are residents of the Commonwealth of Puerto Rico, the Virgin Islands, Guam, and American Samoa, and all other jurisdictions within the same class.

- A corporation organized under the laws of the Commonwealth of Puerto Rico, the Virgin Islands, Guam, and American Samoa (and all other jurisdictions within the same class) or of the District of Columbia (and all other jurisdictions within the same class).

Isn't it amazing how things change when we actually know the definitions and apply them?

The final description of what constitutes "covered employment" is "service performed that is recognized as *employment* under section 233 of the Social Security Act". Hmmm. How can we know what that is? Simple; we look at section 233 of the Social Security Act. And here is how that section begins:

"The President is authorized to enter into agreements establishing totalization arrangements between the social security system established by this title and the social security system of any foreign country...."

Section 233 is about coordinating coverage of U.S. Social Security with social security-like programs in foreign nations. In other words, a person is "covered" if he is a foreigner, and his country and the U.S. have worked out a "totalization agreement".

We've now covered all three elements of Social Security's "covered employment". To recap, the three elements are:

- Employment within the *United States*
- Employment outside the U.S. for an *American employer*
- Service performed that is recognized as employment under section 233 of the Social Security Act

You've now learned what *United States* means (as defined for the purposes of FICA), what *American employer* means, and what section 233 of the Social Security Act addresses. There is just one more element to FICA "employment" of which you should be aware, though it applies to very few people. There is a provision for those who work on vessels or aircraft registered under U.S. law. But of course this is all international as well. (If you think it may involve you and you'd like to look it up, it is addressed at 3121(b)(A)(ii).)

One can summarize the FICA tax as being imposed upon those who work for the U.S. government (with those at the highest levels of government being excepted), those who work in U.S. possessions and territories; those who are covered under a totalization agreement; and those who work on U.S. registered vessels and aircraft (under certain specific circumstances).

Do you wonder why FICA has been imposed "there" and not "here"? Simple; based on previous Supreme Court rulings, the U.S. government can legislate differently in each place. This is the legal concept: When legislating in its role of serving the needs of the states of the Union, the U.S. government is constrained by the limits of constitutional power laid out in the Constitution. However, when legislating for places other than the 50 states Congress is free to do anything not specifically prohibited by the Constitution. That is a HUGE distinction!

In his now famous dissent in <u>Downes v. Bidwell</u>, 182 US 244 (1901), Justice Harlan said:

> "The idea prevails with some, indeed it has found expression in arguments at the bar, that we have in this country substantially two national governments; one to be maintained under the Constitution, with all of its restrictions; the other to be maintained by Congress outside and independent of that instrument, by exercising such power as other nations of the earth are accustomed to…I take leave to say that, if the principles thus announced should ever receive the sanction of a majority of this court, a radical and mischievous change in our system of government will result. We will, in

that event, pass from the era of constitutional liberty, guarded and protected by a written constitution into an era of legislative absolutism…IT WILL BE AN EVIL DAY FOR AMERICAN LIBERTY IF THE THEORY OF A GOVERNMENT OUTSIDE THE SUPREME LAW OF THE LAND FINDS LODGEMENT IN OUR CONSTITUTIONAL JURISPRUDENCE. No higher duty rests upon this court than to exert its full authority to prevent all violations of the principles of the Constitution." [emphasis in original]

In other words, Congress is free to impose a "nanny state" tax such as FICA (without regard to issues such as whether or not it is an excise) because places like Puerto Rico, Guam, American Samoa, etc. ***belong*** to the United States.

The states of the Union, however, do ***not*** belong to Congress.

Possibly you think I am mistaken about those places "belonging" to the U.S.?

Title 48, section 731, of the United States Code:

> *"The provisions of this chapter shall apply to the island of Puerto Rico and to the adjacent islands belonging to the United States…."*

Or phrased another way, U.S. territories and possessions are not parties to the contract known as the U.S. Constitution. The various protections that exist in that document for the states of the Union (and by association for the citizens of the states of the Union) are not applicable to the territories and possessions. In short, the President and Congress rule the territories and possessions much like King George III and Parliament ruled the 13 colonies.

This legislative distinction of "here versus there" is not used only in tax law. Not by a long shot!

The Federal Firearms Act, passed in 1938, relies on the same masquerade. The Act is written to give Congress regulatory control over certain movements of firearms and destructive devices. However, those who drafted the legislation were crafty with their legislative language. Their choice of words was very subtle and requires a practiced and discerning eye to see it for what it is. Nevertheless, the reality is that they wrote the law to give Congress regulatory authority over firearms and destructive devices moving from one federal "place" *within a state* to another federal "place" *within a state*. So what are these federal "places"? They're spelled out for us in the U.S. Constitution!

Congress will "exercise exclusive legislation in all cases whatsoever…over all ***places*** purchased by the consent of the legislature of the state…." Article I, Section 8, Clause 17 of the U.S. Constitution.

The handshake provision is:

"The Congress shall have power to dispose of and make all needful rules and regulations respecting the territory or other property ***belonging*** to the United States…." Article IV, Section 3, Clause 2 of the U.S. Constitution.

Is this coming into focus for you now? There's a shell game being played on you. Congress is passing legislation for one *United States* and then people in the other *United States* are being harassed and even jailed for non-compliance with it. And what permits this? Ignorance and fear.

In the Federal Firearms Act, Congress put forth a novel "species" of interstate commerce authority. The Federal Firearms Act gives Congress control over firearms and destructive devices that move between:

1. One federal "place" in a state, and any location outside that state.
2. A federal "place" in a state, and any U.S. possession or territory (and visa versa, of course).
3. Any U.S. possession or territory and any other U.S. possession or territory.

In its Statement of Purpose at the beginning of the Federal Firearms Act, Congress expressed a desire to assist the states in controlling crime associated with firearms. You will note that the Constitution grants Congress no power to assist the states with ordinary crime. (Remember Jefferson and Madison's remarks about the role of the federal government being almost entirely restricted to matters of foreign intercourse?)

Some very enterprising lawyers within government decided to use the "exercise exclusive legislation…over all ***places***" clause and the "all needful rules and regulations respecting…property ***belonging*** to the United States" clause of the U.S. Constitution to structure restrictions upon firearms being transported from, or between, various ***places*** that belong to the *United States*. They then made a special definition (which they entitled "interstate or foreign commerce") to constrict the Act to just that limited scope. Federal courts have been ruling it constitutional and putting people in jail under its various provisions for 7 decades! But why not? Not one person has *ever* argued its special limited scope. What is the old adage? "You snooze, you lose." When dealing with Congress maybe it should be, "You snooze, you go to prison". How's that for a servant government of a free people?

My point is that this "here/there" distinction is neither new nor rare in federal law. It is a common legislative ploy by Congress and it works well. And guess what? The courts know all about it and never say a word! Their position is that if you don't raise the issue, they'll laugh heartily as you get marched off to prison in chains. (Some folks contend that if you raise the issue you'll still get marched off in chains, but since no one has ever raised it, that's speculative.)

We have concluded our examination of the first part of the con-job by exploring the inane claims of those who control payroll matters in the private sector within the states of the Union; claims that they have to deduct and withhold FICA. Not only do they not "have to", they are not ***allowed*** to do so!

Let us move on to the rest of the "payroll withholding" issues.

Most Americans who work for a company, or another person, are familiar with a Form W-4. It is entitled "Employees Withholding Allowance Certificate". The "common wisdom" (i.e. ignorance) is that every worker must complete a Form W-4 when he begins working for a company.

Many companies will violate the law and say that you cannot work for them unless you complete a Form W-4. Remember the story of the CEO?

I say "violate the law" because in reality there is no law in existence that requires – *or permits* – an American working in the private sector to fill out a Form W-4. If the Secretary's regulations say that *only* government workers are to complete the Form W-4, then they are the only people *permitted* to do so.

This is tax law we're talking about. People who work in accounting, payroll, human resources, the legal dept. etc., are not permitted to just make it up as they go along. They are not permitted to say, "Well, I know there's no actual requirement in the law but the company insists on this as a condition of working here." Oh, really? Do you also require Jews to convert to Christianity as a condition requisite to working for the company? If you can't insist that a Jew convert to Christianity as a condition for employment, then you can't insist that a person surrender his property rights as a condition for employment. And again, **_there is no law that requires a Form W-4 to be completed by a worker in the private sector_**!

As stated earlier, the regulations for all "Employment Taxes" are found in Part 31 of the CFR. So let's look at these regulations and see what the Secretary has to say about completing a Form W-4!

We have already explored FICA in great detail so we will begin by looking at the rest of "Employment Taxes".

Any investigation of the regulations should begin with a review of the foundational statements the Secretary felt compelled to make in the opening sections of Part 31. These "foundational" sections speak to certain specific definitions as well as the scope of the regulations in Part 31. The sections to which I refer are 15 pages in length, so I'll simply share with you the relevant items. (As always, if you have questions, read the entire section at a law library or on the internet.)

The first of these sections is 31.0-2, entitled . At 31.0-2(a)(1) the Secretary states:

The terms defined in the provision of the law contained in the regulations in this part shall have the meaning so assigned to them.

What the Secretary is saying is that definitions provided elsewhere in the Code, or "general definitions", are not applicable to Part 31 if the Secretary has provided specific definitions within Part 31.

Part 31 serves a particular purpose and in order to achieve those ends Congress and the Secretary have adopted definitions that suit their purpose – and we must adhere to them.

At 31.0-2(a)(7) we find the definition of :

> *District director means district director of internal revenue. The term also includes the Director of International Operations in all cases where the authority to perform the functions which may be performed by a district director has been delegated to the Director of International Operations.*

Once again we see that any time we read that a "district director" is given authority to do something, that same authority is given to the "Director of International Operations" (whose title was later changed to "Assistant Commissioner, International").

This is repeated and reinforced in the general "Procedures and Administration" regulations in Part 301. 301.7701-10 reads:

> *The term district director means the district director of internal revenue for an internal revenue district. The term also includes the Assistant Commissioner (International).*

What we see is that this "dual role" is operative in tax administration generally (Part 301) as well as in "Employment Taxes" specifically (Part 31).

The next foundational definition provided by the Secretary is at 31.0-2(a)(10) and is the definition of "Account number". The definition states:

> *Account number means the identifying number of an employee assigned, as the case may be, under the Internal Revenue Code of 1954, under Subchapter A of Chapter 9 of the Internal Revenue Code of 1939, or under Title VIII of the Social Security Act. See also Sec. 301.7701-11 of this chapter (Regulations on Procedure and Administration).*

Clearly this is indicating a Social Security Number (SSN). Although a reference that uses the word "see" is not controlling, it is provided for clarity. So let us "see" what 301.7701-11 has to say.

> *For purposes of this chapter, the term social security number means the taxpayer identifying number of an individual or estate which is assigned pursuant to section 6011(b) or corresponding provisions of prior law, or pursuant to section 6109, and in which nine digits are*

> *separated by hyphens as follows: 000-00-0000. The terms "account number" and "social security number" refer to the same number.*

So, the Secretary's general regulations (i.e. Procedures and Administration) at 301.7701-11 say that "account number" and "social security number" refer to the same number. Then, when the Secretary writes his regulations for "Employment Taxes" (Part 31), he gives us the definition of account number that is exact and specific to "Employment Taxes".

Directly after *Account Number* we find 31.0-2(a)(11), which is entitled "Identification number".

> *Identification number means the identifying number of an employer assigned, as the case may be, under the Internal Revenue Code of 1954, under Subchapter A or D of Chapter 9 of the Internal Revenue Code of 1939, or under Title VIII of the Social Security Act. See also Sec. 301.7701-12 of this chapter (Regulations on Procedure and Administration).*

You will notice that this description is identical to the description of *account number* except that "301.7701-11" has changed by just one digit, to "301.7701-1".

301.7701-12:

> *For purposes of this chapter, the term employer identification number means the taxpayer identifying number of an individual or other person (whether or not an employer) which is assigned pursuant to section 6011(b) or corresponding provisions of prior law, or pursuant to section 6109, and in which nine digits are separated by a hyphen, as follows: 00-0000000. The terms "employer identification number" and "identification number" (defined in Sec. 31.0-2(a)(11) of this chapter (Employment Tax Regulations)) refer to the same number.*

I won't go into the specifics of the language because I'm sure you'll see it for yourself, but the **only** difference between an account number and *identification number* is that the former is assigned to "an individual or estate" while the latter is assigned to "an individual or other person". What the Secretary is saying is that an *account number* is for a human or the estate of a human, and the *identification number* is for either a human or an entity.

Employment Taxes, like everything else in the Code, rely on specific narrow definitions in order to tailor a statute's application to Congress' intended purposes. The terms *"employee"* and *"employer"* feature prominently in this methodology. Not only do these terms have specific narrow definitions, but these definitions change considerably as one travels through the Code!

Those who mistakenly believe there is just one meaning for such terms might do well to ask themselves why Congress (as well as the Secretary) chose to change the definitions throughout the Code. Since some of these definitions are not even remotely similar, the only logical reason to change the definitions is to adjust the meanings into alignment with Congress' intended purpose for each area of tax law.

Let me give you an example.

At 7701(a)(20), *"Employee"* is defined as:

> *For the purpose of applying the provisions of section 79 with respect to group-term life insurance purchased for employees, for the purpose of applying the provisions of sections 104, 105, and 106 with respect to accident and health insurance or accident and health plans, and for the purpose of applying the provisions of subtitle A with respect to contributions to or under a stock bonus, pension, profit-sharing, or annuity plan, and with respect to distributions under such a plan, or by a trust forming part of such a plan, and for purposes of applying section 125 with respect to cafeteria plans, the term ''employee'' shall include a full-time life insurance salesman who is considered an employee for the purpose of chapter 21, or in the case of services performed before January 1, 1951, who would be considered an employee if his services were performed during 1951.*

Compare that to the definition we've already covered at 3401(c) - (addressing payroll withholding):

> *For purposes of this chapter, the term "employee" includes an officer, employee, or elected official of the United States, a State, or any political subdivision thereof, or the District of Columbia, or any agency or instrumentality of any one or more of the foregoing. The term "employee" also includes an officer of a corporation.*

Section 3231(b) defines *"employee"* as:

> *For purposes of this chapter, the term "employee" means any individual in the service of one or more employers....*

So who is the *"employer"* in the above case? 3231(a) states:

> *For purposes of this chapter, the term "employer" means any carrier...which operates any equipment or facility or performs any service...in connection with the <u>transportation of passengers or property by railroad [underline added]</u>*

That makes *"employee"* (at 3231(b)) someone who works for the railroads.

Hopefully you have already noticed that these three examples (of which there are many more) are all completely different definitions. Although they use the same word – *employee* – each has a completely different meaning!

And you'll notice that each section qualifies its limited application by language such as "For purposes of this chapter" or "For the purpose of this section" or "For the purpose of applying the provisions of section…." If every time Congress used the term *"employee"* (or any term) the meaning was to be the same, Congress would not have provided separate and distinct definitions, nor would Congress have specifically limited the definitions to a particular segment of the law.

If it seems I am belaboring this point, it is because some people will want to reject narrow meanings of the definitions and the limited application of the statutes thereunder. They will want to do so because it's easier to maintain the facade if one rejects the truth. To accept the definitions means two things. First, it means that no private company in the 50 states has any legal justification to take money out of the paychecks of American citizens under the guise of "tax law". Second, it means the U.S. government cannot be trusted. For decades now the U.S. government has sat by and received more money than we can even contemplate based on promoting a lie; based on allowing the "myths" to continue to be propagated.

You will remember that I call the income tax "the largest financial crime in the history of the world." The root of this crime is fraud.

- contracts, torts. Any <u>trick or artifice employed by one person to induce another to fall into an error</u>, or to detain him in it, so that he may make an agreement contrary to his interest. <u>The fraud may consist either, first, in the misrepresentation, or, secondly, in the</u> [emphasis added] Bouvier's Law Dictionary

Let's break that definition down in light of what the U.S. government is doing.

- Congress and the Secretary have re-defined words from their ordinary meaning to special legal meanings. While lawyers see this as standard operating procedure (and indeed it is) you have intentionally been kept in the dark about it. I'd certainly call that a "trick or artifice".

- The government has watched people wrongly apply the "plain meaning" of these terms for at least 50 years without uttering so much as a single corrective peep. I'd certainly call that intentional "concealment of a material fact."

- And finally, who is the recipient of the property illegally taken by trick or artifice; said trick and artifice kept operative by concealment of a material fact? It is the U.S. government.

It is Congress who created the special definitions that no one ever told you about. It is Congress and the Treasury Department who have chosen to remain silent all these many decades about the misapplication of the Code. And it is Congress and Treasury who receive the massive, illegally acquired wealth.

And what did the famous U.S. Supreme Court justice, Joseph Story, write about fraud?

"An actual or positive fraud is the intentional and successful employment of any cunning, deception, or artifice, used to circumvent, cheat, or deceive another."

Is there anyone who understands the reality of subtitles 'A' and 'C' who does not believe that Justice Story's description fits the government's actions to a tee?

But I digress. Back to payroll withholding.

At 31.3401(f)(1)-1, the Secretary discusses the exemptions one can take from payroll withholding. In 31.3401(f)(1)-1(a)(1) he states:

> *"In general... an employee receiving wages shall on any day be entitled to withholding exemptions as provided in section 3402(f)(1)."*

OK; that's clear enough. What are these exemptions in 3402(f)(1) of the Code? At 3402(f)(1)(a)(1) it states:

> *An employee receiving wages shall on any day be entitled to the following withholding exemptions:*
> *(A) an exemption for himself unless he is an individual described in section 151 (d)(2);*

Huh? What was that?

According to this statute we are to refer to an equation in subtitle 'A'. How can that be? We already know that subtitle 'A' has been imposed by Congress on *foreign persons* and *U.S. citizens residing abroad with foreign-earned income*. Isn't payroll withholding affected upon various government workers who are American citizens living and working in the 50 states? If so, then how can we be commanded to use an equation that is about *foreign persons* and *U.S. citizens residing abroad with foreign-earned income*?

But wait! How did you come to the conclusion that section 3402 commands withholding on various government workers who are American citizens living and working in the 50 states? Ah, yes – you made an ***assumption***! Need I say more?

By directing us to chapter 1 of subtitle 'A', Congress is telling us that we need to use the "rules of computation" (which are chapters 1 and 2) for the tax that is upon *foreign persons* and *U.S. citizens residing abroad with foreign-earned income* in order to determine the proper exemptions for the *employee* being withheld from under 3402. How very interesting – and informative.

Furthermore, sections 3402 and 151 are "handshake" sections. In other words, they work together for a common purpose. Allow me to explain.

It is not Congress' intent to take more from a person in withholding than that person may owe in taxes. Thus, Congress permits "withholding exemptions" in order that one may adjust the amount taken from his paycheck to be roughly equivalent to what he anticipates he will owe at the end of the year.

But how might one reasonably anticipate the amount one owes at the end of the year? This should not be guesswork, nor does Congress intend it to be so.

This brings us directly to section 151, entitled "Allowance of deductions for personal exemptions". Under section 151 the "taxpayer" – and we know who those are under subtitle 'A' – is entitled to an "exemption amount" of $2,000.00 a year.

That's the amount for one single person. Accordingly, the "***withholding*** exemption" for a single (non-married) person is set to adjust one's payroll withholding to reflect that person's "***personal*** exemption". Or phrased another way, there is an intentionally designed one-to-one relationship between the "***withholding*** exemption" at 3402 (subtitle 'C') and the "***personal*** exemption" at 151 (subtitle 'A').

I can almost hear you thinking, "Hmmm. But wouldn't that mean that the *withholding exemption* and *personal exemption* both pertain to *foreign persons* and/or *U.S. citizens residing abroad with foreign earned income*?" Now you're getting it!

And, since you are starting to get the picture, let's go back and look at the opening words of 3402(a)(1):

> *Except as otherwise provided in this section, every employer making payment of wages shall deduct and withhold upon such wages a tax determined in accordance with....*

Earlier in this chapter we looked at a number of sections that imposed taxes. In each case there was language such as, "There is hereby ***imposed*** a tax upon…." Now compare that to the language in 3402: "…every *employer…shall deduct and withhold upon such wages a tax….*" Clearly this section dictates a "collection mechanism", not the imposition of a tax.

Since it does not impose a tax, but simply commands the collection of "a tax" already imposed elsewhere in the code, what tax is it?

You notice I put the phrase "a tax" in quotes. That's exactly how Congress worded it! Congress said that the employer is to withhold "a tax". Clearly the men who drafted 3402 intended to be evasive by that language. There is no *legislative draftsman* on the planet who would adopt that language for a tax statute unless he was setting out from the inception to deprive the reader of necessary information – such as which tax "a tax" actually is!

Despite this intentional act of vagueness and evasion, these l*egislative draftsmen* know there has to be <u>something</u> in the statute to direct the reader to what tax the phrase "a tax" is describing.

And let's be frank, in this instance the *legislative draftsmen* did set out to hide something from the reader. But, if they hide it in one place, they have to reveal it elsewhere in the statute. *Legislative draftsmen* may lead us on an Easter egg hunt to find the prize, but which tax is being collected has to be revealed somewhere, in some manner, or Congress' purpose would be rendered "unknowable" – and that Congress does not permit. *Legislative draftsmen* can play games with "construction" of a statute to some extent, but Congress will never allow the *draftsmen* to shorn the statute of Congress' intended purpose.

The subtle mechanism used in this case is to tie the exemptions back to subtitle 'A'. In doing so Congress is telling us that "a tax" is the tax imposed in subtitle 'A' – in other words, the "income tax".

Let's explore these a little further.

In chapter 7, I explained that section 61 – the definition of *gross income* – only applied to those upon whom Congress had imposed subtitle 'A'. So let's revisit section 61 for a moment.

The very first item on the list is

Compensation for services is a phrase that is used repeatedly in the Code and the regulations.

The phrase "compensation for <u>labor</u>" was long ago addressed by the U.S. Supreme Court and denotes our **unalienable right to contract** and to receive the remuneration agreed upon in the contract.

Because *compensation for labor* has a well-settled meaning, *legislative draftsmen* settled on the phrase *compensation for services* to describe work that is subject to an excise [privilege] tax. *Compensation for services* is the labor earnings from *trade or business*.

This is great time to revisit 3401(a) – the definition of "wages" for the purpose of payroll withholding.

> *For purposes of this chapter, the term "wages" means all remuneration (other than fees paid to a public official) for services performed by an employee...*

You will note that it says, *"remuneration...for services"*. "Remuneration" is a synonym for "compensation". (You can verify that with any handy thesaurus.) Sections 61 and 3401 are talking about the same thing. One uses "compensation for services" while the other uses its synonym, "remuneration for services". It should be pointed out that "compensation" and "remuneration" are not defined by Congress in the Tax Code and therefore must be used in their natural meaning. (The exception is that "compensation" is defined in chapter 22 as the earnings of railroad *employee*s.)

In other words, the "wages" defined at 3401(a) is the same type of payment as described in section 61, "compensation for services". But of course the kicker is that subtitle 'A' has been imposed only upon *foreign persons* deriving U.S. source income and U.S. citizens with foreign income.

Are there any other links between the tax imposed in subtitle 'A' and the withholding at 3402? Yes.

> *Section 31(a)(1) - The amount withheld as tax under chapter 24 shall be allowed to the recipient of the income as a credit against the tax imposed by this subtitle.*

It doesn't get much clearer than that!

If one has had payroll withholding performed under the provisions of chapter 24, then the amounts withheld are to be credited against the tax owed under subtitle 'A'. Since section 3402 does not impose a tax, but rather mandates the collection of "a tax", there should now be no question which tax that is.

"Employee" – Who, Me?

[: Chapter 24 contains more than just payroll withholding. It also contains provisions such as *backup withholding*. We are focusing only on payroll withholding here because that is the subject of this chapter.]

Is there still more? You bet.

If you remember, in chapter 7 we spent considerable time in the area of 1.1441, which of course addresses the collection of the income tax from *foreign persons*. Well, at 1.1441-4(c)(2) we find this:

"A withholding agent may elect to withhold on the amounts described in paragraph (c)(1) of this section at the rates applicable under section 3402, as if the income were wages. Such election shall be made by obtaining a Form W-4...from the beneficial owner. The fact that the withholding agent asks the beneficial owner to furnish a Form W-4...shall serve as notice to the beneficial owner that the income is being treated as wages for purposes of withholding tax under section 1441."

In other words, a *withholding agent* [and we know what that terms means!] can choose to withhold from certain income of a *foreign person* as if the income were "wages", simply by having the *foreign person* complete a Form W-4.

Let me ask you a question. If a *withholding agent* can withhold at the rates under 3402 by simply having the *foreign person* fill out a Form W-4, how does anyone tasked with administrating tax law know the difference between a *foreign person's* W-4 and an American's W-4? The simple answer is, they don't. But if the Form W-4's proper use is restricted to withholding by the government on the remuneration paid to *foreign persons* who are working for the government (i.e. the *employee*), then there wouldn't be any need to distinguish between the two, would there? Right! And that is exactly the proper role of the Form W-4. There is no legal role for the Form W-4 outside of government. Or phrased another way, there is no legal role for Form W-4 in the private sector.

The Form W-2 is an "information return". Its purpose is to report amounts subject to taxation under either subtitle 'A' (income tax) or subtitle 'C' (FICA tax), or both. Please note that there is no other purpose for this return. While there are boxes on the form that speak to State taxes, the W-2 is a federal form and the requirement to file one is based on federal taxation, not state issues.

Let's take a moment and go over the typical chronology of events that leads up to the filing of Form W-2.

The traditional routine is that a company unlawfully demands a worker complete a Form W-4 when the worker begins working for the company. When the worker provides the Form W-4 he is attesting (under penalty of perjury no less) to the fact that he is a *foreign person* subject to the payroll withholding under 3402. The worker normally provides his SSN on the W-4, which of course in that context serves as his TIN! The corrupt practice of demanding a Form W-4 as a condition of working in America results in the company receiving what it sees as a "permission slip" from the worker to steal his property. I say "steal" because workers are rarely permitted to obey the law by not completing a Form W-4.

I have worked with many people over the years who have educated themselves concerning who is required to complete a Form W-4 and who is not. The informed worker will often tell the company that he is not required to complete a Form W-4 and that without a signed W-4 and a TIN the company has no legal authority to withhold any taxes from his paycheck. In all my years of involvement with these matters no company has ever claimed to have the legal authority to withhold without a signed W-4 and a TIN. They know they cannot. So what is their response? Normally it is, "You cannot work here without signing a W-4." Really? And where is that in the law? Nowhere, of course! It's just more of the same; people who are tasked with payroll matters and have no idea what the law says. They just make it up as they go because they have no idea what they're talking about.

And let me repeat something. There is no law anywhere that forbids a private sector company in any of the states of the Union from hiring a citizen and paying him his full compensation for labor (with absolutely no deductions) without ever receiving a Form W-4. Or maybe I should phrase it in an alternate manner so that payroll people can understand it. There is no law that authorizes you to terminate a worker because he knows the law and declines to fill out a Form W-4!

"Employee" – Who, Me?

What companies rely on in this circumstance is the "at will" employment statutes that permit companies to fire workers in the first few weeks or months for any reason or no reason at all. But this is a corrupt and illegal application of the "at will" doctrine.

Imagine that a woman is hired to be an administrative assistant at a large architectural firm. Her direct supervisor is a Project Director who works directly with the firm's architects. After a week or so on the job, the Project Director lets the administrative assistant know that if she wishes to keep her job she must perform oral sex on him. She refuses and is terminated under the "at will" law of that state.

Who is it among you who believes this is a moral, proper, and lawful application of the "at will" doctrine? It may seem too obvious to comment upon, but "why" do we see this as wrong?

We see it as wrong for several reasons. We see it as wrong because the Project Director has no moral right to make such a demand of the administrative assistant. We see it as wrong because the Project Director has no legal right to make such a demand of the administrative assistant. And we see this as wrong because the demand has no connection to the business of the firm.

And ultimately we see it as unjust because the worker was harmed – made to pay a price – for standing upon her right to say "no" to a request that was neither moral nor legal. In other words, she was 100% within her rights to resist the illegal request and yet she was punished for doing so.

As you have likely surmised, this is exactly how the informed worker is treated when he declines to complete a W-4.

- The company has no legal right to demand a W-4 as a condition to work.
- The worker is 100% within his right to refuse to sign a W-4.
- Signing or not signing a W-4 does not affect the service or product the company sells to the public.
- There is no law (when applied properly) that permits the company to terminate a worker for following the law.

Despite these plain parallels, most companies don't see any problem with misusing the "at will" doctrine to harm an American who is standing upon his property rights and upon the law.

I say all of that to bring to your attention the reality that the Form W-4 is the prerequisite to issuance of the Form W-2. Without a Form W-4 there can be no payroll withholding under the guise of 3402, and therefore there can be no W-2 at the end of the year.

How do we know that the Form W-2 is tied to payroll withholding?

Section 1.6041-2(a) states:

> *Wages, as defined in section 3401, paid to an employee are required to be reported on Form W-2. See section 6011 and the Employment Tax Regulations thereunder.*

There are a couple of things to consider in that provision. First – and quite significantly – you will note that it says "*Wages, as defined in section 3401....*" In other words, the Secretary is being crystal clear that "wages" is not to be given its "plain meaning", but that the definition in 3401 is the *only* "wages" being addressed. I said earlier that the definitions Congress and/or the Secretary choose to employ are pivotal because the definitions tailor the provision to the exact (limited) purpose intended by Congress/the Secretary. 1.6041-2 is a perfect example of this concept in operation.

We can see that if one is paid "wages" (as defined in section 3401) then a Form W-2 must be prepared and submitted at the end of the year.

Now we come to something truly significant that you may not have immediately realized. This regulation – 1.6041-2 – is in Part 1! Part 1 is the regulations for the income tax. Or phrased another way, Part 1 is the regulations for subtitle 'A'. And upon whom has Congress imposed subtitle 'A'? Nonresident aliens, foreign entities, and U.S. citizens residing abroad with foreign-earned income. Understanding this, we now find a regulation in Part 1 that talks about "wages", as defined in 3401 (which is subtitle 'C')! In other words, the tax that is being *collected* under authority of 3402 is the tax *imposed* by subtitle 'A'.

The regulation then tells us to see section 6011 (in the Code) and the "Employment Tax Regulations thereunder". Since the employment tax regulations are in Part 31, we'd be looking at 31.6011.

So what does 6011 say?

"Employee" — Who, Me?

When required by regulations prescribed by the Secretary any person made liable for any tax imposed by this title, or with respect to the collection thereof, shall make a return or statement according to the forms and regulations prescribed by the Secretary.

You will notice that 6011 states that the responsibility to make a return or statement falls upon the "person made liable". And of course Congress, not the Secretary, designates who is liable.

So…who has been "made liable" in Employment Taxes? Here are the words of Congress:

Section 3403 – *The **employer** shall be liable for the payment of the tax required to be deducted and withheld under this chapter, and shall not be liable to any person for the amount of any such payment.* [emphasis added]

And of course we know that just two sections earlier, at 3401(d), Congress defined "*employer*" as government entities and instrumentalities.

Let's take a moment to summarize what we have discovered so far.

What we can clearly see is that Congress has defined "wages" as only being earned by the "employee". Congress has defined "employee" as various government workers and the "employer" as the entity or instrumentality for which the "employee" works. Form W-4 is only to be filled out by an "employee". The "employee" who is to fill out a Form W-4 is the same person upon whom Congress has imposed subtitle 'A' (income tax), and that is a nonresident alien deriving U.S. source income as well as a U.S. citizen residing abroad with foreign-earned income. When the nonresident alien deriving U.S. source income or the U.S. citizen residing abroad with foreign-earned income has been withheld from after completing a Form W-4, the "*employer*" must (under authority of 6011) report the withholding upon "wages" on a Form W-2.

At this point, let's look at the *Employment Tax* regulations concerning section 6011.

Section 6011 of the Code is entitled "General requirement of return, statement, or list". Remember, the U.S. Supreme Court referred to Congress' words as "the broad language of the statute." And the purpose of the regulations is to provide the specificity that may be lacking in the statute.

Here's the list of regulations for 6011 within Part 31 (Employment Taxes).

31.6011(a)-1 Returns under Federal Insurance Contributions Act
31.6011(a)-2 Returns under Railroad Retirement Tax Act
31.6011(a)-3 Returns under Federal Unemployment Tax Act
31.6011(a)-3A Returns of the Railroad Unemployment Repayment Tax
31.6011(a)-4 Returns of income tax withheld

Let's see now... We know the first one doesn't have anything to do with the average American because we've already covered FICA in detail. The second is exclusive to the railroads. The third deals with federal employees (and state funding). The fourth [3A] is again exclusively about railroads. That brings us to the fifth regulation (numbered 31.6011(a)-4), which is entitled "Returns of Income Tax Withheld." So, what return is required under 31.6011(a)-4?

> "*...every person required to make a return of income tax withheld from wages pursuant to section 3402 shall make a return for the first calendar quarter in which the person is required to deduct and withhold such tax....*" "*...Form 941 is the form prescribed for making the return required under this paragraph.*"

We see that the only section that sounds like it might be general in application – "Returns of Income Tax Withheld" – is actually specific to the "employer" who has withheld from the "wages" of the "employee" (who is a nonresident alien or U.S. citizen residing abroad with foreign-earned income). It is the "employer" (as defined at 3401(d)) who is to file a Form 941 quarterly. (There are others who can be designated to file returns such as the 941, but they are designated to do so in lieu of the actual "employer".)

You should also take note that the requirement for an *information return*, found in the "income tax" regulations at 1.6041-2, is 100% coordinated with the requirement to file a tax return, found in the Employment Tax regulations at 31.6011(a)-4. Section 1.6041-2 requires the *employer* to file an *information return* with the IRS about the withholding that has been affected upon the nonresident alien or the U.S. citizen residing abroad with foreign-earned income. Section

31.6011(a)-4 requires the *employer* to file a tax return with the IRS concerning the liability it incurred under 3403 by the act of withholding the tax.

One might ask what is the status of the withheld tax money between the time it is withheld and the time it is paid over to the Treasury. For that we turn to section 7501 of the Code.

> *Whenever any person is required to collect or withhold any internal revenue tax from any other person and to pay over such tax to the United States, the amount of tax so collected or withheld shall be held to be a special fund in trust for the United States. The amount of such fund shall be assessed, collected, and paid in the same manner and subject to the same provisions and limitations (including penalties) as are applicable with respect to the taxes from which such fund arose.*

We have traveled through a significant amount of information concerning *Employment Taxes*. You can now better understand the title of this chapter - "Employee – Who, Me?"

The statues are the law. Regulations (when properly promulgated) have the "full force and effect of law". Treasury Department or IRS Forms and publications are not law and we are not permitted to rely on them; so says the Treasury Department. We may however look at them to satisfy ourselves that our understanding of the law, and that of the IRS, is commensurate.

IRS Form 8233 is entitled "Exemption From Withholding on Compensation for Independent (and Certain Dependent) Personal Services of a Nonresident Alien Individual". The instructions for 8233 begin with a section entitled, "Purpose of Form". Here is what it says is the form's purpose:

> *In general, section 1441 requires 30% federal income tax withholding on compensation for independent personal services (defined on this page). Sections 1441, 3401, and 3402 require withholding, and sometimes graduated rates, on compensation for dependent <u>personal services</u> (defined on page 2). However, some payments may be exempt from withholding because of a tax treaty or the personal exemption amount. Complete and give Form 8233 to your withholding agent if some or all of your compensation is exempt from withholding.*
> [underline added]

This form is for the exclusive use of a *nonresident alien* (i.e. an "individual" as defined in chapter 3 of the Code). Form 8233 references 1441, 3401, and 3402. It states that payments to the *nonresident alien* may be subject to a withholding exemption under a tax treaty or because of the *personal exemption* amount, which we discussed previously in this chapter.

I underlined the words "personal service" because when section 61 (definition of *gross income*) speaks of "compensation for services" it is referring to the *personal services* of a nonresident alien.

There are some other very informative parts of Form 8233. There is a section entitled "Compensation for Independent Personal Services", which states:

> *Independent personal services are services performed as an independent contractor in the United States by a nonresident alien who is self-employed rather than an employee.*

Whenever you read about an "independent contractor" in the Code or regulations, ***that*** is who it means.

Another section is "Compensation for Dependent Personal Services" which states:

> *Dependent personal services are services performed as an employee in the United States by a nonresident alien. Compensation for such services includes wages, salaries, fees, bonuses, commissions, and similar designations for amounts paid to an employee.*

And yes, *"employee"* as used on the Form's instructions is the *employee* defined at 3401(c).

Here is an "example" given on Form 8233's instructions to provide clarity:

> *A nonresident alien is primarily present in the United States as a professor, but also is occasionally invited to lecture at another educational institution. These lectures are not connected with his teaching obligations but are in the nature of self-employment. For each tax year, the professor must complete two Forms 8233 and give*

> *one to each withholding agent to claim tax treaty benefits on the separate items of income.*

The instructions go on to explain that Form 8233 should only be used when claiming a deduction from withholding pursuant to a tax treaty (as in the example provided above). And then this:

> *For compensation for which you are not claiming a tax treaty withholding exemption, use Form W-4, Employee's Withholding Allowance Certificate.*

There is then a section entitled, "Completing Form W-4":

> *You are required to enter a social security number (SSN) on line 2 of Form W-4. If you do not have an SSN, you must apply for one on Form SS-5, Application for Social Security Card.*

Remember all that political hubbub a few years back about whether to allow aliens to have driver's licenses? DMVs around the country will only issue a driver's license to a person with a SSN because only Americans can get a SSN, right? WRONG! Not only can aliens get a SSN, they are mandated to do so by certain provisions of tax law! How come no one in government told you about *that* when everyone was saying that only an American can get a SSN?

But that is not really the significant point of what 8233 says. The main point is that it clearly states that a nonresident alien is to use a Form W-4! And that means he's the same guy that is to receive a W-2 at the end of the year. Form 8233 is confirming, in plain English, what we've explored in this chapter concerning payroll withholding.

Even at this point some folks might be saying, "But Dave, that form is only about foreigners." Exactly! And this is the kicker – there is **nothing** in the statutes, the regulations, or the myriad of IRS forms that says that a U.S. citizen, living and working in one of the 50 states, is required to fill out a Form W-4.

Given what you have seen (or maybe what you "haven't seen") in Congress' statutes and in the Secretary's regulations, isn't it amazing that *anyone* in the private sector is *ever* asked to fill out a Form W-4? And of course it is often worse than that, because most do not request, but rather a *demand!*

Now you can see how arrogant and abusive of your rights such a demand is. In the next chapter we'll discuss what happens when these functionaries demand – out of raw unadulterated ignorance – that you sign a tax document that doesn't apply to you, and how it affects you when/if you submit to such an unlawful demand!

Working the Marks

Chapter 9

I do not feel obliged to believe that the same God who has endowed us with sense, reason, and intellect has intended us to forgo their use."
~ Galileo Galilei

The title of this chapter – Working The Mark – takes its meaning from the world of con-men who run "confidence games". A "mark" is con-man language for "victim".

Confidence game - *A swindle in which the victim is defrauded after his or her confidence has been won.* Answers.com

It should be clear to you by now that the income tax (subtitle 'A'), and Employment Taxes (subtitle 'C') have nothing to do with the average American. If that is so, how can it be that a nation of supposedly free men and women remains in bondage to a proposition so demonstrably false?

There are many reasons, but here are the leading ones:

1. ***Ignorance/Laziness***. Most Americans would rather be robbed than spend time getting educated.

2. ***Fear***. Since Americans do not bother to get educated, they fear trying to disengage from the tax system, even if they know (or sense) that something is not proper about the income tax.

3. ***Government terrorism***. Americans fear acts of terrorism committed by the U.S. government. Stealing money out of your bank account without a court order is terrorism. Stealing your vehicle out of your driveway

without a court order is terrorism. Getting a company to unlawfully steal your paycheck without a court order is terrorism.

Why do I say these acts are terrorism? Because they are.

There are many definitions of "terrorism". Dictionaries define it differently, statutes define it differently, and virtually every nation defines it differently. But here is a definition from a United Nations resolution that gives what I believe is a suitable general definition.

> *Criminal acts intended or calculated to provoke a state of terror in the general public, a group of persons or particular persons **for political purposes** are in any circumstance unjustifiable, whatever the considerations of a political, philosophical, ideological, racial, ethnic, religious or any other nature that may be invoked to justify them.* General Assembly resolution 49/60, adopted on December 9, 1994 [emphasis added]

Most definitions of terrorism include the word "violence". You'll note that the definition above does not. Violence need not be committed. In order to create terror in a population all that is really necessary is for the public to know that the terrorist will not hesitate to use violence to achieve its ends. If you aren't already aware that the federal government will resort to violence any time it feels threatened, you may as well close this book now and go back to your Rip Van Winkle existence.

I emphasized "for political reasons" in the definition above because that is exactly what the U.S. government is doing concerning the income tax. It is engaged in an active terror campaign against the peaceful law-abiding population of America in order to maintain the facade that the income tax applies to everyone. Its purpose in doing so is to maintain a political system that could not be sustained without the ill-gotten gains from the largest financial crime in the history of the world.

In other words, the U.S. government steals from you (and hundreds of millions of others) in order to prop up a political system. And, not only is violating the Constitution a violation of the Supreme Law of the Land, but the very political system that is propped up by this violation is itself a violation of the Constitution! Or phrased another way, one massive crime is being committed in order to maintain another massive violation of law, by a group with a political agenda.

There are two ways that the con-men work the mark. One is indirectly and the other is directly. And make no mistake, YOU are the mark!

INDIRECTLY WORKING THE MARK

The indirect side of stealing from you is the less violent of the two, but it is completely pervasive in today's society. This mechanism is the one in which your fellow citizens bully you, or outright steal from you, in order to force you to participate in the income tax scheme.

In daily life, the lynch pin of the entire income tax scheme is the TIN. Please re-read the preceding sentence until it is welded into your consciousness. If you take nothing else away from this book, I want you to take that sentence with you. It is that pivotal.

In his regulations, the Secretary has been kind enough to tell us who is required to provide a TIN on request. These regulations can be found at 301.6109-1(b) & (c).

> (b)(1) - U.S. persons. *Every U.S. person who makes under this title a return, statement, or other document must furnish its own taxpayer identifying number as required by the forms and the accompanying instructions. A U.S. person whose number must be included on a document filed by another person must give the taxpayer identifying number so required to the other person on request. For penalties for failure to supply taxpayer identifying numbers, see sections 6721 through 6724.*

There are a couple of things to consider about this section. First, it speaks exclusively of a *U.S. person* and we already know that term is very limited in its meaning, and does **not** embrace the average American. I'm sure you noticed the word "penalties", and we'll be getting into that down the road a bit.

At this juncture we know that a *U.S. person* is required to furnish a number on a return "it" is required to make. Great. No problem. I completely understand why a *U.S. person* would be required to furnish a number. So far, so good.

Section (b)(2) is very lengthy so I reduced the text to the minimum that will make the point. (As always, feel free to look up the entire text on-line or in a law library.)

> (b)(2) - Foreign persons. *The provisions of paragraph (b)(1) of this section regarding the furnishing of one's own number shall apply to the following foreign persons--*

That's it! There ain't no more! I could go on to list the subsections (i), (ii), (iii), (iv), (v), (vi), (vii), and (viii), but why? They all deal with *foreign persons*.

So now we know that two "classes of persons" are required to furnish a TIN if they are required to file a return. One is a *U.S. person* and the other is a *foreign person*. Isn't it satisfying to see how all the various elements dovetail together perfectly when you know what the tax is actually about?

From 301.6109-1(b) we now go to (c). It is also a bit long, but I think it is worth printing most of it here.

> *301.6109-1(c) - Requirement to furnish another's number. Every person required under this title to make a return, statement, or other document must furnish such taxpayer identifying numbers of other U.S. persons and foreign persons that are described in paragraph (b)(2)(i), (ii), (iii), (vi), (vii), or (viii) of this section as required by the forms and the accompanying instructions. The taxpayer identifying number of any person furnishing a withholding certificate referred to in paragraph (b)(2)(vi) or (viii) of this section shall also be furnished if it is actually known to the person making a return, statement, or other document described in this paragraph (c). If the person making the return, statement, or other document does not know the taxpayer identifying number of the other person, and such other person is one that is described in paragraph (b)(2)(i), (ii), (iii), (vi), (vii), or (viii) of this section, such person must request the other person's number. The request should state that the identifying number is required to be furnished under authority of law. When the person making the return, statement, or other document does not know the number of the other person, and has complied with the request provision of this paragraph (c), such person must sign an affidavit on the transmittal*

document forwarding such returns, statements, or other documents to the Internal Revenue Service, so stating.

So...now we know that if a person is required to file a return, and that return requires the TIN of another, the filer must provide the other person's TIN – if they know it – and they are required to tell the other person that they must provide a TIN "under authority of law".

You will note however that the statement "under authority of law" is only permitted if the other person is *"one that is described in paragraph (b)(2)(i), (ii), (iii), (vi), (vii), or (viii) of this section"*. And who is that? We just saw that (b)(2) addresses **only** *foreign persons*! Isn't it interesting that the Secretary only permits that "under authority of law" statement to be used involving *foreign persons*, and no such language is permitted when an American is involved?

That is the sum total of who is required to furnish a TIN under 301-6109-1. According to the Secretary, only two "classes of persons" are required to furnish a number. One is a *U.S. person* and the other is a *foreign person* – and we already know who those "persons" are!

So where's the section that mandates that the average American furnish a TIN in the conduct of his ordinary personal financial dealings? No such section exists and no such mandate exists.

The Code and its regulations are very precise and narrow concerning the income tax, once you know where to look. For the purposes of subtitle 'A', *U.S. persons* and *foreign persons* are required to furnish a number. For subtitle 'C' purposes, "employees" are required to furnish a SSN and "employers" are required to use an EIN. As far as *identifying numbers* are concerned, that's it!

Wow! Those are the only requirements to furnish a number. That's almost too much to fathom, huh? But more importantly, that is not at all how it works on the street. Which brings us to the point of this portion of the book.

As we discussed earlier in some detail, those who deal with the bureaucracy of tax law have rarely ever read any of the actual law; the authority under which they claim to be acting. That can create havoc and frustration for those who have!

Here's a typical American scenario. An American citizen is living and working in one of the states of the Union. He makes his living repairing copy machines and computers. Most of his customers are businesses. We'll call this citizen, Frank.

When Frank is finished with breakfast and helping to get the kids off to school, he kisses his wife goodbye, jumps in his truck and heads to his first service call of the day. He is to repair a copier at a local auto parts store; Lenny's Auto Parts. It is a new account Frank picked up a few months ago. It's not a big account, but Frank values every one of his customers, small or large. Frank is a small businessman and every dollar counts.

Frank walks in and is greeted by Steve, the store manager. Steve tells Frank to go on back behind the sales counter and do his "magic". Frank is an experienced repair tech and the problem is solved in just a few minutes. He fills out an invoice and on the way out hands it to Steve. Raising his hands in mock surrender Steve says, "Not me, buddy. That goes upstairs to Janice." Steve and Frank chuckle and Frank heads upstairs to drop the invoice with Janice. Frank hasn't met Janice, but he's heard her name and knows that she's in charge of the "back office".

When he walks into the office he sees a middle-aged woman sitting at a desk with the name-plate, "Janice". Frank walks over and introduces himself. Janice has a nice smile and a competent way about her. Frank gives her the 10-second version of the work he performed and tells her that he's leaving the invoice with her on Steve's instructions.

Janice tells Frank that in the future it's OK to leave invoices downstairs with Steve, but that he was directed upstairs on this occasion because she wanted to speak with him. As she's explaining this to Frank she's looking down and methodically thumbing through the file drawer in her desk. She pulls out an 8.5 x 11 piece of paper and places it on the desk in front of Frank. Frank looks down and sees that there are big bold letters on the paper which say, "**Request For Taxpayer Identification Number and Certification**". Frank also sees that it says "W-9" in upper left corner, along with the words "Department of the Treasury, Internal Revenue Service". Janice says, "We've paid you roughly $1,000 so far this year Frank, so I need to get your tax number."

At this point in our saga we need to pause. For many of you this is an all too familiar scenario. In your daily life some of you may be "Frank" and some of you "Janice". There are various ways this may proceed. Some good; some not so good. Let's look at the options.

IGNORANT FRANK

"Sure Janice. Do you have a pen handy?" Janice hands Frank a pen and he fills out his name and places his TIN on the form. He then signs on the line under the "Certification Statement" paragraph that begins with the words "Under penalty of perjury I certify that:"

- The number shown on this form is my correct taxpayer identification number, *and*
- I am not subject to backup withholding…*and*
- I am a U.S. citizen or other U.S. person.

You will note that I have emphasized the word "and" as it appears on the form. That is because "and" has a specific meaning in law. And while the form is not law, it is expressing the legal requirement (which IS in the law) to sign a W-9. The word "and" is not defined by Congress for the purposes of the Tax Code and therefore we must use the "Plain Meaning Rule" as instructed by the U.S. Supreme Court.

The U.S. Supreme Court has said repeatedly that the ordinary meaning of "and" is *conjunctive*. In other words, the purpose of "and" is to "join together" the elements that appear on either side of it. "Join together" means that **both** elements must be operative for the statute/regulation to have effect. Or phrased another way, "and" is the opposite of "or". This might seem elementary to most of you, but let me assure you that those who support the continuation of the largest financial crime in the history of the world will twist and argue any and every point left unaddressed.

[**Author's Note**: While I will not quote from the sources, a partial list of citations addressing the proper meaning of "and" is, *Statutes and Statutory Construction*, § 21.14 at 179–80 (6th ed. 2002), by Norman J. Singer; *Bouvier's Law Dictionary and Concise Encyclopedia* 194–95

(3d Revision 1914); *Crooks v. Harrelson*, 282 U.S. 55, 58 (1930); *United States v. Field*, 255 U.S. 257, 262 (1921); *City of Rome v. United States*, 446 U.S. 156, 172 (1980)]

Now that we understand the proper meaning of "and", we can more effectively take stock of the elements listed on the W-9 – that a person must sign under penalty of perjury. If we line them up, here's how it looks:

> *"Under penalty of perjury I certify that: The number shown on this form is my correct taxpayer identification number, **and** I am not subject to backup withholding...**and** I am a U.S. citizen or other U.S. person."*

So what are we to make of this? First off, since the instructions for the W-9 state that it is ***only*** to be used by a *U.S. person*, that should be the end of the discussion for us, but let's continue looking at the text of the form to nail it all down thoroughly.

The first provision is pretty banal; the U.S. person certifies that the number is "correct" (not a fake or contrived number). It is the second and third provisions that warrant examination.

The second provision says, "I am not subject to backup withholding". Only a *foreign person* – or a person *"having the control, receipt, custody, disposal, or payment of any of the items of income...of any nonresident alien individual or of any foreign partnership"* – can be the subject of backup withholding. Clearly that is ***not*** the average American. And it certainly isn't "Frank"!

I should take a moment to clarify what the W-9 means when it says, "not subject to backup withholding". Since the Form W-9 is exclusively for a *U.S. person* – and we know who that is – there is the implicit understanding that the government has the authority under the Code to invoke backup withholding. What the form means when it says, "not subject to backup withholding" is that the IRS has not, as of yet, informed the *payor/withholding* agent to begin backup withholding. In other words, in reality the person is "subject to" backup withholding, but has not yet been "subjected to" it.

The third provision states that the signer is a "*U.S. citizen* or other *U.S. person.*" Notice that I have underlined "other". This is a common little game played in drafting such language. The use of the word "other" limits the scope of *U.S.*

citizen to those who ***are*** *U.S. persons* and excludes those *U.S. citizens* who are ***not*** *U.S. persons*. Government attorneys love to use these subtle little word games on things like public forms because the public never reads the language in the same discerning manner that the IRS attorneys used when they drafted it!

So…what we have here is this: The Form W-9 is only to be used by a person who can state – under penalty of perjury – that he is a person upon whom backup withholding could be effected (but he hasn't yet been notified that it's been placed into effect) ***and*** that he is a *U.S. person*.

Can you attest to those elements under penalty of perjury? I know I can't. For me to sign that form I would have to ***commit*** perjury! Knowing what you know, could "Frank" sign that form under penalty of perjury? Absolutely not. Only an "ignorant Frank" could agree to sign a Form W-9.

INFORMED FRANK

Let us pick up at the point at which Janice has told Frank she needs a TIN from him. Let's see how an "informed Frank" might respond.

"Janice, I'd love to fill that out for you but that form requires me to sign it under penalty of perjury, and I can't sign it without committing perjury. Perjury is a criminal offense. I'm sure you're not suggesting or advocating that I commit a criminal act."

"No, Frank, I'm not suggesting or advocating that you commit a criminal act, but I don't understand. I have vendors like you fill this out all the time. There's never a problem."

"I understand completely, Janice. No one ever reads the law so they sign any ol' paper put in front of them. I've actually read the law and I know what that form is asking me to attest to under penalty of perjury and I'd be committing a federal crime to sign it."

We've reached the point in our scenario where the ball is squarely in Janice's court. So how might Janice respond?

INFORMED JANICE

"OK, Frank. I'm not sure I understand the underlying argument you're relying on, but this form sure does say that you'd be signing it under penalty of perjury, and if you're telling me you can't sign it without committing a criminal act then I guess that's that. We'll just have to let it go."

Or…

"That's OK, Frank. Lenny makes me ask everyone for one of these, but like you, I understand what it's really asking for. It's nice to meet someone who is informed and isn't a lemming like so many of the other vendors I deal with. I've already told Lenny that not everyone is required to sign a W-9 so I'll handle it from here. Have a great day, Frank."

Hopefully that last response will be the one more and more Americans will receive as this book penetrates our society. Now let's look at the ugly side.

IGNORANT JANICE

"Frank, this isn't a debate. I need that form signed by you."

"Janice, you seem like a nice lady, but I've already told you that I can't sign that form without committing a criminal act."

"Frank, that's absurd. I have hundreds of vendors just like you who've signed these. You won't be committing perjury."

"Wow Janice! You're really going out on a limb here. Only licensed attorneys are legally able to tell a person what his or her obligations are under the law, and that's what you're doing. Janice, are you aware that if you're not a lawyer what you just did is a violation of the law? If you think you can determine what is and is not perjury for me, and therefore you can decide what I have to sign and what I don't, why don't you sign that form for me. What you can do is print 'Frank Baker' right there on the signature line, and then write in 'signature signed by Janice Kennedy after Frank Baker refused to perjure himself' and then we'll send it over the U.S. Department of Justice and see what they think of that."

"I'm not going to do that!"

"Why not, Janice? It's OK with you if I commit perjury, but it's not OK for you to get in trouble for counterfeiting my signature on a federal tax form? That's pretty scary, Janice."

"You're *not* committing perjury."

"You keep saying that, Janice, but the law holds me responsible for that decision, not you. Help me understand your thinking, Janice. Can you please cite for me the tax regulations that address who is to furnish a TIN and under what circumstances?"

"What? No, I can't do that. I don't know that stuff."

"Janice, if you don't know where those regulations are, and you've never read them, why are you telling me – someone who *has* read them – that you know better than I do what will constitute perjury for me in this situation?"

You can clearly see how a situation like this develops, so from here we'll move on to the next level.

IGNORANT AND MALICIOUS JANICE

"Frank, I'm not going to put up with this anymore." (I guess "this" is Frank making it apparent that Janice has no idea what she's talking about or what the law says!) "If you won't give me a number then I'm going to have to backup withhold from you."

"Janice, this is where your lack of knowledge about the law is really a problem. There is no provision in the Tax Code that would permit you to backup withhold from me."

"Yes there is, Frank. Don't ask me to quote it or give you any legal mumbo-jumbo, but there's something in the law that allows backup withholding and unless you give me your TIN I'm going to do it!"

"Janice, I don't know why you'd want to do that. But if you do, I'm going to have to sue you. I'm not going to sue Lenny because I don't believe that Lenny supports your violating the law. I'm going to have to sue you, personally. And I'd rather not have to."

"You can't sue me personally."

"Actually, Janice, I can. I don't want to, but I can. Lenny isn't telling you to do this; this is you being bull-headed and malicious. You don't even know where the law is that allegedly supports your actions, but you're going to do it anyway. While I hate suing anyone, at least in this case it'll be quick and easy for me."

IGNORANT AND CRIMINAL JANICE

"Frank, I'm not going to argue with you about this. If you don't give me the number then I'm not going to be able to pay your invoice."

"Really? And where in the law does it say that you can steal my money if I don't give you a number, Janice?"

"Like I said Frank, I'm not going to argue. No number, no money."

"Janice, if you do this I'm going to have to sue Lenny for the money, and I'm going to explain to him that I'm very sorry to have to sue him but that you are acting completely outside the law and that you have left me no choice but to sue Lenny for the money I am rightfully due."

"You can tell Lenny whatever you want but until I get a number you won't be getting a check."

"Janice, I will be getting a check because I'll be getting a court judgment for the amount due me, plus costs."

Obviously none of these "negative encounters" is what we're looking for in the business environment but the negative scenarios I've outlined here are a composite of various conversations that nontaxpayers have had in the marketplace when dealing with people who have no idea what they're talking about yet believe that whatever they have been ***told***, or whatever they have ***done in the past***, is somehow miraculously legal. And this perspective often remains in place even after the law has been laid out before them.

I did not write this book to convince the government of anything. At the highest levels of the Treasury Department and IRS, they already know all of this. And those agencies intentionally keep their rank-and-file troops as ill-informed as they attempt to keep you. After all, if their troops knew the truth, few would be willing to break the law on a daily basis – especially if they believed that the truth was destined to reach the public too!

I wrote this book for America. I wrote this book for every American whose heart yearns for truth and freedom. I wrote this book for Americans who know there's something wrong with this nation and its government and who want to have tools with which to set this once great nation back on its proper course. As we move forward, I will explain why ending the fraud of the income tax is ***the*** tool for accomplishing that task!

It is the American people who will put this criminal conduct in its grave and return freedom and prosperity to America, not the criminals who inhabit every level of Washington, D.C.

I long ago came to the realization that the U.S. government knows all about what is in this book and intentionally terrorizes the American people in order to keep the spigot of ill-gotten gains wide open. That is what makes it a crime; they ***know*** that the tax is being misapplied to hundreds of millions of innocent American victims, yet they continue to commit the acts of terrorism designed to terrify Americans into "compliance".

This brings us to the government's involvement in "working the mark".

DIRECTLY WORKING THE MARK

The Congress is the source of the Tax Code, and Treasury and the IRS are permitted by Congress to viciously attack Americans whenever it suits them. Congress could rein them in if it wanted to, but it doesn't want to. Who is the recipient of the advantages that flow from the income tax? Why Congress of course! (We'll get into that more in an upcoming chapter.)

Having been given free rein by Congress to do all the evil they wish, it is no wonder that Treasury and the IRS have become a massive terrorist organization and a gargantuan propaganda machine.

There are several ways in which these agencies accomplish their goals of terrorizing the American public and keeping the public fed an almost constant diet of disinformation/misinformation about the income tax. I should make the observation that each of these mechanisms is designed to support the other. In other words, the government's domestic terrorism is designed to keep the people accepting its disinformation/misinformation, and the disinformation/misinformation is designed to cause so much doubt and confusion in the minds of the public that the government's domestic terror campaign has a fertile field of ignorance in which to make its full impact.

Let's look at the propaganda aspect first.

TAX TERRORISM SEASON

The most readily noticeable element of the government's propaganda campaign is what I call the "The United States Government's Annual Tax Terrorism Season." This runs from approximately January 1st through April 15th. During the preceding year the government attempts to structure various legal actions so that they come to the "headline point" during Tax Terrorism Season.

A "headline point" in a case is where something has happened that the government's co-conspirators in Tax Terrorism Season – the dominant media – will be able to print for the purpose of terrorizing the American people into staying in the corrupt tax system.

Occurrences that are often considered to have brought a matter to its "headline point" are things such as a grand jury handing down an indictment, a guilty verdict from a trial, an injunction against people in the Tax Honesty Movement barring them from speaking or writing about the income tax.

The government does its best to ensure that these events occur between January 1st and about April 5th. (April 5th still allows time for publication by the government's media co-conspirators and wide dissemination before the 15th.) Often federal judges – who are all too aware of the timing the prosecutors are shooting for – will assist the government in bringing the matter to its "headline point" during Tax Terrorism Season.

It's really rather amazing; federal judges constantly gripe about the case load before the federal courts, yet they seem to have little difficulty arranging their trial calendar to ensure that the "headline point" in a tax case occurs during Tax Terrorism Seasons. I guess they're just that good! Oh…and did I mention that virtually all federal judges are former U.S. government prosecutors? Funny how that works.

Once the "headline point" in a case occurs, the government brings in its co-conspirators in the dominant media to splash the story across America. The "reporters" (can I throw up now?) do the bidding of their masters and run the stories with language such as "tax protestor", "frivolous arguments", and "criminal violation", etc. What do they offer in contrast? Nothing. Is there another point of view to the story? Of course. But they're not interested in showing the American people that side of it. They are knowingly and intentionally co-conspirators in Tax Terrorism Season. They are not interested in unbiased reporting or ensuring that their coverage is fair and balanced. Their only concern is making sure that the government's perspective is presented. After all, that's what Tax Terrorism Season is all about!

Remember, these are often seasoned reporters who work the "tax beat" or the "financial beat", or cover criminal matters. They know *exactly* what takes place every year, and why! They are actually waiting to be fed the stories by their "sources" at the IRS, Treasury, or Department of Justice. They know that these stories are coming every year during Tax Terrorism Season and that these stories allow them to get articles into print with little or no effort. In other words, these stories are simple; they are "pre-packaged" by the government. In many cases, the government gives the reporters CDs with the story all written out! In short, these stories are "easy money" for the reporters. All the reporter has to do to ensure a steady supply of these "easy money" stories is to print the government's perspective without actually looking into anything.

The editors of the dominant media know the game that's being played and they dutifully run the stories. The editors understand the value of pleasing the government. Keep the government happy and the government will keep the stories coming. Stories that can be run without any effort keep costs down. They also know that if they do not run this pre-canned tripe, the next time a big story breaks they will be excluded and their competitor will get the jump on them. As I said, they understand the value of pleasing the government.

Does all this sound too incredible? If it does, you might do well remember back to October of 2007 when FEMA held a "fake" press conference. They filmed the "press conference" and passed the footage out to the media. The problem was that the "reporters" asking the questions were actually FEMA staffers.

Many people were amazed at what they perceived as FEMA's brazenness. In fact, it wasn't all that brazen. From FEMA's point of view they were just taking things to the "next level".

They knew that today's reporters merely parrot whatever the government tells them to say. FEMA knew that they give reporters "press packs" and the reporter merely parrots whatever it says in the press pack. FEMA just took the "reasonable step" of saving the reporters the time of showing up to the press conference. Unfortunately FEMA underestimated the media's response. From the view of the reporters, this was unacceptable. It's one thing to have a job being a shill for the government. It's something else entirely to be cut out of your job as the shill!

So how do you feel about all those "tax evasion" stories now?

First of all, 99% of Americans the government indicts or brings to trial never owed the government a penny in income tax under the law (as you've seen). Second, the stories you're reading are often written by government "media relations" employees and merely "massaged" a bit by the reporter. And lastly, often the timing of these stories is specifically intended to terrorize the American public into staying in a system that does not apply to them.

THE IRS SAYS...

Another form of directly "working the mark" is the IRS call centers. A "call center" is a facility staffed with hundreds (or even thousands) of "phone agents" who are there to respond to your questions. Call centers are used by private industry and government alike. The difference is that IRS call centers are just another tool in the government's propaganda campaign.

Let's look at how these call centers do their part in the propaganda campaign.

Let's imagine that you give a copy of this book to the person in charge of payroll at your company. We will call her Gladys. Gladys is disturbed by what she reads, but after decades of socialization in how "payroll" works, she squirms at the prospect of acting upon the information she's read. Instead of spending the time to research the sources that I've cited and make sure that the information is sound, Gladys turns to that which is familiar (and hence, comforting) to her. She calls the IRS 800-number and asks what she should do.

When an IRS employee working the phone center comes on the line, Gladys tells the employee that she has come across information that has raised doubts in her mind about whether or not she should be conducting payroll withholding, and that one of the company's employees is asking to have his payroll withholding stopped. She tells the call center employee that she is confused and doesn't know what to do.

I hardly need to tell you how this conversation turns out. And this exact type of call happens hundreds of thousands of times a month concerning one issue or another. People are confronted with the truth of what the law says and then call the IRS (of all people) to ask what they should do! Can you say "lemming"?

The IRS employee sternly tells Gladys that the law requires every *employer* to deduct and withhold from the *wages* of *employees*. He warns her that if she follows the advice of "tax protestors", in the end the company will get hit with massive fines and penalties, and that there is always the possibility of criminal prosecution. The IRS employee goes on to tell her that no one ever wins against the IRS in these kinds of things and that she shouldn't put the company at risk by following the illegal advice of "tax protestors". The IRS employee might even throw in that once the company is hit with massive fines and penalties she'll lose her job because she's the one who brought this down upon them.

That's enough for Gladys! Even though she's already read the truth – she's already seen the law with her own eyes – the words of the IRS are all she can hear. In her desire to "comply" – and thus feel safe – she can no longer remember that *employer*, *employee*, and *wages* have special statutory meanings. She can no longer remember that section 3402 is merely a collection mechanism for the tax imposed under subtitle 'A'. All of that has evaporated from her mind in her desire to feel safe by complying with the tyrant. What was that line about "America… land of the free and home of the brave"?

The worst part of this scenario is that the IRS call center employee is following a script! He has absolutely no idea what the law does or doesn't require. Even if he had a clue about what the law requires (which he doesn't), he would be breaking the law if he began giving "legal advice" to Gladys because he is not an attorney.

Has this IRS call center employee received any training? Yes – he has been trained on how to run through the script with people like Gladys! That's it; nothing more. If Gladys had the gumption to ask the IRS employee what the legal definition of *employee* is, and/or where it could be found, he'd have no idea! But Gladys didn't really call the IRS looking for the truth. She called the IRS with the goal of obtaining "justification" for rejecting the truth. Maybe that line should be "America…land of the slave and home of those who cower in fear."

WHAT HAPPENS WHEN…

Earlier we looked at the various options that "Frank" could take when "Janice" asked him to sign a Form W-9. And now we need to discuss the consequences.

There is only one way for a person who must submit an *information return* to acquire another person's TIN. That is to request it. [See 301.6109-1 et seq] There is no provision in either the statutes or the regulations for a TIN to be acquired by any other method. This element – requesting the number – is essential to keeping subtitle 'A' constitutional.

You may have heard it bandied about that the income tax is "voluntary". This is nonsense. If people have had the tax imposed on them, then there is nothing voluntary about it. Could people go to jail for failing to file a return or pay a tax that is voluntary? If there is any voluntary aspect of subtitle 'A' it is whether or not you furnish a TIN upon request. And even this is not really voluntary, because if you are a *U.S. person* or *foreign person* you are required by regulation to furnish the number.

One definition of "voluntary" is that you have a choice. Which choice you make when a TIN is requested depends solely on what you know about the requirements of the Code and the regulations. Generally speaking, when presented with a "choice" one may not always choose wisely. If one is not well informed on the subject upon which one is called to make a choice, the odds increase that the choice one makes will be unwise. In other words, one can unwisely volunteer!

Millions of Americans unwisely "volunteer" every year. The Frank/Janice story (in one version or another) is repeated millions of times each year. So what are the consequences of acting like "Ignorant Frank"?

<u>A TIN being requested from you is your pivotal moment in regard to subtitle 'A'</u>. Re-read that sentence as many times as it takes to retain it and be able to recall it! If you are not a *U.S. person* or *foreign person deriving U.S. source income* or a *U.S. citizen residing abroad with foreign-earned income*, you are ***not*** required to furnish a TIN.

Let me explain a little something about tax law. Tax law is "regulatory law". Regulatory law functions differently than what people think of as "real" law; things such as robbery, battery, rape, murder, etc. In "real" law you actually committed the crime in order to be convicted (all things working the way they should). Let me give you an example. Let's say a person confesses to committing a murder. But shortly after the confession, a local TV reporter discovers a videotape of the murder scene and it shows that someone else committed the murder. Because of the video, the person who confessed to the murder will not be tried for the murder (though he may be tried for lying to a police officer). In other words, whether or not the person confessing actually committed the act is a controlling element. Not so in regulatory law.

In regulatory law, whether or not you are actually, really, truly, the person upon whom the tax has been imposed (or otherwise made liable) is not important! All that matters is what you say in the form of a declaration on a tax form. What is a declaration?

Declaration – 1) any statement made, particularly in writing. 2) a written statement made "under penalty of perjury" and signed by the declarant…

What do you think you create when you sign a Form W-9 "under penalty of perjury?" You create a legal declaration that you *are* a *U.S. person*!

Once you hand that signed W-9 to the requester, he is now bound to do all the things the Tax Code requires of those making payments to *U.S. persons* of U.S. source income belonging to a *foreign person*. One of those things is filing an *information return*.

Shortly after the 1st of the year, the IRS receives a deluge of *information returns* that reflect payment made by *payors* (or at least those who believe themselves to be *payors*). In order to keep the example simple we'll stick to just Form 1099 MISC, which is the most common (non-employee) *information return* in America.

Once you hand a signed W-9 to a requester, you set a series of events into motion. Why? Because you've just made an official declaration, on a federal tax form, that you are a *U.S. person*. As such, the immediate legal presumption arises (though not necessarily understood by the person paying you) that the payment made to you is U.S. source income belonging to a *foreign person*. Suddenly, subtitle 'A' controls all.

Let's revisit "Ignorant Frank".

Shortly after the 1st of the year, the IRS will receive a 1099 with Frank's name on it and his TIN. This tells the IRS computers that Frank is a *U.S. person* who has received a payment of U.S. source income belonging to a *foreign person*. The IRS computers now start tracking whether Frank files a return for the year that the 1099 was filed. Why? Because Frank has been identified as a person who had *"control, receipt, custody, disposal, or payment of any of the items of income…of any nonresident alien individual or of any foreign partnership"*.

If Frank doesn't file a return, the IRS computer (part of the Automated Collection System [ACS]) will kick out a letter asking Frank to file a return or tell the IRS why he did not.

There is a major disconnect at this point. Frank falsely believes the IRS is asking for a return concerning his own personal earnings. If Frank has done a modicum of research into the income tax he may be angry and tell the IRS that his income isn't subject to the income tax. But that's **not** what the IRS is asking for so his response is totally off-point!

The IRS computer is asking for a return from the *U.S. person* who received the income belonging to a *foreign person*. There is in fact no law imposing a tax on Frank concerning his own domestic income, but there **is** a requirement to file if he withheld on the U.S. source income of a *foreign person*.

You'll note that I repeatedly have said, "the IRS computer knows...." That's because the IRS computer is 100% compliant with the law. Also, while the IRS maintains the veneer of constitutionality by having its computers act in accordance with the law, it treats its employees and most of its officers like mushrooms when it comes to subtitle 'A'. In other words, it keeps them in the dark and feeds them excrement. The vast majority of IRS officers and employees are intentionally mis-trained so that they will have the false belief that the income tax is upon the average American and therefore will have no qualms about (illegally) enforcing it upon you.

When the IRS sends out its letter asking where Frank's tax return is, the letter will say that the "type of tax" they're referring to is "1040". It literally says "Type of Tax: 1040". Clearly there is no "1040 tax". 1040 is a form, not a tax. But let's imagine for a moment that they're actually trying to be helpful, and that what they're saying is that the tax they're after is the one that must be reported on a Form 1040. From what you've seen in this book, it sure is easier for IRS to point to a form than it is a section that imposes the tax on you!

Nevertheless, let's look at the 1040.

As I stated in earlier chapters, the only reference to the Form 1040 made by the Secretary has been for *nonresident aliens*, the withholding agent for a *nonresident alien*, and certain Americans residing abroad (under very limited circumstances).

At this juncture some "tax professionals" [uh, yeh] may say I'm being silly. Today a *nonresident alien* is to use a "1040-NR" and *withholding agents* are to use a myriad of different forms, including the "1040-S". And I would agree with those examples. Certainly over the years new forms have been created as the Treasury Department has sought to improve the efficiency of tax administration. And as these new forms have been created some of those who were formerly directed to file a generic 1040 have been directed to use the new specialized variants. No doubt about it.

But does that mean that nonresident aliens are to no longer use it? Here's what the instructions say from the 2009 version of IRS publication 570:

> Nonresident alien. If you are a bona fide resident of Puerto Rico during the entire tax year, but <u>a nonresident alien of the United States</u>, you generally must file the following returns:
>
> - A U.S. tax return (Form 1040) reporting income from worldwide sources, but excluding Puerto Rican source income…

Well what do you know! Nonresident aliens are still directed to file a Form 1040! And this is just one handy example as I'm writing this. There are more, but I'm simply making the point that there are specific instructions for a nonresident alien to file a Form 1040.

In contrast to these clear directions for a nonresident alien to file a 1040, there exists no authoritative citation anywhere directing an American citizen living and working in one of the 50 states, earning only his own domestic source income, to file any return whatsoever.

Because the income tax has not been imposed upon average American citizens living and working in one of the 50 states, earning their own domestic source income, there is no citation directing them to file a tax return of any kind. However, the IRS uses the confusion over the nature of the tax, and whom it has been imposed upon (or otherwise made liable) to have its computers enforce the tax on those who are ignorant of the law and have therefore made legal declarations that they are within a class of person who must file a return.

Hopefully you now understand why the phrase "under authority of law" is reserved to TIN requests made to *foreign persons*. When a TIN request is made to an American, that American is expected to make a determination as to whether he is acting on behalf of a *foreign person* or is receiving ordinary payments not subject to the authority of subtitle 'A'. If he is acting on behalf of a *foreign person* then he must furnish a TIN. If he is merely going about his own financial affairs, not addressed by subtitle 'A', then he **must** decline to furnish a TIN in order to be in compliance with the law. If he is merely going about his own financial affairs not addressed by subtitle 'A', then to sign a Form W-9, he would be committing a federal crime; i.e., perjury.

Many IRS/Treasury officials, as well as federal judges, have referred to the income tax as a system of "self-confession". And indeed it is. Often times there is no way for the person making a payment to know whether or not the recipient is acting on behalf of a *foreign person*. If an American citizen invested funds in your company that actually belonged to a *foreign person*, how would you know unless he/she "confessed" it? You wouldn't. The Form W-9 is that confession. What have *you* improperly confessed to lately?

Let's now continue exploring what happens after the IRS sends you a letter inquiring about your tax return.

Let me begin by saying that because the IRS has intentionally mis-trained their workers, if you explain all of this to them, it will fall on deaf ears. This is the point where the veneer of constitutionality (if it exists at all) falls apart.

The IRS has long relied upon the doctrine that by keeping their computers in compliance with the law their tax "enforcement" methods will always be declared constitutional by the courts, and they can blame individual misconduct on employees if a significant constitutional challenge ever arises. However, there is now more than sufficient evidence to support the reality that the IRS intentionally keeps its workers in the dark concerning the true limitations of the tax so that they will attack and steal from innocent Americans every day.

Clearly all the IRS would have to do would be to tell their employees that subtitle 'A' is imposed upon the exercise of a privilege and that making money is almost never a privilege subject to subtitle 'A' taxes when the person is an American citizen living and working in one of the 50 states, earning his/her own domestic income. Since the solution is just that simple, there is no rational justification possible for why it has not happened.

IRS publication 54 is entitled, "Tax Guide for U.S. Citizens and Resident Aliens Abroad". It's very thoughtful of the IRS to offer that assistance to U.S. citizens and resident aliens residing abroad. However, it seems that thoughtfulness does not extend to regular ol' Americans here in America. I scoured the IRS list of publications, and golly gee wiz, as hard as I tried I could not find a publication entitled, "Tax Guide for U.S. Citizens and Resident Aliens In The 50 States" or anything that could remotely be construed as such. Hmmm. Obviously just an oversight by the IRS!

Despite all these crystal clear indicators that the IRS knows damn well to whom the tax is limited, if an *information return* has been filed against you it is virtually impossible to get the IRS to understand this! This is because in regulatory law all that matters is the declaration you made under penalty of perjury when you signed the W-9.

Once the examiner has rejected your explanation for why you haven't filed, the matter will be forwarded to the appropriate IRS regional Service Center. When the file arrives there, the IRS's "claim against you" begins its journey toward becoming a "procedurally valid assessment". This means that the IRS will supposedly conform to various statutory and regulatory requirements as they process their claim that you owe them a tax return and didn't pay the tax on the "reportable payments".

This process begins with something called the Automated Substitute for Return Program, known as the ASFR program.

Here's what happens at the Service Center in the ASFR program:

An IRS employee grabs a blank Form 1040. (Remember they've already said that the "type of tax" is "1040", and we know who has been directed to fill out a 1040, yes?) The employee then writes your name and SSN on the form and uses that form – which contains nothing but your name and SSN – to open a "tax module" in the IRS computer for the year in question. The 1099 data is then keyed into the newly opened "tax module" and now the IRS computers are locked onto you like a cruise missile locked onto its target!

Because I made several *Freedom of Information Act* requests on this subject, I know that the IRS refers to that nearly blank 1040 that they use to open the module as a "dummy return".

Working the Marks

From this point on everything is completely automated. In the later stages, when the law requires signatures of certain designated IRS officers in order to proceed, the IRS simply places those signatures on the necessary forms automatically, without the actual IRS officer even being aware of the file/paperwork or having any knowledge of it! In other words, just as they violate the law by the use of "dummy returns" (which no statute or regulations permit), they then violate the law by placing "dummy signatures" on forms that attest to your liability!

How's that for a big ol' stinky violation of Constitutionally mandated "due process of law"?

Section 6020(b) of the Code deals with the Secretary/IRS making returns for people who are liable, but have not filed. Here's what 6020(b) says:

> Execution of return by Secretary
>
> (1) Authority of Secretary to execute return
> If any person fails to make any return required by any internal revenue law or regulation made thereunder at the time prescribed therefor, or makes, willfully or otherwise, a false or fraudulent return, the Secretary shall make such return from his own knowledge and from such information as he can obtain through testimony or otherwise.
>
> (2) Status of returns
> <u>Any return so made and subscribed by the Secretary</u> shall be prima facie good and sufficient for all legal purposes.

You'll notice I've underlined the part about these substitute returns being "subscribed by the Secretary". So what does subscribe mean?

Subscribe - to sign at the end of a document. (Nolo.com)

In other words, Congress built some accountability into the *substitute return* process. Congress permits the Secretary (which includes those to whom he may delegate authority) to complete returns that are *"required by any internal revenue law or regulation"*.

So the very first requirement under the law is that the Secretary has knowledge that the returns are required by law. Then, if such return is to be considered as valid for the purposes of tax administration, it must be signed by an officer of the Treasury/IRS to whom the Secretary has delegated his authority to do so.

In the ASFR program the 1040 "dummy return" is never signed by anyone. In fact, no signed return exists at all. Later, when the computer spits out a report containing cumulative figures on how much a large group of "taxpayers" allegedly owes (RACS006 report) the computer automatically places on the report the signature of a person who has been delegated *substitute return* authority by the Secretary.

The problem here is two-fold. First, the person whose signature appears there has zero information about anything in the report. Even if one supposes that a signature on a RACS006 report fulfills the requirements of 6020(b) – which is a huge stretch – no one in his right mind could imagine that Congress' requirement to "subscribe" the return permits computers to affix signatures to documents of which the "signature party" is not even aware. Second, Congress said clearly that the "return" is to be subscribed, not some report kicked out by a computer involving the cumulative amount allegedly owed by thousands of taxpayers. This is the "dummy signature" to which I referred earlier.

Those who support "the largest financial crime in the history of the world", and want to see it continue, would likely argue that these are trivialities. I doubt any rational person would agree.

So what has the IRS said about its own ASFR program? I have a copy of a memo from the IRS Office of Chief Counsel which states on page 3, "…the ASFR program is not 6020(b) compliant." In other words, the way the ASFR program operates does not meet the requirements laid out by Congress when it enacted the legislation we now know as 6020(b). Given what Congress said in 6020(b), how could anyone imagine that ASFR would be 6020(b) compliant?

If ASFR does not meet the requirements laid out by Congress in 6020(b), then it is an illegal program. Why? Because Congress has not enacted any other law permitting the Secretary to create *substitute returns* for anyone! In other words, if it isn't done under the authority of 6020(b), then it isn't legal.

Furthermore, if Americans upon whom Congress has never imposed the tax (or otherwise made liable) are being consistently assessed taxes through the ASFR program, and hounded for taxes they do not owe, then we have reached the point that U.S. Supreme Court Justice White warned about in Brushaber, when he wrote:

> "*Pollock*... recognized the fact that taxation on income was in its nature an excise entitled to be enforced as such <u>unless and until it was concluded that to enforce it would amount to accomplishing the result which the requirement as to apportionment of direct taxation was adopted to prevent</u>...." [emphasis added]

With the ASFR program we have exactly that. The ASFR program uses *information returns* as the "fig leaf" that covers the government misapplying an excise tax (the income tax) in such a way that it really operates as a direct tax, which of course the constitution requires to be apportioned and which, of course, the government is not doing.

The IRS has an *information return* (such as a 1099), which it assumes (but cannot prove) is the result of the person named as the "payee" having certified under penalty of perjury that he is a *U.S. person*, and then railroading that person (who in fact is not a *U.S. person*) through the examination process and then on into assessment, followed by seizing property under the "collection" authority.

In other words, the IRS is using *information returns* and the ASFR program as its means to effect the "con-job"; the means to impose upon the American people an unconstitutional direct tax absent apportionment, while claiming that it is in compliance with the Constitution because its process is "procedurally" correct.

Clearly this is precisely the kind of "enforcement" that Justice White was referring to when he cautioned that there could be a circumstance in which the method of enforcement would be *"accomplishing the result which the requirement as to apportionment of direct taxation was adopted to prevent."* We are there; and have been for some time now.

Everyone who understands the income tax, and looks at its enforcement, knows that it is being enforced as a direct tax. The government disingenuously pretends that the manner of enforcement is "within constitutional boundaries" simply by the "procedures" that are used. These procedures exist for no other purpose than to keep the con-job hidden and moving forward.

If we are to accept the government's position that it is "innocent" because of the procedures it uses, then we must also accept that it is just hunky-dory for a man to have sex with a 12 year old girl (who looks 12) simply because the man claims she said she was 18!

If we believe that the man has a moral duty to verify the age of the little girl before having sex with her, then we must also hold that the U.S. government has the same duty to determine if the income tax actually applies to you before it #%@&'s you! But that doesn't happen. In fact, just the opposite happens!

Try going to an IRS meeting and telling an "examiner" that you are not a *U.S. person* and that you did not sign a Form W-9 and that the person who submitted the *information return* "pirated" your SSN from some other source (such as a medical insurance form or a background check form). The IRS does not care what you have to say. The fact that they have a 1099 on file is *all* they care about.

IRS employees are *not* trained in the law. They are trained *only* in procedure. Because they are not trained in the law, like the general public they believe the "socialized view" that if you make money in America you owe some to the IRS.

Is it not the height of irony that the very people who are tasked with administrating/enforcing U.S. tax law are not taught anything about "the law" they are to enforce? There is a reason that the U.S. government does not teach its officers/employees anything about the law they are to enforce!

Clearly, it would be simple enough for the IRS to spell out to its officers/employees the limited applicability of the income tax. Since it would be so amazingly simple to do, the only conclusion a reasonable person can come to as to why it hasn't been done is that the U.S. government *wants* the largest financial crime in the history of the world to continue being perpetrated against **YOU**!

But wait! Why are we talking about the IRS telling its employees the truth? What about the IRS telling **YOU** the truth? How might they do that? Simple. Here's all they'd have to do. On its website, the IRS would center a message on the screen, in bright red, that would say, "***The income tax does not apply to the vast majority of Americans. Click on this sentence to learn more.***" That's all it would take. How long do you think it would take for virtually every American to read/hear the truth?

I know many of you are saying, "Come on, Dave; the government would never do that." Exactly!!! You're right! The U.S. government will never do that. It will never do that because it *desires* that the illegal, unconstitutional theft of your property continue! Telling the truth is startlingly simple and you yourself were just thinking the government will never do it. Stop a moment and think about that. The government could end the theft within an hour by posting the information to the IRS website, but it won't. And it won't do that because it *wants* to steal your property from you. How does that make you feel about "your" government?

And now, back to the ASFR program. What happens after ASFR has illegally opened a "tax module" against you and their computer starts sending you letters?

If you respond correctly, my experience is that you stand a 50/50 chance of the IRS ending its persecution against you. By "correctly", I mean a written response to the proper authority, which contains the relevant information from this book.

Why 50/50? Who knows. My personal opinion is that it depends on whose desk your letter lands upon. Some IRS employees will be unable to disprove what you have said, and will thus enter a code in the computer to end the persecution. Other IRS employees will simply ignore what you're saying because it's above their heads. In that event, the IRS will simply keep on persecuting you because of the ignorance of its employees, which, remember, is intentional.

If the IRS ignores your initial explanation, they will then do what I refer to as "steamrolling". To steamroll you is to ignore anything and everything you say and to keep attacking you without any law to support their actions. If it were being done to you by anyone other than the IRS, federal prosecutors would call it "an on-going criminal enterprise".

The "steamroller" routine looks like this. The IRS sends you a series of letters. This is to create the illusion in the IRS computer records that you were extended "due process of law". Of course if they ignore everything you say back to them (which is what they do when "steamrolling"), there is no "due process" being provided. As I said, it is only the *illusion* of due process that appears in the IRS computer records.

This sequence of letters will end with something the IRS calls a "Notice of Deficiency", known commonly as a NOD. The NOD is your final "opportunity" (cough, cough) to make your case to the IRS.

The NOD relies on section 6211 of the Code for its legal authority. 6211 is entitled, "Definition of deficiency" and looks like this:

> 6211(a) – In general – For purposes of this title in the case of income, estate, and gift taxes imposed by subtitles A and B and excise taxes imposed by chapters 41, 42, 43, and 44 the term "deficiency" means the amount by which the tax imposed by subtitle A or B, or chapter 41, 42, 43, or 44 exceeds the excess of— (1) the sum of (A) the amount shown as the tax by the taxpayer upon his return, if a return was made by the taxpayer and an amount was shown as the tax by the taxpayer thereon, plus (B) the amounts previously assessed (or collected without assessment) as a deficiency, over—
>
> (2) the amount of rebates, as defined in subsection (b)(2), made.

The first thing we want to take note of is that it says, "For the purposes of this title...." This "title" is Title 26 – the Internal Revenue Code. In other words, Congress is saying that this definition controls the entire Code, in reference to what a deficiency is, when it comes to subtitles 'A' and 'B', as well as chapters 41 (Public Charities), 42 (Private Foundations, and Certain Other Tax Exempt Organizations), 43 (Qualified Pensions, Etc., Plans), and 44 (Qualified Investment Entities).

Now that we know what Congress is applying it to, what is a ***deficiency?***

It means, *the amount by which the tax imposed by subtitle A...exceeds the excess of—*

> (1) the sum of
> (A) the amount shown as the tax by the taxpayer upon his return, if a return was made by the taxpayer and an amount was shown as the tax by the taxpayer thereon, plus
> (B) the amounts previously assessed (or collected without assessment) as a deficiency, over—

(2) the amount of rebates, as defined in subsection (b)(2), made.

Over the years I've noticed that people have trouble grasping what all that means. We could go over it phrase by phrase, but I think a better way to address it (for the purposes of the point at hand) is to simply lay it out in plain English.

There is a statutory "deficiency" if:

a) The amount of tax properly owed under subtitle 'A' exceeds that which the taxpayer has stated he owes on his return.
b) The amount of money assessed and/or collected from you by the government is less than the amount properly owed under subtitle 'A'.

In short, when all the math is done – to include what is really owed, how much has been paid, the amount of credits owed, rebates that have been paid, etc. – the amount a person owes is more than the amount the IRS has received in regard to that person, there is a deficiency.

But here's the kicker. Congress has chosen some very specific language in 6211. Congress has said that a *deficiency* is based on "the amount shown as the tax by the taxpayer upon his return, if a return was made by the taxpayer and an amount was shown as the tax by the taxpayer thereon." Specific language indeed!

We might reasonably ask ourselves why Congress didn't just say, "the amount shown on the return". What would the difference be between the actual words Congress used and the shorter 6-word version I just brought up?

It has to do with 6020(b) – the authority to create substitute returns.

If Congress had simply said that a *deficiency* is the difference between the amount owed and the amount shown on the return, it would be reasonable to interpret that as meaning that the IRS could create a *deficiency* if the amount actually owed was more than the amount shown on the return, whether said return was made by the taxpayer or by the Secretary under 6020(b).

But that is **not** what Congress has said!

Instead, Congress made the decision to use very specific language that limits the definition of *deficiency* to those cases in which the taxpayer filed a return.

Not only did Congress state specifically "*...the amount shown as the tax by the taxpayer upon his return...*" but then Congress went to an additional length by saying, "*...if a return was made by the taxpayer and an amount was shown as the tax by the taxpayer thereon.*" Clearly Congress has limited the Secretary's authority to create a deficiency to "***if*** *a return was made by the taxpayer and an amount was shown as the tax by the taxpayer thereon.*"

Some folks may doubt that a little word, such as "if", can affect the meaning of a statute.

> "Tax laws are clearly in derogation of personal rights and property interests and are, therefore, subject to strict construction, and any ambiguity must be resolved against imposition of the tax." Billings v. U.S., 232 U.S. 261, 34 S. Ct. 421 (1914),

> "...in statutes levying taxes the literal meaning of the words employed is most important, for such statutes are not to be extended by implication beyond the clear import of the language used. If the words are doubtful, the doubt must be resolved against the Government and in favor of the taxpayer." Gould v. Gould, 245 U.S. 151, 153.

> "The primary and general rule of a statutory definition *construction* is that the intent of the lawmaker is to be found in the language that he has used. He is presumed to know the meaning of the words and the rules of grammar" United States v. Goldenberg, 168 U.S. 95

Obviously *statutory* construction would be impossible (or completely chaotic) unless every word the legislature uses is taken into account and given its proper meaning, whether statutory or "common usage". Since "if" is not defined in tax law, we must rely on the "plain meaning rule". There are several meanings in the dictionary for the word "if", but only one fits grammatically and gives Congress' use of the word any meaning in 6211. That meaning is "on condition that". (Using any of the other definitions renders Congress' sentence both nonsensical and grammatically incorrect.)

If we use the proper meaning, then the clause in question reads like this:

> *"...the amount shown as the tax by the taxpayer upon his return, on the condition that a return was made by the taxpayer and an amount was shown as the tax by the taxpayer thereon...."*

I see no other rational conclusion than this: In section 6211, Congress has limited the creation of a *deficiency* to those cases in which a return is filed by the taxpayer, and that excludes the use of a return prepared by the Secretary under 6020(b). However, since there are few if any Form 1040 returns legally prepared by the IRS under 6020(b), the point is somewhat moot.

So let's tie all of this together and see what the IRS process really looks like.

- An American citizen working in the private sector, in one of the 50 states, (who has never read this book) mistakenly gives another person in the private sector his TIN (or the person making the payment has illegally "pirated" a SSN from another source).
- The person who received the TIN prepares a 1099 and sends it to the IRS.
- The IRS cannot find a tax return for that year concerning the person named on the 1099.
- The IRS sends letters to the person named on the 1099.
- Having by now read this book, the citizen responds properly to the letters.
- The IRS ignores the citizen's responses.
- After ignoring the citizen's responses, the IRS computer kicks the matter over to a Service Center operating the "ASFR program".
- An IRS employee assigned to the ASFR program then creates a "dummy return" (Form 1040) containing only the alleged taxpayer's name and TIN.
- The IRS employee then uses the *existence* of the "dummy return" (which he just created without any legal authority to do so!) to open a "tax module" in the IRS's computer for the person named on the 1099.
- Once the "module" is open, the computer uses the 1099 information to calculate an amount due under subtitle 'A'.
- In the best fashion of a con-artist, the IRS places a "dummy signature" on a few computer reports in an attempt to pretend to comply with 6020(b). The IRS officer (whose name appears on the reports) is totally unaware of any information about you or your alleged tax debt.
- The IRS is 100% aware that the process it is using is outside the law because it does not comport itself with the clear requirements of 6020(b), and the Chief Counsel has said as much.

- The IRS is 100% aware that there is no law in existence that allows it to do what it is doing.
- After ignoring the person's proper responses, and creating a claim of taxes due by knowingly violating the law, the IRS then sends the person a NOD.
- The NOD is also not authorized by law because Congress has limited a *deficiency* to those cases in which a taxpayer filed a return.
- The NOD gives you the choice of appealing the matter to someone in the IRS or going to Tax Court. No one ever wins in either case.

How's that for a straightforward tax system? The whole process, from beginning to end, is one giant con-job that requires the IRS to violate the very tax laws that it tells you it is there to enforce. And of course in the process it is violating your rights.

So what is the solution to all this? We'll get into that shortly!

FINANCIAL INSTITUTIONS

One of the most onerous aspects of how you are victimized under the guise of U.S. tax law is the part financial institutions play.

Banks, credit unions, and brokerage firms are making demands on their depositors that are not in compliance with the law. Or phrased another way, they are demanding that you falsely declare yourself to be a "person liable" for the income tax, whether you are or not!

When you fill out a "signature card" at the bank, within that document there is an "imbedded Form W-9". Allow me to explain.

IRS regulations permit a private document to serve as a federal tax form, provided that the private document contains language that is "substantially similar" to the language used on the form as it is published by the government.

On the bank's signature card you will find a spot where your TIN is requested. When you compare the language on the bank's card with the language on the actual Form W-9, you will see that it is virtually identical. In other words, while the signature card is a private document and serves the private purposes of the bank, it *also* serves as an official W-9 for tax purposes. (There are a few institutions that do not have the "imbedded W-9" on their signature cards, but instead will simply hand you a W-9. This is the exception to the rule.)

Is there an intrinsic problem with the signature card containing an imbedded W-9? No. The problem (as usual) is that financial institutions don't really make a "request" for a TIN; they make a demand. They do this by refusing to open an account for anyone who refuses to furnish a TIN.

There are three reasons banks claim that this is acceptable. None of the reasons holds any legal or moral merit.

First, banks take the position that everyone is a taxpayer and every account contains monies subject to a U.S. tax. This is absurd on its face.

Let's say for the sake of this illustration that the income tax has been imposed on every American. That said, a man receives an inheritance. Not understanding how that tax really operates, he pays the inheritance tax. What he has left after paying the inheritance tax is known in the accounting world as "post-tax" proceeds. In other words, the tax has already been paid on the original amount and what is left over is the sole property of the owner and there is no further claim by the government of any taxes being due on that amount.

Our fictitious American takes his post-tax proceeds to a local bank and asks to place his post-tax proceeds in a non-interest-bearing checking account. In this illustration, there is no tax due on the funds and he is opening a non-interest-bearing account, so there is no basis in the Tax Code for demanding a TIN to open the account – even given the context that all Americans are subject to the income tax.

Despite the fact that there is no basis within the Tax Code for asking for the number, the bank will refuse to open the account without a TIN. If there is no law requiring each depositor to furnish a number, then the bank is acting outside the law.

This is no esoteric discussion. By acting without the force of law in this manner, the bank is forcing you to declare something that is not true under penalty of perjury! In other words, the bank takes the position that if you perjure yourself, they will open an account for you, but if you refuse to perjure yourself, you cannot have an account. This is damn close to the legal definition of *subornation of perjury*, and it is certainly *subornation of perjury* in a moral sense.

This conduct rests on the nonsensical presumption that everyone who walks into a bank in America is either a *U.S. person* or a *foreign person*. Of course you know that premise is ridiculous.

The banks act as if there are but two hemispheres concerning who an American is: either a *U.S. person* or a *foreign person*. But of course they've framed the issue improperly. There are things that would fit the "only two hemispheres" model, such as whether you are a man or a woman (though even that seems to be slipping these days).

But there are in fact three "hemispheres" when it comes to how the income tax relates to Americans. One may indeed be a *U.S. person* if engaged in certain specific conduct relating to payments of U.S. source income to foreigners. One may be a *foreign person* if one is not a U.S. citizen or U.S. corporation and is deriving U.S. source income.

But what of the third "hemisphere"?

> "The revenue laws are a code or system in regulation of tax assessment and collection. They relate to taxpayers and not to nontaxpayers."
> Economy Plumbing and Heating Co. v. United States, 470 F.2d 585 (1972)

In other words, the third hemisphere is the vast majority of Americans upon whom Congress has ***not*** imposed the income tax!

If a financial institution demands you sign a W-9, it is telling you that it has made the determination that you are a *U.S. person*. But it has no facts with which to make such a determination, nor does the law permit it to make that determination for you. The regulations clearly state that a TIN is only to be ***requested***. There is no mechanism for the requester to force anyone to furnish a number! This is a critical point.

If you are in fact a U.S. person (i.e., receiving U.S. source income that belongs to a foreign person) and you refuse to furnish a TIN, then the payor is <u>required</u> to initiate *back up withholding*. And of course *withholding at the source* is required if the *reportable payment* is being made directly to a *foreign person*. That's it. That's their recourse for not receiving a TIN!

But, if you are just a plain ol' American who is working in one of the 50 states, earning just your own domestic income, then you are in that third hemisphere – the persons upon whom the income tax does not operate – and as the federal court stated in *Economy Plumbing and Heating*, you are a **nontaxpayer**. A **nontaxpayer** cannot be required to sign *any* tax form in order to open a bank account!

Before we go on to the other two lame excuses the banks give for suborning perjury, let's take a moment and talk about the word "nontaxpayer". The government hates this word. It makes them froth at the mouth and want to do bad things to people. The government takes this position for two reasons. First, the government wants to keep getting your money – even if you've never owed a penny in income tax and never will in your entire lifetime. Second, the government sees the use of the word "nontaxpayer" in a very backward sense.

The government chooses to view the matter in this way: people who *are* taxpayers simply say the word "nontaxpayer" out loud and – viola – they magically no longer owe any tax. This is of course absurd, and no one does this. But this ridiculous approach is the mechanism the government uses as its foundation from which to brand all *nontaxpayers* as "Tax Protesters" or "Tax Deniers".

In point of reality, it works just the opposite. For the purposes of the income tax, the appellation of *nontaxpayer* quite properly and legally belongs to those upon whom Congress has *not* imposed the income tax. It's just that simple, but the government won't concede that because to do so threatens its "house of cards".

But, back to the banks!

The second reason banks think they are right to demand a TIN in order to open an account for you is an unbelievably stupid reading of the regulations behind the Patriot Act. Bank employees/officers will tell you that they *must* have a TIN because it is *required* under the Patriot Act. Oh really? Let's explore!

The silliness begins with the requirement for financial institutions to "*verifying the identity of any person seeking to open an account, to the extent reasonable and practicable*" and "*maintaining records of the information used to verify the person's identity, including name, address, and other identifying information"*. You'll notice that the requirement is modified by the standard of "to the extent reasonable and practicable". That's critical – as we shall see!

Section 103.121(a)(6) of the Patriot Act regulations states that a TIN has the same meaning as in 6109 of the Internal Revenue Code. This of course tells us that our understanding of a TIN is the same for the purposes of opening an account under the provisions of the Patriot Act as it is for the purposes of the Tax Code.

The *final rules* (regulations) for the Patriot Act use a modified version of the definition of U.S. person. (This is why I mentioned earlier that terms that sound identical may be defined differently when used in different laws.) It defines a U.S. person as *"an individual who is a U.S. citizen, or an entity established or organized under the laws of a State or the United States"*. This definition merely excludes a resident alien from the definition given in the Tax Code.

So…how much does that matter to us? Not at all.

Shortly after the definition of *U.S. person* is given, some "commenters" discussed proposals concerning modification of the definition of U.S. person. Treasury explains why it rejected those proposals and then states the following:

"The bank will have to ask each customer for a U.S. taxpayer identification number (social security number, employer identification number, or individual taxpayer identification number). If a customer cannot provide one, the bank may then accept alternative forms of identification. For these reasons, the definition is adopted as proposed." http://www.ustreas.gov/press/releases/reports/326finalrulebanks.pdf (page 22)

This rule is fine. There is nothing wrong with asking for a number. Unfortunately, the banks act like this paragraph doesn't exist. The bank will tell you that they **must** get a TIN from you as a requirement for opening an account; that it is **the law**. As you can see, that is not remotely true.

Some may be asking why the regulation is written that way. After all, aren't we trying to detect/catch terrorists? First of all, anyone who believes the Patriot Act is about detecting/catching terrorists should go back to dreaming. It's about monitoring and controlling Americans. Why do you think it is misapplied on a wholesale basis by the banks? The people who work in banks can read the English language. Are you telling me that you think every bank in America, and all of their attorneys, just happened to miss the paragraph of the *final rule* that I just shared with you? Come on! Get real!

So why would Treasury write its regulation to permit the banks to open an account without a TIN? Simple. Because most Americans are not required to have one at all! There is no legal basis (that would pass constitutional scrutiny) for demanding that every American who wants to have a bank account acquire a TAXPAYER Identification Number, when every American is not a taxpayer.

The *final rules* Treasury issued mandate a minimum identification verification requirement. The minimum requires four items:

1. Name
2. Address (a residential and mailing address for individuals, and principal place of business and mailing address for a person other than an individual)
3. Date of birth for individuals; and
4. An identification number.

You will note that while earlier discussions within the regulation were specific about requesting a *"U.S. taxpayer identification number"*, the minimum requirement actually adopted by Treasury merely states *"an identification number"*. They have dropped the "taxpayer identification number" and in place of that they simply require *"an identification number"*.

So, what is an *"identification number?"* The regulation states that when a person cannot provide a TIN:

> *"...the bank may obtain an identification number from some other form of government-issued document evidencing nationality or residence and bearing a photograph or similar safeguard."*

There you have it. The *identification number* mentioned in the "minimum requirement" section is not a "U.S. Taxpayer Identification Number" (as mentioned earlier in the regulation), but rather a non-tax-related identification number from some government-issued I.D. – such as a driver's license or U.S. passport.

I should also mention that when the regulation says the person "cannot" provide a TIN, it means that you either don't have one or the account has nothing to do with any income subject to taxation! If an account has nothing to do with any income subject to taxation, I cannot execute a Form W-9 in relation to that account without committing perjury!

In summation, Treasury knows that the average American cannot be compelled (except in very rare and limited circumstances) to acquire or furnish a TIN to anyone, including financial institutions, in order to open an account. Accordingly, they wrote the regulatory "minimum requirements" for *Identification verification* to reflect that reality.

Congress has passed income tax laws that are totally constitutional, and the Secretary has written regulations that are equally so. It is the IRS that misapplies the law. Likewise, Congress' requirements in the Patriot Act (in reference to banking) are non-objectionable (from a nontaxpayer perspective), as are the regulations thereunder. Like the IRS, it is the *financial institutions* that are knowingly and intentionally misapplying the law. They are telling you that you must provide a TIN, when that is ***not*** what either Congress or the Secretary has said!

The third and last reason that a financial institution may give for demanding a TIN – rather than following the regulations and merely requesting it – is as a matter of "policy". This reason is the same grotesque perversion of law and destruction of your property rights as is committed by the company that says you can't work for them unless you commit perjury.

The bank will say that it is a "business decision" that all their depositors must furnish a TIN. They will claim that their computers are set up to identify customers by their TIN and that it doesn't make "business sense" for them to accept customers outside their protocols. Sounds plausible on first blush, right? WRONG!

If these institutions were merely asking for a SSN – not to be used as a TIN – or they were willing to input a "unique personal identifying number" (created by either the bank or the customer and formatted like a TIN) into their computer, then this argument would hold some merit. In fact, were it done in this manner I'd have no problem with it at all.

But that's not what these two-faced liars are doing at all. They are using the *facade* of a "business decision" as a ploy to demand a TIN! These institutions will say that it is fine for you to furnish just a SSN, but then they will demand that you place it in the "imbedded W-9" section of their signature card and sign under penalty of perjury that you are a *U.S. person* for the purposes of the income tax.

Even in the rare instance where they permit you to write it somewhere else on the card, when they enter your data into the computer you can bet your bottom dollar that they'll plug that number right into the "TIN" field on their computer screen. In doing so, this allows the IRS to locate your "taxpayer" account and provides a thin patina of pseudo-legality when the bank turns your property over to the IRS based on a levy that is the result of the corrupt process detailed earlier in this chapter.

The IRS cannot locate a bank account without a TIN. The IRS cannot administratively levy an account that does not have a TIN associated with it. Are you getting the picture? Do you understand why the banks are playing this obscene and illegal game? It is to convert you into something you're not so that the government can steal your money for a tax you never owed. How special.

Here's some good news. The first bank that respects the law and allows accounts to be opened without a TIN (by those who are not *U.S. persons* for income tax purposes) will be the healthiest, best-capitalized institution in America! Millions of Americans will flock to the institution and it will not know what to do with the flood of money that will come pouring through its doors. And since they'd be in compliance with the law, there is nothing the government could do. Once one bank breaks ranks and does it, others will have to do so in order to compete. Let the games begin!

WHAT OF EMPLOYMENT TAXES?

In this chapter I've kept the focus on the business-to-business environment and banking. I haven't discussed Employment Taxes in the context of "Working The Mark" because I believe chapter 8 said it all. And I believe our journey with "Janice" and "Frank" made the point well enough.

The illegal and unconstitutional theft takes place millions of times a week from the paychecks of hardworking Americans, usually at the hands of their fellow citizens. It is sad and it is a disgrace. But most importantly, it needs to end! [More on that soon!]

As I close on this chapter, let me leave you the words of the IRS "Statement of Principles of Internal Revenue Tax Administration".

> "At the heart of administration is *interpretation* of the Code. It is the responsibility of each person in the Service, charged with the duty of interpreting the law, to try to find the true meaning of the statutory provisions and not to adopt a strained construction in the belief that he or she is 'protecting the revenue.' The revenue is properly protected only when we ascertain and apply the true meaning of the statute." [emphasis in original]

I have two observations about this Statement. First, you will note that "interpretation" is only to be done by those "charged with the duty of interpreting the law". That is a very small contingent of people at the very highest levels of the IRS. They have no intention of sharing the "true meaning" of the law with you or even their own officers/employees. The true application of the income tax has been – until now – one of the best-kept secrets in the world. Second, few IRS officers/employees have ever read that Statement and no one in the IRS believes it or adheres to it. From the IRS Commissioner down to the lowliest first-time examiner, everyone at the IRS knows what the ***real*** 'statement of principle' is at the IRS: **GET THE MONEY!!!!**

The Lies They Tell To Cover The Lies They've Told

Chapter 10

"Formerly no one was allowed to think freely; now it is permitted, but no one is capable of it any more. Now people want to think only what they are supposed to think, and this they consider freedom."
~ Oswald Spengler

Who is it among us that imagines the government (or its quislings) is simply going to accede to that which is revealed in this book?

We've discussed how simple it would be for the government to tell the American people the truth, and we all know the government has no intention of doing that. If the government will not take the simple step we talked about in chapter 9 to tell the American people the truth, what do we imagine will be their response to this book? Will they remain silent? Well…yes…and no.

The government and its quislings will have something to say, but little of what they say will address the substantive points of law raised in this book, and most will be attacks on me.

The attacks on me are irrelevant. Calling me names and/or accusing me of every evil thing under the sun does not change the law one iota. Personal attacks on me will only demonstrate that there is no rational response to what is in this book.

That said, the government and its quislings do have a "portfolio" of canned responses they roll out whenever anyone challenges the legality or constitutionality of the income tax (as applied to the average American). A prudent person who wishes to investigate all sides of the issue would do well to explore what the "opposition" has to say. So let's do just that.

The IRS has oodles of "canned" responses on its website. These "canned" responses are meant to convince the readers that what they've heard elsewhere is "wrong" and "illegal" and the only voice that they must adhere to in such matters is the voice of the IRS. Or phrased another way, the only voice that should be heard is that of the government agency that's bent on continuing to perpetrate the largest financial crime in the history of world. Or phrased yet another way, the only voice that should be heard by you – the victim – is the voice of the perpetrator – the IRS. Gee…how reasonable.

If the contents of this book are untrue or inaccurate, I'd expect to find a whole bunch of compelling counter-arguments on the IRS website. After all, they've had more than 90 years to get their position all sorted out! So let's see what they have to say.

Unfortunately, that's going to be tough. Why? Because there is almost nothing on the IRS website that addresses the points I have raised in this book! In response to that startling revelation you're probably thinking "What? How can that be?" It's actually rather simple to explain.

To begin with, this book is the first time that all this material has been laid out in a comprehensive and orderly fashion. Since no one has done this before, the government hasn't yet had a need to concoct screwy arguments in an attempt to overcome or discredit it. Second, it's a bit difficult to argue that 2+2 isn't 4, though I imagine the government will do its best to convince you it isn't.

Because there isn't much on the IRS website that refutes what has been revealed to you here, I find myself in the strange position of having to anticipate what the government and its quislings will say about what is set forth in this book. I'll do my best to think like they do, but I admit that's a challenge. However, before I give you my version of their potential responses, there are a few things on the IRS website that are relevant, so let's look at them.

The Lies They Tell To Cover The Lies They've Told

CURRENT IRS RESPONSES

You may recall that in the Introduction I said, "...you will be shocked at how flimsy and transparent the government's propaganda really is." This is the time for you to judge for yourself.

EMPLOYEE

In chapter 8, we discussed the definition of "employee". Here is the government's response to that reality:

> *Section 3401(c) defines "employee" and states that the term "includes an officer, employee or elected official of the United States . ." This language does not address how other employees' wages are subject to withholding or taxation. Section 7701(c) states that the use of the word "includes" "shall not be deemed to exclude other things otherwise within the meaning of the term defined." Thus, the word "includes" as used in the definition of "employee" is a term of enlargement, not of limitation. It clearly makes federal employees and officials a part of the definition of "employee", which generally includes private citizens.*

Let's see how discerning you have become while reading this book!

You will notice that the government's response only quotes a portion of 3401; the portion that mentions *"officer, employee or elected official of the United States..."* But that's not all of the various persons listed, is it? What happened to *"...a State, or any political subdivision thereof, or the District of Columbia, or any agency or instrumentality of any one or more of the foregoing. The term "employee" also includes an officer of a corporation."* Why would the IRS quote only such a short portion of the statute? We shall see!

The government's argument then states, *"This language does not address how other employees' wages are subject to withholding or taxation."* Absolutely true – because the government intentionally left off the part about a "state" and the "District of Columbia", as well as government-owned corporations.

What the government has done here is to put forth an argument that is indeed false, and then show you that it's false.

The false argument is that payroll withholding only operates upon *federal* workers. The government then points out that there are "others" who are subject to payroll withholding. Well...duh! Officers, employees, and elected officials of a "state" and the "District of Columbia" and officers of government-owned corporations are also subject to it; so says the statute!

But – and this is important – please note that this entire line of response by the government completely neglects the fact that 3402 is only a collection mechanism for the tax when a *foreign person* is receiving U.S. source income in the form of "wages".

The government then trots out a number of court cases to support its position that more than just federal employees are subject to the tax, but since we agree with that position (as far as it goes) we don't need to read them!

WAGES, TIPS, ETC.

The government offers this as a "tax protestor argument":

> *Wages, tips, and other compensation received for personal services are not income. This argument asserts that wages, tips, and other compensation received for personal services are not income, because there is allegedly no taxable gain when a person "exchanges" labor for money.*

As we've seen, "personal services" is a legal term right out of the Code. Those engaged in "personal services" receive "wages". "Wages" is defined at 3401(a) and is a part of the collection mechanism used to collect the tax on U.S. source income earned by *foreign persons* when said *foreign person* works for the U.S. government or the government of a State or the District of Columbia, or is an officer of a corporation owned by the U.S., a State, or the District of Columbia.

The statement about exchanging labor for money is relevant to me because when I do that there is no privilege taking place and my actions are outside of and beyond the taxing power of the United States government. However, such an argument is indeed false when used by a nonresident alien because for him to exchange labor for money is a privilege subject to the taxing authority of the federal government.

As you can see, there really isn't much here to disagree with, other than the smarmy half-truth approach the government is using in order to try to deceive those less informed than you.

FOREIGN SOURCE INCOME

Speaking of smarmy half-truths, this one takes the cake!

> *Only foreign-source income is taxable. Some maintain that there is no federal statute imposing a tax on income derived from sources within the United States by citizens or residents of the United States. They argue instead that federal income taxes are excise taxes imposed only on nonresident aliens and foreign corporations for the privilege of receiving income from sources within the United States.*

This one requires some mental acuity to reason through it. Its sophistry is subtle. Let's break it down.

The first sentence of substance is, "*Some maintain that there is no federal statute imposing a tax on income derived from sources within the United States by citizens or residents of the United States.*" Please note that the government's statement does not address who **owns** the income.

Remember all the information in chapter 7 about *U.S. persons* acting as agents of *foreign persons* and the role of *withholding agents*? When a *withholding agent* withholds U.S. source income from a *foreign person*, whether under subtitle 'A' or 'C', the *withholding agent* is made liable for the tax and must file a return and pay the tax over to the government.

Technically, the government's statement is inaccurate. The tax has in fact been imposed on *foreign persons* deriving U.S. source income. We've seen that in abundance in chapter 7. However, some citizens and residents of the U.S. have been "made liable" for the tax if they act as a *withholding agent*. It would appear that the person tasked with putting together this particular item of IRS propaganda doesn't understand the difference between the phrases "tax imposed" and "made liable". That's not surprising. Few people, even attorneys, understand the difference. They presume the phrases are always synonymous.

The second sentence in the government's argument is, *"They argue instead that federal income taxes are excise taxes imposed only on nonresident aliens and foreign corporations for the privilege of receiving income from sources within the United States."*

There are two key elements in the preceding sentence that must be recognized in order to understand the government's little word game. First, note that it says "income taxes". It's plural. When the government is trying to get beyond a fact it cannot deny, it often blurs the lines in order to confuse or distract the reader. In this case the government is using the phrase "income taxes" loosely, to embrace any number of "internal revenue taxes" other than **the** income tax. Clearly, if we apply the *nonresident aliens* and *foreign corporations* position to taxes such as alcohol and tobacco, the concept is absurd.

Even if one wants to view the plural phrase "income taxes" as referring to ***the*** income tax, we are still faced with their use of the word "only". We already know that the income tax has also been imposed on U.S. citizens residing abroad with foreign earned income. So clearly the contention that the income tax has been imposed **only** upon *"nonresident aliens and foreign corporations for the privilege of receiving income from sources within the United States"* is false.

Possibly some readers think the IRS is saying that the income tax is not an excise. That is not what the IRS is saying here, but we know that no matter what the IRS may say, there is no question that it is an excise. We have already covered *Brushaber* in detail so there should be no question where the U.S. Supreme Court stands on this. But what of the legislative branch? What of Congress?

In 1941, reporting on "The Revenue Bill of 1941," the House Committee on Ways and Means prepared House Report No. 1040. In the section entitled "Constitutionality of Proposal" the report states:

> "It seems clear that Congress has the constitutional power to enact this proposed amendment. Generically an income tax is classed as an excise

(*Brushaber v. Union Pac. R.R. Co.*, 240 U.S. 1). The only express constitutional limitation upon such taxes is that they be geographically uniform."

Then in 1943 we find in '89 Congressional Record 2579-80', a report on the nature of the income tax. This report was prepared by Mr. F. Morse Hubberd. Mr. Hubberd was not only a former member of the Columbia University Legislative Drafting Research Fund, but he was also a former legislative draftsman in the Treasury Department. Clearly he was a man who would understand the income tax because he was in the business of drafting legislation for it! So what did Mr. Hubberd say about the income tax?

> "The sixteenth amendment authorizes the taxation of income 'from whatever source derived'.... So the amendment made it possible to bring investment income within the scope of a general income-tax law, <u>but did not change the character of the tax</u>. It is still fundamentally an excise or duty with respect to the privilege of carrying on any activity or owning any property which produces income." [underline added]

In 1980, the Congressional Research Service (CRS) issued a report on the same subject. The report was entitled, "Some Constitutional Questions Concerning the Federal Income Tax" [Report No. 84-168 A 734/275] and was written by an attorney for the CRS, Mr. Howard M. Zaritsky.

On page 6 of the report it states, *"Therefore, it can be clearly determined from the decisions of the United States Supreme Court that the income tax is an indirect tax, generally in the nature of an excise tax."*

There has never been any equivocation from Congress about the fact that the income tax, which it passed into law, is an excise tax. Congress has been crystal clear on this point.

It is critically important that you understand that the 16th Amendment did not, and could not, convert your right to property and the fruits of that property into a privilege. The 16th Amendment simply made *"the privilege of carrying on any activity or owning any property which produces income"* taxable by the federal government <u>concerning those for whom such activity is a privilege</u>.

What we see is that both the Legislative and Judicial branches have stated unequivocally that the income tax is an excise. That renders immaterial the view of the Executive Branch (which includes Treasury and IRS). Why? Because when it comes to the laws passed by Congress, the sole constitutional role of the Executive Branch is to faithfully execute those laws.

Once both Congress and the U.S. Supreme Court have spoken to an issue, such as the nature of the income tax, the job of the Executive Branch is to administrate those laws in accordance with the determination made by the body that passed the law (Congress) and the branch that interprets the law (the courts).

The job of the Executive Branch is to "enforce", not interpret. There may be times of uncertainty when, in the absence of clear determinations by the Legislative and/or Judicial Branches, the Executive Branch may need to make a judgment call, but that is clearly not the case here. Both Congress and the U.S. Supreme Court have spoken.

Now that we are clear on that, let us return to the IRS's silly "tax protestor" responses.

Do you see how the government goes about its refutations? It states an argument that is plainly not true, and then makes a hullabaloo about the fact that it's not true.

Many of the government's "tax protestor" responses begin with words such as "The taxpayer alleges that...." You should be able to see the little con-job here. By beginning with the word "taxpayer" the IRS is establishing at the outset that the person is one upon whom the income tax has been imposed or a person who has been made liable. Let's switch out "taxpayer" for its definition.

"The *person subject to any internal revenue tax* alleges that...." Clearly, if a person is subject to an internal revenue tax, there is little to argue about and the proper course of action is to file a return and pay the tax!

Although there are a few other items on the IRS website that might touch upon what has been revealed in this book, I won't bother to share more with you because the "game" is so clear that you would immediately see it yourself.

The purpose of this portion is to show you how the IRS plays this game. They present a false argument to the reader and then prove it's a false argument. Gee... isn't that impressive. Unfortunately, at times they do this so subtly that people who aren't steeped in the subject matter can become panicked and think everything they've learned is incorrect.

Having said all that, these are still just statements made on a website run by those who are perpetrating the largest financial crime in the history of the world. Who cares what they say! You have chapters 1 through 8 that review what the *law* says, not what a bunch of criminal thugs say on a website. Only an un-American simpering coward would ignore the law and instead listen to the IRS – but then we've already had that discussion, haven't we?

A DIRECT TAX

In the section above, the IRS does not say the income tax is a direct tax absent apportionment. However, they *do* say that on another page on their website. However, like all of their assertions, it relies on word-trickery.

> "Some assert that the Sixteenth Amendment does not authorize a direct non apportioned income tax and thus, U.S. citizens and residents are not subject to federal income tax laws."

Let's explore that statement. Since we already *know* that the 16th Amendment does not authorize a direct non apportioned income tax, what point is the IRS trying to make here?

The IRS is saying that some people assert that since there is no direct tax absent apportionment in operation as *income tax* in this nation, then "U.S. citizens and residents are not subject to federal income tax laws." Such a contention is of course, silly. While it is true that there is no income tax in America in the form of a direct tax absent apportionment, why wouldn't the actual *income tax* – an excise – apply to those who are engaged in the relevant and specified activities?

Once again we see the IRS making a nonsense argument and then telling us it's nonsense. Very impressive, don't you think?

The IRS then lists a handful of cases from the half of the federal circuit courts that have held the income tax to be a direct tax absent apportionment. BUT the IRS does not mention that the other half of the circuit courts have held the income tax to be an excise! My, how forthright of them!

They then tell us that one of those "direct tax" courts said that *Brushaber* ruled the income tax to be a direct tax without apportionment. But of course we know that any judge that said such a thing has rectal-cranial inversion because we've already read *Brushaber* for ourselves – with our own two eyes – and we *know* what it says!

Apparently the IRS has also forgotten the words of its own former Treasury Department legislative draftsman who said of the income tax, "It is still fundamentally an excise...."

And, the IRS appears to have forgotten the words of the Congressional Research Service: *"Therefore, it can be clearly determined from the decisions of the United States Supreme Court that the income tax is an indirect tax, generally in the nature of an excise tax."*

As I told you in the Introduction, you would be shocked at how flimsy and transparent IRS propaganda really is!

THE QUISLINGS

As I've mentioned repeatedly, the government has very little to say about the income tax. Other than the frivolous nonsense that appears on their website, they are virtually silent. Accordingly, I anticipate most of the supposed "refutations" will come from the government's quislings. These are people who, for whatever reasons, want the "largest financial crime in the history of the world" to continue. These are people who are happy to continue to see your property stolen, if there is some perceived benefit to it from their point of view. These people come from both the Left and Right of our political spectrum.

I should clarify that when I say the "Right", I mean Republicans, not Conservatives. The foundational ethos of true Conservatives is respect for individual rights, and property rights in particular. Conservatives also support the true and correct interpretation of statutes, and adherence to Constitutional boundaries. This book will be a breath of fresh air to Conservatives.

There is no question that those on the Left have no respect for property rights. The vast majority of their agenda cannot be carried forward unless property rights are abolished, or at least weakened to the point where they must give way whenever government says so (which, of course, means there really are no property rights).

But regrettably, the Republicans Party isn't much better. The GOP no longer represents conservative ideals. The only thing that can be said of the GOP these days is that they try (and sometimes fail) to stay just a teeny-weeny bit to the right of the Left. Gee whiz…there's something to be proud of!

Thus, we will find government quislings coming from both the Left and the GOP, albeit for different reasons. Their reasons are unimportant for the purpose of this chapter. The issue is what they have to say about the content of this book.

So what will they say? Hell, I don't know. Trying to think like human vermin who do not respect the *unalienable rights* of their fellow citizens is a challenge. It requires one to think like a liar. It requires one to look at "that which is so" and figure out how to lie to someone so they won't believe it. That's a tall order. The IRS does a fantastic job of it, but I'm at a bit of a loss.

Even after all the years I've been involved in this venue, I really haven't heard too many lies. Those who support the largest financial crime in the history of the world typically don't lie to justify their actions. They just violate the rights of their fellow Americans without much more than some weak-kneed excuse/justification.

This book will change that landscape. Those who support "the largest financial crime in the history of the world" will now feel compelled to attempt some exposition as to why what is in this book cannot be true. Since I haven't heard the opposition tell very many lies (because their M.O. has been to just ignore the law), I'll have to imagine what is to come.

The reason this book changes the landscape is that instead of vague statements about how the tax does not apply to everyone, this book lays out exactly to whom the tax *does* apply, which in turn constitutes a concrete statement about to whom it does *not* apply. If the tax has been imposed on A, B, & C, and you're not within A, B, or C, then it doesn't apply to you. Pretty simple, when you get right down to it.

Admitting that I'm at a loss on this, here goes my best effort.

Stupid Refutation #1 – Statutory definitions do not control.

We've been through all this, but I'll give you another supporting reference (as if the U.S. Supreme Court isn't good enough). There is a publication called "Sutherland Statutory Construction". It is an 11-volume set. Thanks to generous donations (made for this very purpose) from the listeners to my radio show, I own the set. Sutherland is the touchstone for issues of construction and interpretation.

> At 47:6 in Sutherland we find this:
> *It is not unusual for statutes to contain definitions of the terms used in them. Statutory definitions may appear either in separate sections, or in the body of substantive sections. It is commonly understood that such definitions establish the meaning where the term appears in the same act... As a rule, a definition which declares what a term means is binding upon the court.*
>
> And at 47:7...
> *The use of dictionary definitions is appropriate in interpreting undefined statutory terms.*
>
> And at 20:8...
> *When a legislature defines the language it uses, its definition is binding upon the court even though the definition does not coincide with the ordinary meaning of the word.*

We see that Sutherland imparts the identical rules we've already discussed. And what "other" rules exist that would contradict these? None whatsoever.

But Sutherland goes further than I have gone in earlier chapters. At 27:2 we find:

> *The legislature is the primary law-making authority and should be able to declare the law in any form it chooses as long as it is clearly expressed.*
>
> *To ignore a definition section is to refuse to give legal effect to a part of the statutory law of the state.*

But wait...there's more (at 27:1)!

> *In view of the imprecision of language as an instrument of communication, clear expression may often be impossible to achieve without the use of definitions or ancillary explanations and instructions. This is in recognition that unusual or fanciful definitions may be deceptive and misleading to the ordinary reader.*

Wow! Here Sutherland is telling us that statutory definitions not only control and are binding upon the courts, but if these definitions are "unusual or fanciful" they *still* control. Aren't you glad you're no longer an "ordinary reader"!

And finally, this from the U.S. Supreme Court:

> "It is axiomatic that the statutory definition of the term excludes unstated meanings of that term. Colautti v. Franklin, 439 U.S. 379, 392.

Stupid Refutation #2 – The tax doesn't have to be clearly imposed.

I know, I know; it's silly. But I'm guessing some nincompoop is going to say it, so I thought I'd cover it now.

> "Keeping in mind the well-settled rule that the citizen is exempt from taxation unless the same is imposed by **clear** and **unequivocal language....**" Spreckels Sugar Refining Co. v. McClain, 192 U.S.397 (1904) [emphasis added]

Enough said.

Stupid Refutation #3 – Engaging in business is a privilege.

Yes, someone was actually stupid enough to say this one out loud. A friend of mine in California asked an examiner with the State Board of Equalization (which has jurisdiction over all California taxation) what the privilege is that an American exercises when he buys and sells his own property for a profit. (The discussion was about Sales Tax.)

The examiner stated that there is no privilege unless you buy and sell your own property for a profit as a business. When asked where that distinction could be found in the law, he had no idea. (In fact there is no such distinction anywhere in the law!)

While that discussion was about Sales Tax, it highlights the ignorance of the "professionals" who make such absurd claims. Be wary of claims made by "tax professionals", whether in or out of government, that may sound reasonable or even compelling on first blush.

It's easy to rattle off a sentence such as, "There is no privilege unless you buy and sell your own property for a profit as a business." It's a lot harder to back it up. Make them back it up. They rarely ever can.

Stupid Refutation #4 – The IRS should be able to act in any way it wants.

Yes, there will be people who take this position. Their position goes something like this: The IRS is the agency tasked with assessing and collecting U.S. taxes and it shouldn't be hamstrung by any requirements to adhere to specific procedures.

There are a couple of things wrong with this perspective. First, that statement constitutes nothing more than an individual's personal opinion. Happily, such personal opinions do not translate into 'law'.

Second, a person who espouses such an opinion obviously does not care about your property rights. A tax agency that need not follow the procedures laid out in the laws that authorize its actions is nothing more than a thief masquerading as a legitimate agency. All Americans have an absolute *right* to know upon whom any particular tax has been imposed, and how that tax is to be legally assessed and collected. If we are deprived of this information then we lose the ability to hold the government – ostensibly 'our' government – accountable for its actions.

Despite this nation's ugly and meteoric slide toward "collectivism" and away from individual rights, the government knows that these rights still belong to us and are enshrined not only in our national heritage, but also in our jurisprudence. In other words, our unalienable rights are enshrined in our legal precedent. That is the reason the entire income tax scheme is based on disinformation, intimidation, and abusive behavior.

Those who want the IRS to function without exacting legal procedures/ boundaries are really saying that they do not believe in your rights, and that they support you being abused by the government. In short, they believe that the only 'rights' you should have are the rights the government *permits* you to have.

FREEDOM OF INFORMATION ACT AND OTHER IRS SCAMS

Those who hold the view that the IRS can do whatever it wants should be quite pleased at this time. The IRS is doing whatever it wants. Here are some examples.

The *Freedom of Information Act* (FOIA) allows a person to ask a government agency for "a copy of a document". The FOIA does not permit you to ask the government questions. Under the FOIA, the government must respond to your request in one of 3 ways.

1. The government can provide you with a copy of the requested document;

2. The government can tell you that no such document exists;

3. The government can refuse to give you the requested document under the authority of one or more of the statutory exemptions in the FOIA.

FOIA requests are handled by government personnel assigned to the Disclosure Office. Each agency has its own Disclosure Office. The IRS Disclosure Office is a joke. It should be referred to as the Non-Disclosure Office. The IRS Disclosure Office flags certain "requesters" and then the IRS provides nothing responsive to those requesters. That's a violation of the FOIA. There are also certain requests that the IRS long ago decided it will not respond to (in any meaningful way). All of this is meant to keep the truth from getting out. If there were nothing to hide, why violate the law in this manner? Let the information out and let the American public look at it.

Here's a prime example of their non-disclosure practices. After I learned about the ASFR program and its use of "dummy returns", I made a FOIA request. My request began with a background section in which I referenced the memo from the IRS Office of Chief Counsel in which it was revealed that the ASFR program was not 6020(b) compliant. (In other words, returns created by the IRS in the ASFR program are *not* created under 6020(b)). I then asked for a copy of any internal IRS document that spoke of, or referenced, IRS authority to create substitute returns under any provision of U.S. law other than, or in addition to, 6020(b).

Look again at the 3 options (shown above) that the IRS has for responding to a FOIA request. Since there is no statutory exemption that fit my request, the IRS was limited to either providing me with the requested document or admitting that no such document exists. There is no other option under the FOIA.

I think we would all agree that providing me with the requested document would have gone a long way to clearing things up. (Of course that's a tough one when no such document exists.) It would have provided even greater clarity if the IRS had declined to furnish me the requested document under the provision that no such document exists (which is, of course, the truth of the matter). But the IRS has a problem with that last option.

To admit that no such document exists is to also admit that the ASFR program is completely illegal – which it is. Instead of simply stating (as they have on less critical issues), "No document exists that is responsive to your request", they wrote me a letter in which they assured me that the ASFR program was legal! There is no provision in FOIA for that type of response. They also provided *zero* legal evidence to support their statement. (No surprise there.) In essence, they wanted me to believe the ASFR program is legal without actually providing a law that permits it. Their response was an illegal dodge so that they did not have to admit that the ASFR operates outside the law. Or phrased another way, it was an illegal act intended to hide another illegal act.

IRS Chief Counsel Notice #CC-2004-009 states, *"The current Automated Substitute for Return ("ASFR") procedures do not alone create a section 6020(b) return...."* Yet when the IRS is asked to provide a document that authorized them to create a substitute return under any other provision of law they refuse to provide such a document while merely alleging that what they are doing is legal.

Can you spell C-O-N-S-P-I-R-A-C-Y? Oh, and by the way, the act of engaging in a criminal 'conspiracy' is a felony. However, since in this case the felons are the ones deciding who gets prosecuted, I wouldn't hold your breath for any of these felons to be prosecuted.

The Lies They Tell To Cover The Lies They've Told

They prefer to prosecute innocent Americans who've never owed a penny in income tax! Can you spell T-E-R-R-O-R-I-S-M?

A few years back, I was invited to speak before several hundred people at a function in Sacramento, California. During my speech, I asked the audience how many had sent the IRS a FOIA request. About a third of the audience raised their hands. I then asked how many had received responses from the IRS that were completely non-responsive. Virtually every hand that had risen in the first instance went up again in response to the second.

I have peers in the research community who have stopped bothering with FOIA because they have personally been 'flagged' by the Disclosure Office and the IRS now routinely gives them non-responsive responses.

The IRS has turned the FOIA process on its head. While Congress intended FOIA to allow citizens to have access to internal records of an agency, the IRS Disclosure Office exists for no other purpose than to make sure that **nothing** gets out that will reveal the truth about the income tax.

And this obfuscation is not just a FOIA issue. Anyone can write a letter to the IRS and ask a question. On one occasion I asked a room full of people how many had sent letters to the IRS asking questions about the income tax. Many in the crowd raised their hand. I then asked how many had been told by the IRS that their question was "frivolous". Virtually every hand that had risen in the first instance went up again. How can an American citizen's honest and sincere question about the nature of the income tax be considered "frivolous"?

In reality, the IRS doesn't see the questions as frivolous. It uses 'frivolous' as a catchall word. Anything the IRS doesn't want to hear – or respond to – is 'frivolous'. It has gotten to be such a routine response that it has now literally become a joke within research circles and with plain old law-abiding Americans who are seeking information from the IRS. People get a response that says 'frivolous' and they just start laughing at the ludicrous conduct of the IRS. Unfortunately it's really not a laughing matter. It is an ugly and craven act of an agency that is violating the law and is dedicated to keeping the truth from getting out.

At this point I confess that I am out of ideas on what the opposition might say. Frankly, I don't know what they can say. It's all there in black and white.

COURT PRECEDENT

As I close this chapter I wish to caution you about trial court rulings. Trial court rulings do not establish precedent – and for good reason. The trial court is the lowest court in the system; what I call the "entry level court". In the federal court system that court is known as the United States District Court (USDC). There are 89 district court "districts" with 2,645 district judges (2009).

Do you want 2,645 men creating legal precedent each year? No. In fact, neither does the federal judiciary. That would create utter chaos.

By comparison, there are only 11 (numbered) federal appellate courts, known as the Circuit Courts of the United States. It is these "Circuit Courts" that establish precedent (though decisions of the U.S. Supreme Court are binding upon all Circuit Courts). If the various Circuit Courts create rulings that conflict with one another, the matter becomes ripe for appeal to the United States Supreme Court. Nothing is more 'ripe' at this time than the division in the circuits concerning the nature of the income tax. Half the Circuit Courts hold it to be an excise and the other half hold it to be a Direct tax absent apportionment. However, it should be noted (as shown in earlier chapters), the U.S. Supreme Court has already ruled on this issue. It held in 1916 that the income tax (subtitle 'A') is an excise. The judges in the Circuits who have said otherwise are either fools or criminals. There is no third choice.

My point is that you should not be misled by those who attempt to dissuade you from the truth by offering up trial court decisions. The IRS does this routinely on its website. They feel safe in doing so because few Americans know that trial court decisions do not establish precedent.

So why don't trial court decisions create precedent? Because any judge can say anything he wants to on any given day. He could be ill that day. He could have gotten up on the wrong side of the bed. He could have no legal expertise in that area of law and his clerks did a lousy job of research. The parties may have done a lousy job of briefing the issue. He might have some personal interest in the outcome, etc. For all these reasons (and more), the decisions of trial courts do not establish precedent.

Conversely, appeals to the Circuit Courts are heard by a panel of judges. There are the traditional 3-judge panels in most cases, and the "full panel" (known as 'en banc') in others. Only after a matter has been appealed and ruled upon by the Circuit Court does it establish 'precedent'. I should also point out that the precedent is only controlling within that Circuit, but may be considered by other Circuits when deciding the same type of matter or a similar legal question.

I say all of this because there is a trial court decision out there to support just about any claim any person wants to make. That's because the decisions of the USDCs are all over the map. Trial court judges have wildly divergent views which come through in their rulings.

Do you remember the discussion about the language used to impose taxes? Every statute that imposes a tax begins with the words, "There is hereby imposed a tax..." (or substantially similar language). Years ago I saw a trial court ruling in which a federal judge said that the following sentence imposed a tax:

"*...every employer making payment of wages shall deduct and withhold...*"

If that looks familiar to you, it should. That's the critical segment of section 3402; the collection mechanism for the situation where a person, upon whom subtitle 'A' has been imposed, is receiving his domestic source income in the form of *wages*. Clearly it is nothing more than what it says – a command to collect a tax. It is equally clear that it does ***not*** impose a tax – but a federal judge once said that it did. Even you – having read this book – know better than that!

The point is that these guys (and gals) are not infallible. Far from it! I've actually been present when a federal trial court judge (Percy Anderson) sat on the bench and blatantly lied to everyone in the courtroom. Why? For no better reason than that he wanted to empower the U.S. Department of Justice to gets its way in a particular matter, and the only way to hand them that power was to blatantly and intentionally mischaracterize the law. Everyone in the court knew what he was doing and why. There was no hiding it. Not only are these folks fallible, but many are also liars of the highest order.

The Good, The Bad, And The Mistaken

Chapter 11

"The road to truth is long, and lined the entire way with annoying bastards."
~ Alexander Jablokov

The road to the truth of the income tax has been a long one. The primary reason for this is the government's unwillingness to engage in an open dialogue about the true nature and proper (limited) applicability of the income tax. In the absence of an open and forthright dialogue, the American people have been left to find the answers themselves.

In an effort to explain what they do not understand, many Americans have found "the answer" in legal theories that are incorrect. Some are slightly off base. Others are simply inane.

In this chapter we will look at a number of these incorrect legal theories. We will not explore them in-depth. There is no need to do so. We will touch on each incorrect theory and I'll explain its basic concepts, as well as briefly address why it is unsound. That should be sufficient to arm you against them, or even allow you to refute them if any of these theories are presented to you or to someone you care about.

Most of the people who propound such concepts honestly believe them. Yes, they are mistaken – but they do not know that. The people who believe in these incorrect theories know that something about the income tax is wrong (as it operates in this nation). They see clearly that the Constitutional limits upon the government, coupled with the unalienable rights of the American people, could not possibly permit the income tax to lawfully operate as it does.

In their sincere quest to understand what is happening, they have gone to the limits of their understanding – or the information available to them – and have settled upon a particular "explanation". With the level of understanding they have attained, or to the extent that information is available to them, they feel that the "position" they've settled upon explains the problem.

These people mean no harm. They are good Americans seeking to understand the truth behind what they believe in their heart and soul is "the largest financial crime in the history of the world". They are attempting to find the truth that the government is hiding from them. Unfortunately, when one faces a government attempting to continue such a gargantuan criminal act, it is extremely dangerous to be wrong. Actually, it can even be dangerous to be right!

All that said, not everyone who propounds these incorrect doctrines is honest and sincere. There is a small minority who promotes false arguments for personal gain. To put it bluntly, these are scam artists. They could care less whether the concepts they promote are legally accurate or not. All they want is money. Fortunately, these unscrupulous people comprise a tiny minority within the Tax Honesty community. I do not even consider them a part of the Tax Honesty community. Rather I see them as shysters who have merely found some easy "marks" within the Tax Honesty community.

Isn't it ironic that these shysters *and* the U.S. government are both promoting a false understanding of tax law in order to fleece the American people!

UCC CONTROLS

The adherents to this theory believe that the Uniform Commercial Code (UCC) controls everything in the United States. They believe that all federal law operates within the structure of the UCC, and is subordinate to the UCC, and that Americans can regain their "sovereignty" by using various provisions of the UCC to fight federal claims/demands.

This argument is typically accompanied by statements asserting that "bankers" quietly overthrew the legitimate United States government in 1939, that there is no longer any legitimate U.S. Treasury, and that every aspect of law is now actually "commercial" in nature.

This argument is appealing to some because the adherent believes he knows something that the rest of the population doesn't. The adherent feels like he is "in the know", while everyone else is missing the boat. It is also appealing to those who have fixed 100% of the nation's problems on the existence of the Federal Reserve, which of course is not "federal" at all, but a legalized cabal of private banks.

The UCC is real. It has a very specific purpose. It addresses, controls, and offers legal remedies concerning various types of commercial transactions. Most Americans will never engage in any transaction governed by the UCC.

The UCC is *not* federal law. It is a *private code* written to provide uniformity in certain types of commercial transactions. The UCC is merely a voluntary guide that states can use as they enact their own state laws. The goal of the UCC is to promote uniformity in the principles that states will enact into law governing certain types of commercial transactions.

Since the UCC has not been passed into law by Congress we can clearly see that the imposition of taxes is not in any way controlled by the UCC, nor can the UCC be used to determine upon whom the tax has been imposed or who has been made liable. If a person is within a *class of person* upon whom Congress has imposed the income tax, or otherwise been made liable, the UCC cannot "undo" that reality.

EXPATRIATION/REPATRIATION

This theory entails expatriating your status as a "US citizen" and then declaring yourself to be solely a citizen of the state in which you live. Some even go so far as to say that they are merely "inhabitants upon the land" and take the position that to claim to be a citizen of any government body is to diminish their natural rights.

This incorrect theory is the result of the confusion about the term "US citizen". That confusion is very real.

The Good, The Bad, and The Mistaken

Most Americans presume that our citizenship comes from our birth within one of the 50 states of the Union. And that is true – as far as it goes. However, in 1857 the U.S. Supreme Court held [in *Dred Scott*] that there really is no such thing as a "Citizen of the United States" but that such phrase – as used in the main body of the U.S. Constitution – is merely shorthand for describing all those who are "citizens of the states of the Union". The Court made it clear that there are ***only*** citizens of the states, and that if one is a citizen of a state of the Union, then under the federal constitution said citizen has certain national rights and privileges as he travels from state to state.

> [**Author's Note**: Many people falsely believe that the 14th Amendment (1868) "repealed" or "overruled" or otherwise nullified *Dred*. That is incorrect. The 14th Amendment merely addressed the <u>constitutional reality</u> ***revealed*** in *Dred* by creating a second class of citizenship. Since the *Dred* Court had ruled that blacks held in slavery (even if later freed) could never be considered "citizens" under the main body of the Constitution (because the Founding Fathers did not intend the term "citizen" to embrace blacks held as slaves). Congress, by the 14th Amendment, simply created a second form of citizenship. The 14th Amendment calls this new form of citizenship, "citizen of the United States". This has led to much confusion.]

The 14th Amendment (1868) created another class of citizen. This new (second) class is called a "citizen of the United States". This has led to much confusion. And to this we add to the fact that people who are not "Americans" can still be "citizens of the United States".

An example of this is Puerto Ricans born in Puerto Rico. Federal law permits Puerto Ricans born in Puerto Rico to be *U.S. citizens*, but of course Puerto Rico is not "a party to the contract between the states, known as the U.S. Constitution." And we must remember that places such as Puerto Rico ***belong*** to the United States; the states of the Union do ***not!***

Clearly, a citizen of a state of the Union is what the Founders were referring to in the main body of the federal Constitution. If the states created the federal government, and merely delegated some of their sovereign powers to it, then the states of the Union (and their citizens) are something entirely different than the people born in places that Congress owns – even if they are called "US citizens".

And, we find this in the United States Code; Title 42, Section 1981:

All persons within the jurisdiction of the United States shall have the same right in every State and Territory to make and enforce contracts, to sue, be parties, give evidence, and to the full and equal benefit of all laws and proceedings for the security of persons and property <u>as is enjoyed by white citizens</u>, and shall be subject to like punishment, pains, penalties, taxes, licenses, and exactions of every kind, and to no other. [Underline added]

The authority for Congress to create section 1981 is Section 1 of the 14th Amendment. The "persons" being spoken of are the recently freed black slaves (and others similarly situated) and the 14th Amendment gives these "persons" the title "citizen of the United States". You'll notice that these *persons* are guaranteed a very short list of "rights" which they are permitted to enjoy to the same extent as "white citizens". The "white citizens" referred to are the *original class of citizen* – the citizens of the states of the Union. (This is not a racist position; this is a legal and historical reality. Whether we like that reality is irrelevant except with regard to possibly demanding that Congress change it. Good luck with that!)

Because of the confusion that is rife concerning the use of the term "US citizen", some Americans have felt the need to clearly distinguish which type of citizen they are. That said, there is no reason to engage in the expatriation/repatriation process.

Furthermore, as you've learned, the income tax is an international tax; it involves *foreign persons* with US source income and citizens who are "resident" in some other location within federal jurisdiction. Therefore, it is clear that expatriation/repatriation does not impact whether the tax has been imposed on you or not.

861 POSITION

This theory has most notably been championed by Larken Rose. This is a perfect example of someone for whom I have the greatest personal respect being honestly mistaken in a legal theory about the income tax.

The Good, The Bad, and The Mistaken

The "861 position" rests on the proposition that section 861 of the Code (and its related sections) are the controlling laws concerning what income is subject to the income tax, and what income is not. Section 861 (and its related sections) discuss the "source" of income. Section 861 addresses income from "sources within the United States" and section 862 addresses income from "sources without the United States". The premise is that these "source rules" are all-controlling concerning who owes the income tax and who does not.

The problem is that 861 does not control the imposition of the income tax. Section 861 (and its related sections) are exactly what they purport to be – "source rules" – no more, no less.

So, how do these rules affect American citizens? Here are some examples.

861(a)(C)(3)(ii) addresses income from personal services that is not considered from sources within the U.S. when:

> ...*an individual who is a citizen or resident of the United States, a domestic partnership, or a domestic corporation, if such labor or services are performed for an office or place of business maintained <u>in a foreign country</u> or <u>in a possession of the United States</u>....* [underline added]

863(c)(2)(B) addresses certain transportation income in the course of providing personal services:

> (i) *begins in the United States and ends in a possession of the United States, or* (ii) *begins in a possession of the United States and ends in the United States. In the case of transportation income derived from, or in connection with, a vessel, this subparagraph shall only apply if the taxpayer is a citizen or resident alien.*

861(b)(1)(B) is part of the definition "trade or business within the United States" and states:

> ...but does not include the performance of personal services — for an office or place of business maintained in a foreign country or in a possession of the United States by an individual who is a citizen or resident of the United States or by a domestic partnership or a domestic corporation...

Section 872 further clarifies "gross income" received by foreign persons. Subsections (a)(1) and (a)(2) state:

> ...*gross income includes only—*
> *(1) gross income which is derived from sources within the United States and which is not effectively connected with the conduct of a trade or business within the United States, and*
> *(2) gross income which is effectively connected with the conduct of a trade or business within the United States.*

Of course we know that the "list of items" of *gross income* appears at section 61. Is it all dovetailing for you?

And a bit further down in 872:

> *For purposes of this paragraph, the term "foreign employer" means—*
> *(A) a nonresident alien individual, foreign partnership, or foreign corporation, or*
> *(B) an office or place of business maintained in a foreign country or in a possession of the United States by a domestic corporation, a domestic partnership, or an individual who is a citizen or resident of the United States.*

And yet further down:

> *To the extent provided in regulations, a possession of the United States shall be treated as a foreign country for purposes of this subsection.*

And here's something from section 896, entitled, "Adjustment of tax on nationals, residents, and corporations of certain foreign countries":

> *Whenever the President finds that -*
> *(1) under the laws of any foreign country, considering the tax system of such foreign country, citizens of the United States not residents of such foreign country or domestic corporations are being subjected to more burdensome taxes, on any item of income received by such citizens or corporations from sources within such foreign country, than taxes imposed by the provisions of this subtitle on similar*

income derived from sources within the United States by residents or corporations of such foreign country...

You may be getting the picture that 861 (and its related sections) do not control the income tax, but they do provide significant clarity on it. The theme is clearly that the income tax is upon citizens when their income is from foreign sources (which often means places belonging to Congress), and to *foreign persons* with income from sources within the U.S.

Congress' purpose in creating 861 is not to "completely control" the imposition of the tax as the devotees of the "861 position" would assert, but rather to provide some necessary and appropriate clarity about it.

Furthermore, when we read the regulations for chapter 3 of the Code, there are various types of financial transactions addressed in some detail. At the end of many of these regulations we are instructed to go to section 861 (et seq) to determine the source of the income.

In other words, section 861 is something of a "traffic signal" that provides a "red light" or "green light" for moving forward or not. We can be reading a regulation in chapter 3 and think that the description of the transaction may apply to us. Then we reach the end of the regulation and are directed to go to section 861 (et seq) to determine whether the income is from a source *within* or *without* the United States.

We can go to section 861 and determine our status – i.e., citizen, resident, nonresident alien, foreign corporation, etc. – and then determine if the fruits of the transaction are *gross income* or not, based upon what the *source rules* say about our status and the source of the income.

Not every regulation for chapter 3 directs us to 861; only certain types of activities do. And as the regulations for section 861 state, using the *source rules* is particularly important in cases in which a person has income from sources both within and without the U.S. In such cases, section 861 is there as a resource to prevent us from falling into error.

In summation, 861 is clearly a significant tool, but it is not the "completely controlling" provision of law that some make it out to be.

FILING A "ZERO" RETURN

This method involves filing a Form 1040 but ending up showing "$0.00" as the amount due, no matter what one's actual income was.

You've already seen that very few people are required to file a Form 1040. The important element to keep in mind is that when a person files a 1040, he is certifying – under penalty of perjury – that he is within a *class of person* required by federal law to file a Form 1040.

There is no provision in tax law – anywhere – that permits people who are *not* within a *class of person* required to file, to file a return "just because" they feel like it or because they are working from some theory they cooked up in their own mind. In other words, when you file a return, the IRS takes the position that you know the law and that you have determined that you are within a *class of person* who is required to file. Whether you actually are within a *class of person* required to file or not is totally irrelevant to the IRS. You said (under penalty of perjury) that you are, and boy-oh-boy, they are going to hold you to it!

Since filing a 1040 is viewed by the IRS as **proof-positive** that you are within a *class of person* required to file, you cannot then claim to owe nothing.

And in most cases in which people file a zero return, *information returns* have already been filed against them which serve as additional evidence (from the IRS perspective) that they are within a *class of person* who is required to file.

As an example of this method, an American living and working in one of the 50 states, earns his own domestic income [his ***property***] of $82,000.00. He has *information returns* filed against him reflecting $58,800. He files a 1040, thus *declaring* himself – under penalty of perjury – to be within a *class of person* upon whom Congress ***has*** imposed the tax, but then claims that he owes the IRS nothing whatsoever. Possibly you can see why there is a problem here.

Many people who have filed zero returns over the past decade have done so (ironically) because they have had *information returns* (e.g. 1099 or W-2) filed against them! Talk about going about something backwards.

The concept that's at play here can best be illustrated by the actions of those upon whom the tax has ***not*** been imposed, yet who still receive a W-2. People who know the law will feel angry (deservedly so) when the private sector firm for which they work refuses to stop withholding, and refuses to stop filing an *information return* (i.e., the company intends to continue violating the law). The workers are then told (by someone who does not know what he is talking about) that they can overcome the company's illegal behavior by simply filing a "zero" return.

This concept was popularized by Irwin Schiff almost a decade ago. Despite my affection for Irwin, this method has harmed more people than I care to contemplate. For years it was seen as a boon by those upon whom the tax has *not* been imposed, yet who felt (usually correctly) that the actions of ignorant and/or stubborn third parties were continually turning these lawful nontaxpayers into IRS victims. In reality it was not a boon, it was a disaster.

The stated purpose of the zero return method is to avoid a potential criminal charge of "Willful Failure To File" [26 USC 7203] by being able to say that one *did* file a return. But here's the kicker – the IRS does not accept or process zero returns. The IRS rejects the return and then imposes a $5,000 frivolous return penalty on the filer!

The reality of it is that a zero return is a "gimmick" used by those who do not understand how the tax system actually operates and/or cannot get a third party to follow the law and stop illegally *filing information* returns.

The law is clear. If the income tax has not been imposed upon you, or you have not otherwise been made liable (such as acting as a withholding agent), then there is *no requirement* to file a form 1040 or 1120 (or any other return for that matter).

Every section of the Code that speaks of a requirement to file any tax return (including income tax) uses language such as, "Every person liable shall file a return…." There is no tax law in existence that says anything such as, "Persons upon whom the tax has not been imposed, or who have not been made liable shall file a return." Get it?

Now, I'm sure many of you are saying, "But Dave, we *are* stuck in the system by the ignorant and harmful acts of third parties!" I know you feel that way. I hear that every week and have for almost two decades. We'll talk about potential solutions very soon.

THE "CRACKING THE CODE" METHOD

This method has been conceptualized and promoted by Pete Hendrickson. Under this method one files a "zero return" but also files an IRS Form 4852 along with the 1040. Hendrickson's contention is that the Form 4852 "corrects" the erroneous *information returns* that have been filed against you.

The Form 4852 is entitled, *"Substitute for Form W-2, Wage and Tax Statement, or Form 1099-R, Distributions From Pensions, Annuities, Retirement or Profit-Sharing Plans, IRAs, Insurance Contracts, etc."*. (I guess no one every told the IRS about brevity.)

The instructions for the 4852 contain a statement of the form's purpose:

> "Form 4852 serves as a substitute for Forms W-2, W-2c, and 1099-R and is completed by taxpayers or their representatives when (a) their employer or payer does not give them a Form W-2 or Form 1099-R, or (b) when an employer or payer has issued an incorrect Form W-2 or Form 1099-R. Attach this form to your income tax return."

Clearly the IRS means for this form to be used in the absence of a required *information return*, or when a clerical mistake has been made. Equally as clear is that the IRS did not create this form to be used by those who have had *information returns* filed against them in violation of the law. If that were the intent of the IRS when it created the form, the statement of purpose would also say, *"or (c), when an information return has been filed in violation of the law."*

Pete Hendrickson takes a form created by the IRS to serve one purpose and suggests that people use it in a manner inconsistent with that purpose. In other words, Pete has decided that the form is to be used for a purpose never contemplated by the IRS when it created its form. Unfortunately, the law doesn't work that way. The IRS is the sole arbiter of how its forms are to be used.

Imagine that you own a company and you create various forms to help the company run smoothly. You create "Form XYZ". You specify that this form is for the purpose of requesting "compassionate leave". "Compassionate leave" is cases in which a spouse, child, or immediate family member is seriously ill.

The Good, The Bad, and The Mistaken

One day a department manager brings you a Form XYZ completed by a worker at your firm. In the field where the worker is to state the specific reason for the request he has written, "*Want to go to Disneyland. I've been promising the kids for some time but I can never seem to fit it into our weekends, so I need this time off.*"

You have the worker come to your office and you explain that Form XYZ is for a very narrow and limited purpose and that requesting time off for recreational activities is not the purpose of the form. The worker responds with, "*My kids have been waiting a long time and they're really counting on this. This would definitely be a 'compassionate leave' so it is appropriate for me to use Form XYZ*".

The worker is attempting to cast his own purpose for the form; a purpose you did not create the form to serve. You would be completely within your rights to tell the worker that his interpretation of what constitutes "'compassionate leave'" and his perception of how Form XYZ is to be used are not controlling – yours are. Likewise, the IRS has a right to determine what purposes its forms are to serve and to what extent. And they have.

The IRS is rejecting all the "Cracking The Code" returns it can identify, and hitting those filers with the $5,000.00 frivolous filing penalty.

Pete Hendrickson has made much of the fact that the IRS has sent out refund checks to thousands of people who have used his method. In reality, one shouldn't read anything into the fact that the IRS has done so. Tax returns are processed automatically, not by hand. The IRS computers are issuing these refunds under the presumption that the Form 4852 has been completed in accordance with the proper IRS understanding of the purpose of the form.

It has taken the IRS some time to devise a method to separate returns with legitimate 4852's from the "Cracking The Code" returns. That system is not yet perfect, but they are catching most. And remember, the IRS is free to demand repayment from anyone and everyone to whom it issued refund checks based on the use of its Form 4852 outside its intended purpose!

All that said, in light of the fact that we have a national crisis of pandemic proportions concerning the filing of *information returns* not sanctioned by the law, the U.S. government should create an official form by which an innocent party – someone upon whom Congress has not imposed the income tax – can officially communicate to the IRS that the *information return* was created and filed illegally and its content must be disregarded. But don't expect that – it would be counterproductive to continuing the largest financial crime in the history of the world!

There are many more oddball arguments out there concerning ways to file or not file a return. Some are the result of confusion and/or frustration. Some are just plain fraudulent. Some are promoted by folks who are nothing more than con-artists. The content of this book should give you a good foundation from which to avoid such painful problems. If you find what is in this book to be logical, rational, and truthful, then avoid anything that deviates from what is here and you will not run afoul with these harmful concepts and methods.

"Some boast of being friends to government; I am a friend to righteous government, to a government founded upon the principles of reason and justice; but I glory in publicly avowing my eternal enmity to tyranny."
~ John Hancock

There are a number of mechanisms that are used in the furtherance of the **largest financial crime in the history of the world** that we have not yet discussed, or have not discussed in terms of how one might want to respond.

When the IRS wants to see the "books and records" of a *taxpayer*, and the *taxpayer* has not voluntarily made these "books and records" available, the IRS will send out a "Summons".

When issued to a person in the private sector, an IRS summons is merely an administrative request for a *taxpayer* to produce records or furnish testimony. An IRS summons does ***not*** have the force of law and does not compel a private [non-governmental] person to do anything.

Please note that the IRS's authority to summons is only upon a taxpayer. And what is the definition of taxpayer?

> 7701(a)(14) - *The term "taxpayer" means any person subject to any internal revenue tax.*

In Economy Plumbing and Heating Co. v. United States (470 F.2d 585 (1972)), the federal court ruled that tax statutes and regulations "relate to taxpayers, and not to nontaxpayers". Since the authorization for the IRS to summons for income tax is contained within a tax statute [26 USC 7602], then under *Economy Plumbing and Heating* an IRS summons can only be applied to taxpayers.

Whether or not *Economy Plumbing and Heating* existed, however, you should now be savvy enough to understand that tax laws only apply to taxpayers and those with a reasonable nexus to the taxpayer's taxable activities (such as a *US person*). If it were otherwise, tax statutes would then effectively render moot all of our unalienable rights and our constitutionally enumerated protections from government power. If it were otherwise, all 308,000,000 Americans would have to lay open their lives to the IRS upon demand.

I know some of you are saying, "Well, Dave, isn't that the way it is today?" Well, yes…and no.

The reality is that the law, both statutory and case law, protects nontaxpayers from the IRS intruding into their personal affairs by issuing an IRS summons. However, since this is **the largest financial crime in the history of the world**, do not expect the IRS or the United States District Courts to follow the law. Remember, the key word in the italicized phrase above is "crime" – and crimes are committed by criminals!

Let's take a moment and look at the summons statute.

> 7602(a) – *For the purpose of ascertaining the correctness of any return, making a return where none has been made, determining the liability of any person for any internal revenue tax or the liability at law or in equity of any transferee or fiduciary of any person in respect of any internal revenue tax, or collecting any such liability, the Secretary is authorized…*

Let's break it down by clause. For the purpose of this exercise we'll place the words "*For the purpose of*" before every clause.

- For the purpose of <u>ascertaining the correctness of any return</u>. Clearly this means a return that has been filed by the taxpayer. Given that the taxpayer has filed a return, the IRS certainly has a right to determine if the return is accurate and otherwise comports itself with law. No problem here.

- For the purpose of <u>making a return where none has been made</u>. Plainly this is speaking of a return under 6020(b), which we have already discussed in detail. Section 6020(b) begins with, "If any person fails to make any return <u>required</u> by any internal revenue law...." The key word being "required". This does not permit the Secretary to make returns for people who *might* be required. The Secretary can only make substitute returns concerning persons he <u>knows</u>, as a matter of fact and law, *are* required.

- For the purpose of <u>determining the liability of any person</u>. This means determining the amount of the liability. In other words, determining how much the "person liable" owes to the IRS.

- For the purpose of <u>collecting any such liability</u>. This means that a summons can be used not only to determine the amount owed by a taxpayer, but may also be used to acquire information for the purpose of affecting the collection of the amount owed.

So what do all these clauses have in common? They all require the Secretary to *know* – before a summons is issued – that the person being summonsed is, under the law, a taxpayer. There is nothing in 7602 that permits the U.S. government to use its summons authority as a "general warrant" and thus render moot the prohibitions placed on the national government by the 4th and 5th Amendments to the U.S. Constitution.

Let me say this plainly: <u>There is no "tax exception" to any of the restrictions which the 4th and 5th Amendments to the U.S. Constitution have placed on the conduct of the government</u>. There is nothing in the Constitution, federal statutes, or any judicial decision, that provides a "tax exception" to these restrictions.

However, if the Secretary *knows* that a person is a *taxpayer*, then the Secretary may summons the *taxpayer*, or any person the Secretary has reason to believe has information that may assist the Secretary in determining the *taxpayer's* liability. In short, if the Secretary knows the person is a *taxpayer*, his power to summons is essentially plenary.

But how can the Secretary *know* that a person is a taxpayer?

The layout of today's Tax Code is merely a rearrangement of an earlier Code. The first Tax Code was created in 1939 and has a completely different numbering scheme. In 1954 Congress reorganized the Code. Congress did not change the legal meaning of various sections of the Code, but merely re-numbered the sections;

ostensibly to better organize the Code. Today we still use the format put in place in 1954.

Congress also used the 1954 reorganization of the Code to alter the language of many sections. Again, this was not intended to change the meaning, or alter what a statute was applicable to, but merely to "simplify" the language.

Do you smell a rat?

Section 7602 (summons authority) of the current Code is found to have its origins in several sections of the 1939 Code. Those sections are 3614, 3615(a)-(c) and 3632(a)(1).

These 3 sections appear within subtitle 'D' (Administration), chapter 34 (Information and Returns), subchapter 'B' (Determination of Tax Liability).

> [: We can trace the current section numbers back to their original sections of the 1939 Code by using a table published by the U.S. Government Printing Office for exactly that purpose.]

In order to understand these sections we need to see them in context. That context begins with 3611(a)(1):

> "It shall be the duty of any person made liable to any special tax or other tax imposed by law, to make a list or return, verified by oath... of the articles or objects including the quantity of goods, wares, and merchandise, made or sold and charged with a tax...."

The language of this section makes it clear that it is not talking about "income tax", but taxes imposed on the manufacturing or sales of certain products (such as alcohol and tobacco). That is why the "person made liable" must make a list *of the articles or objects including the quantity of goods, wares, and merchandise, made or sold and charged with a tax...."*

The next section is 3612, entitled, "Returns Executed By The Commissioner or Collector". If you're wondering if 3612 is the original version of 6020(b), you're right! The section begins with these words:

> *"If any person fails to make and file a return or list..."*

And what "return or list" is it referring to? It is, of course, the same "return or list" described just one section earlier, which is *"the articles or objects including the quantity of goods, wares, and merchandise, made or sold and charged with a tax...."*

Section 3613 permits the Collectors to make lists if the property upon which the tax has been imposed is not owned or controlled by anyone within the Internal Revenue District.

> "Whenever there are in any district any articles not owned or possessed by or under the care or control of any person within such district, and liable to be taxed, and of which no list has been transmitted to the collected, as required by law, the collector or one of his deputies shall enter the premises where such articles are situated…and make lists of the same."

There is no 3614, which brings us to 3615 – Summons Authority.

Section 3615(a) is the broad "general" statement of authority. Subsection (b) then describes the actual limited authority. Subsection (b) looks like this:

> (b) Acts Creating Liability – *Such summons may be issued –*
> (1) If any person, on being notified or required as provided in section 3611, shall refuse or neglect to render such list or return within the time required…

What we can see is that the summons authority is based on a person being *"notified or required as provided in the section 3611"*. We just looked at 3611 a moment ago. It's the one that requires the making of a list or return concerning *"articles or objects including the quantity of goods, wares, and merchandise, made or sold and charged with a tax...."*, which of course has nothing to do with the income tax!

Subsection (b) goes on to talk about false or fraudulent information on the list or return, failure to render the list or return on time and refusal to allow examination of books relating to the objects taxed, but all of these are directly related to and dependent upon the person being required to provide a list or return upon *"articles or objects including the quantity of goods, wares, and merchandise, made or sold and charged with a tax...."* This is clearly unrelated to the income tax.

In reality, today's section 7602 (IRS summons authority) pertains only to "*articles or objects...made or sold and charged with a tax.*" Of course, who is it in today's government that cares about the law's actual meaning when misapplying it can intimidate the American people and allow the U.S. government to continue committing the **largest financial crime in the history of the world**?

Now that we know what section 7602 actually is limited to, let's talk about how things work in today's corrupt environment.

When used within the government, a summons is "as the Word of God". In other words, if the IRS serves a summons on a federal officer/employee in the scope of his official duties, that summons is not a mere administrative request (as it is when served to someone in the private sector). The government officer must respond to the summons as if it is an order from a court.

If you are an American, living and working in the 50 states, earning your own domestic income, and you receive an IRS summons, what are your options? First, if you filed a return, then you should provide the IRS with the documents they have requested. If you have not filed a return, because you are not within a *class of person* upon whom Congress has imposed the income tax, then you are not under any duty to provide your **private** financial records.

What may happen if you refuse to furnish those records? The IRS has the option of filing an action with the U.S. District Court to seek enforcement of the summons by a court order. That is relatively rare. However, if it occurs you have two choices. One, you can argue in the U.S.D.C. why the summons should not be enforced. Two, you can do nothing, in which case the court will grant the IRS's request and you will then receive another summons with a court order attached. You must comply with the court order or risk a contempt action.

We'll discuss this further in just a bit when we explore what all Americans should be doing to end the largest financial crime in the history of the world.The IRS levy is one of the most feared weapons in the government's arsenal. Sadly, it is not the IRS's power to levy (which is very narrow) that is the problem – it is the robotic thug-like conduct of our fellow Americans that creates the false impression the IRS has power it really doesn't have under the law.

The fact that it is our fellow Americans who are joyfully doing the IRS's "dirty work" in these matters is as disappointing as it is disgusting. Americans need to wake up and consider whether they want to be a free people, or whether they want to illegally impose chains on their fellow citizens – and have their fellow citizens illegally impose chains on them!

Anyone who has watched TV crime dramas knows that "the cops" need a warrant to seize your property. And most Americans know that the cops have to submit their request for a warrant to a judge. The officers have to show the court that "probable cause" exists that a crime has been committed, and that the person whose home/business they intend to enter, and the property they intend to seize, is connected to the alleged criminal activity.

If the court agrees that *probable cause* exists, the judge will issue a warrant to enter the person's home/business and seize the designated property. The warrant must specify the address where the warrant will be "served", as well as a reasonable description of the property sought for seizure under the warrant.

As you can see, the requirement to seize property has some powerful "checks and balances" built in to ensure that Americans are not subjected to arbitrary seizures at the discretion of a government officer, which would, of course, be unconstitutional.

But somehow – when it comes to the IRS – Americans lose track of the fact that their property is being seized without a court order (warrant). The IRS no more possesses the power to seize your property based on a piece of paper entitled "Notice of Levy" than a cop would if he created a form on his computer and entitled it "Notice to Search and Seize".

When the IRS sends out a *Notice of Levy*, the levying officer simply pulls a piece of paper out of the desk drawer, writes your information on it, gets the paper counter-signed by his superior, and sticks it in the mail to someone he believes has possession of your property. The levying officer does this because his computer screen tells him that it is now appropriate to do so.

The IRS never sends a *Notice of Levy to you*! They only send it to others. If the *Notice of Levy* actually compelled the recipient to turn over your property to the IRS, why not just serve it on you and demand that you comply?

The IRS does not do this because the *Notice of Levy*, when used in the private sector, is similar to the Summons in that it is nothing more than an administrative request that compels no one to do anything.

Let's look at the IRS's levy authority, which is found at section 6331.

> *If any person liable to pay any tax neglects or refuses to pay the same within 10 days after notice and demand, it shall be lawful for the Secretary to collect such tax (and such further sum as shall be sufficient to cover the expenses of the levy) by levy upon all property and rights to property (except such property as is exempt under section 6334) belonging to such person or on which there is a lien provided in this chapter for the payment of such tax.* <u>Levy may be made upon the accrued salary or wages of any officer, employee, or elected official, of the United States, the District of Columbia, or any agency or instrumentality of the United States or the District of Columbia, by serving a notice of levy on the employer (as defined in section 3401(d)) of such officer, employee, or elected official.</u>
> [underline added]

I have broken the section into two parts. The italicized text is the "general authority" and as usual contains no specifics. The underlined text is the language that specifies how the authority may actually be used.

Please note that the specific language is taken almost verbatim from the definition of *employee* at 3401(c), which we addressed in detail in chapter 8. In other words, the IRS has the authority to levy the property of the very same people from whom the government has the right to affect payroll withholding. And that makes perfect sense! If the government has the legal authority to take a person's property in the form of payroll withholding, then it would also have the authority to take the person's property for unpaid taxes.

You will notice that the specific language of the statute states that the *Notice of Levy* is to be served upon the "employer (as defined in section 3401(d))". Nowhere in 6331 (or any other provision of law) does Congress specify that a Notice of Levy may be served on anyone other than the *employer* of an "*officer, employee, or elected official, of the United States, the District of Columbia, or any agency or instrumentality of the United States or the District of Columbia".*

In order for someone to say that a *Notice of Levy* may be legally served upon anyone other than the *employer* stated above, the person would have to make it up out of thin air because the law never says any such thing! There is a reason that the "general language" does not speak about whom the *Notice of Levy* may be served upon, but the "specific language" does. The specific language is there to restrict (limit) the general language. That is a fundamental aspect of how law is written.

In the regulations, the Secretary has expanded a bit on the words that Congress employed. He included banks and other entities regarding service of a *Notice of Levy*, **but** the person whose property is being levied must still be within a *class of person* from which the government had/has the authority to take his property in the first place through the mechanism of payroll withholding or backup withholding.

Payroll withholding and backup withholding represent the government's authority to withhold (i.e., seize property) administratively (i.e., without having to get a court order). U.S. tax law has been structured to keep that authority very narrow and thus within constitutional boundaries. If it were applied to the average American it would be patently unconstitutional by violating the restrictions placed on the national government by the 4th and 5th Amendments. Let's look at the 4th Amendment.

> *"The right of the people to be secure in their persons, houses, papers, and effects, against unreasonable searches and seizures, shall not be violated, and no Warrants shall issue, but upon probable cause, supported by Oath or affirmation, and particularly describing the place to be searched, and the persons or things to be seized."*

There is no way that seizing property – whether it is taking a percentage of your profit or withholding from your paycheck – could possibly stay within the boundaries of the 4th and 5th Amendments without pre-deprivation judicial review and/or an order from a court.

Here is the 5th Amendment (in its relevant part):

> *"No person shall be...deprived of life, liberty, or **property**, without <u>due process of law</u>..."*

Some people may be saying to themselves, "But Congress passed the law permitting the IRS to just come take your property." Wrong!

First, if you've understood the previous chapters, you know that Congress hasn't done any such thing concerning the average American. Second, even if Congress were inclined to do so, it doesn't have the authority.

The 4th and 5th Amendments deprive Congress of the authority to seize property without *probable cause* and *due process* of law. If all Congress had to do was enact a statute and those two standards were then considered to have been met, the 4th and 5th Amendments would be rendered meaningless.

Furthermore, those restrictions were placed in the Bill of Rights as an acknowledgement of the unalienable rights of the citizens of the states of the Union, which the government can never legislate against or around. The men who wrote the Bill of the Rights, and the state legislatures that ratified the amendments, meant them as a prohibition against Congress being able to enact statutes that violate our unalienable rights.

Because of our unalienable rights, and the restrictions imposed upon the government by the 4th and 5th Amendments, not only is Congress' authority to seize property administratively very narrow, but they have applied it narrowly in the Tax Code. Sadly, when it comes to *levy*, it is not the IRS that is the primary evil-doer, it is your fellow citizens.

After the IRS employee completes the *Notice of Levy*, he drops it in the mail to someone he believes has possession of your property. The recipient opens the envelope and says, "I just got a form in the mail from the IRS. I have to take your property from you now." Wow! If that statement isn't utterly shocking and disgusting to you, you need to get your head in the right place and start being an American!

Few, if any, people ever even wonder whether the form actually compels them to do anything.

> *- to cause to do or occur by overwhelming pressure and **especially by authority or law**.* [emphasis added] <u>Findlaw legal dictionary on-line</u>

> *- not compelled by law: done as a matter of choice or agreement.* <u>Findlaw legal dictionary on-line</u>

The two words shown above embody two opposite and mutually exclusive concepts. These concepts are particularly relevant to a discussion about how Americans respond to a *Notice of Levy*.

Being compelled means that you are "required" or otherwise "forced" to do something. Or phrased another way, you have no discretion in the matter.

Voluntary is just the opposite. When you do something on a voluntary basis, you do it freely, **without** being compelled.

Almost everyone in America who receives a *Notice of Levy* acts like they are compelled to steal the property of their fellow Americans. That is absolutely **not** true. You are not compelled to do anything just because you receive an IRS *Notice of Levy*!

Much as with the IRS Summons, the government has the option of going to court to enforce their "administrative" actions. The IRS is free to file an action with the United States District Court seeking an official court judgment (and subsequently a court order for seizure of property) if they want the legal power to **compel** you to turn over to the IRS the property of another person. The process by which the IRS can do this is called, "reducing assessment to judgment" and the IRS is free to go to court and do this any time it wants.

Do you know why the IRS rarely ever does this? Because stupid Americans **voluntarily** hand over to the government the property of their fellow American citizens when they receive a *Notice of Levy*! Yes, I said "***voluntarily***" hand over the property of their fellow Americans. What a travesty!

For an American to take property away from another American when compelled to do so by law is understandable (though distasteful). For an American to *voluntarily* **steal** the property of another American because he received an administrative form in the mail is disgusting and reprehensible. And yes, I said "steal"!

If there is no legal force – no legal compulsion – causing you to take (seize) the property of your fellow Americans, then you are doing it ***voluntarily***. To do it voluntarily means you are doing it without being required to do so. If you are taking the property of your fellow Americans without being required to do so by law, you are a thief! The fact that you didn't keep the stolen property hardly means you are any less a thief! If I come to your house and steal your BBQ grill off your patio, am I any less a thief because I gave your BBQ grill to my neighbor?

Some people will claim innocence because they mistakenly believed at the time that the income tax was imposed upon everyone and the IRS was appropriately enforcing the tax upon the person named on the *Notice of Levy*. Well…if that helps you sleep at night. But the U.S. Supreme Court has stated that when a government officer purports to have authority, it is the citizen's responsibility to determine whether that officer does, in fact, have that authority.

How many Americans who have received a *Notice of Levy* ever made any effort to determine if it actually compelled them to harm a fellow citizen? Almost none. This is a sad commentary on the condition of the American mindset in reference to liberty and freedom. We jump to be compliant and obedient to the government, but we can't be bothered to stand up for the rights of our fellow Americans. Many Americans today believe that we are losing our freedom in America. If that is true, how much responsibility rests with the government and how much is the result of how pathetic we are as free men and women?

This and That

Chapter 13

"Do not be too severe upon the errors of the people, but reclaim them by enlightening them."
~ Thomas Jefferson

In the flow of a book such as this, it is not possible to stop and include every fact this author might want you to know. In fact, it is unlikely, even if this book were three times its size, that I could impart to you everything I'd like you to know about the income tax and subjects relevant thereto. However, we are now at the point where we can slow down a bit and touch upon information that I feel is important but didn't fit into the "flow" of the dialogue in earlier chapters.

WILLFUL FAILURE TO FILE

Section 7203 is entitled *"Willful failure to file return, supply information, or pay tax"* and is the section of the Code under which most criminal tax prosecutions occur. This is significant because Americans who ponder the illegal and corrupt misapplication of the Code – and would like to do something about it – sometimes hit a personal roadblock when they consider that fighting for what is right might land them in jail.

Let's look at the statute (in its relevant part).

> *7203 – Any person required under this title to pay any estimated tax or tax, or required by this title or by regulations made under authority thereof to make a return, keep any records, or supply any information, who **willfully** fails to pay such estimated tax or tax, make such return, keep such records, or supply such information, at the time or times required by law or regulations, shall...be guilty of*

a misdemeanor and, upon conviction thereof, shall be fined not more than $25,000 ($100,000 in the case of a corporation), or imprisoned not more than 1 year, or both, together with the costs of prosecution. [emphasis added]

The "failure" aspect is pretty clear. If a person is required by law to do any of the things listed in the statute, and fails to do one or more of them, then he has "failed" to meet his duty. Clear enough.

However, the standard under 7203 is not just that one has failed to do something. The standard is that one has *willfully* failed to do something. How does that change things?

Most of you reading this book have children or have had experience with small children. If someone were to say, "That child is willful", there would be little doubt in your mind what that means. It carries the connotation that the child knows what is right, or knows what his parents (or other adults) expect of him, but intentionally chooses to do that which he knows is wrong. The same definition applies in 7203!

> **Willful** – *Said or done on purpose; deliberate. Obstinately bent on having one's own way.* The American Heritage® Dictionary of the English Language, Fourth Edition

> **Willful** – *Referring to acts which are intentional, conscious and directed toward achieving a purpose. Some willful conduct which has wrongful or unfortunate results is considered "hardheaded," "stubborn" and even "malicious." Example: "The defendant's attack on his neighbor was willful."* Law.dictionary.com

This is one of the rare occasions in which the standard English dictionary definition and the legal definition are virtually synonymous.

Of course, when it comes to 7203, we must keep in mind that the "failure" is failure to do a known or recognized legal duty, and therefore the *willful* choice to evade that duty constitutes a criminal offense.

With all that said, 7203 is possibly the most abused criminal statute in U.S. law. While there are very few prosecutions each year under 7203 (in relation to the nation's population), almost no one who is prosecuted under this section – including those who are convicted – ever violated it!

[**Author's Note:** Section 7203 can be used for taxes other than income tax, but is used almost exclusively in reference to the income tax, and we will limit our review of the subject to its use in income tax cases.]

You will notice that the statute's opening words are, "Any person *required* under this title....". I'll assume that by now you understand that Congress has never imposed the income tax upon the average American. Therefore the average American cannot be "required" to do anything concerning the income tax. Yet that is exactly who is usually prosecuted under 7203!

Since the average American has not had the income tax imposed upon him, and therefore he cannot be "required" to do anything, why is he prosecuted? For one reason and one reason alone – to terrorize the American people into continuing to be complacent sheep who allow the parasite (government) to continue sucking the life out of them. These 7203 prosecutions – conducted by the U.S. Attorney's Office – are nothing more than the "mob enforcers" for organized crime, breaking knee caps of those who don't want to pay the "protection" money to the mob.

Let me speak plainly: The U.S. Department of Justice and the U.S. Attorney's Office conspire to prosecute and jail innocent Americans upon whom Congress has never imposed the income tax. And you thought you lived in a free country!

On my radio show, I frequently refer to January 1st through April 15th as "The United States government's annual Tax Terrorism Season". This is because during that time the U.S. government uses all its media resources to create a campaign of fear directed at the American people. And the government attempts to structure its court actions in such a way that it will be able to publicize its criminal tax case victories as part of its terror campaign.

Let's explore 7203 a bit more. There are a few legal elements that are necessary for the government to support a "willful failure to file" case.

First, as we just covered, there is the *required* element. The government must show that the defendant was *required* to do the thing that the government contends he didn't do.

Second, the government must show that the defendant *failed* to do the thing required.

Third, the government must show that the defendant knew he was under a legal duty to do the thing and *willfully* chose not to do it.

These things that the government must show/prove are commonly referred to as the "burden of proof", and in criminal cases that burden is always upon the government. In a criminal trial the accused does not need to prove he is innocent; the government must prove he is guilty.

Most of you are probably wondering how the government can ever get past point #1 – being *required* to do the thing. How the government gets past this is a two-part equation.

The first part of the problem is that the judge looks at things such as W-2s, 1099s, etc. and finds that the government has made a prima facie case that the defendant is a person required to file. In the rare instances in which the defense challenges the "required" element, the judge sees the W-2s, 1099s, etc., and decides that it is the jury that must decide whether the person was *required*.

While the judge leaves it to the jury to decide whether the defendant is a person who was required to file, he doesn't *really* leave it to the jury. While it is true that the jury must decide whether the government has met its burden on all 3 elements, the judge always gives the jury "instructions" about how the jury is to consider the question of a legal "requirement". And what does the judge tell the jury about this? He tells the jury that they **must** take the law as he gives it to them. In other words, he tells them that they must decide the question of the defendant being "required", but that they must decide it as directed by him! In many cases, federal and state judges have instructed juries that the defendant was required to file and that they (the jury) must use his determination of the law when deciding the defendant's innocence or guilt.

Now let's take a moment and think this through. The prosecutor is a government employee. The judge is a government employee. The prosecutor (gov't employee) is under the legal burden of proving every element of the crime. (For the purposes of 7203, there are 3 elements to be proven.) If he cannot prove *every* element of the crime, then the jury must acquit.

All too often the problem is that in reality the prosecutor is alleviated from his burden to prove the "required" element because the judge (just another government employee) tells the jury that the defendant <u>was</u> required by law to file, and then tells the jury that his determination is the only one that they are permitted to apply in their deliberations.

When judges do this, they are gutting the defendant's ability to put on a credible defense by removing one of the most important prosecutorial burdens, and preventing the jury from reaching an impartial verdict! The judge's actions are nothing more than institutionalized jury tampering.

How significant is this "judicial jury tampering"? It would be hard to overstate how injurious this practice is to the American citizen sitting at the defense table. In cases in which the juries have been savvy and have demanded to see the statutory evidence that the defendant was required to file, the judges have not been able to provide the juries with anything credible and the juries have frequently acquitted the defendant.

Is it my opinion that federal prosecutors could care less about railroading the innocent into jail? Hardly. Here is what a former top-ranking Treasury Department official has to say about what is taking place in the courts today:

> *"Americans are no longer secure in law - the justice system no longer seeks truth and prosecutors are untroubled by wrongful convictions."*
> -- Paul Craig Roberts (former Asst. Secretary of the Treasury)

Mr. Roberts is being kind when he says that prosecutors are "untroubled" by wrongful convictions. After nearly two decades of watching what they do, it is my opinion that at times they intentionally seek out wrongful convictions. Harsh words, yes, but I believe the facts bear out the conclusion.

Let's now look at the element of "knows or has reason to know", which is an essential element of having acted *willfully*. This is a standard legal phrase. It is used in a number of different legal applications. In 7203, it is one of the elements that the government **must** prove at trial in order for the jury to convict. Well…sort of. It would be a necessary element for the government to prove if the jurors would open their eyes and stop acting like sheep!

In a *Willful Failure to File* trial the accused will sometimes take the stand and testify as to why he did not file a return. In these instances the accused (in response to questions by counsel) tells the jury why he doesn't believe he was/is required to file a tax return. By this testimony the accused is attempting to show the jury that he did not act *willfully* because he truly did not believe he was required to file a tax return.

The U.S. Supreme Court has already stated that when *willfulness* is an issue it is not important whether the jury agrees with the views of the accused; it is only important that they believe the accused truly thought that he was not required to file.

In some cases, the accused has years of written communications back and forth with the IRS attempting to have the agency establish that he has a legal duty to file (or not) and the IRS has never given him anything that shows he has any legal duty to file. In other cases, defendants have written books or produced successful videos detailing their legal views about the income tax and why they believe they are not required to file. Others have audio tapes of meetings with the IRS in which they've asked these questions and the IRS has been unable (or unwilling) to respond.

A number of my clients have asked the IRS – face-to-face – at live meetings, one simple question: "Can you provide me with a citation in the law that requires an American citizen, living and working in a state of the Union, earning nothing but his own domestic income, to file a 1040?" Never once has the IRS provided the requested citation. Usually they say things such as, "That's a frivolous argument" or "I see you didn't come here to cooperate" or some other such non-responsive reply. I want to reiterate that no IRS officer/employee has *ever* provided a response to that simple, direct, and forthright question.

A couple of years ago I was at a meeting with the IRS in Los Angeles, California. An IRS officer asked me to explain what a nontaxpayer was. I told her that section 7701(a)(14) is Congress' definition of *taxpayer*: "*The term 'taxpayer' means any person subject to any internal revenue tax.*" I explained that if a taxpayer was "any person **subject to**" the tax, then a nontaxpayer would simply be any person **not** subject to the tax. She seemed stunned by the simplicity of my response. (I think "embarrassed" would have been a more appropriate reaction; embarrassed that they hadn't figured that one out on their own.)

Next, she asked me what I believe causes a person to be a nontaxpayer (aka, a person **not** subject to the tax). I told her that I found the question to be ridiculous. I responded, *"It is not for the American people to tell the IRS why they are not subject to the income tax. It is for the IRS to tell the American people what makes them subject to the tax, and that is something the IRS has been unable or unwilling to do for 50 or 60 years now."*

She started to respond but before she could get the first word out, the Area Counsel (an IRS attorney) reached over, touched the officer on the arm and said, "We don't need to get into that." Here was a perfect opportunity for the IRS to set me straight (from their perspective), but the IRS attorney strangled that discussion in the cradle. This is standard IRS policy; they will never talk about what makes the average American subject to the tax - because they can't!

Regrettably, Americans are so brainwashed to believe that "everyone" is required to file a return that they don't really listen to the defendant's testimony. I don't think they care what the accused has to say.

I believe there is some petty small-mindedness on the part of the jurors. I believe they are saying to themselves, *"Everyone knows you have to file! Hell, I file every year. I pay my taxes. Who does this guy think he is coming in here trying to tell me he doesn't have to file. If I have to file, he has to file!"* There's only one problem with this. The juror who is saying that has never read a word of tax law in his life. He has absolutely no idea what he's talking about. And the government LOVES it!

This brings us to the final part of the problem. It's a shame juries (both grand and petite) don't understand that one of their primary roles is to **protect** Americans against just this sort of government abuse. Yes, a trial (petite) jury's number one job is to determine whether the accused has committed the crime alleged, but a huge part of that process is also to determine if the government is attempting to railroad the accused by "trick or device".

When one government bureaucrat makes the allegation, and then another government bureaucrat (wearing a black robe) tells the jury that they **must** "take his word for it" instead of the first bureaucrat meeting his "burden of proof", there is some seriously stinky stuff going on and the jury should be astute enough to take stock of that and acquit the defendant. There is only one reason for the government to cheat in these trials. That is to send innocent Americans to jail as an act of <u>domestic terrorism</u> meant to intimidate the American public into complacently continuing to be the victims of the largest financial crime in the history of the world.

SYSTEM OF RECORDS

U.S. government agencies maintain what are called "systems of records". That's an awkward title that merely describes the "information catalogue system" by which agencies keep all the data they accumulate.

Have you ever put something on your computer, but then months or years later couldn't remember what folder/file you placed it in? I know I have. The *system of records* is the government's way of preventing that problem.

As you can imagine, the government collects and amasses a gargantuan amount of data. Each agency must not only store that data, but also be able to locate and retrieve it on demand. The *system of records* is the "information catalogue system" by which they keep all that data in an organized fashion.

Most of the government's *systems of records* are dull and unimportant. Some are not!

We just discussed *Willful Failure to File* in some detail. In chapters 6, 7, and 8, we discussed that the income tax is only upon a *foreign person* with domestic source income and U.S. citizens with foreign-earned income. And of course, the *withholding agent* is made liable for the *foreign person's* tax.

Let's see how all that ties in with the IRS's *system of records*.

Where does the IRS keep all of its records concerning taxpayers who the IRS believes have committed *Failure to File*? We find those records are kept in a system of records designated as "Treasury/IRS 49.007" and entitled "Overseas Compliance Projects System".

The information in this system of records (which appears in the Federal Register) states the following:

- The system is maintained by the *Assistant Commissioner, International*.
- The system manager is the *Assistant Commissioner, International*.
- The system pertains to income tax, gift tax, and estate tax.
- Categories of individuals covered by the system are U.S. citizens, Resident Aliens, and Nonresident Aliens.
- Item #4 in the description of records covered by the system is "failure to file required returns or pay tax due."

There are some interesting issues to note here.

First, we can see that *failure to file required returns or pay tax due* essentially mimics the language of 7203, thus allowing us to have confidence that this *failure to file* is the same as 7203 – even though we know it must be because there is no other section in the Code that addresses *failure to file*.

Second, the individuals covered in the system are exactly those we have discussed, i.e. nonresident aliens with domestic source income, and U.S. citizens and resident aliens with foreign-earned income. (I know we haven't addressed resident aliens much, but tax law treats lawfully admitted aliens in a manner virtually identical to U.S. citizens.)

Third, this *system of records* is maintained **exclusively** by the *Assistant Commissioner, International*.

I have saved the best for last. There is no other *system of records* in existence in which records are maintained concerning people the IRS believes have committed the offense of *failure to file*! Or phrased another way, the only records that the IRS keeps about people it believes have committed *failure to file* are under the sole and exclusive authority of the *Assistant Commissioner, International*.

MORE SYSTEMS OF RECORDS

Do you remember that in chapter 7 we discussed the various components within the *Office of the Assistant Commissioner, International*? One of the components was the *Office of Taxpayer Service and Compliance*.

IRS *system of records* number 49.008 is entitled "Taxpayer Service Correspondence System". Care to guess who maintains this system of records and who is its manager? You're right; it's the *Assistant Commissioner, International*.

What records does this file cover? "Correspondence from taxpayers."

And of course there is no other *system of records* entitled *Taxpayer Service Correspondence*, nor any other system that contains "correspondence from taxpayers." What this means is that all "correspondence from taxpayers" is maintained by the *Assistant Commissioner, International*.

Are you getting it?

STATE INCOME TAX

Most people who discover the truth about federal income tax ask how those truths relate to state income tax.

Most states have an income tax: some don't. A better description than, "Most states have an income tax" would be "Most states have piggybacked onto the federal income tax scheme." In a practical sense, there is no such thing as state income tax. It's really just another jurisdiction deciding to also tax the same privilege.

Here's an analogy to help clarify the point for you.

Let's say you're driving down the road and you get stopped by a police officer for speeding. He writes you a $300.00 ticket. The area in which you were stopped and cited is one in which the city and county exercise *concurrent jurisdiction*, so each is entitled to a share of the revenue generated from the "rolling revenue officer". When you pay the fine, the city receives $100.00 of it, and the county $200.00.

In this example, two entities received a cut of your hard-earned money. Was there one violation, or two? Since you were only cited for speeding, there is clearly only one violation. Despite the fact that there was only one violation, two jurisdictions got a piece of the action.

That is exactly how state income tax works. There is one privilege, with two jurisdictions (federal and state) claiming their share.

State personal income tax is based 100% on the same criteria as federal income tax. Many states even have statutes, regulations, or other authoritative statements that say things such as, "The requirement to file a state personal income tax return is predicated on the requirement to file a federal return".

The states use the same definitions as the federal government. Terms such as *gross income, taxable income, taxable year,* etc. are the same.

Here are some examples from California law.

> 17071. Section 61 of the Internal Revenue Code, relating to gross income defined, shall apply...
>
> 17073(a). Section 63 of the Internal Revenue Code, relating to taxable income defined, shall apply...
>
> 17020. "Trade or business" includes the performance of the functions of a public office.
>
> 17074. Section 64 of the Internal Revenue Code, relating to ordinary income defined, shall apply...

And we could go on and on. The point being that the income taxes of the states are tied to the federal tax in virtually every way.

Remember that *gross income* is merely a definition of a species of income. That species is income received by a person upon whom Congress has imposed the federal income tax (and you know who that is). There is no way for the states to adopt the language of *gross income* from the federal Tax Code while leaving the context behind. The context is ***the*** pivotal element of the definition! That is why the states specifically cite the Internal Revenue Code as the source of the key definitions. If the states simply re-printed the definition of *gross income*, then arguably it would lose the original context. However, by specifically stating that the definition is the same as section 61 of the Internal Revenue Code, the context is preserved.

Although I used California law as an example, it is the same for every state that has an income tax. The pivotal definitions are specifically cited as being the same as the relevant sections of the Internal Revenue Code.

Do the states admit that their income tax is imposed upon the same *class of persons* as the federal income tax? Well, it depends. If a person believes that the federal income tax applies to everyone, then the states will admit that their income tax statutes are keyed to the Internal Revenue Code.

However, if you begin to make a case that you are not within a *class of person* upon whom the federal income tax has been imposed, then the state will lie and say that its income tax is different than the federal income tax.

I was present at an appeals hearing before the Arizona State Tax Board and personally heard a member of the Board lie through her teeth and say that Arizona income tax is its own tax, unrelated to the federal income tax. Despite her lie, section 105 of the Title 43 of the Arizona Revised Statutes (Taxation on Income) makes all of the definitions of the Internal Revenue Code applicable to Arizona income tax law.

The member of the Arizona State Tax Board lied through her teeth because the states that have the income tax are just as dedicated to continuing the largest financial crime in the history of the world as the United States government.

Thrashing About

Chapter 14

"When the government violates the people's rights, insurrection is, for the people and for each portion of the people, the most sacred of rights and the most indispensable of duties."
~ Marquis De Lafayette

    Because the income tax is so obnoxious, there has been an almost constant cacophony of suggested or recommended "alternative taxes". What is conspicuously absent from every one of these discussions is any explanation of the constitutional grounds upon which such tax schemes could be erected.

    There is good reason for this silence. There is an old expression that goes, "It is better to remain silent and be thought a fool than to speak and remove all doubt." Those who propose various alternative taxes do not want any discussion about how their pet alternative would fair constitutionally.

    If there is no discussion about the constitutionality of the types of tax they propose, then these folks enjoy being seen as wise and progressive. Once one raises the question of how the tax will fair constitutionally, they have no answers and they are revealed for the fools they are.

    Many a reader may be offended by what I just said because so many Americans support the various alternative taxes that have been offered over time. Please don't be offended.

    If you are an ordinary American, because you are living in this era you have not been taught anything meaningful about the Constitution. And that is intentional. Not being taught anything meaningful about the Constitution hardly prepares you for the task of testing proposed tax schemes (or any other government schemes for that matter) against the standard of the Constitution. Hopefully, this book has provided some additional insight for you in that area.

Additionally, my criticism is aimed far more at the state and federal politicians who make such proposals than at you for possibly supporting them. Although most Senators and Congressmen today know about as much about the Constitution as I do about astrophysics, they have a *duty* to know; a duty concerning which they have been, and remain, derelict.

So let us examine some of the more popular "alternative taxes".

FAIR TAX

The Fair Tax is merely a marketing name for a *national retail sales tax*. "Fair Tax" sounds so much more…fair…than the concept of adding yet another tax on everything you buy.

Another name for this tax is a "consumption tax". In other words, you get taxed based on the value of what you purchase. The advocates of this type of tax would tell you that the more you consume, the more tax you pay. The less you consume, the less tax you pay. That's not true.

The tax would be a percentage of the dollar value of any purchase you make, not how much you purchase. That means that in reality, with time, it would result in people purchasing the least expensive items they can live with. So we would not necessarily consume less, we would consume less quality: lower-ticket items.

A high quality blender for your kitchen? Not any more. A cheap one will do.

Fashionable clothing? Nope. Bland, unattractive, no-name clothes will be what most people turn to.

A nice, safe, roomy, comfortable car? Not a chance. The smaller, cheaper car that will get the kids to school and you to work will be the order of the day.

The beautiful, spacious home you've always been dreaming of? Forget about it. The new tax will put it out of reach. Gee whiz, isn't that "fair"!

I only offer these tidbits to give you a glimpse into life under such a "fair" arrangement. The economic fallout would be dramatic. Yet these are only the practical effects of such a scheme, and have nothing to do with whether or not it is constitutionally sound.

"Sales tax" is simply another *excise* tax. It is a tax upon the exercise of a privilege. The California statute that imposes the sales tax in that state is worded in a manner that makes this principle clear.

> "For the **privilege** of selling tangible personal property at retail a tax is hereby imposed upon all retailers...."
> Section 6051, California Revenue and Taxation Code. [emphasis added]

Do not be confused and believe that the State of California is there declaring (making into law) that selling your property to the public is a privilege. They are not. They would, I'm sure, but they know they do not have the power to do so.

The meaning of section 6051 is that the State has imposed a sales tax **_only_** when the sale constitutes a privilege – which is almost never!

> [**Author's Note**: I have used the California statute because it clearly makes the point. However, sales tax is always an excise. There are state statutes that impose sales tax without ever mentioning the word "privilege", but that omission does not in any way change the fact that sales tax is always an excise.]

We have already discussed that as Americans we have *unalienable rights*, which include the right to acquire property, own property, use property (in any manner that does not interfere with the equal rights of others), and dispose of property. The U.S. Supreme Court has acknowledged these rights time and again. So, if we have these rights, where's the privilege? Good question!

There are plenty of government privileges. But most have nothing to do with sales tax. The government considers driving a vehicle with a license to be a privilege. Do we pay sales tax because we have a driver's license or because we drive? Of course not. Engaging in prostitution with a license from the state is a privilege. Do we charge licensed prostitutes sales tax while others are not required to pay it? No.

You can clearly see that exercising any of the myriad of government privileges does not give rise to liability for sales tax.

Here it should be noted that sales tax is imposed upon the seller, not the buyer. Usually the public misperceives that and thinks the sales tax is imposed upon the buyer. Not so. The seller passes along the tax to the buyer, but the tax is actually imposed on the seller, and the seller is "made liable" for the tax. This is a critical element to understand because the privilege – whatever it may be – is enjoyed by the seller, not the buyer. The seller merely passes his tax obligation along to the buyer as a "cost of doing business". (Most states mandate that the tax passed on to the buyer be clearly indicated on the sales receipt.)

Now that we know the tax is imposed upon the seller, what privilege is the seller enjoying?

The same *unalienable rights* that you and I have to acquire (buy) property applies to our disposing of (selling) said property, so can there be any privilege for us in doing either buying or selling? No. And I want to point out that your *unalienable right* to buy and sell property exists anywhere and everywhere in America!

Some of you are probably as flabbergasted by what I'm telling you about sales tax as you've been regarding the income tax. You're thinking that everyone charges sales tax on almost everything! Yup, no doubt about it. And the reasons are the same as why everyone files income tax returns and pays income tax – because they have no idea what the law says, or what their rights are, and the government has been lying to them about it, damn near forever.

If we have the *unalienable right* to buy and sell property, and exercising any old privilege is not what gives rise to sales tax liability, what is sales tax really all about?

The crux of the sales tax is what does (and does not) constitute a privilege with regard to selling your personal property to the public. The only privilege that is relevant to sales tax is the circumstance in which you, the seller, are indeed exercising a privilege when selling at retail to the public.

Since being charged sales tax is so ubiquitous it may be hard for you to break away from that way of thinking. But remember, a "privilege" is something that is not a right! "Rights" and "privileges" are mutually exclusive.

Does this mean that every store with which you do business, and which charges you sales tax, is exercising a privilege? Far from it. What it means is that most of the owners of the stores you do business with wouldn't know a "right" if it bit them in the rear end! Additionally, they've always been told (by people who've never read the law) not only do they have to charge sales tax, but they also need a Resale Permit.

There are quite a few books and websites out there that purport to teach people how to start their own business. Two things that such books and websites always say are that the prospective new business owner must get a TIN and a Resale Permit. This has always amazed me.

Whether or not a person needs a TIN or a Resale Permit is controlled by law. But the person who is "advising" people on what is (allegedly) necessary to start their own business ***never*** addresses what the law says about getting a TIN or a Resale Permit. This is the same mindset that causes people to say, "I have to withhold from your paycheck; it's the law," while they have never read the law, do not know where the (alleged) law is, nor can they tell you what it says! So much for "experts".

Also contributing to the misunderstanding of this issue in the business community is that there are "wholesalers" (who also have never read the law) who take the absurd position that they cannot sell to you unless you have a Resale Permit. Further exacerbating an already bad situation are enterprises such as trade shows (and even some large swap meets) that take the position that they cannot provide you with a booth unless you provide a TIN, a copy of a Resale Permit, and a business license. In point of fact, most Americans are not legally required to apply for, or have, any of those three items. As I said earlier, our fellow citizens are usually the "thugs" who attempt to keep us from living a life of freedom and liberty.

So, we come to this question: Who is it that does not have a "right" to sell their property to the public within your state? You have the right. I have the right within my state. So who doesn't have the right?

Each state creates its own corporations. Corporations do not have any *unalienable rights* as do you and I. Corporations only have the (so-called) 'rights' vested in them by the legislature of that state, and those rights are only operative within that state. A corporation created in one state has no 'right' to do business in any other state. Under the law, a corporation created in one state is a "foreign corporation" to any state other than its home state of incorporation.

By law, each corporation that wishes to do business in another state must petition that state's *Secretary of State* for permission to enter the state and do business with the inhabitants of that state. If this legal requirement is unfamiliar to you, that's understandable. While this legal requirement is still on the books, it is often ignored these days, even by the states themselves. Why? Because under the *subjective theory of contract*, a corporation that enters another state and begins "doing business" (there's that phrase again!) is presumed to have submitted itself to the laws and policies of the state in which it is *doing business*.

Nevertheless, a corporation that wishes to begin *doing business* in a state other than the one in which it is incorporated is "required by law" to submit an application to that state's Secretary of State seeking consent to enter the state and begin *doing business*. Since consent can be granted or withheld by the state government, we can see that the requesting corporation has no 'right' to enter that state and begin *doing business*. If the corporation had the right, then it would have no need to request permission. Clearly such a corporation is exercising a privilege when *doing business* in a state other than its state of origin.

As an example, is it a privilege for a Delaware corporation to begin *doing business* in Florida? Absolutely. Is it a privilege for me (a citizen of Nevada) to sell my property in Florida? Absolutely not. Let's use this book as an example. I could put several boxes of this book (my property) into my vehicle and drive to Florida. Once in Florida I could sell my books just as if I were in Nevada. As an American, my *unalienable right* to acquire, use, and dispose of property is just as operative in Florida as in Nevada. In short, as long as I am within one of the 50 states of the Union all of my *unalienable rights* remain inviolable.

That is **not** true for a "foreign corporation". A *foreign corporation* (a corporation created under the laws of another jurisdiction) has no such rights. A *foreign corporation* is exercising a privilege when "selling at retail" to the inhabitants of a state other than the one in which it was incorporated.

I should add that applying for and possessing a Resale Permit creates the legal presumption that you are within a *class of person* upon whom the sales tax has been imposed. Having that Resale Permit then places a duty upon you to collect the sales tax and pay it over to the state on a timely basis. If you are not within a *class of person* upon whom the sales tax has been imposed, and you cancel your Resale Permit, you are then no longer obligated to collect the tax.

Now that you have some perspective on state sales tax, how does that impact the proposed *national retail sales tax*?

First, let's examine what the rate of the tax would be. In a 2004 Congressional Democratic Leadership press release, Nancy Pelosi is quoted as saying that the rate of a national sales tax would be "at least 30 percent and as high as 50 percent or more on all goods, including homes and cars." Imagine that $35,000 Ford Explorer suddenly becoming a $70,000 SUV! And a $300,000 house leaps to $600,000 the day after a national sales tax takes effect.

Some might say the increase in cost of goods is irrelevant because you would no longer be paying the income tax, so it would all balance out. Not so. (In the upcoming section on VAT, you'll see why that is not true at all!)

As we've covered, sales tax is an excise. However, simply because sales tax is, in its nature, an excise doesn't mean that Congress would impose it as such. Congress only has two choices; it can impose it as an excise, which of course means there has to be a privileged activity taking place, or Congress can enact it as a direct tax, which of course would be unconstitutional because "direct tax", as such term is used in the U.S. Constitution, is limited to real property (and slaves).

(Although we've already treated the direct tax question thoroughly, if you still question the "real property and slaves" limitation, allow me to share a few words with you from the January 25, 1916 New York Times article detailing the Brushaber decision. The article states, *"The Chief Justice said that…a direct tax was a tax on real estate and other property…."* "Other property" was, in the polite manner of the day, how the NY Times alluded to the ownership of slaves. And let me remind you that no one has found a single word ever uttered or written by the men who wrote the Constitution that a direct tax applied to anything other than real estate and slaves.)

In summary, Congress has very little latitude in enacting a *national retail sales tax*. If enacted in its ordinary nature it would be an excise, which would require there to be a privilege in order for the tax to apply. Want to see people start to discover the truth about sales tax? Ratchet it up to 30% and see how fast people learn that they don't have to participate in it any more!

There is, of course, the question of whether or not Congress has the Constitutional authority to impose an internal tax without apportionment (other than upon alcohol and tobacco). Remember the discussion in which I pointed out that Madison and Jefferson, who were responsible for most of the theory and principle behind the Constitution, designed a system in which the federal government's sphere was primarily international in nature and scope. That is one of the fundamental reasons that today's income tax is international and not domestic.

My personal opinion is that Congress does not have the constitutional authority to enact any internal tax on Americans. Yes, the Constitution gives the national government power to lay direct and indirect taxes (imposts, duties and excises) but that power must be seen within the scope of Congress' primary function, which is international relations. When the Constitution was written the states would never have granted – and did not grant - Congress the power to compete with them in the realm of internal domestic taxation.

If Congress were to enact a direct tax absent apportionment, yet merely entitle it *"national retail sales tax"*, it would be unconstitutional before the ink dried.

FLAT TAX

Another of the alternative taxes being bandied about is the Flat Tax. The sales pitch for this tax is that it, too, is more "fair". Oh…sure.

The basis of the Flat Tax is that the rate of tax would be the same for everyone – sort of. In pure theory, the rich man would pay the same percentage of his income in tax as would the poor man.

Let's look at an example. For the purpose of this example we'll put the tax rate at 10%. One citizen has an annual income of $150,000. Under the proposed

Flat Tax this citizen would pay $15,000 in federal income tax. Another citizen might make $37,000 a year. Under this plan he would pay $3,700 in income tax.

But that's not what would happen in the real world. Once politicians started meddling with the "pure theory" of a Flat Tax, it would no longer be "flat"! And frankly, there are some very good reasons for that.

The man who makes $37,000 a year is unlikely to use any of his money to invest in the economy. That's because he's living off of virtually every penny he makes. By contrast, the man who makes $150,000 a year may very well plow a significant percentage of that back into the economy in the form of investments, which is a form of capitalizing business ventures. Capitalizing industry is a vital part of any free-market economy. That $15,000 the government takes away from the more well-to-do American may be the money he was intending to invest in America. So what will Congress do about that? They'd likely create an investment deduction or exemption!

And what of the man with the more modest income? He will claim that his $3,700 is more important to him than the $15,000 is to the more well-off citizen. He will make a case that even after having $15,000 taken from the other man, the other man still has far more money than he does. He will claim that taking $3,700 from him will mean less food on the table for his family, the inability to secure a good education for his children, etc. He will make the case that the $15,000 taken from the other man does not "harm" that man in the same way that taking $3,700 will hurt him and his family. So what will Congress do? Congress will likely raise the Flat Tax rate several points and then exempt people with an income that is below whatever threshold Congress finds politically expedient. And of course, they will tamper with the new Flat Tax every year until in the end the original concept of the Flat Tax is totally obliterated.

But of course all that is irrelevant anyway. People can call it a Flat Tax (or any other name they want), but in reality it is the same old "income tax". All Congress would be doing would be repealing a lot of the complexities of the existing Code and setting a rate that would (allegedly) be applicable to everyone. But let me say this again – from a legal and constitutional perspective it's the same old *income tax*, it's just being handed to you in a shiny new box. Or phrased another way, it is merely a modified version of **the largest financial crime in the history of the world.**

VALUE ADDED TAX – VAT

VAT is a variation on the sales tax theme. It is a variation that is used in places where, due to various circumstances, other forms of taxation, such as income tax, are not deemed to be the best way to extract revenue from the people.

There is no need in this book to go into the details of VAT. It is sufficient to say that it is a version of sales tax; a version that simply operates to extract the tax during production rather than at the point of sale, yet it is still a form of sales tax. It is nothing more than a modification of a *national retail sales tax* – just remove the word "retail".

Both the *national retail sales tax* and VAT are insidious forms of taxation. They can be made to sound attractive, but in reality they are poison. One of the ways they are made appealing is to claim that they offer some perceived benefit (which can only be accepted by a dumbed-down, ignorant populace) coupled with a low initial rate. The "benefit" is always political nonsense, the low rate is merely a teaser, and the politicians have no intention of keeping the rate low!

Let's look at a prime example.

In 1967 Sweden instituted a VAT. The initial VAT rate was 10%. However, by 1992 the Swedish government had increased the rate to 25%. Because the Swedish VAT operates on a percentage basis, inflation is not a factor. The rate of tax increased from 10% to 25% over a 25 year period for one reason, and one reason alone – the Swedish government wanted to spend more money – so it decided to take more money from its people. It's just that simple.

In the minds of the American people these "alternative taxes" are thought of as options to replace the income tax. That's because American politicians have always framed the discussion of such taxes as a replacement for the income tax. But that is **not** what they really intend. They intend one or more of these taxes to be implemented in **addition** to the income tax!

In October 2009, as a part of the debate on nationalized health care, Nancy Pelosi stated that in order to pay for government-provided healthcare Congress should be looking at instituting a national VAT. She was not talking about doing this as an alternative to the income tax, but as an additional tax to fund the bloated and ever-growing debts of the federal government. So much for "free" healthcare.

And keep in mind that there is no way for you to avoid a VAT because it is paid at various stages in the production of the goods and then passed on to you in the final price. How'd you like to pay income tax <u>and then</u> have 25% added to everything you buy?

I have several friends who have emigrated from various European countries where they are taxed in the manner that American politicians are now planning for you. All of them say that the reason they came here is because it is still possible to work hard and increase one's standard of living here. They are very concerned about the rumblings they hear about additional forms of taxation here in America.

They say that America is heading down the same path as their native countries. They tell me that if the U.S. government is permitted to add more taxes this country will become just like the countries they left, where no matter how hard you work you can never get ahead.

One of these men owns his own small business and recently bought a home for himself, his wife, and their 2 children. Additionally he owns a mini-van and a plain old Dodge pick-up truck. He tells me that he could never have acquired any of these things in his native country of Ireland because the tax burden is so crushing that he essentially worked to fund the government while he barely eked out a living. Is that what you want in America? Well, that's what your politicians in Washington DC have in mind for you!

And The Answer Is...

Chapter 15

"What shall a free people do?"
~ Bob Schulz

As you've been reading the previous 14 chapters you may have been wondering where this has all been leading. You may have been asking yourself what this country would do for money if the income tax were to go the way of the Dodo bird. You may have been questioning what every loyal patriotic American can do to stop the largest financial crime in the history of the world from continuing. It's time for some answers.

Let's tackle the practical issues first.

Because Americans know so little about taxation in general, not just the income tax, I have heard people give voice to all sorts of concerns when they consider ending the income tax. Let's explore some of them.

1. <u>If there is no income, tax who will pay for the roads</u>? Income tax does not pay for roads. Each gallon of gasoline or diesel you buy at the fuel pump has both federal and state motor fuel taxes added to the price. It is primarily these taxes that pay for highways and roads.

2. <u>If there is no income tax, how will we pay for police and fire protection</u>? Income tax does not pay for police and fire protection. Although the formula differs a bit from state to state, the general rule is that local property taxes pay for police and fire protection.

3. <u>Schools will not have needed money if there is no income tax</u>. Income tax does not pay for schools. K1 through K12 education is paid for almost exclusively from local property taxes.

So now that we know you will still have roads, highways, police, fire, and educational services, how much do you still feel you need to give to the federal government?

Another concern I sometimes hear is that we will no longer be able to maintain our "world dominance" without an income tax. This statement is really saying that these people believe the income tax is necessary in order to maintain our military might. Well…possibly. It depends on what your military goals are.

Over the last decade or so, we Americans have become very proud of our military. We have come a long way from the days after Vietnam when many Americans were ashamed of the U.S. military.

Much of this newfound enthusiasm is a result of our being able to see fascinating technological victories in the media and on the internet. All of us have seen, and been impressed with, the ability of U.S. bombs and missiles to hit targets with pinpoint accuracy. It's very impressive. And who doesn't like to be on the winning team!

While I appreciate the technology and the thrill of perceived victory, I'm less thrilled about the fact that some people believe that if we can't wipe out an entire village on the other side of the planet with the push of a button, Americans will no longer be free. I question whether being able to push a button and kill people on the other side of the planet has much to do with your liberty or mine in our own land. I'm infinitely more concerned about personal liberty at home than I am with "projecting power" around the globe.

In this post-9/11 era, Americans often misguidedly imagine that they must surrender their liberty in order to ensure it. This is an odd thought process indeed.

On September 11, 2001 approximately 3,000 Americans lost their lives. Tell me something – how does that compare to 300,000,000 being slaves every day?

If there is a fight to fight, should it be to prevent 3,000 from being killed in a one-time incident, or should it be to free 300,000,000 from life-long slavery? While I do not mean to trivialize the tragedy of 9/11, the reality is that it affected less than .00001 percent of the population. And it was an anomaly. By contrast, the income tax affects well over 100,000,000 Americans every year! And the vast majority never owed a penny of income tax in their lives!

Just a moment ago I used the word "slave". You may guffaw at my use of that word in reference to the income tax. But that is only because you have become so conditioned to its existence and operation upon you that it seems "normal" – and you cannot possibly imagine that you have permitted your own enslavement to become "normalcy". I am here to tell you that you have done exactly that!

What is a slave? The simple answer is that a slave is one who is owned by another. But that's a superficial answer one might expect from a school child. Let's get down to what slavery is all about. <u>The only value a slave has to his master is his labor. If the slave does not perform labor he is worthless</u>. 300 years ago, this would have been simple economics. Today we have lost touch with this reality.

What is the key distinction between master and slave? That which differentiates the two is that the slave has no legal right to the fruits of his own labor and the master takes the fruits of the slave's labor for himself without the consent of the slave. In order for slavery to operate, the law must not contemplate that the slave has the right to the fruits of his own labor, nor restrict (or punish) the master who seizes the fruits of that labor.

Is there anyone reading these words who does not believe slavery is immoral?

"Tax Freedom Day" is the phrase used to describe the day that Americans start working for themselves rather than working for the government, i.e., working to pay taxes. Depending on various influences, Tax Freedom Day fluctuates a bit every year. In 2009 Americans worked 103 days for the government. There are a number of taxes included in the formula, but in rough numbers, based on what you've learned in this book, the average American works 86 days a year to pay taxes that he never owed under the law, including the income tax.

That means for 86 days you worked and received nothing in return. Someone else took the fruits of your labor. You received nothing for your labor. (Some might say that they did in fact receive something for their labor in the form of government services but I will throw cold water on that fantasy in just a few minutes.)

The fruits of your labor have been taken from you by another without your consent. What does that sound like to you? I can almost hear some of you saying, "But Dave, how can you call it slavery, when it's the law?!" Let us recognize first and foremost that slavery is a ***moral*** issue. Are you so out of touch with morality that you overlook an immoral act simply because the government says it's "legal"?

One of the elements of slavery is that the "authorities" must refuse to acknowledge that the slave has the right to the fruits of his own labor while at the same time protecting the master from all consequences of stealing the fruits of the slave's labor. Without these elements slavery cannot succeed. And make no mistake, in every case both the "authorities" and the master know what they are doing is immoral. They choose to do it anyway because there is a reward for them in doing so – usually an economic reward.

In the case of the income tax, the "authorities" and the "master" who is stealing the fruits of your labor are the same entity. Which person (or entity) is it who will declare himself to be a thief and order himself to stop stealing when he is the one being enriched by the theft?

Of course some will say that it is not slavery because the people voted into office the men/women who voted for the tax. In other words, we have taxed ourselves and it is impossible to make slaves of ourselves. That would be true enough if the underlying premise were factually accurate, but it is not.

As you've learned in this book, Congress has **not** passed any laws that tax your labor, so you did not make slaves of yourselves! Second, a moral wrong is still a wrong, no matter what you, or what some elected idiot, may have done. Remember, if you don't have the right to take my property from me, then 1,000,000 people who don't have that right can't do it any more than you could acting alone.

Some might say that the American people have acquiesced to the tax and so it has somehow become legitimate. Again, the basic premise is flawed. The American people have never freely acquiesced to the income tax. Being ignorant of the law, and being faced with an implacable adversary, they have chosen not to be gunned down in the streets by evil men with guns and a license to kill. You think I exaggerate? Try resisting arrest by federal agents for a crime you've not committed and see how fast you will be gunned down.

The only reason more innocent Americans aren't gunned down by these evil bastards is because the citizen surrenders, is tried in a corrupt federal court, and then spends years in jail – but he's alive. What happens, however, when you know you're innocent and you decide to fight back and refuse to be put into the corrupt meat-grinder? Ask the survivors of Ruby Ridge and Waco what happens! You'd have to ask the survivors because it's impossible to ask those who were shot to death or intentionally burned alive by the government. And I should add that not one single person in either incident has ever been convicted of the alleged crimes the government trumped up as justification to attack them in their homes.

> [**Author's Note**: If you think I am overstating the case, watch the documentary "Waco: Rules of Engagement" in which a retired U.S. general, who was known as the "father of FLIR" [Forward Looking Infrared camera technology] and who was the acknowledged world expert at FLIR interpretation, gives his interpretation of government FLIR footage. He says that as women and children were attempting to escape the flames of the main Waco building, armed U.S. personnel (out of sight of the media cameras) were shooting at them with automatic weapons, forcing them back into the building to be burned alive in the flames.]

The U.S. government loves to manipulate you. And of course the American people aren't very hard to manipulate. For decades now you've been bombarded by "sound bites" from TV and radio. Sadly, too many Americans now don't really think beyond the length of a sound bite. If the sound bite makes a person feel good, no further thought process is necessary. Of course the sound bites are designed with the intent of making you feel good about whatever the issue or position is. Critical analysis is an essential skill of free men and women that is on the endangered species list in America.

Here's a perfect example of how a manipulative sound bite works. In a 2008 press release, then Assistant Attorney General (Tax Division) Nathan Hochman announced a new initiative to go after "Tax Defiers". In that press release he states that the purpose of the initiative is *"stopping those tax defiers who do not meet their federal tax obligations and seek to transfer those obligations to their neighbor's back."* In support of this premise he quotes former U.S. Supreme Court Justice Oliver Wendell Holmes who said, "Taxes are what we pay for a civilized society."

How many Americans blindly bought into the pathetic manipulative crap being peddled by Hochman? Probably almost every one who heard it. Why? Because too many Americans don't think.

Hochman's manipulation began by hitting one of the basest of all human emotional responses – that someone is getting away with something and in doing so is increasing your burden. No one likes that scenario, so Hochman's manipulation plays well. It resonates with millions of people. Hochman then tossed in the famous words of Holmes to make you feel good about your being turned into government slaves. The problem is that not a word of it is factually accurate! Millions of Americans however bought it hook, line, and sinker, which is precisely what Hochman was shooting for!

As you now understand, Americans who know the truth about the income tax are not failing or refusing to meet their federal tax obligation. They have no federal tax obligation! The only thing these people are "defying" is being a victim of the largest financial crime in the history of the world.

Hochman paints a picture that these 'defiers' (i.e., Americans who know the truth about the income tax) are increasing the burden on "good Americans". In reality, that's like a person asserting you have to keep paying "protection money" to the Mob so that the Mob doesn't demand more from him – and insinuating that if you don't keep allowing yourself to be victimized, you're selfish. Talk about manipulative!

As to Justice Holmes's quote, possibly we should look at some other quotes and see if this is a man we should admire.

> "A new untruth is better than an old truth."
> "I hate facts."
> "It is very lonely sometimes, trying to play God."
> "This is a court of law, young man, not a court of justice."

How come Nathan Hochman didn't share those quotes with us? Hochman also fails to reveal that Holmes believed in "outcome based law"[1]. *Outcome based law* is a concept in which a judge determines what he wants the outcome of a case to be and then structures his decision in such a way as to make it seem as though the law supports his decision, when in fact it really doesn't matter to him whether the law supports the decision or not. It is fitting that the U.S. government would use a quote from Holmes because it wants its own raw power, not the law, to rule the day.

---

1 Outcome based law is often referred to in legal academic circles as "Legal Realism". The use of the phrase outcome based law is too revealing so the phrase "Legal Realism" was instituted so you won't understand what is taking place.

Let us nevertheless examine Holmes's quote: "Taxes are what we pay for a civilized society." In so far as that goes, it may well be true. But "taxes" are not a guise under which slavery may be imposed - at least in America.

History is replete with every type of tax imaginable. And our nation has its own tax history. As far as the federal government is concerned, that history – as well as present and future – is controlled by the U.S. Constitution. And that document (including the 16th Amendment) does not give the federal government the authority to tax the labor of Americans working at home in the 50 states. So, while Holmes' quote may indeed be accurate, it has absolutely nothing to do with you or me and the income tax. Gee…I wonder why Hochman didn't explain that to you! Could it be that if he told you the truth his press release would lose its ability to manipulate its target audience – millions of non-thinking Americans?

Before I move on, let me share one additional quote from Holmes that I don't think Hochman would like (since Americans own roughly 250,000,000 firearms).

"Between two groups of people who want to make inconsistent kinds of worlds, I see no remedy but force." -- *Oliver Wendell Homes*

The choice is between a world in which you are free, the government obeys the Constitution, and it respects your unalienable rights – and a world in which you are the continuing victims of the largest financial crime in the history of the world and "the system" closes ranks to prevent you from being able to obtain any just remedy.

While we're on the subject of judges, let's examine how they play into this crime.

It is sad but true that many federal judges actually believe that "the law" is whatever they say it is. To these judges it does not matter what language Congress adopts, or how a statute's boundaries are limited by the Constitution, or what your unalienable rights are. The only thing that matters to these judges is that they can make the world work the way they think is best, even if it means twisting and distorting the law.

You might think this is judgmental of me, but I am not alone in this view. Do you know who also holds this view? Lawyers. More often than I can count I've had lawyers tell me that the law is not what it says in the statute or the regulation, but whatever the judge says it is.

Under federal law, every case that is filed at the District Court level is to be assigned to one of the various judges in that District by means of a "lottery". In other words, there is no way for a party in a legal action to "judge shop" as they can do in some state court systems. In the federal system your case is assigned by luck of the draw. Or is it?

You see there is an exception to the "lottery" rule. The Chief Judge of the District (who is in charge of the court system there) can reassign cases as he sees fit "in the interest of the efficient administration of the courts." So who is the sole arbiter of what is "the efficient administration of the courts?" The Chief Judge of course.

The "lottery" requirement is yet another part of the propaganda you are fed so that you will incorrectly believe that the federal courts are fair, impartial, and your case can be judged on the merits. And that may be true – if your adversary in the courtroom is not the United States.

I have watched criminal tax cases very carefully for more than a decade. I watch intently the cases involving people who are notable in the Tax Honesty Movement. In virtually every one of these cases the Chief Judge has reassigned the case. I'm sure you will be shocked to learn that the judges to which these cases have been reassigned are almost always judges who have a track record of twisting and mutilating not only the law but also court procedure in order to guarantee that the government gets a conviction. In the Tax Honesty Movement the names of these judges are notorious and well known. Isn't it amazing that with more than 2,000 federal judges on the bench this same small circle of judges keeps getting the high-profile Tax Honesty cases!

Of course I was presenting the information a bit tongue-in-cheek. It is not a coincidence that this small circle of "government hatchet men" (judges) keeps getting Tax Honesty cases. The U.S. government knows these judges are not dedicated to following the law. The U.S. government knows these judges are dedicated to maintaining the raw power of the United States government, and the law be damned.

Every venue in life has its deviants who are willing to sell their integrity for various rewards. Judges are not immune from this ugly trait. In fact, they seem to be more prone to it because of the inordinate power they wield. As Lord Acton said, *"Power corrupts, and absolute power corrupts absolutely."* Federal judges have nearly absolute power.

There are countless stories I could tell you about the corrupt actions of judges but this book would be considerably longer if I were to detail all the illegalities of judges I have witnessed; therefore I will only share a few stories with you.

In 2008, the IRS initiated a summons enforcement proceeding against me in the United States District Court in Los Angeles. I fought the action because I knew that their "end game" was to silence me.

> [**Author's Note**: My response to their allegations can be read at http://www.taxrevolt.us/media/incourt.pdf. I'm sure you will find it enlightening.]

For various reasons I decided that invoking my right to remain silent in response to certain questions was the best course of action. I have nothing to hide, but anything and everything a person says to the government will be used against him, so to say nothing can be at times the wisest course of action. I'm sure you are all aware that the right not to be compelled to be a witness against yourself is enshrined in the 5th Amendment of the U.S. Constitution.

Judge Percy Anderson, one of the judges who practices *outcome based law*, dismissed all of my arguments and ruled in favor of the government, ordering me to provide documents and give testimony before the IRS. When the IRS asked me certain questions that I considered imprudent to answer, I invoked my right to remain silent.

The IRS didn't like that I exercised my right to remain silent and went back before the judge seeking to have me jailed for "contempt of court". I thought this a silly and wasteful tactic because a person cannot be jailed for exercising a constitutionally protected right. As it turned out, I discovered that in Percy Anderson's court there is "law" that doesn't exist anywhere else in the known universe. It is special law that Percy makes up as he goes along.

It's not real law – it's "Percy's law". Percy's law is actually just Percy violating the law – and the Constitution – for the purpose of intimidating an American citizen out of relying upon his constitutionally protected rights.

When we were all back in front of good ol' Percy, he informed me that I had no right in his courtroom to remain silent. He stated that if it was my intention to invoke my right to remain silent, I needed to tell him that during my first appearance before him months earlier. Since I had not done so, I no longer had the right.

But there's a little problem with his ruling. There is no provision of the Constitution, no statute, nor any case law that says anything like that! He was simply sending me a message that if I intended to thwart any part of his order to give evidence to the IRS – even if it was my constitutional right not to furnish the evidence – the price for that in his court was to go to jail. In other words, the Constitution can go screw itself. What Percy Anderson wants Percy Anderson gets in his courtroom – and *that* is the law!

Of course it's even worse than it sounds because not only is there no legal support anywhere in existence for Percy's deprivation of my *unalienable right* to remain silent, but there is a boat-load of case law stating exactly the opposite!

It is a well-settled point of constitutional law that a person **cannot** exercise his right to remain silent until he has been asked a question. If you walk in and say, "I intend to take the 5th", before you've heard the questions, that is called a "Blanket 5th" and there is no constitutional right to do that. Of course that is a silly rule because if a person doesn't want to answer *any* questions for the government why wait to hear each one? But that is the law as it stands today. I should also point out that there is no law of any kind in existence that says a person must pro-actively tell the judge that he *might* take the 5th before hearing the questions the government intends to ask.

In pursuance of this well-settled point of law, I quite properly – and under guidance of counsel – waited for the government to ask each question. Most I answered, some I did not, in those instances invoking my *unalienable right* not to be a witness against myself.

You will note that the 5th Amendment does not grant me any rights. My *unalienable rights* pre-exist the formation of the states or the federal government and therefore cannot be modified, altered, or abolished by the government – so says the U.S. Supreme Court. <u>The 5th Amendment is a prohibition on the actions of the federal government</u>.

The relevant part of the Amendment for the purpose of this story states, "*… nor shall be compelled in any criminal case to be a witness against himself….*" [Although my case was not criminal, the government is free to later use anything they get from me for the purpose of a criminal prosecution, which is why the Amendment applies in this type of case.] Please note the words, "*nor shall be compelled*". We've already addressed the issue of being "compelled" so you know what that means.

Under the restrictions placed upon him by the U.S. Constitution, Percy could do nothing that would "compel" me to give testimony after I'd invoked my right to remain silent. But Percy doesn't give a damn about the Constitution. Instead of obeying the Constitution (to which he took an oath) he threatened me with jail time if I wished to actually invoke my right not to be compelled. Or phrased another way, if I invoked my *unalienable right* not to be compelled, then Percy would compel me to stop demanding I not be compelled!

[**Author's Note**: If you would like to hear the whole sordid tale from beginning to end, go to http://www.taxrevolt.us/media/incourt.mp3]

The next story involves the criminal trial of Irwin Schiff. Schiff's trial was before United States District Court Judge Ken Dawson. During the trial, members of Irwin's defense team observed the prosecutors in the case coming out of the side door of Judge Ken Dawson's chambers. The very men who were prosecuting Irwin were in a private meeting with the judge outside the presence of the defense. This is about as corrupt as it gets, and the prosecutors and the judge both knew it. What would cause them to do that? Well, a personal meeting leaves no phone records or e-mail trail. Much cleaner if you're illegally conspiring behind the defendant's back. Fortunately, they got caught. But to what end?

The defense requested that Judge Dawson recuse himself. Dawson refused. What was his reason for not recusing himself? He said he need not recuse himself because they were not discussing Irwin's case. When asked what else those particular prosecutors and the judge could be talking about, the judge became angry and stated that he was not to be questioned further on the matter and that he was staying on the case.

Of course he was staying on – there was some dirty dealing to be done to Schiff, and how that was to be accomplished had already been agreed upon during the meeting. Dawson couldn't recuse himself at that point. What if the case went to a judge who wasn't a whore for the government? Dawson couldn't let that happen. There was a high-profile defendant that needed railroading!

So how does a judge make sure a defendant gets railroaded? By doing just what Dawson did in the Schiff case; by sustaining virtually every objection made by the government (thus preventing the defense from effectively presenting its position to the jury) and overruling virtually every objection made by the defense (thus allowing the government to say anything it wanted in front of the jury).

So what is the proper standard for recusal? I think it was best articulated by the Tennessee Supreme Court when it said, "Even if a judge believes he can be fair and impartial, the judge should disqualify himself when *"the judge's impartiality might be reasonably questioned"* or because *"the appearance of bias is as injurious to the integrity of the judicial system as actual bias."*

After discovering the Schiff prosecutors in a private meeting with the judge, and the judge being unwilling to explain what else they could possibly have been talking about, do you think Dawson's impartiality *"might be reasonably questioned"*?

And amazingly, that's what the federal statute says as well! 28 USC 455(a) states, *"Any justice, judge, or magistrate judge of the United States shall disqualify himself in any proceeding in which his impartiality might reasonably be questioned."* But of course because the law means whatever Dawson says it means (not what's written by Congress), then it doesn't really mean that he should recuse himself if *"his impartiality might reasonably be questioned."*

And one last thing on the Schiff case. After Dawson slanted the playing field almost entirely toward the government, the jury obligingly convicted Schiff of 14 charges. He was 77 at the time. He will likely die in jail for "violating" laws that never applied to him, and because a corrupt federal judge conspired with corrupt federal prosecutors to convict an innocent man – all to intimidate *you* into continuing to be good obedient slaves.

Another example involves a California state judge and happened in a case in which I was an interested observer. A friend of mine filed an answer to the government's initial filing. Much as I did in the response to which I provided you a link (above), the defendant challenged the jurisdiction of the court based on the insufficiency of the government's pleading. The judge was noticeably angered by the filing (just as "Percy the Constitution-violator" was angered with mine).

During a pre-trial conference (at which I was present) the prosecutor stated that he'd spoken with the judge about the case and the judge assured him that if the defendant were convicted he would receive jail time. The judge had decided on jail for the defendant before the trial began and before one shred of evidence had been presented to the court. Additionally, the judge had quite obviously been in private consultation with the prosecutor about the case, without the defense being present. The judge had threatened the defendant with jail time because the judge was angry over the defendant's filing, not because of any facts of the case!

When the defendant next appeared in court he requested the judge recuse himself and spelled out the indiscretion that gave rise to the request. The judge did not admit that the conversation had taken place and attempted to bluster his way past the allegation. Only after the prosecutor admitted on the record in open court that the conversation had occurred did the judge finally recuse himself. (I feel compelled to observe that this prosecutor showed integrity by voluntarily confirming the allegation in open court.)

Please note that once it was on the record that a private meeting had taken place between the judge and prosecution, the judge **did** recuse himself, unlike Dawson. This state judge knew that to hold a private meeting with prosecution created a circumstance in which *"the judge's impartiality might be reasonably questioned"*. Of course Dawson knew that too, but he had some railroading to do that he felt was more important than the law.

Sometimes judicial crimes involve multiple judges. In 1994, Edward Dufresne, Chief Judge of the U.S. 5th Circuit Court of Appeals took charge of all *pro se* appeals. *Pro se* means that an individual is bringing an action before the court in his own name, without using an attorney.

Dufresne had clerk Jerrold Peterson prepare rulings denying writs for all of them and signed off "without so much as a glance." "No judge ever saw the writ application before the ruling was prepared by me," Peterson wrote.

Over 13 years we're talking about more than 2,500 appeals dismissed without ever being read by a judge! And the Court was charging local jurisdictions $300 per appeal. In other words, the 5th Circuit billed cities, towns, and counties $750,000 for appeals it never legitimately acted upon. What would happen to you if you knowingly took three quarters of a million dollars from people when you'd never provided the service for which you charged? Can you spell F-E-L-O-N-Y?

But it gets worse than that. The only reason we know any of this is that Jerrold Peterson could no longer live with the guilt of things he had done at the direction of the judges of the 5th Circuit so he blew his brains out. He left one general suicide note for police and a second note for the federal Judiciary Commission. Both detail the actions of the judges of the 5th Circuit.

Upon hearing of Peterson's suicide and the notes that he left, Chief Judge Dufresne had Peterson's computer seized and taken from Peterson's office. When law enforcement showed up to take possession of the computer as evidence in their investigation, they were made to wait days while Dufresne did whatever he wanted to do with the contents of Peterson's computer. If you did that it would be called "evidence tampering", which is a felony.

Jerrold Peterson took his own life on May 21, 2007. It is now 2010. And where is Judge Edward A. Dufresne Jr. today? He is still sitting as the Chief Judge of the very same court. No legal action or disciplinary measures of any kind have been taken against him.

My final example focuses on Tennessee judge Durwood Moore. It seems that Durwood had a bad habit. He would arbitrarily pick out a citizen sitting in the public gallery of his courtroom and order police officials to seize the stunned citizen, take him to another part of the building against his will, and force him to take a urinalysis drug test. It should be noted that the citizens he selected were not involved in any action before the court. They were just there as spectators observing the proceedings.

Durwood's criminal conduct finally came to light when one of his victims, Ben Marchant, filed a complaint against the judge for being seized by court police and forced to take a drug test on January 2, 2009. What was Durwood's response to the allegation? He did not deny it. He stated that arbitrarily seizing spectators from the court's public gallery and forcing them to submit to drug testing was "the routine policy of the court."

The Tennessee Supreme Court stated that Durwood had violated Marchant's constitutional rights. Specifically, the Court stated that Durwood had *"violated [Marchant's] privacy and freedom under both the United States Constitution and the Tennessee Constitution."* Since the judge had done the same to many other innocent Americans seated in his courtroom, that means he violated the constitutional rights of those citizens as well.

So what was the outcome in this matter? Is Durwood resting comfortably in a federal prison for his felonious conduct and flagrant violation of the constitutionally secured rights of Americans? No. Is he sitting in a state penitentiary for violating the Tennessee constitution? No. Was he removed from the bench? No. Was he disbarred? No. Today Durwood Moore continues to sit as a judge in that very same court. All he received was a letter of censure from the Tennessee Supreme Court. Oh, and he was ordered not to do it again.

There is no judicial accountably for **The People** of the United States. Judges commit heinous acts from the bench and no one in "the system" cares. It is the epitome of the "good-old-boy network". It is said that in America no man is above the law. That is clearly a farce. In America many men are above the law, most especially judges.

There's an old adage about the "one rotten apple in the barrel." When it comes to federal judges, the barrel has more "rotten apples" than you'd care to know about. The judges who actually care about fidelity to the Constitution, who care about your rights, who care about what the law actually says and what Congress intended by its laws, are few and far between.

Now that we know judges are no more law-abiding than your common neighborhood pedophile, let us return to the issue of your enslavement. And yes, I promise this is all leading somewhere!

If your labor is taken from you by another, you are that person's slave. Period. There is no "but…" about it. You can deny it, but denying it doesn't make it any less so.

I know that some of you are saying, "Well, it's only for a portion of the year. It's no big deal". If you are thinking that, then just close this book and go on with your life. If being made into a part-time slave is acceptable to you then you are lost and nothing I say can save you.

There are several ways to look at being a part-time slave. You're either a slave for a couple of months a year, or you're a slave for about an hour and a half out of each 8-hour day. If you work more hours each day, then the time you are enslaved also increases.

Let's think about this. If we look at the monthly perspective, then for all of January and February, and a part of March you are working as a slave and 100% of the fruits of your labor are being seized by someone else without any law that authorizes/permits it. How does that make you feel?

We can also look at it from the daily perspective. If you work the average 8-hour day, then each work day roughly 1½ hours of the fruits of your labor are taken from you illegally – without any law that authorizes/permits it.

Money is not the driving factor here, but just think about how much is being illegally stolen from you. If your job pays $60,000 per year, then almost $11,000 is being illegally **stolen** from you! What could you do with $11,000 of your own property if it were not being stolen from you in the course of the largest financial crime in the history of the world?

While money is not the issue, money has an impact on our lifestyle, sometimes referred to as "quality of life". Let's explore what your quality of life might look like were it not for the largest financial crime in the history of the world.

If you have children, think about what you could do for them if the government wasn't illegally stealing $11,000 per year from you. If you saved $11,000 per year for your child from the time he was born, when he reached 18 you'd have close to $200,000 put aside for him – and that doesn't include interest over all those years! But instead of having $200,000+ for your child, that money has been **stolen** from you. Or phrased another way, the opportunities that $200,000 could have provided for your child have been stolen from him! Don't you owe it to your children and to yourself to end this crime spree?

What if you don't have children? What might you do with that money? Use it to open that small business you've been dreaming about for years? Work a bit less and go back to school so you can achieve more in life? Donate it to help find a cure for some destructive disease such as diabetes, Alzheimer's or MS? Or maybe use it just to enjoy life a little more by doing the things you love to do but for which you rarely have the time or money. Whatever you would do with it, you can't do those things now because it is being illegally stolen from you. All those opportunities have been missed because of the largest financial crime in the history of the world.

We know that going to the Judicial Branch to stop the largest financial crime in the history of the world is very likely a waste of time. But what about the Legislative Branch?

In 2001, We The People Foundation For Constitutional Education detailed many of the issues concerning the unconstitutional misapplication of the income tax. We The People Foundation then submitted these facts to every sitting federal legislator in Congress in the form of a Remonstrance[2].

This Remonstrance was submitted to each legislator under the doctrine expressed (and protected) in the 1st Amendment to the U.S. Constitution.

> Congress shall make no law respecting an establishment of religion, or prohibiting the free exercise thereof; or abridging the freedom of speech, or of the press, or the right of the people peaceably to assemble, and to petition the Government for a redress of grievances.
> [underline added]

While the 1st Amendment bars Congress from making any law that would prohibit the citizens of the states from petitioning the government for redress of grievances, it should be noted that there is no requirement in the constitution for the government to respond. Congress may do exactly what Parliament and King George III did in the decade preceding 1776; they may ignore the petition.

And that, Congress did!

---

[2] An earnest presentation of reasons in opposition to something; *specifically* : a document formally stating points of opposition or grievance. *Merriam-Webster's Dictionary of Law*, © 1996 Merriam-Webster, Inc.

There was very nearly no response whatsoever from Congress. We The People Foundation received some perfunctory "feel good" letters from several of our servants in Congress, but most ignored the Remonstrance. Congress did not lift a finger to end the largest financial crime in the history of the world.

The exception was Congressman Roscoe Bartlett, representing Maryland's 6th Congressional District. (Of course, Texas Congressman Ron Paul has long been a supporter of ending the income tax and has lent his support for that cause in various ways over the years.)

Allow me to tell you the story.

In August of 2000, I attended a Tax Honesty research conference organized by Bob Schulz, President of We The People Foundation For Constitutional Education. Thirty-nine of the nation's top tax law researchers from within the Tax Honesty community met to create a list of 300 questions addressing various aspects of the illegal and unconstitutional misapplication of the income tax upon the American people.

The researchers broke into working groups and created questions on a large variety of issues. The questions that were produced by the different working groups were then submitted to a committee of attorneys whose job was to distill the questions down to the most significant issues and word the questions in the most productive manner.

Once the initial work was complete, these questions and concerns were placed into a formal Remonstrance. This Remonstrance was personally hand-served to every office of every Congressman and Senator in America. Enter Congressman Roscoe Bartlett.

After reading the questions and concerns, Congressman Bartlett felt that they were worthy of answers from the government. With Bob Schulz in the background, Congressman Bartlett arranged for a meeting to be held in a congressional committee room, in which attorneys from the IRS and The U.S. Department of Justice (DOJ) would publicly answer questions about the income tax put to them by a panel of individuals.

Congressman Bartlett secured a written commitment from the IRS and DOJ to attend the meeting. As part of the agreement, IRS/DOJ told Congressman

Bartlett that they required the list of questions two weeks in advance of the meeting date in order to have their answers researched and available for the meeting.

Bob Schulz had arranged for the entire proceeding to be "televised" over the internet. Anyone with internet service and $25.00 could view the entire event "gavel to gavel." (It was estimated that the meeting would be two or three days in length.) Additionally, Schulz arranged for the event to be placed on DVD and made available to anyone for a modest price. In so doing, Schulz had made it possible for virtually every American to hear the questions and watch the IRS and DOJ respond. I have no doubt this would have been a watershed moment in American history.

As per the government's request, Congressman Bartlett provided the questions to the IRS and DOJ two weeks in advance. These were the questions that had been constructed at the Tax Honesty research conference in August.

Within days of receiving the questions, IRS and DOJ notified Congressman Bartlett that they would not attend the meeting. That was it. They read the questions and cancelled. Gee…what a surprise. The government is willing to point a gun at your head to terrify you into paying a tax you've never owed, but they're not willing to engage in an open discussion about the income tax laws they claim give them that power. Funny how that works.

Some DOJ and IRS apologists have posited that DOJ/IRS broke their signed agreement because the meeting was scheduled to take place in late September, and of course we had the events of 9/11 that year. But that explanation is specious. The attorneys in DOJ's Tax Division, and the attorneys at the IRS, were no more involved in any post-9/11 related activities than was your local dog catcher. Life at the DOJ's Tax Division and in the legal offices of the IRS continued on as normal after 9/11. After all, they couldn't let a little foreign-sponsored terrorism interrupt their far more important domestic terrorism!

Bob Schulz and We The People Foundation For Constitutional Education did a fantastic job of getting the American people's concerns about the income tax to every legislator in Congress. The net result? Congress doesn't give a rat's behind about you, your property, or your liberty. Congress did nothing.

Since the Judicial Branch is worthless, and the Legislative Branch is useless, shall we then take this information to the Executive Branch? Maybe they will care.

Sorry, they don't care either (I won't even discuss the lunacy of trying to take the information to the IRS or DOJ since they are the "mob bosses" who are enforcing the largest financial crime in the history of the world upon YOU!).

Bob Schulz did not overlook the Executive Branch in his endeavor. During an official visit to the White House, Bob personally discussed the illegal misapplication of the income tax with Bill Clinton's economic advisor, Jason Furman. Bob asked that representatives from the White House be involved in the hearings to investigate the income tax. Several weeks later Bob again spoke with Furman. Furman informed him that the White House had decided "the issue of the legality of the income tax is not a high priority matter for the White House" and that the White House would not participate in the upcoming hearing. Of course not.

So there you have it. The grievances concerning the government perpetrating the largest financial crime in history have been brought to all three branches of the federal government. They don't care. They don't give a damn about you. But just stop and think about it for a moment; why should they? Not only are they the perpetrators – the very people who benefit from it – but hundreds of millions of Americans just go along with being victims year after year, decade after decade. Tell me something; which crime is it that a criminal will stop committing if he is offered no resistance or acts of self-defense by the victim?

I told you this was all going somewhere, and we've arrived.

IT IS 100% UP TO **YOU** TO STOP THE LARGEST FINANCIAL CRIME IN THE HISTORY OF THE WORLD.

There is no one else. We're on our own. This is an "us against them" battle. "Them" is officers of the United States government (and the states) who are trampling the rights of hundreds of millions of Americans every day, and enslaving a supposedly free people, in order to continue to commit the largest financial crime in the history of the world – and you are the victims. This is real Hitler type stuff and it needs to be stopped – today – by me and you, and millions of our countrymen!

This is not some vague call to action. I am about to give you some steps to take to end this felonious crime spree of unparalleled dimensions.

Before I do that, let me take just a moment to show you that what I'm asking of you is exactly in line with the political theory of the founders of this nation. In other words, we will not be acting against our nation, but in support of it!

> "*If money is wanted by Rulers who have in any manner oppressed the People, they may retain it until their grievances are redressed, and thus peaceably procure relief, without trusting to despised petitions or disturbing the public tranquility.*" Journals of the Continental Congress, 1:105-113 (1774)

Let's break that down. Because the men who wrote these words were still "colonists" at the time (1774) they used the word "Rulers". Today we would say "government" (though possibly we should also use "Ruler" if we are unwilling to stand up against our own enslavement).

The men of the Continental Congress say that if the government is practicing oppression (such as enslaving free men and women), then **The People** have the right to withhold their money from the government until their "*grievances are redressed*" by the government.

The Continental Congress also makes the point that by using this method we do not need to expose ourselves to insult and humiliation by submitting Petitions For Redress Of Grievance (i.e., remonstrance) only to have them ignored by our oppressors.

And lastly, Congress makes the point that by utilizing this method we can "*peaceably*" steer clear of "*disturbing the public tranquility.*" This means that withholding our money in an effort to solve the problem is preferable to shooting government officials. "*Disturbing the public tranquility*" means armed revolt. And I would draw your attention to the fact that the Continental Congress did not say that violence shouldn't be used to throw off an oppressor. In fact the Continental Congress initiated violence against the oppressive government just two years later for exactly that purpose. The Congress is simply saying that this method, i.e., withholding money from the government, is the preferred method. If the oppressor does not respond as **The People** demand, well then…

We see that the Founders recommend this method to the people of the Colonies as a means of addressing their own oppression, hoping it would stave off something far uglier.

Since we're all in this together, what are we to do?

Let's start with "criminal" matters and we'll work our way to life's everyday affairs.

GRAND JURY

If you sit on a Grand Jury, <u>never again indict an American for a tax crime who has earned only his own domestic source income</u>! Also, <u>never again indict an officer of a domestic corporation that has only domestic source income</u>. While some cases may be more complex, this simple rule will end the fear Americans have of going to jail for not filing or paying a tax they never owed.

Explain the reality of the income tax to your fellow Grand Jurors. If need be, buy each doubter a copy of this book. Remember, a Grand Jury sits for anywhere from several months to two years, depending on the jurisdiction. Your fellow Grand Jurors should have plenty of time to read this book.

If the case is presented late in the session, ask your fellow Grand Jurors not to indict until they've read the book. If they don't feel they can read it before the panel expires, explain that the government is free to ask another future Grand Jury to indict the "target", so there is no harm to the community or society in declining to indict a non-violent *target* until **all** the information is on the table.

Also, don't buy into all that nonsense that your decision as a Grand Juror must be restricted to only what is brought to you by the government or presented in the Grand Jury setting. Your #1 job is to protect the innocent from the wrongful or overzealous acts of the prosecutor.

It is critical that you have a correct understanding of the law under which the government is asking you to indict. To rely on the government's interpretation of the law is irresponsible and downright un-American. In point of fact, it is blindly believing in the government's misrepresentations of tax law that has brought us to this dangerous moment in history. Educate yourself as to the true meaning and application of the law and make sure your fellow Grand Jurors do the same.

TRIAL JURY

If you sit on a trial jury, <u>never again convict an American of a tax crime who has earned only his own domestic source income</u>! Also, <u>never again convict an officer of a domestic corporation that has only received domestic source income</u>. While some cases may be more complex, this simple rule will end the fear Americans have of going to jail for not filing or paying a tax they never owed.

In a trial setting, it only takes one informed juror to end the tyranny and terrorism of the government in criminal tax cases. That's because a criminal jury must bring in a verdict unanimously. If even one juror refuses to convict, the defendant cannot be found guilty!

If all members of a trial jury find the government has not proven its case beyond a reasonable doubt, then the defendant is found "not guilty" (acquitted). When this happens the defendant can never be tried again for that crime. In other words, the government took its shot and lost.

By contrast, if some jurors vote "guilty" and some "not guilty" then you end up with what is called a "hung jury". In other words, the jury cannot reach a unanimous decision that the defendant is guilty.

In this circumstance the government has the prerogative to try the defendant again in a new trial for the same offense. Various factors go into the government's decision to try the defendant again or not. One factor is the results of "polling the jury". This is where the trial attorneys ask the jurors (after the trial is over) how they voted and why. As a juror you are not required to answer these questions. Answering is 100% voluntary.

However, if enough Americans look the government attorneys in the eyes and say, "*I didn't convict because I know the truth about whom Congress (or the state legislature, in a state case) has imposed the tax upon and I will not convict an innocent man*", then eventually the government will stop prosecuting criminal tax cases. No one likes banging his head against the wall. This applies to DOJ Tax Division attorneys too. And remember, these immoral bastards thrive on their conviction rate. If the American people prove to these vermin that they won't get any more convictions, the vermin will stop prosecuting, if for no better reason than to protect their own precious conviction rate!

The same thing applies in a trial court about limiting the interpretation of the law to what the government says, though it operates a little differently.

In a trial setting, the judge will tell you (falsely) that you must take the law as he gives it to you. In other words, the judge is telling you that whatever he says the law means is what you must believe it means. And who pays the judge's salary? The U.S. Treasury, just like every other government employee. And what have we learned about judges? We've learned that they can be no more law-abiding than your local neighborhood pedophile. So why would you accept the meaning of the law from a law-breaking government bureaucrat wearing a black robe?

Americans typically have no love of attorneys. In fact, most every instance of bending, twisting, and mangling of the law that we've discussed in this book has been concocted by lawyers. Even in William Shakespeare's day (1564 –1616), lawyers were despised. That sentiment is expressed in the famous Shakespearean quote, "The first thing we do, let's kill all the lawyers."

So, let me ask you a question. What was every single judge before he put on that black robe? That's right – a lawyer. And in many cases not even a very good one! But somehow, when a lawyer walks into a courthouse and puts on a black dress, in the eyes of the average American he suddenly becomes the all-knowing, all-seeing, god of law. What rubbish. These "judges" are nothing more than lawyers in black dresses. Never forget that.

When the judge tells you that you must take the law as he gives it to you, he is lying to you. (I know you're shocked.) Let's find out what the law really is in America on this subject!

In State of Georgia vs. Brailsford (1794), U.S. Supreme Court Chief Justice John Jay instructed the jury as follows:

> "It is presumed, that juries are the best judges of facts; it is, on the other hand, presumed that courts are the best judges of law. But still both objects are within your power of decision." "...you have a right to take it upon yourselves to judge of both, and to determine the law as well as the fact in controversy".

Nothing has changed since that time. In fact, as recently as 1972, the U.S. 1st Circuit Court of Appeals stated that the jury has an "unreviewable and irreversible power...to acquit in disregard of the instructions on the law given by the trial judge...."

In <u>US vs. Moylan</u> (417 F 2d 1002, 1006 (1969)), the court engaged in an even more forthright discussion of the matter:

> *"We recognize, as appellants urge, the undisputed power of the jury to acquit, even if its verdict is contrary to the law as given by the judge, and contrary to the evidence. This is a power that must exist as long as we adhere to the general verdict in criminal cases, for the courts cannot search the minds of the jurors to find the basis upon which they judge. If the jury feels that the law under which the defendant is accused, is unjust, or that exigent circumstances justified the actions of the accused, or for any reason which appeals to their logic or passion, the jury has the power to acquit, and the courts must abide by that decision."*

So you see, you do ***not*** have to take the law as given to you by the judge! If you know that the judge is full of excrement, then you are under no obligation to follow either his instructions or his version of the law.

In reality, when sitting on a jury, ***you*** are the boss! The entire historic (as well as current) purpose of a jury is to ***protect*** your fellow citizens from the government! But we've lost sight of that. Americans have mistakenly come to see their role as a juror as an opportunity to put people in jail. That is ***not*** the role of a juror.

The proper role of a juror is to ***ensure*** that the government has sufficient evidence to convince you that the defendant is guilty of the alleged crime <u>beyond a reasonable doubt</u>. After reading this book, how could anyone believe that an American with only domestic source income could have committed a tax crime?

Forget what they tell you in court. The federal court system (and to a lesser extent the state system) is rigged to produce the outcome the government wants. If you are sitting on a jury, it is ***you*** who must protect your fellow Americans.

In some cases, especially if the case has gone on for some time, you may find yourself pressured by other jurors to cast the same vote as the rest of them. <u>Don't do it</u>! <u>Follow your conscience</u>! Do not allow the irritation or intimidation of other jurors to sway you. Most of the time these other jurors just want to get home, or back to work, and therefore they want the matter settled right now. <u>Take the extra time</u>. <u>Stick to your guns</u>. <u>Protect that innocent American accused of a tax crime</u>. *That* is your job!

The practice of deciding all matters for yourself as a juror is called "Jury Nullification". Its name is derived from its original practice (which is still valid today) of declaring a man innocent – even when the facts say otherwise – because the law is simply not what you want your community to live under. In other words, you – the citizen – the boss in a free country – have decided that the law is bad or wrong and that you will not convict anyone of violating a bad law. Now *that's* American!

Do *not* tell your fellow jurors that you are engaging in *jury nullification*. One of them may ask to speak with the judge and report what you are doing. The judge will then remove you from the jury and seat an alternate juror in your place. Yes, you heard me right. If the judge finds out that you are exercising your right as an American to engage in jury nullification, he will remove you from the jury! To remove a juror for exercising a right is nothing more than judicial corruption. But by this point are you really surprised?

It is fine to attempt to convince your fellow jurors of the defendant's innocence, but do not explain to them, or hint to them, about jury nullification. That will likely get you removed from the jury and that will not help the innocent American at the defense table one bit. Keep quiet. Do your job. Set that man free. Set a nation free. Then go home knowing what a tremendous service you have provided to your countrymen.

IN THE MARKETPLACE

The next essential step is to stop the vicious cycle of Americans harming their fellow Americans by acting as the "enforcement thugs" for the IRS. That is so un-American it makes me want to vomit.

You may be wondering how you can do this. First of all, take a stand! Killing the largest financial crime in the history of the world is not something that can be done in complete safety. But there are steps that are safe and legal.

First, <u>stop using a TIN and stop demanding a TIN from your fellow Americans</u>!

The entire income tax scheme pivots off of the use of a **TAXPAYER** Identification Number. Get it?

A TIN is only to be used – can only be used legally – by a person upon whom the tax has been imposed, or a person who has been made liable (such as a *withholding agent*) or a *US person*, i.e., one who is involved in the flow of U.S. source income to its foreign owner. That's it. So stop using the damn number and be an American – a free American!

People generally have two questions about not using or demanding a TIN.

As far as not using a TIN, people want to know how to address/overcome the objections of others who do not understand the law and demand a TIN. This question usually comes in one of two flavors; it is addressed by people who are in business, and people who work for others.

When it comes to not demanding a TIN from others, the question is also two-fold. First, will I get in trouble for not demanding a TIN? Second, can I still write off the expense? These questions typically come from an American who has no idea what tax law is about but is cautiously willing to follow the law and accommodate the nontaxpayer.

Let's start with, "Will I get in trouble for not demanding a TIN?" The answer is a resounding "NO!" There is nothing in the Tax Code that instructs anyone to demand a TIN. The language in the Code tells *payors* (and we now know who that is, don't we?) to **request** a TIN. The vast majority of you have never been and will never be a *payor* so the entire issue should be moot. Even if one actually is a *payor*, the only requirement is still merely to "request" a TIN, not demand.

26 CFR 301.6109-1(c), in its relevant part:

> "*If the person making the return, statement, or other document does not know the taxpayer identifying number of the other person, and such other person is one that is described in paragraph (b)(2)(i), (ii), (iii), (vi), (vii), or (viii) of this section, such person must **request** the other person's number. The **request** should state that the identifying number is required to be furnished under authority of law. When the*

> *person making the return, statement, or other document does not know the number of the other person, and has complied with the request provision of this paragraph (c), such person must sign an affidavit on the transmittal document forwarding such returns, statements, or other documents to the Internal Revenue Service, so stating."*

You'll notice that the only time the "person making the return" is instructed to say that a TIN is required *"under authority of law"* is when the person is described in (b)(2)(i), (ii), (iii), (vi), (vii), or (viii). What are those sections? They address various issues concerning trusts, and they are predicated on the trusts being owned by persons described in section 671 – 678. And where do we find 671 – 678? That's right, within chapter 1 of subtitle 'A', and we already know that chapters 1 and 2 of subtitle 'A' are merely the "rules of computation" for the tax imposed on the U.S. income of *foreign persons*, and the foreign-earned income of a U.S. citizen residing abroad!

But are there provisions that instruct a person to furnish a TIN? Yes there are. The question is, do they address you? For the vast majority of you the answer is again, "NO!"

26 CFR 301.6109-1(b), in its relevant part:

> "Every U.S. person who makes under this title a return, statement, or other document must furnish its own taxpayer identifying number as required by the forms and the accompanying instructions. A U.S. person whose number must be included on a document filed by another person must give the taxpayer identifying number so required to the other person on request. For penalties for failure to supply taxpayer identifying numbers, see sections 6721 through 6724."

Do you get it now? A TIN is required of/by *foreign persons* and *US persons* – no one else! I included the final sentence about penalties because we're going to be getting into that in just a moment.

As you can see, the vast majority of Americans are **not** required to furnish a TIN to anyone at any time. It is the complete misunderstanding of whom the tax has been imposed upon, who has been made liable for it, and who is required to furnish a number that is the foundation of your enslavement. And the government has continuously promoted this misunderstanding to accomplish exactly that – your enslavement.

When I told you earlier that you've been relegated to a slave, I wanted you to understand what is happening to you. However, the pure unadulterated truth of it is that your own ignorance has enslaved you. The information in this book is designed to set you free. But that will only happen if you act upon it!

Most Americans are aware that the commonly understood version of slavery in America ended with the conclusion of the Civil War and the ratification of the 13th Amendment to the U.S. Constitution. Have you ever read the 13th Amendment?

> *Neither slavery nor involuntary servitude, except as a punishment for crime whereof the party shall have been duly convicted, shall exist within the United States, or any place subject to their jurisdiction.*

You will note that the Amendment bans "slavery" and "involuntary servitude". It does *not* ban voluntary servitude. Voluntary servitude is exactly what you'd imagine. It is serving as a slave or servant to another voluntarily. Welcome to your status in America! Now you have the power to be free again. All you have to do is use it!

Every tax form in existence in this country is for the exclusive use of taxpayers, i.e., those upon whom the tax *has* been imposed or who otherwise have been made liable. And every single one of those forms requires you to declare the content true "under penalty of perjury". But you cannot declare the content to be true unless you are also declaring the context to be true. In other words, for the content to be true, you must also be within a *class of person* upon whom the tax has been imposed or otherwise made liable. When you sign "under penalty of perjury" that the form's content is correct, you are also declaring that you have read the law and determined that you *are* within a *class of person* upon whom the tax has been imposed.

Let me give you an example. We've already discussed that the term *gross income* does not mean all income, but designates a particular species of income, i.e. income received by those upon whom the tax has been imposed. A person upon whom the income tax has been imposed, or otherwise made liable, must declare his *gross income* on a Form 1040. By signing a Form 1040 "under penalty of perjury", you are not merely swearing that the math is correct (or that you're not lying), you are also swearing that you received *gross income*, which can **only** be the case if you are within a *class of person* upon whom the tax has been imposed or otherwise made liable. Do you see how you have been falsely making this declaration for years?

When you fill out a Form W-9 you are likewise declaring yourself to be a *US person*, and that places you within Congress' taxing jurisdiction for the income tax. When you fill out a Form W-4 you are declaring that you are a *foreign person* subject to the income tax or a U.S. citizen residing abroad and earning foreign income, requiring the government to deduct the tax from your paycheck.

When you sign these forms you are saying, "Please take my property from me. Please render me a slave." I know you've not seen it in that light before, but that is exactly what you've been doing – and the government loves it and wants you to keep doing it!

So now that you know that these forms are not for you, how do you go about not signing them in a world where everyone thinks they know about tax law, but doesn't have a clue what they're talking about? This brings us to the "penalty" provisions for failing to file an information return. Those provisions are 6723 and 6724.

> 6723 – In the case of a failure by any person to comply with a specified information reporting requirement on or before the time prescribed therefor, such person shall pay a penalty of $50 for each such failure, but the total amount imposed on such person for all such failures during any calendar year shall not exceed $100,000.

We can see that the failure to file an *information return* (e.g. 1099 or W-2) is $50 each. However – and this is a huge "however" – this penalty section only relates to the filing of information returns that are **required** by regulation. For the vast majority of Americans there is no *information return* required to be filed!

That said, no one wants to get hit with a $50 penalty, and certainly no one wants to get hit with a lot of $50 penalties. But do you have to get hit with such penalties? Again, "NO!"

First off, if you understand this book you know that not only can you leave the income tax behind; it is your legal and moral duty to do so. (This of course exempts the tiny percentage of Americans who are involved in some activity that puts them into the *class of person* upon whom the tax has been imposed or otherwise made liable.)

If you take yourself out of the income tax system then you won't be asked about why you didn't file *information returns* because your activities will no longer be subject to IRS scrutiny. At that point what you do or don't do is your personal and private business. Uncle Sam will no longer be looking over your shoulder. How nice does that sound!

However, as Americans learn the truth there will be a period of transition. During the transition some people will have left the income tax system behind while others will still be a victim or participant, or immoral enforcement thugs for the IRS. In this environment you will need to explain to the person making the payment (who is not actually a *payor* under the law) that you are not required to furnish a number and that he is not required to receive one from you. This process can be accomplished in a few different ways.

If you know the person making the request, the very best thing you can do is to give him a copy of this book. I think you will agree that you could talk about it all day long and never give the subject as complete a treatment as it is given in this book. Your goal in giving him the book is two-fold. First, you're giving him information to help him make the right decision concerning you. Second, you're helping to make the national transition happen as quickly as possible by "spreading the word". There may be many ways to spread the word, but getting every American you know to read this book is likely the best way to move the process forward as rapidly as possible.

But what of the person you do not know, or a person who refuses to read the book? Then let's look at section 6724(a).

> *No penalty shall be imposed under this part with respect to any failure if it is shown that such failure is due to reasonable cause and not to willful neglect.*

As you can see, if the failure to file an *information return* is "due to reasonable cause" then there is no penalty. So, what is *reasonable cause*?

And The Answer Is...

This is one of those things that Congress has attempted to hide by altering the statute over time. This was almost certainly at the urging of the IRS. (Congressmen and Senators rarely read or understand the amendments that Treasury wants to make to thousands of tax statutes each year, but they blindly vote to approve them anyway!)

Sections 6723 and 6724 are not the first sections to address penalties for failing to file an *information return*. 6723 and 6724 are relatively new. They replaced old section 6676. Congress repealed the old 6676 and re-enacted it as 6723 and 6724. The stated purpose for this change was to establish a uniform penalty for non-filing of required *information returns*.

While 6723 is just one paragraph today, it was originally 3 paragraphs, each communicating a different aspect of the statute. Congress amended section 6723 in 1989 so that the three paragraphs were condensed to one. What didn't survive that amendment was paragraph 3, which said that 6723 and 6724 should be read in such a way as to coordinate with the old 6676. In other words, with the exception of establishing a uniform penalty, 6723 and 6724 were to operate in accordance with the old 6676.

The old 6676 isn't so important on its own, but the former regulations for 6676 are. The regulations created by the Secretary of the Treasury for old section 6676 state:

> "If, after such a request [for a TIN] has been made, the payee does not furnish the payor with his identifying number, the penalty will not be assessed against the payor."

It doesn't get any clearer than that! The Secretary is saying that if a person asks for a TIN, and none is provided, then that person shall not be penalized. In short, the failure of the payee to furnish a number is a bar to being penalized for failing to file an *information return*, or filing an incomplete *information return*.

So what do today's regulation say? The regulation today is found at 301.6724-1 and it is very lengthy and ominous sounding. It is also worded more vaguely. (Gee…what a surprise!) Yet the same message is still there.

One of the reasons for which the penalty cannot be assessed is found at 301.6724-1(c)6(i), which states:

> *"That the failure resulted from the failure of the payee, or any other person required to provide information necessary for the filer to comply with the information reporting requirements...."*

Same message; just less specific because they don't want the American public to figure it out. I should also add that 301.6724-1 has been made unnecessarily long and difficult to read. What was less than a quarter of a page in the old regulations is today more than 12 pages! Hidden in the midst of that mess is the provision shown above. That is the way your government treats you.

The point is this: even if a person falsely considers himself a *payor*, he is still protected from any penalty if he requests the number and the recipient of the payment refuses to furnish the number. Since he is protected from any penalty he should have no reason to be upset about your refusal to furnish a TIN. At that point his position should be, "That's between you and the IRS, and if I'm not being injured in any way by your decision then I see no reason to get in the middle." Fair enough!

In order to give the false *payor* something to rely upon (in the unlikely event he ever gets asked about it by the IRS) your refusal should be in writing. The false *payor* can then place your written communication in his files for his reliance. Keep the refusal letter simple. If it's more than a couple of moderate size paragraphs you're not doing it right. And most of that should be dedicated to explaining (in a slimmed down version) why your refusal to provide a TIN means he cannot be subject to the penalty. Remember, you're not writing a nontaxpayer manifesto; you're succinctly addressing one narrow subject and nothing more.

What if it is you who is making a payment to another? What then?

Today most firms just hand a Form W-9 to the person who is to be paid. Sadly, most Americans do not understand that they are not a *US person* and complete the form thinking they are doing the right thing. So what can you do to stop this ugly and illegal cycle?

In the overwhelming majority of cases the person who is receiving the payment is not a *foreign person*, and not a *US person*, so there is no issue. But how would you know if an American you were paying was a *US person* serving as an agent of a *foreign person*? The odds are infinitesimal for most of us, but some people worry about these things. Accordingly, instead of initially giving the ill-informed American a Form W-9 (thus perpetuating the problem), give him something else. You might consider giving him a document entitled "Tax Notice". It might say the following:

"If you are any of the following described persons, you are required to inform this company of your status as a condition of doing business with us, and in order to comply with U.S. tax law."

1. If you are a nonresident alien to the U.S. you are required to notify this company of that status prior to engaging in any work for us or receiving any payments from us. The general definition of nonresident alien can be found at 26 USC 7701(b).

2. If you are a foreign entity (such as a trust or corporation) you are required to notify this company of that status prior to engaging in any work for us or receiving any payments from us. The general definition of nonresident alien can be found at 26 USC 7701(31)(B) and 7701(a)(5).

3. If you are a U.S. citizen or U.S. corporation and you are acting as a representative or agent of a *foreign person* (items 1 or 2 above) and the payment being made to you actually belongs to a *foreign person*, then you are required to complete and submit to this company an IRS Form W-9 prior to engaging in any work for us.

4. If you are not a person described in items 1-3 (above) then no IRS forms or a TIN is required from you.

That's pretty succinct, yes? And it gets the job done! Have each person you pay sign that form confirming only that they read it, nothing more. In the incredibly unlikely event that the IRS claims you made a payment to a *foreign person* without filing an information return, you'll have this document to show that you exercised *due diligence* in determining if the person was within a *class of person* upon whom *information reporting* is required. Of course for the average American business this would simply be a complete waste of time, but for those who worry about such things, there you go.

Now we come to a more challenging task. Getting ignorant companies to follow the law when you work for them as a worker. Because of the statutory definition of *employee* at 3401(c), in this discussion I will use the word "worker" to designate an American citizen working within one of the 50 states, earning his own domestic income while working for another.

This book provides all the information/evidence that anyone should ever need that the law does not permit payroll withholding from a worker. But not everyone will read this book. There are people who simply do not read. (These are most likely the most ill-informed people you know.)

Others will not read it because they've been told about it and feel threatened by it. This will likely exclude accountants, CPAs, payroll managers, and the like. Just a few days before writing this section of the book, a listener to my radio show told me a story that is relevant to these "tax professionals". He told a CPA customer of his about the criminal misapplication of the income tax. The CPA became demonstrably upset. He said he didn't care if Americans were being ripped off by a corruptly applied tax system. He stated forthrightly that all he cared about was maintaining his clients and keeping his income coming in. With fellow countrymen like that, who needs enemies?

That listener's experience is just a fraction of the disheartening (and might I say, disgusting) attitudes I have seen in the last 17 years. These are the worst type of Americans (I even find it hard to call them Americans). They are happy to rape you as long as they get what they want from the rape. They rely on the certificate (or license) on the wall and the expensive suit they're wearing to camouflage their despicable conduct.

Now don't get me wrong, I have nothing against CPAs, accountants, or tax attorneys, per se. I have some great friends who are CPAs and accountants. I understand and appreciate that they have trained in a particular discipline. After undertaking years of such rigorous training, and being considered an "expert" (or at least a professional) at what they do, they naturally feel quite confident of what they know. And that's fine.

CPAs and accountants go to school to learn their profession. Most work hard to learn what they need to know to go out into the marketplace and succeed at their chosen profession. The schools they attend typically do a good job of teaching them. These schools put out good solid information to their students. The problem is that the schools neglect to tell their students "the whole story". The information taught to accounting students today is tied almost 100% to tax law. That's to be expected, considering the current climate in which everyone thinks they're *taxpayers*. The gargantuan multi-billion dollar accounting industry is built on the concept of tax compliance.

Much like the CPA in the story above, there is every reason for the accounting industry to eschew the truth of tax law, and no reason whatsoever to acknowledge the existence of nontaxpayers, or to discuss who those people are. The millionaires in the accounting industry – the guys who call the shots – know that the truth is kryptonite to their industry. They're not going to give that information to the "unwashed masses" who come through accounting school. All this is easily understandable.

My problem is with CPAs, accountants, payroll managers, etc. who have read the law – the parts that they were never taught in school – and simply ignore it. Sadly, that's most of them. Some feel threatened financially, as in the story above. Others feel threatened in the sense that they cannot hold onto their position as "the expert" if you – a mere layperson – actually know critical information they do not. Therefore even when they see the information with their own two eyes, they must reject it to protect their fragile egos and maintain their own self-image. And some are just too "simple" to make the leap. They are men and women of limited ability and the reality of the subject is too overwhelming for them to grasp. In their highly structured world the introduction of such information represents chaos in their life – and they'll have none of that

I have no empathy for any of them in this situation. Once they have been shown the truth, their "reasons" for rejecting it are irrelevant. To reject it is to reject the law – <u>and in so doing to attack the rights of their fellow Americans</u>. Their rejection also makes them hypocrites.

Accountants are not lawyers. They do not go to law school to become accountants; they go to accounting school. In their accounting schools they are taught only the "rules of computation" in chapters 1 and 2 of the Code. Who exactly those rules are applicable to is never taught in accounting school. That is left un-addressed. The students then naturally function from the "everybody knows" concept, which we have learned is a sure-fire way to go astray in tax law.

The most common mantra I have heard from accounts (and the like) over the years is, "I have to; it's the law". I can't think of a single case in which the accountant (and the like) who has said that to me ever actually knew the law.

Those who hire accountants generally put their trust in them. So, when the accountant says, "That's the way it has to be done; it's the law" the client (falsely) assumes the accountant knows the law. In point of fact, the only "law" the accountant knows is the regulatory standards that comprise the "rules of computation" in chapters 1 and 2.

We might analogize this to a person who has taken geometry in high school. He may be able to tell you the correct postulate/theorem to use in an equation, but that doesn't qualify him to know when/if/how those postulates/theorems are to be used in constructing a bridge or a building. Taking geometry in high school gives you the "rules of computation" without the broader context of applicability. That's exactly the situation accountants are in.

If a person is a taxpayer, a good accountant will know just what to do for that person, but the accountant has no education or experience that qualifies him to determine as to whom those "rules of computation" should be applied, i.e., who is a taxpayer and who is not. In fact, some of the largest accounting firms in America have been unable to respond to questions about what law imposes the income tax on the average American.

When a businessman hires an accountant, it is proper that he should trust the accountant to do a good job of accounting. But for the businessman to trust the accountant well beyond the accountant's skills, knowledge, or training is improper and unwise.

My problem with accountants is that in some circumstances they mistakenly believe they are attorneys. They give "legal advice" to their clients (which is a crime in most states). If you were to say to a business owner, "I am not required to provide you with a TIN", the accountant should never say to the business owner, "Yes he is", because that is a legal question. It is a point of law, not an accounting issue. The accountant should certainly know what do with a TIN if one is provided, but it is well beyond his "scope of practice" to determine whether or not you are required to furnish one.

The only reason the accountant tells the business owner that you must furnish a TIN is because receiving a TIN is all the accountant knows. He has no idea what to do if he doesn't get one. He has only been taught about taxpayers. The school he attended never told him (no less taught him) about nontaxpayers. His demand for a TIN does not come from his expertise in law, but rather from the limited education he received in accounting school.

When the law is working correctly, it follows a moral path. The business owner also has a moral obligation when it comes to tax law. His duty is to do that which is demonstrably right. He is not merely to defer to the words of a "paid resource" when he can clearly see what the law says.

Over the years I have lost count of the times business owners have blindly deferred to their "paid resource" and done the immoral thing. Actually, they didn't do it "blindly". They had already seen the law. They were cowards. Their perspective was, "I don't want any problems". With that mindset in place, they simply used the (incorrect and illegal) advice of their "paid resource" as a cowardly excuse; "My account said I have to...."

The owners I'm speaking of have seen the law. They just don't like what they've seen because it takes them outside their comfort zone. So how important is their "comfort zone"? Apparently important enough to violate the property rights of their fellow Americans and steal from them.

Most Americans would agree that our nation has many problems today. Yet so many people seem baffled as to exactly where these problems originate. In other words, how did we get here? If we live in a nation of citizens who are so timid, fearful, and cowardly that they are willing to violate the property rights of their fellow Americans and steal from them for no better reason than "I don't want any problems", is it any surprise that this nation is in trouble? Liberty – or freedom – or whatever term you'd like to use, cannot be had, or maintained, by timid fearful, selfish, little men.

These accountants and business owners (and various other parties such as CFOs, payroll managers, etc.), who have seen the law and rejected it, are hypocrites. One cannot see the law, reject it, and then rely on some "procedure" intended exclusively for taxpayers as justification for their actions. They say, "I have to follow the law", yet they reject the law when it is shown to them. What they really mean is, "I must blindly follow the dictates of others and if the law conflicts with my blindly following others, I will cast the law into the trashcan."

We send our young men and women around the globe to fight and die in other nations for "freedom", but this is the pathetic state of Americans at home. If this is what America has become, what are those young men and women fighting for? Is "I don't want any problems" the brave American principle that you want your son or daughter dying for? Worse yet, are you one of the masses who hold such a timid and pathetic view? Are you one of the ones willing to violate the rights of your fellow citizens because you "don't want any problems"?

Remember the old adage, "You've got to break a few eggs to make an omelet"? How come is it that virtually every American I know feels this nation is heading down the wrong path but very few are willing to *break any eggs* to get it back on track? Correction: They're willing to break as many eggs as it takes, as long as not one single egg of their own is broken.

During this transition period there will be those in business who are still in the tax system but are aware of the growing public movement away from it. Many of these folks will agree with what is happening and will want to "contribute" to it but are too cautious to make any bold and decisive moves themselves. (They will act only when it's completely safe.) Their form of "contribution" will be to respect your rights and accommodate your proper status. However, they will only do so when assured there is no cost to them. As I mentioned earlier, they will want to be assured that they can still "write off" payments to people for whom they do not have a TIN and/or have not submitted an *information return*.

This may sound silly, but people think this way. You can reassure them by pointing out a couple of quick and easy-to-understand examples.

1. Every business has telephone service. Every month they pay the phone bill. At the end of the year they write off the phone bill as an expense even though they don't have a TIN for the phone company and didn't 1099 it. This shows them that "services" can be written off without a TIN from the payment recipient or having filed an *information return*.

2. Most businesses rely on computers. These computers are often times purchased from large providers such Dell, Best Buy, Apple, CompUSA, etc. These computers represent a capital investment (not a service).

Companies write off these new computers every year without having a TIN from the sellers or having filed an *information return*.

As can clearly be seen, no TIN is required from the person to whom the payment was made in order to claim the payment as a business expense, nor is it necessary to have filed an *information return* in relation to the payment. Put simply, the only standard that has ever existed for claiming a business write-off on a tax return is that (if challenged by the IRS) the taxpayer can show the expense was realistically related to the operation of the business.

FINANCIAL INSTITUTIONS

Back in the early days of the Tax Honesty movement, there were stories of IRS Criminal Investigators visiting banks and obtaining copies of a person's bank signature cards before initiating criminal action against that person. Some folks claimed that this was evidence that there was some murky link between having a bank account and being made liable for the income tax. That of course was utter nonsense. But it does point out a link in the *legal presumption* of your status as a taxpayer.

I have repeatedly made the point that a nontaxpayer cannot run around town all year long handing out his **TAXPAYER** Identification Number and then imagine that he can convince the IRS that he isn't a taxpayer.

We have already covered the fact that the financial institutions are lying to you when they assert that the Patriot Act (and its regulations) require them to obtain a TIN from you in order to open an account. However, at this moment in time virtually every American who has a bank account (business or personal) has provided a TIN and signed the W-9 certification statement at the bottom of the signature card. (We discussed the "embedded W-9" on a bank's signature card in chapter 9.)

Here's what I suggest one do to rectify this situation.

Open an account without a TIN using the Treasury regulations discussed earlier to show the bank that the Treasury Department says you do ***not*** need a TIN to open an account. Once the account is open, close your existing account and move the funds to the new account. Of course, if you really like your current bank you may wish to extend them the courtesy of informing them of your planned action and asking them to close your old account and open a new one without your SSN. However, my experience with banks is that they'll say, "OK" but since they already have your SSN (on the old account) they'll key it into your new account as your TIN as soon as you walk out the door.

And guess what? The IRS cannot administratively levy a bank account that does not have a TIN associated with it. Why? Because the bank cannot be assured you are the specific person being levied without a TIN. Let's say the IRS wants to levy the bank account of Robert Franklin, SSN 344-45-4321. They send a Notice of Levy to a bank where they know there is an account with that name. Since the bank doesn't have a SSN for you, it cannot be certain you are the targeted "Robert Franklin" or some other Robert Franklin. And without a SSN associated with the account the IRS cannot verify to the bank that the account-holder is the specific Robert Franklin upon whom they have an [alleged] assessment. As I said, the entire income tax system pivots off the use of a TIN. So stop using it!

These realities apply to all "financial institutions". That includes banks, credit unions, brokerage accounts, etc., and I tend to use the word "bank" generically to include all such institutions.

A bank might say to you, "If you're earning interest from this account that's reportable and we'll need a TIN." Despite the fact that the bank has no idea what it's talking about, the fast and easy solution is to just tell them to make it a non-interest bearing account. For most Americans any interest from a standard bank account is a trivial amount, well worth sacrificing to gain freedom from the presumption that the account-holder is a *US person*.

A moment ago I said that the bank doesn't have a clue what it's talking about when it says that it has to get a TIN and file an information return regarding interest paid to you on an interest-bearing deposit account. Let's see what regulations say about that!

> 1.861-2(a)(1) – *Gross income consisting of interest from the United States or any agency or instrumentality thereof (other than a possession of the United States or an agency or instrumentality of a possession), a State or any political subdivision thereof, or the*

> *District of Columbia, and interest from a resident of the United States on a bond, note, or other interest-bearing obligation issued, assumed or incurred by such person shall be treated as income from sources within the United States. Thus, for example, income from sources within the United States includes interest received on any refund of income tax imposed by the United States, a State or any political subdivision thereof, or the District of Columbia.* <u>*Interest other than that described in this paragraph is not to be treated as income from sources within the United States.*</u> [underline added]

You can see that the Secretary has determined that unless the interest is paid by the *"United States, or any agency or instrumentality thereof...a State or any political subdivision thereof, or the District of Columbia, and interest from a resident of the United States on a bond, note, or other interest-bearing obligation..."*, it is not to be considered as income from sources within the U.S. If it is not U.S. source income (for the purpose of subtitle 'A') why would the banks be reporting on it at all? The only other option is that these banks imagine they are part of the United States government when paying interest. That, of course, would be a ludicrous contention.

At this point we have covered the following:

- Not giving out a TIN
- Not demanding a TIN
- Not signing/furnishing a TIN or signing a Form W-4 if you are an American living and working in any of the 50 states.
- Not demanding a TIN or a W-4 from a worker who is an American living and working in any of the 50 states.
- Addressing the *legal presumptions* that arise from furnishing a TIN when opening a bank account.

I'm sure you can think of many more questions to ask. I wish this book could be long enough to address every facet of the issue. But I think you will agree that the information provided thus far comes close to being overwhelming. In "How To Read This Book" I pointed out that many readers will want/need to read some or all of this book several times in order to gain a firm understanding of the issues. I'm sure you can look back and see why I raised that possibility.

Let's now shift away from the individual and explore some national issues.

For many Americans, even those who know the truth of the income tax, one of the biggest fears is "fear of the unknown". What will happen to America without an income tax? That is a reasonable question. After all, this is our country; we live here. So to wonder what the effects might be of no longer having an (illegally applied) income tax is an understandable concern. My response will come in several forms.

First, as a moral people, can we allow the largest financial crime in the history of the world to continue now that we know the truth? My answer is 'no'.

Second, the only way for the crime to continue is for you to continue to be a part of the criminal enterprise by depriving your fellow citizens of their property rights and disregarding the law you have seen, just like the disgusting hypocrites we've discussed. I pray that you are not the kind of person who could do such a despicable thing to your fellow Americans. If someone is such a person, and chooses to continue preying on his fellow Americans, who could be blamed if his fellow citizens put a bullet in him? I certainly would have no sympathy for the criminal and would see the victim's actions as a defense of his liberty. And since there is no court that would order the criminal to stop his illegal conduct (because the government desperately wants the largest financial crime in history to continue) this may be the way in which honest American are forced to resolve the situation. Hopefully not.

Imagine that you purchased a home in a fashionable neighborhood that has a Homeowner's Association. Shortly after you move into your new home your next-door neighbor approaches. He says he wants to make sure you don't forget to pay him the $2,000 you owe him each month. At first you think it's some weird "welcome to the neighborhood" gag. But you soon realize that he's serious. He pulls out a copy of the Homeowners Association rules (to which you are bound because of the terms of your purchase contract) and shows you where it says you must pay him $2,000 a month. You are floored!

After discussing the matter with several people, including an attorney, you begin paying the neighbor $2,000 per month, on top of making the mortgage payment on your house. Every month you think about what you could be doing with that money, and it really chaps your hide, but you feel trapped by "the law".

A year or so later you have some friends over for a BBQ. In the course of a discussion your $2,000 monthly payment to the neighbor comes up. Your friends are aghast but you assure them that this terrible situation is actually legal. You tell them that you've read the law with your own two eyes. One of your friends asks if you have a copy of the Homeowner's Association rules handy. You get him your copy and point out the section that requires your $2,000.00 per month payment to your neighbor.

Several minutes later your friend approaches you and tells you that you do *not* have to pay your neighbor $2,000.00 per month. He says the law does not say what your neighbor said it says. Having read the rules for yourself you know your friend is mistaken and you tell him as much. He quietly asks, "Did you check the definition section to determine the meaning of the various 'legal terms' used in that part of the rules?" Definitions? What is he talking about?

Your friend sees the confused look in your eyes and sits down with you and explains what he has found. He points out that the definition section that controls the meaning of the terms being used in that part of the rules is located 70 pages away from the actual part that supposedly created the legal obligation to pay your neighbor. He points out that only someone who'd read the Rule Book cover-to-cover would be likely to have come across these special definitions. He also points out that the meanings given to the words in the definition section are considerably different than the meaning in the English dictionary.

You read the definitions, make some notes about the most relevant terms, and then re-read the section of the rules that supposedly created the obligation to pay the neighbor $2,000.00 a month. As you re-read the section with the proper meanings, your blood begins to boil. You now understand that your instincts were correct – that no law could require such a thing – and that when the proper meanings are read into the rules there is no obligation whatsoever to pay the neighbor anything!

The next day the neighbor knocks on your door and demands his $2,000.00 payment. Despite your anger you calmly explain to him that you've read the definitions and now you know you don't owe him a penny – and never did. He tries to convince you that you don't understand what the definitions really mean and that you do indeed still owe him the money. You harshly shut him down and tell him that he'd better leave before you lose your temper and that he will *never* be getting another penny from you.

The next words of his mouth are, "But my family and I have come to live a certain lifestyle based on that money. We'll have to really lower our lifestyle if you stop paying that money." Would you give a damn about his objection? Would you continue to pay him $2,000.00 a month that you don't owe him, thus taking opportunities away from your own family, because he'd built a 'house of cards' with the money he was stealing from you? Of course you wouldn't.

I want you to keep this story in mind when people say, "But what will happen if we don't have an income tax?" With that said, let's explore what would happen to this nation without an income tax.

In order to answer that question we need to know what happens to/with the revenues obtained from subtitle 'A'. Most Americans presume that income tax pays for federal government services that Americans want. By this point in the book you are wise enough not to make such a presumption, right?

Not one penny of income tax pays for even one federal service to the American public. If you're one of those people who felt paying income tax was OK because it came back to the American public in the form of federal services, I'm sorry to burst your bubble. In 2007 the U.S. government collected $1,116,000,000,000 in income tax. That's $1,116 billion dollars! If that fantastic amount of money didn't provide services to the American public, where did it go?

Are you ready? Hold on to your pants. Are you sure you're ready? OK, here we go! <u>100% of each and every year's income tax revenues goes the member banks of the Federal Reserve (and others) as the interest payment on the national debt</u>. That's it. Every single penny of income tax collected goes to bankers. (Can you better understand now why the banks lie to you about the requirement for a TIN in order to trick you into falsely declaring yourself a taxpayer?)

Of course I would never expect you to take my word for it. It's the United States government that says so! During Ronald Reagan's presidency he empanelled a commission to research certain specific issues and provide Congress with solutions. The proper name of the commission was "Private Sector Survey on Cost Control", but it is more commonly known as the *Grace Commission*, having been named after its Chairman, J. Peter Grace.

Here is the quote from the Commission's report (1984) that is significant to us. Speaking of the income tax, the report states:

> *"...100 percent of what is collected is absorbed solely by interest on the Federal debt and by Federal Government contributions to transfer payments. In other words, all individual income tax revenues are gone before one nickel is spent on the services which taxpayers expect from their Government."*

While the report characterized this situation as a problem in need of a solution, in fact it is not a problem. The income system was devised to operate that way from the start. Only the ever-foolish and ill-informed American public imagines that the income tax exists to serve their needs. Everything about the income tax is 'smoke and mirrors' and that includes the public perception that the income tax is there to fund government operations for your benefit.

Stop and think this through; do you really imagine that a tax system which profits by violating your unalienable rights and turning you into slaves is there to benefit you? Don't you think that a tax system that violates your unalienable rights and turns you into slaves is actually there to benefit someone else? Here's a hint: There are no systems set up to benefit slaves. All such systems are designed to benefit the master at the expense of the slave.

It is no coincidence that the 16th Amendment and the Federal Reserve Act were adopted in the same year. They are inter-dependent.

You may have heard the phrase "Keynesian economics". This is a system of economic theories named after its originator, John Maynard Keynes (1883–1946). It is the economic/monetary theory under which most of the nations on Earth now function. It is also a complete flim-flam job on the public.

Economists construct "economic models". This is a fancy term for creating a contrived construct based on someone's theory or hypothesis. Economists create "economic models" for various reasons. The links between an "economic model" and reality are tenuous at best. An economic model can at times provide some enlightenment on a narrow issue, but its main appeal is in the realm of academia.

The problem arises when one starts to fantasize that an economic model can supplant, or even significantly impact, the real world. No matter how much one believes that his economic model can supplant or significantly impact the real world, it is still just a deluded egomaniacal fantasy. Enter John Maynard Keynes.

Keynes was an Englishman who studied at Cambridge University just after the turn of the 20th century. There he joined a secret organization, the Cambridge Apostles. It is little known who else were members of the Cambridge Apostles at that time. What is known of them is that they take a loyalty oath to the other members. One member, Michael Straight, stated, "I held up my right hand and repeated a fearful oath, praying that my soul would writhe in unendurable pain for the rest of eternity if I so much as breathed a word about the Society to anyone who was not a member...." Keynes remained an active member of the Apostles throughout his life.

The identity of a number of members did come to light shortly after WWI when it was discovered that they were spies for the Soviet Union. Quite a number of the members were (are?) Marxists. Donald McCormick (author of "The Cambridge Apostles: a history of Cambridge University's elite intellectual secret society") refers to Keynes and some others members as "predatious pederasts". So there is no confusion, "pederast" is one who seeks out sex with young boys, and "predatious" (British spelling) means "predatory in nature". In today's language we'd call Keynes a predatory homosexual child molester. In addition to its members being pederasts, communists, and traitors to their country, McCormick wrote that members also "sought out drugs as devotedly as the undergraduates of the 1960's".

The impact of the Apostles even extended to America. Michael Whitney Straight was an American member of the Apostles. He was also a communist covertly working for the KGB. Straight worked in the Franklin Roosevelt administration while under KBG control. In other words, Straight was a traitor to America.

And so, out of this pristine environment was born *Keynesian economics* – the economic system that is used in most of the world, including the U.S. *Keynesian economics* is too broad and complex a subject to explore in this book, but some of its foundational elements are important to understand in reference to the income tax.

Everyone knows that if they continually spend more than they bring in, they will end up broke. Under the flim-flam scheme that is *Keynesian economics* a sovereign nation may continually spend more than it brings in without ever reaching the point of bankruptcy. If you're scratching your head and wondering how this can possibly be true, welcome to the world of *economic modeling*.

Keynes's concept is, of course, ridiculous. A nation is nothing more than a group of individuals in a political compact. The government is nothing more than an agent of the people. If each of us will become bankrupt should we continue spending more than we bring in, then that is equally true of 300,000,000 million of us collectively. In other words, if 300,000,000 of us continuously spend more than we bring in, all 300,000,000 of us will end up bankrupt. To presume that an entity that acts collectively for all of us (government) can somehow be more, or different, than its constituent parts is absurd. But so says the economic model of a drug-using homosexual, predatory child-molesting communist. Makes you feel all warm and fuzzy about the road your government has taken you down, doesn't it?

In a political sense, Keynes was a Marxist, a collectivist, an institutionalist, and a "central planner". Most of Keynes' economic theories relied on the notion that the people of a nation would simply surrender their liberty and do as the government instructs. In Keynes' "models" the government is the "ruler", not the servant of the people, as it is to be in America. It is much easier for an economic model to have effect in the real world if the citizenry are nothing more than pawns to be moved about a conceptual chessboard, and not real people with rights, property, and liberty.

The dangers of Keynes' approach were spelled out in F.A. Hayek's 1944 book, "The Road to Serfdom". Hayek (a Nobel laureate economist) proved that "central planning", (as advocated by Keynes) must inevitably result in an ever-increasing loss of personal liberty, and eventually totalitarianism. Armed with Hayek's book, Winston Churchill attempted to check the rise of *Keynesian economics* in England after WWII, but the floodgates had already been opened and could not be closed, even by someone with the post-war eminence of Churchill.

Now that we know the corrupt beginnings of *Keynesian economics* and that *Keynesian economics* rely on the concept that your unalienable rights must yield to whatever the government says should happen in order to achieve the government's view of what is "good" for the economy, let's examine what has happened since WWII.

Let us begin with the understanding that a government has to possess money in order to spend money. So how does it acquire its money?

The first method is taxation. However, a government can only acquire so much revenue through taxation. If a government over-taxes its people, one (or more) of three things will happen: the nation's economy will tank, the people will vote out the offending officials (if possible), or there will be rebellion and the government will be changed by violence. Therefore, taxation alone will not permit a government to engage in an obscene level of spending.

The other method by which government acquires money is by borrowing. Here we begin to see America's Achilles' heel. Unless constrained by wisdom or a constitutional prohibition, a government may borrow as much as its lenders will tolerate. This, of course, presumes the lenders to be independent, non-governmental entities who are free to shut off credit to a government that has shown itself not to be credit-worthy.

Remember I told you that it was no coincidence that the "Income Tax Amendment" and the Federal Reserve Act where adopted in the same year? I told you that they are inter-dependent. Now I will explain.

The 16th Amendment was allegedly ratified on February 3rd of 1913. Ten months later the Federal Reserve Act became law.

The Federal Reserve Act was pitched to the American people as a measure to protect them from financial panics, unemployment, and business depression. We can easily look back and see what a con-job such representations were. They were, in fact, blatant lies. Since the creation of the Federal Reserve we've had the Great Depression, numerous recessions ranging from mild to deep, and as I'm writing these words the world is in the midst of suffering an unparalleled worldwide financial crisis, predominantly created by government and the financial industry. The Federal Reserve has obviously done a fine job of preventing financial panics, unemployment, and business depression! If those are the reasons for its creation, and it has been such a blatant failure at its stated purpose, why is it still in existence? Why do the American people continue to allow its existence?

Those who structured the Federal Reserve Act, and those who understood what it would actually achieve, knew that the welfare of the American people was the furthest thing from the true objective of the bill. The purpose of the bill was to give the banks a complete lock on the nation's economic and monetary policies. But the biggest coup of the Act was that it allowed private bankers to "create money" for the United States and made these notes "obligations of the United States".

Even though the bill was pitched as being a benefit to business, the pro-business Republican Party of that time opposed it. The "benefit for business" pitch was yet another lie unless your business happened to be banking.

Remember that a modern government can only attain money in two ways; taxation or borrowing. What the Federal Reserve Act really did was to create a never-ending source of loans to the United States government. A never-ending source of borrowing permits (in the minds of loan-drunk politicians) the ability to engage in never-ending spending.

I doubt I need to tell you that U.S. borrowing is completely out of control. The debt per man, woman, and child in America is staggering. If you cannot pay off your share of the national debt – which most Americans cannot – then as a nation we are bankrupt. If that isn't sobering enough, since the 2008 national elections government's borrowing has soared!

Let me just take a moment to share with you what Thomas Jefferson said about government debt.

> *"I place economy among the first and most important virtues, and public debt as the greatest of dangers. To preserve our independence, we must not let our rulers load us with perpetual debt."*

Also,

> *"The principle of spending money to be paid by future generations, under the name of funding, is but swindling futurity on a large scale."*

And,

> *"I believe that banking institutions are more dangerous to our liberties than standing armies."*

I will not go into the question of whether massive national debt is healthy for America. I'm sure you can figure that out on your own. Instead I will ask this question: <u>How does the interest on the debt get paid?</u>

Have you ever heard of a lender allowing a person to borrow more money in order to pay the interest on the original loan? Of course not; it is not permitted. Nor do the banks that loan money to the United States government allow the U.S. Treasury to borrow money to pay the interest on the money it has already borrowed.

Interest is always something separate and distinct from capital. Interest is the profit the lender makes from loaning the money. A shoe store makes a profit when it sells shoes. Banks (and other lenders) make profit when they sell you money. They have it, you want it, and they'll give it to you – for a price. That price is called "interest".

Since the federal government lives substantially and continuously beyond its means, where does it get the funds to pay the interest on the national debt? <u>It never gets the funds to pay the interest; that obligation is paid directly by you in the form of income tax.</u> And I should point out that the U.S. government hasn't paid back a penny in capital on its debts in decades, and the lenders (banks) have had to "restructure the debt" several times when the U.S. hasn't even been able to make its interest payments!

Why is the U.S. government addicted to borrowing money like a meth addict is addicted to methamphetamine? Because most people in high public office are craven, shallow people who want to stay in power at any cost. Allow me to explain.

We know that there are inherent boundaries on taxation that limit how much money the government can extract. If government had to work with just the money derived from taxes (which include many more things than just income tax), they would have to live within a true budget, just like many American families do. In that environment, every expenditure would have to be considered in light of the question, "Do we have money to pay for this?" Thus, the scope of government action would be considerably smaller and much closer to that specified in the U.S. Constitution (and ignored by Congress today).

In order to free themselves from the shackles of any true budget constraints, Congress now simply turns to the Federal Reserve and commands, "Give me money", and money magically appears in the Treasury's general fund. You may have heard the old facetious adage, "I can't be out of money, I still have blank checks." When we hear that, we laugh at the silliness of it. Congress lives exactly that way.

Congress has never-ending blank checks from the Federal Reserve. Congress keeps writing checks and the Federal Reserve keeps cashing them. The problem is that what the Fed is really doing is creating money out of thin air. To print currency because productivity in the private sector is expanding is one thing. To print money so that a profligate government can continuously live beyond its means is something else entirely. It is destructive to our economic survival.

Make no mistake, despite Keynes' (clearly false) theory that nations cannot become bankrupt, if we do nothing to stop it, there **will** be a day of reckoning. And it will be a disaster for America. It will be a disaster for you. It will be a disaster for your children.

[**Author's Note**: In fairness to Keynes, he would not have approved of the profligate spending of the U.S. Congress. Despite his concept that a sovereign nation cannot become insolvent, he did not approve of large deficits and believed that running such deficits would have substantial negative consequences. I guess Congress picks and chooses the parts of *Keynesian economics* to which it wants to pay attention.]

Thus far I have attempted not to delve into political issues that are typically thought of as "left" or "right" because this book is not about politics, but about the largest financial crime in the history of the world. However, it is important to understand what all this borrowed money is being spent on.

Without the income tax paying the interest on the debt, there could be no more borrowing. After all, what bankers would continue to make loans when they could no longer receive interest?

No interest = no more loans.

That is why the government fears the truth about the income tax more than it fears any other single thing. If no more interest were being paid on the debt, no more loans would be forthcoming. If no more loans were forthcoming, the government would have to live within its means. Living within its means would result in a dramatic reduction in government spending. A dramatic reduction in government spending would mean most, if not all, "entitlement programs" would end.

You cannot find any provision of the U.S. Constitution that permits the federal government to engage in social welfare spending (i.e., entitlement programs) <u>of any kind</u>. I stress "of any kind" because even Americans who say they believe in fidelity to the Constitution seem at times to weaken in that resolve when the discussion turns to eliminating an entitlement program they favor.

Proponents of such spending say it is permitted by the General Welfare clause. They are liars. Let's examine what the men who knew something about the meaning of the words used in the Constitution had to say about this issue.

> "Money cannot be applied to the General Welfare, otherwise than by an application of it to some particular measure conducive to the General Welfare. Whenever, therefore, money has been raised by the General Authority, and is to be applied to a particular measure, a question arises whether the particular measure be within the <u>enumerated authorities vested in Congress</u>. If it be, the money requisite for it may be applied to it; if it be not, no such application can be made. (James Madison" -- James Madison [underline added]

> "[O]ur tenet ever was, and, indeed, it is almost the only landmark which now divides the federalists from the republicans, that Congress has not unlimited powers to provide for the general welfare, but were to those <u>specifically enumerated</u>; and that, as it was <u>never meant they should raise money for purposes which the enumeration did not place under their action</u>; consequently, that the specification of powers is a limitation of the purposes for which they may raise money." -- Thomas Jefferson [underline added]

> "If Congress can do whatever in their discretion can be done by money, and will promote the General Welfare, the Government is no longer a limited one, possessing enumerated powers, but an indefinite one, subject to particular exceptions." -- James Madison (Letter to Edmund Pendleton, January 21, 1792)

Davy Crockett served in the U.S. Congress for nine years prior to his death at the Alamo. During his tenure, Congress considered a bill to provide "relief" (money) to the widow of a distinguished U.S. Naval officer who had just died. Here is a part of Crockett's speech on the floor of the House:

"Mr. Speaker, I have as much…sympathy as…any man in the House, but Congress has no power to appropriate this money as an act of charity. Every member upon this floor knows it. We have the right, as individuals, to give away as much of our own money as we please in charity; but as members of Congress we have no right so to appropriate a dollar of the public money…. Mr. Speaker, I have said we have the right to give as much money of our own as we please. I am the poorest man on this floor. I cannot vote for this bill, but I will give one week's pay to the object, and if every member of Congress will do the same, it will amount to more than the bill asks." Edward S. Ellis, *The life of Colonel David Crockett*...(Philadelphia: Porter & Coates, 1884), pp. 138-39.

Interestingly, while the bill failed to pass, not one member of the House provided any personal money for the widow's relief fund. In other words, then as now, politicians are willing to spend your money on anything and everything, but not a penny of their own money. This obscenely hypocritical behavior alone should convince you that the government must live within its means and be strictly limited to its enumerated powers, as the Constitution requires. As Jefferson so eloquently stated, *"Put not your faith in men, but bind them down with the chains of the constitution."*

According to U.S. Treasury Department figures, the expenses by the Department of Health and Human Service, Social Security, and interest on the federal debt consume the largest block of the federal budget. The Department of Health and Human Service does nothing but administer entitlement programs. And we spent quite a bit of time earlier in the book discussing the truth about Social Security.

The debt – and consequently the interest payments on the debt – would be a fraction of what they are today if not for decades of borrowing to fund unconstitutional entitlement spending. So…what we see is that the majority of government spending – and hence government borrowing – is the result of entitlement spending. Possibly the Founding Fathers weren't as stupid as those on the Left believe them to be. They knew that the public purse could never be used to provide charity. And make no mistake, when the government gives a person money which that person didn't earn, that's charity. You can call it welfare, WIC, Medicaid, Social Security or whatever, but its still charity. It's the same thing that Davy Crockett said every member of the House knew was impermissible under the Constitution. It is noteworthy that not one Congressman stood to counter Crockett's statement.

How many of you felt concern at doing away with the programs listed above? I'm sure many of you. How many of you said, "But I need that!" or "That's an important program!" You're right – they are important. They are inarguably important when these programs are bankrupting our nation. But the important part is not that people like them, or that people feel they are needed. The important part is that they are destructive to the entire fabric of our nation.

These programs require the government to be the agent of "wealth redistribution". Can you find anything in the Constitution that gives the government that power? The People did not give the government this power. Yet the government is engaged in it, through the largest financial crime in the history of the world.

The government acts as if the income tax is imposed on persons upon whom it is clearly not imposed. The government does this so that the illegally-gained revenues can be used to pay the interest on the federal loans (which have been taken out to pay for unconstitutional government charity). The government then engages in domestic terrorism to convince a frightened American public that they must continue to allow themselves to be its slaves and the victims of its extortion scheme. With the scheme still operating, the government uses the criminally obtained revenue to ensure tomorrow's loans (which are used to fund tomorrow's government charity). And so the cycle continues.

But why would the government continue this practice if the outcome is inevitable? Because any nationally recognized politician who would speak out against it would lose the support of his party and would be voted out of office at the very next election. This is the elephant in the room that no one will talk about.

The real motive behind entitlement spending is not charity – it is power.

> *"The democracy will cease to exist when you take away from those who are willing to work and give to those who would not."*
> -- Thomas Jefferson

Any time the Constitution is breached, it diminishes our personal and individual liberty. The Constitution was written in such as way as to bar the federal government from infringing on our rights, whether those rights are political, civil, or unalienable. That is why you will find no power granted to the government to engage in wealth redistribution or charity. When you have your rights intact and secure, the government is thusly limited. Whenever the government expands its powers, your liberty is diminished. That is the way of it.

Because the government produces nothing, everything it has, and anything it gives in charity, must first be **taken** (seized) from someone else. In order to *seize* your property the government must breach your unalienable right to your own labor and property. Every time the government breaches your rights it becomes more powerful and **The People** become less powerful. Every time you allow the government to violate the constitution and illegally seize your property, you agree to being made less powerful and you agree to hand over to the government that power which you rightfully possess. Do this often enough, or long enough, and the government will have everything and you will have nothing.

This entire game boils down to one question. There are only two groups that can hold power in this country. One is you and your fellow Americans. The other is politicians and professional bureaucrats. You can't have it both ways. <u>Them or you – which will it be</u>? It's your choice.

That choice can be exercised by your decision to stop participating in the largest financial crime in the history of the world; to stop participating in the income tax system; to follow the law and insist that others do so too.

If you continue to participate, you are perpetuating the system that will be the demise of your own liberty and the destruction of America as we know it.

If you stop participating, you are saying that you will no longer be a party to the whole sordid, immoral, illegal, and unconstitutional conduct that constitutes the largest financial crime in the history of the world. To stop participating is the first step to setting America back on the path to restoring its former greatness. To stop participating is you telling Congress that you are in charge of America, not them.

> "The government is merely a servant -- merely a temporary servant; it cannot be its prerogative to determine what is right and what is wrong, and decide who is a patriot and who isn't. Its function is to obey orders, not originate them."
> -- Mark Twain

SHUNNING

This is a momentous battle. The stakes are high and the consequences grave for our nation – and in fact the world. That means that we do not have the luxury of sitting by idly while selfish and timid Americans attempt to avoid complying with the law. There are many avenues to gain their compliance. I leave many of those to you to decide upon. I would however like to talk about one in particular. That is shunning.

Much has been made of "tolerance" in the last decade or so in America. As far as I can see, the Left has used the concept of "tolerance" only to intimidate its opponents into tolerating the Left's intolerance of our unalienable rights. I sure as hell am not tolerant of the Left's intolerance of my unalienable rights, nor should you be! When it comes to the largest financial crime in the history of the world, and your decision to end that crime by your refusal to participate and your commitment to follow the law, evil-doers (those who wish to continue to violate the law and your rights) will be from both sides of the fence and every walk of life, and you must not let that sway you from your course!

On a personal and social level I strongly urge you to actively shun anyone and everyone who continues to be a co-conspirator in the largest financial crime in history. It is important, however, to give them an opportunity to know the law and make a choice ***before*** you engage in shunning. Having read this book you understand how few people know the truth of the income tax. That is what we need to change if America is to pull back from the brink.

There are numerous and various ways to share the truth with people. Obviously the method I favor is to get a copy of this book into their hands. As stated earlier, I know of no more thorough treatment of the subject than this book.

There is, of course, the option of sharing the information verbally. While this may be a good method by which to broach the subject, in most cases it will not have the power to change behavior. Most people will not change their ingrained behavior (no matter how harmful or illegal) simply because someone else said so.

In the business environment a professional well-written business letter is the preferred method. The letter should be long enough to lay out the law and the particulars, but short enough that the recipient will take the time to read it. Most busy professionals would need some serious motivation to read a letter that is more than 3 pages in length. Remember, such a letter should be written only if the person is breaking the law and infringing on your rights. As an example, if you are working for a person and all is well, do not write such a letter. However, if he suddenly asks for a TIN or commits some other act that telegraphs he is about to violate your rights, that is the time to professionally communicate the situation to him, not before.

If you communicate to a business associate and he refuses to follow the law, if you have the latitude simply decline to do business with him. During my nearly two decades in this venue I have noticed that the brightest and most professional of our society are those who gravitate to the truth about the income tax. Those who seek out the truth in general, and the income tax in particular, are those who tend to be the best in their fields. Accordingly, if you can afford it I suggest you deprive the co-conspirator of your services. Of course I do not suggest that course of action until you have worked diligently to give him an understanding and it becomes apparent that he has no desire to follow the law which he has seen.

There is also an opportunity here for companies that understand the truth and act upon it. If a company follows the law and does not withhold from its workers, then it will have a substantial edge in hiring the most talented workers.

Imagine that an American has skill/experience in a job that typically pays $5,000.00 per month. He applies at company 'A' and asks if they intend to demand a W-4 and illegally withhold from his paycheck. They say that they will indeed illegally seize his property each pay-period. He then applies at company 'B' and asks the same question. Company 'B' assures him that they would never violate his rights and if he declines to complete a W-4 then there will be no withholding. Where do you think this talented American will go to work? By following the law, and not violating the rights of Americans, company 'B' will have its pick of the best workers. Company 'A' will get whoever is left over.

Aside from the practical aspects, there is a moral component. It is for this reason that we must shun those who reject the truth and choose to be an active part in violating the law and continuing the largest financial crime in the history of the world.

Today we have become such a "delicate" and politically correct[3] society that most people no longer really understand what shunning is about, or how to go about it. Today people are more concerned about being perceived as intolerant – even to an immoral criminal – than they are about the actual wrong committed. Some people feel it is a bigger social faux pas to be (supposedly) insensitive to the feelings of a rapist rather than condemning the rapist for his crime. Needless to say, I do not suffer from that asinine view.

Before I explain shunning in more detail let me say that shunning is (at least in my mind) only appropriate when a person has committed a moral wrong, and generally when they know it is wrong (or have reason to know) and have chosen to commit the moral wrong anyway. Their "justification" for committing the moral wrong should be completely irrelevant to you. Everyone who commits a moral wrong has some excuse they use to justify their actions to others.

Once a person has been <u>sufficiently</u> exposed to the truth about the income tax, and you determine they have chosen to continue violating the law and violating the rights of their fellow Americans, that is the time to begin shunning him.

That said, let me give you another cautionary note.

Simply telling someone what you discovered does not constitute being <u>sufficiently</u> exposed to the truth. Telling a neighbor over a hotdog and couple of beers at a community BBQ is ***not*** sufficiently exposing him to the truth. And of course for shunning to work, it must create some level of uncomfortableness for the person being shunned. If you shun a neighbor living a block away who barely knows you, it will have no effect and you'll look a bit foolish. You must be able to put a sufficient amount of information in front of them and have them reject it. Only then are they ripe for shunning.

Shunning can also be uncomfortable for you. Because shunning only has an effect on someone who usually has some personal interaction with you, it may be emotionally trying for you as well. Tough it out. The issues here are far bigger than your personal comfort.

---

[2] Political Correctness is a doctrine, fostered by a delusional, illogical minority, and rabidly promoted by an unscrupulous dominant media, which holds forth the proposition that it is entirely possible to pick up a turd by the clean end.

Shunning can be done on a number of levels. On one end of the curve it can be complete absence from the offending person. On the other end it can involve being at the same location but having little or nothing to do with that person. If questioned by others about your conduct it is important to firmly (yet politely) explain your actions.

Let's say you've had several discussions with your uncle about the income tax and you've given him a copy of this book. He owns a small business and it becomes apparent to you that he simply doesn't care about the law or the rights of his fellow Americans. He's going to keep on harming people even though he now knows the truth of what he is doing. This is the time to shun.

In this scenario let's say that it is unrealistic to completely avoid him because of frequent family get-togethers. That is no reason not to shun him.

You arrive at one of the family get-togethers and your uncle is there. You've made the decision to shun him and he walks over to you to say 'hello'. How do you handle that situation? Yes, it's awkward. Yes, it's a difficult moment. Here's the way you handle it. First of all, if he puts out his hand to shake yours, do not take it. Leave it extended. That's part of shunning.

Ask him to join you somewhere relatively private. Once you are somewhere relatively private, remind him of what has transpired in the past, i.e., you have laid the evidence out before him and he made the decision to continue violating the law and harming innocent Americans. Calmly explain that you find his decision immoral and loathsome. Explain that you find the violation of the rights of your fellow Americans to be a despicable act. Explain that you used to hold him in regard but now you see him as someone who is more than willing to break the law ***and*** violate the rights of his fellow Americans at the same time. Express how disappointed you are to find out that he is that type of person. Explain that you now find it difficult to be close with him or conduct a conversation with him as if he were a moral person. Let him know that because of his choice, you will be keeping your distance from him. <u>And most importantly</u> – let him know that you are looking forward to the day that he will choose to be a good, honest, and moral American so that you and he can get back to the closeness you used to feel for one another.

Be prepared to explain (again) exactly why what he is doing is illegal and why his choice is immoral. Remember, he can only make the decision to change if he understands what he is doing wrong and what is the proper legal/moral choice.

Be prepared for his excuses. It is a virtual certainty that he will attempt to overcome your decision by hammering you with any number of excuses. Although I cannot anticipate every excuse, a pretty safe response to most any excuse offered is, "That is no excuse for violating the law and violating the rights of your fellow Americans."

Most people in such circumstances will deny violating the law. That is generally just one of their excuses. Don't get frustrated. Simply say, "Yes you are. I've already shown you that you are. However, because I care about you I'll go over it with you again. Let's do it right now so this ugliness doesn't have to go any further."

You may get the response, "I don't agree with your interpretation of the law." The simple answer is, "Uncle, I've already covered this with you. It's all in the book and I'm willing to go over it with you page-by-page if need be. It is not my interpretation; it is the interpretations of Congress, the U.S. Supreme Court, and the Secretary of the Treasury. Would you like to go over it again right now? I care about you enough to go over it with you again." If he declines, simply say, "I'm sorry to hear that", and walk away. There's nothing more you can do at that moment.

And remember, you should not be the only person shunning him. Everyone else who knows the truth should be treating him exactly the same way.

What is the purpose of shunning? It serves several purposes. Unfortunately some people will not do the right thing unless they experience a negative consequence for failing to do so. Having friends, family, and business associates distance themselves from that person, with a clear message as to why, is one method of making the wrong-doer feel the consequences of his actions.

Second, it protects you from continuing to associate closely with an immoral person. That may seem like a trite concept in today's world, but there is significant value in it. It is not healthy for you (or anyone else) to continue socializing with any person who has denied fundamental rights to others or who rejects truth out-of-hand.

And The Answer Is...

Third, it sends a message to others. It sends a message about who you are, and what your standards are, and it conveys to others how significant this issue is.

If you do this, are others going to be critical of you? Sure. So what's new? Someone is going to say you're taking this too seriously, or you're taking it too far, or you're being a jerk. Here's the response.

> <u>You're taking this too seriously</u>: *"Really? So if someone came into your house and stole all your possessions and violated your rights – and maybe even sexually assaulted you – you'd want me to treat that person in a warm and endearing manner?"* But that's not what happened! *"True, but the legal and moral violation is on a par. I'm sorry you can't see that."*

> <u>You're taking it too far</u>: *"No, actually I'm not taking it far enough. What he's doing is disgusting, reprehensible, and immoral. And frankly it reflects poorly on you that you aren't joining with me against his immoral conduct. I guess if someone is a friend or a family member of yours he can do any immoral thing and it's OK with you. I'm not built that way."*

> <u>You're being a jerk</u>: *"It's a shame you feel that way. I guess it doesn't matter to you how many people he screws over as long as it's not you. That's a sad perspective. I guess that means that I can be great friends with someone who screws you over as long as he's ripped you off and not me."*

These are just examples, but I'm sure you get the gist. Stand your ground.

Standing up for what is right is never easy. If it were easy everyone would do it. There's an expression, "If you're not the lead dog the view is always the same." Break free of the herd. Get out in front. Be the lead dog on this issue. The truth is, it's not going to change unless you take a stand. You taking a stand, along with millions of other Americans, **will** change this nation. Don't wait for anyone else. If everyone waits for someone else to stand up first...

The examples we just covered are in a family or friends environment. What about at work?

Work is trickier. No matter how we feel, we need to maintain our professional relationships at work. Yet this doesn't mean you can't let an immoral person know you object to their conduct. The work environment just means that you likely need to be more subtle and less confrontational.

Let's say you're speaking to the payroll manager and she is the decision-maker concerning whether or not the company will attempt to illegally force you to sign a W-4. At the conclusion of the discussion the manager insists that you sign a W-4 or she will terminate you.

> [**Author's Note**: You should know there is a completely legal way to sign such forms that completely divests the company paying you of any legal force or effect.]

Using the correct legal mechanism to divest the form of any legal effect, you sign the form. When you hand the form to the manager you say, "It's disappointing for me to discover you're that type of person." She may leave your comment alone or she may respond with, "What kind of person is that?" Your response should be something such as, "A person who ignores the law and does harmful and violative things to others just to protect herself. But I have to look at the bright side – I have a perfect example of the type of person I don't want my children to grow up to be like!" Turn and walk out.

The important thing at this point is that you follow through by being a good worker and not act inappropriately because of the immoral scumbag who is the payroll manager. As long as you choose to stay there, do a good job. If possible, start looking for that honest company that will respect your rights. When you find it, go! Eventually the companies that violate the law and people's rights will be left with only the untalented and unprincipled working for them. Karma!

It is impossible for me to give you examples for every conceivable situation. I've given you these few examples because this sort of fight may be new to you. I want you know that you can fight this fight successfully, and you can do so with firmness and character.

There is no sudden climactic end to this book, just as there will be no sudden climactic end to the criminal misapplication of the income tax. There is an adage that says, "Freedom is not free." Our forefathers paid a heavy price for liberty.

We are not called upon to pay such a price. Nevertheless, freedom and liberty do require courage and dedication. Do you possess these attributes? I pray you do.

In the Introduction I said, "I long ago came to the realization that the only way to end the fraudulent application of the income tax was to come directly before the American people and provide them with the necessary information in such a way that they can see the situation for what it is, and act accordingly."

We have come to the end of the book and have returned to the opening premise. Ending the largest financial crime in the history of the world cannot be solved by pleading with the perpetrators. It can only be ended by you and me.

In this book I have done my duty as an American who loves and respects his fellow citizens and wants America to again be the shining light of liberty it once was.

Now it's your turn.

Happiness and moral duty are inseparably connected.
George Washington

It is the duty of the Patriot to protect his country from its government.
Thomas Paine

"*Hold on, my friends, to the Constitution and the Republic for which it stands. Miracles do not cluster, and what has happened once in 6,000 years, may not happen again. Hold on to the Constitution, for if the American Constitution should fail, there will be anarchy throughout the world.*" Daniel Webster

"*If ye love wealth better than liberty, the tranquility of servitude better than the animating contest of freedom, go home from us in peace. We ask not your counsels or arms. Crouch down and lick the hands which feed you. May your chains set lightly upon you, and may posterity forget that ye were our countrymen.*"
Samuel Adams – August 1, 1776

This book is about the legal and moral issues involved in the income tax.

It is **not** a "how to" manual on leaving the income tax system behind. Many people would do well to seek experienced guidance, especially companies that intend to stop withholding from their workers.

Should you decide that experienced guidance is the wise course for you, please feel free to contact my office at (775) 751-0811.

The Dave Champion Show and Other Resources

For information about the
Dave Champion Show -
such as how to listen - go to
www.davechampionshow.com.

Facebook.com/DaveChampionFanPage

Twitter.com/Dave_Champion

Youtube.com/TheDaveChampionShow

PLEASE TURN TO THE NEXT PAGE

The Right Handgun

I believe the ***right to keep and bear arms*** is not merely a "right", but also a duty. George Washington referred to firearms as "[T]he peoples' liberty's teeth."

On my radio show I encourage Americans to purchase combat grade firearms and invest the time and money to learn how to employ them effectively in a violent confrontation. After all, George Washington was not talking about firearms for "sporting purposes"!

"The strongest reason for the people to retain the right to keep and bear arms is, as a last resort, to protect themselves against tyranny in government" ~ *Thomas Jefferson,* 1 *Thomas Jefferson Papers, 334*

Most combat grade rifles will serve you well. The majority of combatants around the world use the AR15 or the AK47. Either will serve you well. My combat rifle of choice is the AK47.

A handgun tends to be a more personal weapon because we carry it daily. Quality handguns are just too expensive to keep purchasing until you find the right one. A large part of your confidence, comfort, and expertise with a handgun is tied to selecting the right pistol.

In order to help you select one handgun you can count on in every situation, I have teamed up with firearms manufacturer Ed Brown Products. Ed Brown Products is now offering the *Champion/Molon Labe* 1911 pistol.

The *Champion/Molon Labe* pistol is a fighting tool! It is the product of more than 100 years of firearms evolution, coupled with Ed Brown Product's advanced technology and top-quality craftsmanship.

Not only is this pistol a top-of-the-line uniquely American fighting tool, but it is hand-built to my specifications – specifications that are the result of my 30 years of experience with combat firearms and training. It is the pistol I carry.

You can purchase this pistol with the assurance that you will never need to buy another (though you may love it so much you decide you want another)! And you're buying it from an American family business that manufacturers the components and assembles your pistol right here in the good ol' US of A!

Here are the attributes of this outstanding fighting pistol:

- Classic 1911 design.
- Hand fit and assembled by master pistolsmiths.
- Front and rear cocking serrations.
- "Molon Labe" laser engraved on the left side of the slide.
- "Champion" laser engraved on the right side of the slide.
- The famous Spartan battle helmet engraved in the custom G10 grips.
- Ed Brown's custom "snakeskin" treatment on the front strap and mainspring housing for both comfort and a rock-solid grip in any situation (without chewing up your hands in long hours/days of training).
- Tritium (night sight) front sight. Having tritium only in the front sight allows for faster and more reflexive close quarters response in low-light situations.
- Wide notch (non-tritium) rear sight by "10-8". The wide notch provides faster front sight acquisition at typical handgun fighting distances. (Also great for older shooters whose eyes may not be quite as sharp as they once were.) The rear of the sight is serrated to prevent glare across the back of the rear sight.
- Solid aluminum trigger.
- Ambidextrous thumb safety is available so you can fight effectively with either hand.
- Ed Brown's famous high-rise beavertail grip safety with memory grooves.
- Ed Brown Maxi-well magazine funnel for rapid magazine changes – because at pistol fighting distances time matters!
- Pistol is finished with Ed Brown's high quality "Gen III" coating for a gorgeous appearance and fantastic wear resistance.

In order that you may be confident that I truly believe in this pistol, I want you to know that I do not make a penny from your purchase of the Champion/Molon Labe pistol. Ed Brown Products does the work; they make the money. Letting you know about this outstanding American fighting tool is simply my gift to you as freedom loving American.

You can view this one of a kind all-American pistol at **http://www.edbrown.com/champion.htm**.

"Firearms are second only to the Constitution in importance...."
~ George Washington

"As to the species of exercise, I advise the gun. While this gives moderate exercise to the body, it gives boldness, enterprise, and independence to the mind. Games played with the ball and others of that nature, are too violent for the body and stamp no character on the mind. Let your gun, therefore, be the constant companion to your walks."
~ Thomas Jefferson

Acknowledgments

There have been so many people who have been influential in bringing this book into creation that I hardly know where to start and who to thank. I wish to apologize in advance for not being able to remember everyone who has been of influence to me on this subject over the last 17 years.

The first person I'd like to thank and acknowledge is **Wayne Scott**. For many years Wayne carried a tremendous workload, which permitted me to keep my nose in the law books. His unflinching efforts and quiet perseverance provided me with the time and money to continue seeking out the truth. Without Wayne's kindness, patience, and friendship this book would not exist. I hope one day he will understand that he is the true unsung hero. Whatever good this book may do, Wayne is a tremendous part of that.

Leonard Simon was the first person to introduce me to the Tax Honesty Movement (though that term had not yet been coined at the time). His excitement over the truth was infectious! In 1993 we had a discussion over dinner at a Mexican restaurant. None of us realized that discussion would eventually lead to this book.

Murray Crews was the first Tax Honesty researcher to whom I was introduced. Murray's dedication, methodology, and fervor set a fantastic example for a person burning to discover the truth. Not only did Murray provide me with a powerful example to follow, over the years a rich friendship ensued. He has been invaluable to me throughout the development of this book.

Jeff Tokaji has been an amazing friend since my teens. Not only has he always supported my efforts to uncover the truth of the income tax, but in the later years he never let me forget how important it was to get this book done. No matter how busy my life would get, Jeff would always re-focus my attention on the book. I don't think we've had a conversation in the last several years that didn't include the line, "How is the book coming along?"

Vladimir Diaz is an incredible man whose heart burns for liberty. He is also one hellacously fine paralegal. He has been with me every step of the way in writing the book. His critical eye has provided invaluable insight throughout the book's development.

Jennifer Averett performed the most demanding element of getting the book ready for print. Jen labored untold hours compiling every correction, critique, commentary, editorial suggestion, etc., from every test reader and proofreader. And much of that had to be batted around with the persnickety author before each issue could be concluded! Aside from the actual writing of the book, Jen's task was the most time consuming and detail oriented. During this grueling and highly detailed work I never heard a single complaint. I am forever grateful for her hard work, support, and caring attitude.

Robert Morrow is a treasure trove of technological talent as well as being filled with fantastic insights. There was nary a problem I encountered that Robert couldn't solve, or at a bare minimum offer a productive direction to pursue. Robert was a God-send when it came to getting this book properly formatted for the printer. When I think of the words "How may I be of service", I think of Robert.

Ernie Fowlke and **Bill Fowler** opened my eyes to an entirely new world. They have worked diligently behind the scenes to create a marketing infrastructure with newer internet technologies. They have shown patience and kindness in the face of my lack of technological savvy. They are both true gentlemen.

Bill Carns is one of the most intelligent, insightful, energetic, creative, resourceful men I've ever known. Bill never helps with one thing; he helps with everything. Need a solution? Bill has it! It would be hard for me overstate the value of his assistance in so many matters surrounding the creation of the book. Thank you Bill!

My appreciation to **Ben Vanderklooster** for the back cover photograph.

There are a number of others patriotic Americans who have contributed to this project, yet fear that if they are named they will be become targets of an angry U.S. government. They pitched in with ideas, suggestions, or assistance concerning software, marketing, printer resources, layout, formatting, etc. I am grateful for their assistance because this is my first book and I did not have ready answers to many of the challenges that a first-time author and self-publisher faces. Although I cannot name them, I thank them for their contributions. [It is telling that at this point in our nation's history Americans fear the government when they've done nothing more than assist an author with a book containing a message the government doesn't want people to hear.]

Test Readers: A number of people provided their time and effort to read the book as it was being developed and provided me their feedback. Their efforts have been invaluable. I will not name them because I'm not certain that all of them would wish to be named, but I want each of them to know how much I appreciate their important contribution to this project.

Not one person who contributed to the creation of this book asked for a penny! Every one of them is a volunteer. What makes men and women volunteer their valuable time in such copious amounts to work with such a complex subject? It is their desire to see the lie end! Nothing more. They want the truth to prevail in America. They want America restored to a condition of freedom and individual liberty. They want to do their part to see that occur. They are men and women who do not merely talk about principles; they are men and women who put them into action! **They are true Americans!**

I have been privileged to have several published authors I respect "test read" the book. Their feedback was valuable in that it came from men who had already done what I was attempting to do – write that first book. These men are not only wonderful authors in their own right, but each is a fiercely patriotic American. I am flattered that they consider me a peer and honored that they are my friends.

Michael Lemieux – Michael Badnarik – John Carpenter –

There are, of course, many others who deserve acknowledgement. Much of the research was performed by the dedicated Americans who came before me. There is no way for me to adequately express my respect and appreciation to the tens of thousands of researchers who put their lives on hold to pursue the truth. How do you thank men and women who were brave enough to take a stand against "common wisdom", when that common wisdom is enforced by cruel men with guns? I hope that all those who have contributed so much over so many years will forgive me for not being able to include each by name, but know that their contributions are not forgotten, nor their efforts unappreciated.

Dave Champion

Table of Authorities & Notes

Chapter One - Rules of the Game
1. U.S. Constitution, Amendment IX
2. U.S. Constitution, Amendment IV and V
3. McCulloch v. Maryland, 17 U.S. 327 at 431 (1819)
4. The Declaration of Independence (July 4th, 1776)
5. Butchers' Union v. Crescent City, 111 U.S. 746, at 756-758 (1884)
6. 26 U.S.C., Subtitle A
7. 26 U.S.C., Subtitle C
8. U.S. v. Alpers, 338 U.S. 680 (1950); U.S. v. Rodgers, 466 U.S. 475, at 481-482 (1984)
9. U.S. v. Mersky, 361 U.S. 431, at 437-438 (1960); National Muffler Dealers Assn. v United States, 440 U.S. 472 (1979); U.S. v. Murphy, 809 F.2d 1427, at 1430 (9th Cir. 1987)
10. Fawcus Mach. Co. v United States, 282 US 375, at 378 (1931); Commissioner of Internal Revenue v. South Texas Lumber Co., 333 U.S. 496, at 501 (1948); California Bankers Assn v. Shultz, 416 U.S. 21, at 25 (1974)
11. United States v. Murphy, 809 F.2d 1427, at 1430 (9th Cir. 1987)
12. Chrysler Corporation v. Brown, 441 U.S. 281, at 307-309 (1979)
13. Meese v. Keene, 481 U.S. 465, 484-485 (1987); Sutherland on Statutes and Statutory Construction § 47.07, p. 152, and n. 10 (5th ed.1992).
14. Stenberg v. Carhart, 530 U.S. 914 at 942-943 (2000); Colautti v. Franklin, 439 U.S. 379, at 392-393(1979).

Chapter Two - Origins and Evolution
1. U.S. Constitution, Art. I, Sec. 2, Cl. 3
2. U.S. Constitution, Art. I, Sec. 8, Cl. 1
3. U.S. Constitution, Art. I, Sec. 9, Cl. 4
4. American Airways v. Wallace, 57 F.2d 877, at 880 (1932)
5. Bank of Commerce v. Senter, 149 Tenn. 569, 260 S.W. 144 (1924)
6. Knowlton v. Moore, 178 U.S. 41 (1900)
7. Hylton v. U.S., 3 U.S. 171, at 176-177 (1796)
8. Pollock v. Framers' Loan & Trust Company, 157 U.S. 429 (1895)

9. U.S. Constitution, Amendment XVI

Chapter Three - Interpretations and Perceptions
1. Brushaber v. Union Pacific Railroad, 240 U.S. 1 (1916)
2. Hylton v. U.S., 3 U.S. 171 (1796)
3. Pollock v. Framers' Loan & Trust Company, 157 U.S. 429 (1895)
4. American Airways v. Wallace, 57 F.2d 877, at 880 (1932)
5. http://dictionary.law.com/Default.aspx?selected=1613
6. http://dictionary.lp.findlaw.com/
7. Stanton v. Baltic Mining Co., 240 U.S. 103 (1916)
8. Murphy v. U.S., 373 U.S. App. D.C. 143 (2006)
9. Murphy v. U.S., 377 U.S. App. D.C. 197 (2007)
10. William E. Peck & Co. v. Lowe, 247 U.S. 165 (1918)
11. South Carolina v. Baker, 485 U.S. 505 (1988)

Chapter Four - Income v. Income
1. Corn v. Fort, 95 S.W. 2d 620 (1936)
2. Butchers' Union v. Crescent City Co., 111 U.S. 746 (1884)
3. Coppage v. Kansas, 236 U.S. 1 (1915)
4. American Heritage Dictionary, Fourth Edition
5. United States Constitution, Article IV, Section 4
6. Stratton's Independence, LTD. v. Howbert, 231 U.S. 399, at 414 (1913)
7. Doyle v. Mitchell Brother, Co., 247 U.S. 179 (1918)
8. Towne v. Eisner, 245 U.S. 418 (1918)
9. Eisner v. Macomber, 252 U.S. 189 (1920)
10. Merchants Loan & Trust v. Smietanka, 255 U.S. 509 (1921)
11. Adair v. United States, 208 U.S. 161, at 172 (1908)
12. Gould v. Gould, 245 U.S. 151 (1917); United States v. Wigglesworth, 2 Story, 369, Fed. Cas. No. 16,690; American Net & Twine Co. v. Worthington, 141 U.S. 468, at 474 (1891); Benziger v. United States, 192 U.S. 38, at 55 (1904).

Chapter Five - Then as Now
1. 26 U.S.C. §1(a)
2. 26 C.F.R. §1.1-1(a)
3. 26 C.F.R. §1.1-1(b)
4. 26 U.S.C. §7701(b)(1)(A)

5. http://dictionary.law.com/Default.aspx?selected=1152
6. http://dictionary.law.com/Default.aspx?selected=1365
7. Eisner v. Macomber, 252 U.S. 189, at 206 (1920)
8. 26 U.S.C. §6001
9. 26 C.F.R. §1.6001
10. 26 U.S.C. §6151(a)
11. 26 U.S.C. §61(a)
12. 26 U.S.C. §6012
13. 26 U.S.C. §6072

Chapter Six – If Not You, Then Who?
1. www.quatloos.com (Jay Adkisson, Esq.)
2. www.freedomabovefortune.com (Joe Banister, CPA & Former IRS C.I.D. Agent)
3. Spreckels Sugar Refining Co. v. McCain, 192 U.S. 397 (1904)
4. Black's Law Dictionary, 3rd Ed. (1933)
5. Hale v. Henkel, 201 U.S. 43, at 74 (1906)
6. Corn v. Fort, 95 S.W.2d 620 (1936)
7. 26 C.F.R. §1.1-1(a)

Chapter Seven – In Their Own Words
1. 26 U.S.C. §7601
2. 26 U.S.C. §7602
3. 26 U.S.C. §7621
4. Executive Order 10289, Section 1(g)
5. Treasury Order 150-01
6. 19 C.F.R. Part 101
7. 26 U.S.C. §§7601 – 7606
8. 27 C.F.R. Part 70
9. 27 C.F.R. Parts 170, 296
10. 26 C.F.R. Part 301
11. 19 C.F.R., Part 101, pages 314 through 323 (1998 ed.)
12. 26 C.F.R., Part 601
13. 26 C.F.R. §601.101
14. 26 C.F.R. §601.102
15. 26 C.F.R. §601.103
16. 26 C.F.R. §601.104(a)(2)

17. 26 U.S.C. §3406
18. 26 U.S.C. §1441
19. 26 U.S.C., subtitle 'A', chapter 3, subchapters 'B'
20. 26 U.S.C. §7701(a)(16)
21. 26 U.S.C. §1464
22. 26 U.S.C. §6414
23. 26 C.F.R. §1.1441-1(c)(19)
24. 26 U.S.C. §31.3406(a)-2
25. 26 U.S.C. §6041(a)
26. Treasury Decision 8734
27. 26 U.S.C. §1461
28. 26 C.F.R. §1.1441-2(b)
29. 26 U.S.C. §701
30. 26 U.S.C. §706(a)
31. 26 U.S.C. §264(a)
32. 26 U.S.C. §272
33. Internal Revenue Manual, Part 1100 (1998 ver.)
34. Treasury Decision 1928
35. Treasury Decision 2313
36. Treasury Decision 2401
37. Treasury Decision 2382
38. Treasury Decision 2815
39. Treasury Decision 2988
40. Treasury Decision 6500
41. 26 C.F.R. §602.101 (OMB Control Number)

Chapter Eight – "Employee" – Who, Me?
1. 26 U.S.C., Subtitle 'C'
2. 26 C.F.R., Part 31
3. 26 U.S.C. §7701(a)(26)
4. Meese v. Keene, 481 U.S. 465, at 484-485 (1987)
5. Colautti v. Franklin, 439 U.S. 379, at 392 (1979)
6. 26 U.S.C. §7701(c)
7. 27 U.S.C., et. seq.
8. 27 C.F.R. §72.11
9. Mein Kampf, vol. 1, ch. 10 (1925)
10. 26 U.S.C. §162

Table Of Authorities & Notes

11. 26 U.S.C. §3402
12. 26 U.S.C. §3401(a)
13. 26 U.S.C. §3401(c)
14. 26 U.S.C. §3401(d)
15. 26 U.S.C. §6331(a)
16. http://www.legal-explanations.com/definitions/ejusdem-generis.htm
17. 26 U.S.C., Subtitle 'A', Chapter '3'
18. 26 U.S.C., Subtitle 'C', Chapter '24'
19. 26 C.F.R. §31.6051-1
20. Charles C. Steward Machine Co. v. Davis, 301 U.S. 548 (1937)
21. 31 U.S.C. §1321
22. 26 U.S.C., Subtitle 'C', Chapter '21'
23. 26 U.S.C. §3111
24. 26 U.S.C. §§3121-3128
25. http://www.socialsecurity.gov/history/InternetMyths.html
26. 26 U.S.C. §3121(b)
27. 26 U.S.C. §3121(e)(2)
28. Hooven & Allison Co. v. Evatt, 324 U.S. 652, at 671-672 (1945)
29. 26 U.S.C. §3121(e)(1)
30. 26 U.S.C. §6103(b)(5)(A)(i)
31. 26 U.S.C. §3121(h)
32. Section 233, Social Security Act
33. 26 U.S.C. §3121(b)(A)(ii)
34. Downes v. Bidwel, 182 U.S. 244 (1901)
35. 48 U.S.C. §731
36. United States Constitution, Art. 1, Sec. 8, Cl. 17
37. United States Constitution, Art. 4, Sec. 3, Cl. 2
38. 26 C.F.R. §31.0-2
39. 26 C.F.R. §31.0-2(a)(7)
40. 26 C.F.R. §301.7701-10
41. 26 C.F.R. §31.0-2(a)(10)
42. 26 C.F.R. §301.7701-11
43. 26 C.F.R. §31.0-2(a)(11)
44. 26 C.F.R. §301.7701-12
45. 26 U.S.C. §7701(a)(20)
46. 26 U.S.C. §3231(b)
47. 26 U.S.C. §3231(a)

48. Bouvier's Law Dictionary
49. 26 C.F.R. §31.3401(f)(1)-1(a)(1)
50. 26 U.S.C. §3402(f)(1)
51. 26 U.S.C. §151
52. 26 U.S.C. §31(a)(1)
53. 26 C.F.R. §1.1441-4(c)(2)
54. 26 C.F.R. §1.6041-2(a)
55. 26 U.S.C. §6011
56. 26 U.S.C. §31.6011
57. 26 C.F.R. §§31.6011(a)-1 – 31.6011(a)-4
58. 26 U.S.C. §7501
59. CWT Farms, Inc. v. Commissioner of Internal Revenue, 755 F2d 790, at 803-804 (11th Cir. 1985)

Chapter Nine – Working the Marks

1. http://www.answers.com/topic/confidence-trick
2. United Nations, General Assembly resolution 49/60, adopted on Dec. 9, 1994
3. 26 C.F.R. §301.6109-1(b)
4. 26 C.F.R. §301.6109-1(c)
5. Sutherland Statutory Construction, §21.14, at 179-80 (6th ed. 2002); Bouvier's Law Dictionary and Concise Encyclopedia 194-95 (3rd revision 1914); Crooks v. Harrelson, 282 U.S. 55, at 58 (1930); United States v. Field, 255 U.S. 257, at 262 (1921); City of Rome v. United States, 446 U.S. 156, at 172 (1980)
6. IRS Form W-9 (Rev. October 2007)
7. http://www.lectlaw.com/def/d106.htm
8. IRS Publication 570 (2009 ver.)
9. IRS Publication 54 (2009 ver.)
10. 26 U.S.C. §6020(b)
11. http://www.nolo.com/dictionary/subscribe-term.html
12. Pollock v. Framers' Loan & Trust Company, 157 U.S. 429 (1895)

Chapter Ten – The Lies They Tell To Cover The Lies They've Told

1. 26 U.S.C. §3401(c)
2. The Revenue Bill of 1941, The House's Committee on Ways and Means

prepared House Report No. 1040 in 1941, Section entitled "Constitutionality of Proposal".
3. 89 Congressional Record 2579-80 (1943) by F. Morse Hubberd
4. Congressional Research Service, Report No. 84-168 A 734/275, page 6 by Congressional Research Attorney, Howard M. Zaritsky (1980).
5. Sutherland of Statutory Construction, §47:6
6. Sutherland of Statutory Construction, §47:7
7. Sutherland of Statutory Construction, §20:8
8. Sutherland of Statutory Construction, §27:2
9. Sutherland of Statutory Construction, §27:1
10. Colautti v. Franklin, 439 U.S. 379, at 392 (1979)
11. Spreckels Sugar Refining Co. v. McCain, 192 U.S. 397 (1904)

Chapter Eleven - The Good, The Bad, And The Mistaken
1. Dred Scott v. Sandford, 60 U.S. 393 (1856)
2. 42 U.S.C. §1981
3. 26 U.S.C. §861
4. 26 U.S.C. §861(a)(C)(3)(ii)
5. 26 U.S.C. §863 (c)(2)(B)
6. 26 U.S.C. §861(b)(1)(B)
7. 26 U.S.C. §872
8. 26 U.S.C. §7203
9. IRS Form 4852

Chapter Twelve – Tricks Of The Trade
1. 26 U.S.C. 7701(a)(14)
2. Economy Plumbing and Heating Co. v. United States, 470 F.2d 585 (Ct. Cl. 1972)
3. 26 U.S.C. §7602(a)
4. U.S. Constitution, Amendment IV
5. 1939 Internal Revenue Code
6. 1954 Internal Revenue Code
6. 26 U.S.C. §3614 (1939 IRC)
7. 26 U.S.C. §3615(a)-(c) (1939 IRC)
8. 26 U.S.C. §3632(a)(1) (1939 IRC)
9. 26 U.S.C. §3611(a)(1) (1939 IRC)
10. 26 U.S.C. §3612 (1939 IRC)

11. 26 U.S.C. §3613 (1939 IRC)
12. 26 U.S.C. §3615 (1939 IRC)
13. 26 U.S.C. §6331(a)
14. U.S. Constitution, Amendment V
15. http://dictionary.lp.findlaw.com/

Chapter Thirteen – This And That
1. 26 U.S.C. 7203
2. The American Heritage® Dictionary of the English Language, Fourth Edition
3. http://dictionary.law.com/Default.aspx?selected=2250
4. 26 U.S.C. §7701(a)(14)
5. Treasury/IRS 49.007 (Overseas Compliance Projects System)
6. IRS system of records number 49.008, entitled "Taxpayer Service Correspondence System."

Chapter Fourteen – Trashing About
1. Section 6051, California Revenue and Taxation Code
2. January 25, 1916 New York Times article detailing the Brushaber decision

Chapter Fifteen – And The Answer Is
1. U.S. Constitution, Amendment V
2. 28 U.S.C. §455(a)
3. U.S. Constitution, Amendment I
4. http://www.givemeliberty.org/
5. Merriam-Webster's Dictionary of Law, © 1996 Merriam-Webster, Inc.
6. Journals of the Continental Congress, 1:105-113 (1774)
7. State of Georgia v. Brailsford, 3 U.S. 1 (1794)
8. U.S. v. Moylan, 417 F2d 1002, at 1006 (4th Cir. 1969)
9. 26 C.F.R. §301.6109-1(c)
10. 26 C.F.R. §301.6109-1(b)
11. U.S. Constitution, Amendment XXIII
    12. 26 U.S.C. §6723
13. 26 U.S.C. §6724
14. 26 U.S.C. §6724(a)
15. 26 U.S.C. §6676 (old statute)
16. 26 C.F.R. §301.6724-1

17. 26 C.F.R. §301.6724-1(c)6(i)
18. 26 U.S.C. §7701(b)
19. 26 U.S.C. §7701(31)(B)
20. 26 U.S.C. §7701(a)(5)
21. 26 U.S.C. §3401(c)
22. 26 C.F.R. §1.861-2(a)(1)
23. President Ronald Reagan's Grace Commission's report (1984)
24. U.S. Constitution, Amendment XVI

Index

Symbols

5th Amendment 66, 308, 342, 343, 344
16th Amendment 22, 23, 24, 25, 30, 31, 32, 33, 34, 35, 36, 37, 39, 46, 47, 48, 49, 50, 51, 55, 57, 74, 75, 84, 85, 97, 273, 275, 340, 379, 382
121 262
483 262
1040 iii, 148, 149, 150, 151, 152, 153, 154, 155, 156, 157, 158, 160, 161, 245, 246, 248, 250, 257, 272, 294, 295, 296, 316, 362, 413
1040NR 157
1098 120
1099 363, 372

A

Aaron Russo 78
Account number 206
accredited 120
accumulations of property 26, 27, 28
ACS 26, 27, 28
Adair 26, 27, 28
Adolph Hitler 175. *See also* Hitler
agency 8, 9, 83, 110, 112, 148, 150, 178, 182, 183, 184, 187, 209, 268, 269, 280, 281, 283, 306, 307, 316, 318, 374, 375
alien 57, 58, 60, 93, 94, 97, 115, 122, 125, 126, 135, 136, 150, 151, 152, 153, 154, 155, 156, 159, 199, 219, 220, 221, 222, 223, 232, 244, 245, 246, 262, 271, 291, 292, 293, 367
alternate juror 359
alternative i, 18, 24, 262, 323, 324, 330, 332
Amendment 2, 22, 23, 24, 25, 30, 31, 32, 33, 34, 35, 36, 37, 38, 39, 40, 46, 47, 48, 49, 50, 51, 52, 55, 57, 66, 74, 75, 84, 85, 97, 176, 273, 275, 289, 290, 307, 308, 340, 342, 343, 344, 350, 362, 379, 382, 407, 408, 413, 414, 415
American 5, 8, 9, iii, iv, 2, 3, 5, 6, 8, 10, 17, 18, 22, 23, 27, 29, 37, 39, 41, 42, 44, 54, 55, 56, 58, 60, 69, 70, 71, 75, 79, 80, 84, 88, 93, 95, 98, 99, 101, 103, 106, 110, 113, 115, 116, 117, 118, 119, 120, 123, 124, 126, 127, 131, 132, 133, 134, 135, 137, 149, 151, 154, 159, 161, 163, 164, 165, 166, 168, 170, 180, 185, 186, 188, 192, 194, 195, 197, 198, 200, 201, 202, 205, 209, 211, 215, 218, 220, 223, 225, 227, 229, 230, 232, 237, 238, 239, 240, 245, 246, 247, 251, 252, 257, 259, 260, 261, 263, 264, 267, 268, 275, 279, 281, 283, 286, 287, 291, 294, 304, 307, 308, 309, 310, 312, 313, 315, 316, 317, 318, 323, 328, 331, 332, 333, 334, 336, 337, 338, 343, 351, 352, 355, 356, 357, 358, 359, 360, 364, 366, 367, 368, 370, 372, 373, 375, 376, 378, 379, 380, 382, 384, 388, 391, 393, 397, 400, 401, 402, 405, 407, 408, 414
American Radio 80.
See also Dave Champion Show
apportioned 14, 15, 26, 40, 47, 251, 275
apportionment 15, 16, 20, 21, 23, 25, 26, 27, 28, 30, 31, 32, 33, 34, 35, 38, 40, 48, 50, 61, 62, 64, 65, 72, 73, 74, 75, 85, 251, 275, 276, 284, 330
arbitrarily 19, 347
Arizona State Tax Board 322
Articles of Confederation 12, 13, 14, 96
ASFR program 248, 250, 251, 253, 257, 281, 282
assessment 66, 70, 112, 114, 174, 248, 251, 254, 260, 309, 374
Assistant Commissioner 80, 113, 114, 115, 145, 146, 147, 148, 206, 319, 320
authority 2, 3, 4, 5, 6, 7, 15, 16, 20, 21, 23, 24, 25, 26, 33, 38, 39, 40, 41, 48, 49, 50, 59, 70, 74, 83, 84, 86, 87, 88, 89, 90, 91, 96, 97, 98, 105, 106, 107, 108, 109, 110, 111, 112, 113, 114, 115, 117, 120, 121, 126, 129, 138, 141, 143, 144, 145, 146, 148, 160, 165, 177, 183, 202, 203, 206, 216, 218, 219, 228, 229, 232, 246, 247, 249, 250, 251, 253, 254, 255, 256, 257, 271, 278, 281, 282, 290, 299, 301, 302, 303, 304, 306, 307, 308, 309, 310, 311, 319, 330, 340, 360, 361
Automated Collection System 245.
See also ACS
Automated Substitute for Return Program 248

Index

B

backup withholding 118, 119, 120, 121, 123, 124, 126, 129, 130, 133, 134, 136, 215, 231, 232, 233, 236, 307
Baker 39, 40, 408
Baltic Mining Co. 33, 39, 408
bank account 225, 261, 263, 265, 373, 374, 375
Banks 258, 384
Ben Marchant 347
Billings v. U.S. 256
Blanket 5th 343
Bob Schulz 334, 351, 352, 353
books and records 105, 111, 112, 113, 144, 146, 299
bribe 178, 179
brokerage firms 258
Brushaber 25, 26, 27, 30, 31, 32, 33, 34, 35, 39, 43, 47, 49, 52, 53, 55, 61, 64, 66, 73, 74, 151, 152, 251, 272, 273, 276, 329, 408, 414
burden 22, 26, 27, 31, 32, 38, 40, 74, 116, 314, 315, 317, 333, 338, 339
Butcher's Union Co. 44, 52

C

Cambridge Apostles 380
capitation 15, 19
census 15, 23
certified 22, 23, 134, 178, 251
chapter 3 121, 122, 137, 139, 140, 141, 151, 152, 158, 161, 185, 222, 293, 410
chapter 24 122, 181, 185, 214, 215
Charles C. Steward Machine Co. 188, 411
Chief Counsel 78, 80, 250, 257, 282
Chief Justice John Jay 357
circuit court 34, 35
citizens of the United States 57, 60, 93, 94, 97, 289, 292
civil action 63
Civil War 20, 196, 362
classes 15, 16, 22, 94, 114, 116, 184, 228, 229
class of person 123, 138, 157, 246, 288, 294, 304, 307, 322, 329, 362, 363, 364, 367
class warfare 21, 22

D

Dave Champion Show 80, 399
David Cay Johnston 80, 82
Davy Crockett 386, 387
debates 14, 96, 170
declaration 244, 248, 363
deficiency 254, 255, 256, 257, 258
Department of Health and Human Service 387
Department of Justice 65, 68, 80, 235, 239, 285, 313, 351
direct iv, 14, 15, 16, 19, 21, 25, 26, 27, 28, 32, 33, 38, 40, 47, 75, 85, 97, 124, 213, 217, 251, 275, 276, 316, 329, 330
Director 112, 113, 114, 115, 144, 145, 206, 217
Director of International Operations 206
disbarred 83, 348
Disclosure Office 281, 283
disinformation iv, 64, 75, 238, 280
dissent iv, 64, 75, 238, 280
District Courts 74, 300
district director 112, 114, 115, 206
District of Columbia 36, 182, 183, 184, 187, 192, 198, 200, 209, 269, 270, 306, 307, 375
dividends 21, 72, 129, 132, 152
doing business 85, 87, 88, 92, 112, 113, 158, 159, 326, 328, 367
DOJ 68, 74, 351, 352, 353, 356
dominant media ii, iii, 63, 64, 238, 239, 240, 392
Douglas H. Ginsburg 36
Downes v. Bidwell 201
Doyle v. Mitchell Brother, Co. 47, 408
Dred Scott 288, 413
due process of law 92, 249, 253, 308
dummy return 248, 250, 257
Durwood 347, 348
duties 15, 16, 17, 21, 32, 46, 108, 111, 129, 304, 323, 330

E

Economy Plumbing and Heating Co. 260, 300, 413
Edward Dufresne 346
Eisner v. Macomber 48, 408, 409
Ejusdem Generis 184
employee 84, 104, 105, 161, 167, 178, 179, 180, 181, 182, 183, 184, 185, 186, 187, 193, 194, 197, 198, 206, 208, 209, 211, 214, 215, 218, 219, 220, 222, 241, 242, 244, 248, 257, 269, 304, 306, 307, 308, 314, 315, 316, 357, 368
employer 181, 182, 183, 185, 186, 187, 191, 192, 194, 198, 201, 207, 208, 209, 212, 213, 219, 220, 221, 241, 242, 262, 285,

292, 296, 306, 307
employment 6, 44, 52, 114, 146, 178, 188, 191, 193, 194, 198, 200, 201, 205, 210, 217, 219, 223
Employment Tax 122, 190, 207, 218, 219, 220, 221
enforce 10, 13, 27, 28, 246, 251, 252, 258, 274, 290, 309
enforcement 8, 64, 91, 110, 118, 145, 147, 247, 251, 304, 342, 347, 359, 364
enjoin 63
entitlement spending 387, 388
enumerated powers 46, 164, 386, 387
Everson 80
evidence tampering 347
excepted subjects 39
excise 17, 25, 27, 28, 29, 30, 31, 32, 33, 40, 43, 44, 46, 47, 49, 50, 51, 52, 57, 58, 59, 61, 62, 64, 65, 66, 72, 73, 74, 85, 87, 88, 92, 93, 95, 97, 105, 110, 111, 114, 117, 146, 152, 191, 202, 214, 251, 254, 271, 272, 273, 274, 275, 276, 284, 325, 329, 330
Executive Branch 7, 274, 352, 353
Executive Orders 102, 108, 162
exemptions 192, 211, 212, 213, 281
expatriation 290

F

F.A. Hayek 381
Fair Tax 324
Fannie Mae 179
Farmers' Loan & Trust 20
FDIC 20, 92, 184
Federal agencies 8
federal authority 2, 6
Federal corporation 179
federal courts iii, 10, 35, 46, 239, 341
Federal Deposit Insurance Corporation 92, 184. *See also* FDIC
Federal Firearms Act 203
federal government iii, 2, 5, 6, 12, 22, 23, 24, 35, 39, 46, 50, 53, 55, 62, 63, 64, 75, 76, 91, 92, 95, 96, 98, 104, 110, 160, 162, 164, 176, 196, 197, 204, 226, 271, 273, 289, 321, 330, 332, 335, 340, 343, 344, 353, 378, 384, 386, 388
Federal Insurance Contribution Act 190, 191. *See also* FICA
federal Judiciary Commission 347
Federal National Mortgage Association 179, 184
federal "place" 203
Federal Register 9, 10, 107, 108, 318
Federal Reserve Act 379, 382, 383
Federal Trade Commission 176
Federal Unemployment Tax Act 190, 191, 220
felony 170, 282, 347
FEMA 240
FICA 187, 188, 189, 190, 191, 192, 193, 195, 197, 198, 200, 201, 202, 204, 205, 216, 220
filing requirement 73, 158
financial crime iv, 24, 40, 97, 99, 101, 127, 163, 165, 182, 210, 226, 231, 250, 252, 268, 275, 276, 277, 287, 298, 299, 300, 304, 318, 322, 331, 334, 339, 340, 349, 350, 351, 353, 359, 376, 385, 388, 389, 390, 391, 397
firearms 181, 203, 204, 340, 400
Flat Tax 330, 331
FLIR 338
F. Morse Hubberd 273, 413
FOIA 142, 148, 281, 282, 283
foreign 6, 17, 56, 58, 87, 88, 95, 96, 97, 98, 103, 108, 110, 112, 113, 115, 116, 117, 119, 120, 121, 122, 124, 125, 126, 129, 130, 131, 132, 133, 134, 135, 136, 138, 140, 141, 143, 146, 147, 150, 152, 154, 155, 157, 158, 159, 160, 161, 162, 163, 178, 179, 180, 186, 200, 201, 204, 211, 212, 214, 215, 216, 218, 219, 220, 221, 228, 229, 232, 243, 244, 245, 246, 247, 260, 261, 270, 271, 272, 290, 291, 292, 293, 318, 319, 328, 352, 360, 361, 363, 366, 367
foreign branch 96, 135
foreign corporations 87, 88, 112, 113, 115, 122, 158, 159, 160, 271, 272
Foreign Earned Income 161
Foreign Operations District 112, 113, 114, 115
foreign person 56, 58, 98, 103, 120, 124, 130, 131, 134, 135, 136, 141, 150, 157, 163, 180, 215, 216, 228, 229, 232, 243, 244, 245, 247, 260, 261, 270, 271, 318, 363, 366, 367
foreign persons 88, 98, 103, 110, 116, 117, 119, 120, 121, 122, 126, 129, 131, 132, 133, 134, 135, 136, 138, 140, 143, 147, 155, 157, 161, 162, 186, 211, 212, 214, 215, 228, 229, 246, 270, 271, 290, 291, 293, 361
Form 2555 161

Index

Form 4852 296, 297, 413
Founders 27, 46, 53, 64, 75, 289, 354
Founding Fathers 5, 18, 27, 46, 64, 289, 387
Franklin Roosevelt 380
fraud 64, 81, 84, 99, 104, 111, 137, 210, 237
Freedom of Information Act 103, 142, 248, 281. *See also* FOIA
Freedom to Fascism 78
frivolous 36, 176, 185, 239, 276, 283, 295, 297, 316
fruits ii, 4, 21, 31, 32, 45, 46, 53, 273, 293, 336, 337, 349

G

general applicability 9, 107
general government 96, 97, 98, 110, 120
general language 129, 158, 193, 307
General Welfare clause 386
George Mason 45
Goldenberg 256
Gould v. Gould 53, 256, 408
Grace Commission 378, 415
grand jury 238
green card 94, 97
gross income 66, 67, 68, 71, 72, 73, 95, 103, 115, 122, 137, 138, 153, 156, 186, 213, 222, 291, 292, 293, 321, 362, 363
Guam 150, 192, 195, 196, 197, 198, 200, 202

H

Hale V. Henkel 92
Hamiltonians 20, 39, 40
Happiness 4, 5, 397
head tax 18, 19
Hitler 175, 353
Hooven & Allison Co. v. Evatt 195, 411
Howard M. Zaritsky 273, 413
hung jury 356
Hylton 19, 26, 407, 408

I

imposed i, 6, 10, 15, 17, 20, 28, 29, 31, 32, 43, 44, 47, 48, 50, 52, 53, 54, 55, 56, 57, 59, 60, 61, 62, 64, 65, 68, 69, 70, 71, 72, 73, 74, 83, 93, 94, 95, 97, 98, 102, 103, 104, 110, 112, 115, 117, 122, 137, 138, 140, 141, 143, 148, 152, 153, 161, 162, 163, 185, 186, 191, 194, 201, 211, 212, 213, 214, 218, 219, 242, 243, 244, 246, 247, 251, 254, 259, 260, 261, 271, 272, 274, 277, 279, 280, 285, 288, 290, 292, 294, 295, 297, 302, 303, 304, 308, 310, 313, 321, 322, 325, 326, 329, 340, 356, 360, 361, 362, 363, 364, 375, 388
imposes 6, 57, 58, 59, 92, 93, 97, 161, 245, 285, 295, 325, 370
imposition 19, 87, 174, 212, 256, 288, 291, 293
imposts 15, 16, 21, 32, 46, 330
includes i, 2, 44, 45, 75, 115, 123, 124, 125, 130, 137, 145, 172, 173, 174, 175, 181, 182, 184, 195, 197, 198, 199, 206, 209, 222, 249, 269, 274, 292, 321, 374, 375, 379
Income Tax Act of 1913 47, 49
independent contractor 222
individual 2, 3, 6, 7, 12, 55, 56, 57, 58, 59, 69, 73, 81, 90, 92, 93, 94, 97, 98, 115, 122, 125, 126, 135, 136, 138, 150, 151, 155, 156, 159, 160, 161, 162, 174, 182, 183, 191, 196, 198, 199, 200, 207, 208, 209, 211, 222, 232, 244, 247, 262, 263, 276, 280, 291, 292, 346, 376, 379, 388, 405
information returns 70, 120, 125, 126, 128, 129, 131, 244, 251, 294, 295, 296, 297, 363, 364, 365
instrumentalities 92, 199, 219
interest 13, 21, 22, 46, 67, 72, 77, 79, 129, 132, 135, 144, 150, 152, 210, 259, 284, 341, 349, 374, 375, 378, 379, 383, 384, 385, 387, 388
Internal Revenue Code 10, 106, 121, 122, 124, 130, 162, 206, 207, 254, 262, 321, 322, 413
Internal Revenue Manual iii, 10, 102, 143, 157, 410. *See also* IRM
IRM 143, 146
IRS call centers 241
Irwin Schiff 77

J

James Madison 95
Janice Rogers-Brown 36
Jason Furman 353
Jay Adkisson 81, 409
Jay D. Adkisson 80. *See also* Jay Adkisson
Jefferson 8, 45, 95, 98, 203, 311, 330, 383, 386, 387, 388, 400, 402
Jerrold Peterson 346, 347
Joe Banister 83, 147, 409
John Locke 45

John Maynard Keynes 379
Joseph Story 45, 210
J. Peter Grace 378
Judicial Branch 35, 350, 352
Judicial Conferences 68
judicial corruption 359
Judith Rogers 36
jurisdiction 35, 87, 88, 145, 197, 279, 290, 320, 328, 346, 355, 362, 363
Jury Nullification 359
jury tampering 315
Justice Harlan 201
Justice Story 45, 211
Justice White 25, 26, 27, 33, 35, 38, 52, 251

K

Ken Dawson 344
Keynesian economics 379, 380, 381, 385
kickback 178, 179
King George III 202, 350
Knowlton 18, 407

L

labor 4, 5, 41, 44, 51, 52, 72, 93, 214, 216, 270, 271, 291, 336, 337, 340, 348, 349, 389
language of the statute 7, 140, 220, 307
legal advice 8, 242, 370
legal hit teams 63
legal precedent 280, 284
legal presumption 128, 244, 329, 373
legal terms 11, 138, 140, 180, 181, 195, 377
legislation 6, 96, 107, 172, 188, 195, 197, 203, 204, 250, 273
legislative draftsman 213, 273, 276
legislative draftsmen 6, 7, 61, 140, 213, 214
legislative history 40
levy 183, 187, 265, 305, 306, 308, 374
liability 29, 68, 75, 83, 105, 114, 115, 142, 154, 159, 162, 221, 249, 300, 301, 326
liable 57, 59, 60, 61, 65, 66, 67, 68, 69, 70, 71, 72, 73, 93, 94, 98, 103, 104, 105, 111, 136, 138, 142, 152, 155, 163, 185, 219, 244, 246, 249, 251, 258, 271, 272, 274, 288, 295, 301, 302, 303, 306, 318, 326, 360, 361, 362, 363, 364, 373
liberty 5, 8, 9, 4, 5, 44, 45, 46, 52, 100, 101, 102, 165, 202, 308, 310, 327, 335, 352, 376, 381, 388, 389, 396, 397, 400, 403, 405
life iv, 7, 3, 4, 23, 45, 46, 67, 77, 78, 92, 93, 102, 139, 164, 165, 187, 208, 227, 231, 308, 313, 317, 325, 327, 335, 342, 347, 349, 350, 355, 369, 380, 387, 390, 403
Lloyd D. George 176
Lord Acton 342
Lowe 39, 408

M

measure 19, 47, 382, 386
Meese v. Keene 172, 197, 407, 410
Mein Kampf 175, 410
Merchants Loan 49, 408
Michael Straight 380
Michael Whitney Straight 380
money 6, 8, 10, 13, 44, 52, 62, 64, 69, 70, 71, 74, 93, 96, 101, 102, 116, 117, 119, 131, 136, 141, 154, 157, 167, 168, 182, 185, 188, 189, 190, 209, 210, 221, 225, 236, 239, 240, 247, 252, 255, 261, 265, 270, 271, 287, 313, 320, 331, 332, 334, 339, 349, 350, 354, 376, 377, 378, 381, 382, 383, 384, 385, 386, 387, 400, 401, 403
monopolistic 91
Moore 18, 347, 348, 407
Murphy 36, 37, 407, 408
Murray Rothbard 45, 55

N

Nancy Pelosi 329, 332
Nathan Hochman 338, 339
national government 2, 6, 12, 13, 14, 89, 95, 301, 307, 330
nationalized health care 332
national retail sales tax 324, 329, 330, 332
NOD 254, 258
nonresident alien individual 93, 122, 125, 126, 135, 136, 150, 155, 232, 244, 292
nontaxpayers 237, 260, 261, 295, 300, 369, 371
Northern Mariana Islands 150, 198
Notice of Deficiency 254. *See also* NOD
Notice of Levy 305, 306, 307, 308, 309, 310, 374

O

obedience 10
obligation 17, 29, 60, 102, 159, 193, 326, 339, 358, 371, 375, 377, 384
Office of Management and Budget 160
official business 175, 178

Index

Old-Age and Survivors Insurance Trust Fund 189
Oliver Wendell Holmes 338
OMB Control Numbers 160
on-going criminal enterprise 253
outcome based law 339, 342
Overseas Compliance Projects System 318, 414
ownership 25, 26, 44, 329

P

Paperwork Reduction Act 160
Part 31 165, 186, 205, 206, 207, 219, 220, 410
Patriot Act 261, 262, 264, 373
Paul Craig Roberts 315
payor 119, 120, 123, 124, 125, 126, 128, 129, 130, 131, 132, 133, 232, 260, 360, 364, 365, 366
payroll withholding 20, 116, 117, 166, 167, 168, 169, 170, 173, 179, 182, 187, 189, 204, 208, 211, 212, 214, 215, 216, 218, 223, 241, 270, 306, 307, 368
Peck 39, 408
Percy Anderson 285, 342, 343
perjury 133, 134, 216, 231, 232, 233, 234, 235, 244, 247, 248, 251, 259, 260, 261, 264, 265, 294, 362, 363
permanent residency 94
personal liberty 5, 44, 45, 52, 100, 101, 102, 335, 381
personal service 222
person liable 59, 60, 65, 66, 67, 105, 258, 295, 301, 306
Pete Hendrickson 296, 297
Philander Knox 22, 23
pirated 252, 257
plain meaning rule 11, 256
plenary 38, 98, 301
polling the jury 356
Pollock 20, 21, 22, 25, 26, 27, 28, 30, 31, 32, 43, 47, 52, 53, 251, 407, 408, 412
power 9, 1, 3, 4, 5, 6, 13, 14, 15, 16, 22, 23, 26, 27, 36, 38, 39, 40, 45, 46, 48, 53, 66, 71, 75, 85, 86, 89, 90, 92, 93, 96, 98, 105, 106, 110, 117, 148, 165, 201, 202, 203, 271, 272, 285, 300, 301, 305, 309, 325, 330, 335, 339, 341, 342, 352, 357, 358, 362, 384, 387, 388, 389, 390
privacy 23, 106, 111, 348
private citizens 21, 269
private sector 92, 93, 126, 129, 182, 184, 186, 187, 192, 193, 198, 204, 205, 215, 216, 224, 257, 295, 299, 304, 306, 385
Private Sector Survey on Cost Control 378
privilege 17, 29, 30, 31, 40, 43, 44, 45, 50, 51, 52, 57, 62, 66, 72, 73, 85, 86, 87, 88, 91, 92, 93, 95, 97, 110, 117, 152, 214, 247, 270, 271, 272, 273, 279, 280, 320, 321, 325, 326, 327, 328, 330
Procedures and Administration 109, 158, 206, 207
profits 20, 42, 97, 153, 379
Progressive Era 21
property 20, 21, 25, 26, 27, 28, 31, 32, 33, 40, 41, 42, 43, 44, 45, 46, 47, 48, 49, 50, 51, 52, 53, 64, 67, 69, 71, 72, 75, 85, 92, 95, 101, 102, 121, 152, 153, 167, 169, 170, 175, 187, 203, 204, 205, 209, 210, 216, 218, 251, 253, 256, 259, 264, 265, 273, 276, 277, 279, 280, 290, 294, 303, 305, 306, 307, 308, 309, 310, 325, 326, 327, 328, 329, 334, 337, 349, 352, 363, 371, 376, 381, 389, 391
publication 54 248
publication 570 246
Public Law 7
public office 172, 177, 178, 179, 321, 384
Puerto Rico 145, 150, 157, 195, 196, 197, 198, 200, 202, 246, 289

R

RACS006 report 250
Railroad Retirement Tax Act 190, 191, 220
railroads 91, 209, 220
rate 3, 4, 5, 19, 153, 329, 330, 331, 332, 356
ratified 13, 19, 20, 22, 23, 196, 308, 382
real estate 20, 21, 25, 26, 46, 52, 53, 58, 88, 329
reasonable doubt 356, 358
recuse 344, 345, 346
redress of grievances 350
regional service center 114
Regulations 7, 8, 9, 56, 94, 108, 128, 162, 186, 206, 207, 218, 219, 221
Regulatory law 243
Remonstrance 350, 351
remuneration 181, 182, 186, 214, 215
rent 20, 31, 189
reportable payments 120, 129, 132, 248
Republican Form of Government 46
resident 57, 58, 60, 93, 94, 97, 150, 153, 154, 155, 161, 194, 198, 199, 200, 246, 248,

262, 290, 291, 292, 293, 319, 375
resident alien 57, 58, 60, 93, 94, 97, 153, 155, 262, 291
revenue stamp 114
revolt 354
Right of Free Speech 176
right to remain silent 342, 343, 344
Ruby Ridge 337
rules of computation 139, 140, 149, 151, 211, 361, 369, 370
Rules of Construction 184
Rules of Engagement 338
Rules of Interpretation 173, 177

S

sales tax 44, 324, 325, 326, 327, 329, 330, 332
Samoa 151, 192, 195, 197, 198, 200, 202
scope of practice 370
Secretary iii, 7, 22, 57, 59, 60, 65, 66, 67, 68, 69, 70, 73, 80, 94, 97, 104, 105, 107, 108, 109, 110, 111, 113, 114, 116, 119, 120, 122, 125, 126, 127, 128, 129, 130, 131, 132, 133, 134, 135, 136, 137, 147, 149, 151, 156, 159, 160, 161, 181, 183, 187, 193, 205, 206, 207, 208, 210, 211, 218, 219, 224, 227, 229, 245, 249, 250, 255, 256, 257, 264, 300, 301, 302, 306, 307, 315, 328, 365, 375, 394
Secretary of the Treasury iii, 7, 69, 80, 107, 109, 113, 127, 160, 187, 315, 365, 394
section 233 of the Social Security Act 194, 200, 201
seizure 92, 305, 309
self-defense 90, 353
Senate 81
Service Correspondence System 320
Shakespeare 88, 357
Sheldon Cohen 78, 82
shunning 390, 392, 393, 394
signature card 258, 259, 265, 373
slave 242, 336, 337, 348, 349, 362, 363, 379
slavery 26, 289, 335, 336, 337, 340, 362
slaves 12, 18, 19, 20, 25, 26, 46, 52, 53, 54, 289, 290, 329, 335, 337, 339, 345, 379, 388
Socialism 21, 75
socialist 21
Social Security 168, 170, 188, 189, 190, 193, 194, 200, 201, 206, 207, 223, 387, 411
Social Security Administration 189, 193. *See also* SSA
Social Security Number 168, 170, 207. *See also* SSN
Social Security Trust Fund 189
source ii, 23, 32, 38, 40, 51, 67, 84, 86, 89, 98, 102, 103, 110, 115, 117, 120, 122, 124, 126, 131, 132, 133, 134, 135, 136, 137, 143, 147, 152, 154, 155, 157, 159, 161, 162, 214, 219, 238, 243, 244, 245, 246, 252, 257, 260, 270, 271, 273, 285, 290, 291, 293, 318, 319, 321, 355, 356, 358, 360, 375, 383
South Carolina 39, 40, 408
sovereign 12, 13, 195, 196, 197, 289, 380, 385
sovereign nation 12, 195, 380, 385
Soviet Union 170, 380
Speckels Sugar Refining Co. 85
SSA 193
SSN 207, 216, 223, 229, 248, 252, 257, 264, 374
State income tax 187
State of California 83, 325
State of Georgia vs. Brailsford 357
State personal income tax 321
states 9, 2, 4, 5, 12, 13, 19, 21, 23, 34, 47, 67, 70, 73, 75, 87, 89, 98, 110, 115, 124, 125, 128, 129, 144, 157, 164, 175, 188, 193, 195, 196, 197, 198, 201, 202, 203, 204, 205, 206, 209, 211, 216, 218, 219, 222, 223, 230, 232, 246, 247, 250, 257, 261, 262, 263, 269, 272, 273, 274, 282, 288, 289, 290, 291, 294, 304, 307, 308, 318, 320, 321, 322, 326, 328, 329, 330, 338, 340, 343, 344, 345, 350, 353, 365, 368, 370, 375, 378
Statute-At-Large 7
statutory definition 71, 72, 172, 173, 174, 177, 179, 181, 197, 256, 279, 368
Stratton's Independence 47, 408
subornation of perjury 260
substitute return 249, 250, 282
subtitle 'A' 6, 60, 61, 66, 72, 73, 74, 77, 84, 85, 92, 93, 94, 95, 97, 102, 103, 110, 117, 119, 121, 122, 133, 134, 136, 137, 138, 139, 148, 152, 157, 158, 159, 161, 162, 165, 175, 185, 211, 212, 213, 214, 215, 216, 218, 219, 225, 229, 242, 243, 244, 245, 247, 255, 257, 271, 284, 285, 361, 375, 378, 410
subtitle 'C' 6, 117, 165, 166, 180, 185, 212, 216, 218, 225, 229
summons 104, 105, 109, 110, 111, 299, 300,

Index

301, 302, 303, 304, 342
Sutherland Statutory Construction 278, 412
systems of records 318

T

tar and feathering 119
tariff 85, 88
taxable income 55, 56, 57, 93, 95, 138, 139, 321
tax attorney 169, 170
tax fraud 81
Tax Freedom Day 336
Tax Honesty Movement ii, iii, iv, 63, 77, 80, 81, 142, 239, 341, 403
tax module 248, 253
Taxpayer 127, 133, 144, 145, 230, 263, 319, 320, 414
taxpayer identification number 118, 130, 132, 133, 232, 262, 263
tax protestor 36, 68, 176, 239, 270, 274
tax scams 81, 142
Tax Terrorism Season 238, 239, 313
territories and possessions 202
territory 19, 195, 196, 203
terrorism 225, 226, 237, 238, 318, 352, 356, 388
The Law That Never Was 22
The Road to Serfdom 381
The U.S. Department of Justice 68, 313, 351. *See also* DOJ
Thomas Jefferson 45, 95, 311, 383, 386, 388, 400, 402
Title 27 174
Title 31 189
Title 42 289
totalitarian 86
Totalitarianism 177
Towne v. Eisner 47, 408
trade or business 115, 125, 171, 172, 173, 175, 177, 178, 179, 186, 214, 291, 292
Treason 76
treasonous 35
Treasury Decisions iii, 9, 10, 102, 127, 149, 157, 162
Treasury Secretary 7
treaties 13, 145, 196
Treaty of Paris 196
trial court 284, 285, 357
trial jury 356
Tyranny 76

U

UCC 287, 288
unalienable rights 4, 5, 277, 280, 286, 300, 308, 325, 326, 328, 340, 343, 379, 381, 390
unavoidable 17, 18, 29, 30
unconstitutional 9, 6, 8, 20, 21, 30, 31, 33, 34, 36, 39, 40, 43, 44, 47, 52, 53, 65, 75, 120, 129, 188, 251, 253, 265, 305, 307, 329, 330, 350, 351, 387, 388, 389
uniform 15, 16, 40, 273, 365
Uniform Commercial Code 287
uniformity 32, 38, 288
United States 8, 9, 8, 1, 2, 6, 7, 10, 15, 16, 30, 34, 36, 40, 46, 52, 53, 54, 57, 58, 60, 70, 75, 80, 85, 88, 93, 94, 97, 99, 106, 108, 112, 115, 122, 144, 145, 146, 150, 152, 153, 154, 155, 156, 158, 161, 162, 163, 168, 174, 175, 176, 177, 178, 181, 182, 183, 184, 187, 188, 189, 194, 195, 196, 197, 198, 199, 200, 201, 202, 203, 204, 209, 221, 222, 223, 232, 238, 246, 256, 260, 262, 269, 271, 272, 273, 276, 284, 287, 289, 290, 291, 292, 293, 300, 306, 307, 309, 313, 322, 341, 342, 344, 345, 348, 353, 362, 374, 375, 378, 383, 384, 407, 408, 411, 412, 413
United States Circuit Courts 30
United States Code 7, 174, 189, 202, 289
Unites States government 4
U.S. 5th Circuit Court of Appeals 346
U.S. Attorney 80, 313
U.S. citizens residing abroad 94, 143, 144, 146, 147, 157, 211, 212, 218, 272
use of deadly force 90
U.S. government ii, iv, 5, 26, 47, 74, 91, 92, 134, 157, 164, 176, 177, 196, 201, 209, 210, 225, 226, 237, 239, 252, 253, 270, 287, 297, 301, 304, 313, 318, 333, 338, 339, 341, 378, 384, 404
U.S. person 124, 126, 130, 131, 132, 133, 134, 135, 227, 228, 229, 231, 232, 233, 243, 244, 245, 251, 252, 260, 262, 265, 361
U.S. Senate 81
U.S. Supreme Court 8, 3, 5, 6, 7, 11, 15, 18, 19, 20, 23, 25, 26, 30, 33, 34, 35, 38, 40, 43, 44, 47, 48, 51, 53, 54, 57, 72, 85, 92, 93, 98, 151, 152, 172, 173, 174, 177, 182, 188, 195, 210, 214, 220, 231, 251, 272, 274, 278, 279, 284, 288, 310, 316, 325, 338, 344, 357, 394

usurpation 23
US vs. Moylan 358

V

Value Added Tax 332
VAT 329, 332, 333
violence 75, 86, 90, 226, 354, 382
Virginia Declaration of Rights 45
Virgin Islands 151, 157, 195, 196, 197, 198, 199, 200
voluntary 17, 29, 193, 243, 288, 309, 356, 362
Voluntary 309, 362

W

W-2 120, 186, 187, 216, 218, 223, 294, 296, 363
W-4 160, 161, 168, 170, 204, 205, 215, 216, 217, 218, 219, 223, 224, 363, 375, 391, 396
W-9 124, 130, 132, 133, 134, 160, 230, 231, 232, 233, 234, 242, 244, 247, 248, 252, 258, 259, 260, 264, 265, 363, 366, 367, 373, 412
Waco 337, 338
Wages 180, 181, 183, 191, 218, 270
warrant 87, 92, 106, 148, 232, 301, 305
Washington D.C. 24, 197
wealth 23, 27, 64, 74, 84, 101, 102, 165, 210, 388, 389, 397
well-settled 4, 43, 214, 279, 343
We The People Foundation For Constitutional Education 350, 351, 352
White 25, 26, 27, 28, 29, 30, 31, 32, 33, 34, 35, 38, 52, 53, 64, 73, 251, 353
White House 353
Wigglesworth 53, 408
Willful Failure To File 295
William Taft 85
Winston Churchill 381
withholding agent 121, 122, 123, 124, 125, 126, 128, 135, 136, 138, 141, 153, 154, 156, 159, 163, 185, 215, 222, 223, 232, 245, 271, 272, 295, 318, 360
withholding of tax 115, 159

Z

zero returns 294, 295